Strangling the Axis

This is a major reassessment of the causes of Allied victory in the Second World War in the Mediterranean region. Drawing on a unique range of multinational source material, Richard Hammond demonstrates how the Allies' ability to gain control of the key routes across the sea and sink large quantities of enemy shipping denied the Axis forces in North Africa crucial supplies and proved vital to securing ultimate victory there. Furthermore, the sheer scale of attrition to Axis shipping outstripped their industrial capacity to compensate, leading to the collapse of the Axis position across key territories maintained by seaborne supply, such as Sardinia, Corsica and the Aegean islands. As such, Hammond demonstrates how the anti-shipping campaign in the Mediterranean was the fulcrum about which strategy in the theatre pivoted, and the vital enabling factor ultimately leading to Allied victory in the region.

RICHARD HAMMOND is a lecturer at Brunel University and is a vice president of the Second World War Research Group. He is the recipient of the Society for Military History's Moncado Prize and the Corbett Prize in Modern Naval History (proxime accessit).

Cambridge Military Histories

Edited by

HEW STRACHAN, Professor of International Relations, University of St Andrews and Emeritus Fellow of All Souls College, Oxford

GEOFFREY WAWRO, Professor of Military History, and Director of the Military History Center, University of North Texas

The aim of this series is to publish outstanding works of research on warfare throughout the ages and throughout the world. Books in the series take a broad approach to military history, examining war in all its military, strategic, political and economic aspects. The series complements Studies in the Social and Cultural History of Modern Warfare by focusing on the 'hard' military history of armies, tactics, strategy and warfare. Books in the series consist mainly of single author works – academically rigorous and groundbreaking – which are accessible to both academics and the interested general reader.

A full list of titles in the series can be found at:
www.cambridge.org/militaryhistories

Strangling the Axis

The Fight for Control of the Mediterranean during the Second World War

Richard Hammond
Brunel University

CAMBRIDGE
UNIVERSITY PRESS

CAMBRIDGE
UNIVERSITY PRESS

University Printing House, Cambridge CB2 8BS, United Kingdom

One Liberty Plaza, 20th Floor, New York, NY 10006, USA

477 Williamstown Road, Port Melbourne, VIC 3207, Australia

314–321, 3rd Floor, Plot 3, Splendor Forum, Jasola District Centre, New Delhi – 110025, India

79 Anson Road, #06–04/06, Singapore 079906

Cambridge University Press is part of the University of Cambridge.

It furthers the University's mission by disseminating knowledge in the pursuit of education, learning, and research at the highest international levels of excellence.

www.cambridge.org
Information on this title: www.cambridge.org/9781108478212
DOI: 10.1017/9781108784566

© Richard Hammond 2020

This publication is in copyright. Subject to statutory exception and to the provisions of relevant collective licensing agreements, no reproduction of any part may take place without the written permission of Cambridge University Press.

First published 2020
Reprinted 2020

Printed in the United Kingdom by TJ International Ltd, Padstow Cornwall

A catalogue record for this publication is available from the British Library.

Library of Congress Cataloging-in-Publication Data
Names: Hammond, Richard, 1985– author.
Title: Strangling the Axis : the fight for control of the Mediterranean during the Second World War / Richard Hammond, Brunel University.
Other titles: Fight for control of the Mediterranean during the Second World War
Description: Cambridge, United Kingdom ; New York : Cambridge University Press, 2020. | Series: Cambridge military histories | Includes bibliographical references and index.
Identifiers: LCCN 2019051274 (print) | LCCN 2019051275 (ebook) | ISBN 9781108478212 (hardback) | ISBN 9781108747110 (paperback) | ISBN 9781108784566 (epub)
Subjects: LCSH: World War, 1939–1945–Campaigns–Mediterranean Region. | World War, 1939–1945–Mediterranean Region. | Mediterranean Region–Strategic aspects.
Classification: LCC D763.M47 H36 2020 (print) | LCC D763.M47 (ebook) | DDC 940.54/293–dc23
LC record available at https://lccn.loc.gov/2019051274
LC ebook record available at https://lccn.loc.gov/2019051275

ISBN 978-1-108-47821-2 Hardback

Cambridge University Press has no responsibility for the persistence or accuracy of URLs for external or third-party internet websites referred to in this publication and does not guarantee that any content on such websites is, or will remain, accurate or appropriate.

For my parents

Contents

List of Illustrations	*page* viii
List of Maps	ix
List of Tables	x
Acknowledgements	xi
A Note on Terminology: 'British' and 'Allied'	xiii
List of Abbreviations	xv
Maps	xvi
Introduction	1
1 The Descent to War in the Mediterranean	11
2 Resisting *Mare Nostrum*: The Early Anti-shipping Campaign, June–December 1940	31
3 Enter Germany: January–July 1941	52
4 Progress: August–December 1941	82
5 Axis Ascendency: January–August 1942	107
6 The End of the Beginning: Alam Halfa and El Alamein	127
7 The End in North Africa and the Shipping Crisis: December 1942–May 1943	148
8 After North Africa	173
Conclusion	198
Notes	205
Bibliography	252
Index	263

Illustrations

1.1 Benito Mussolini inspects an Italian warship and crew, with Achille Starace and Domenico Cavagnari in tow *page* 18
2.1 The Italian battleship *Conte di Cavour* in port with destroyers, June 1940 31
3.1 A Consolidated B-24 Liberator Mark I bomber 58
3.2 HMS *Taku* returns home after a successful tour of the Mediterranean 72
4.1 Members of the crew of HMS *Utmost* pose with their 'Jolly Roger' success flag on their return from a year's service in the Mediterranean, February 1942 95
5.1 Photograph from an Italian bomber dropping bombs on Hal Far airbase, Malta 110
5.2 A heavily damaged HMS *Penelope* after narrowly escaping from Malta in April 1942 115
6.1 Sunken wrecks of Axis shipping strewn across Benghazi harbour 146
7.1 Sunken vessels litter Bizerte harbour, May 1943 162
8.1 An Allied bombing raid on Messina, Sicily, June 1943 182
8.2 RAF Bristol Beaufighters of No. 201 (Naval Co-operation) Group attack a convoy in the Aegean Sea, February 1944 196

Maps

1 The Mediterranean theatre   *page* xvii
2 Axis sea and air transport routes to North Africa, October 1942–May 1943   xviii
3 The central and eastern Mediterranean, including the Aegean islands   xx
4 The Western Desert battle area   xxii
5 Tunisia   xxiii

Tables

1.1	Principal Axis convoy routes in the Mediterranean	page 25
3.1	Arrivals of RAF bomber reinforcements in the Middle East, January–July 1941	61
3.2	Raids on ports and shipping by aircraft from Egypt and Malta, May–July 1941	69
3.3	Numbers/tonnage of Axis shipping sunk, January–July 1941	70
3.4	Losses in anti-shipping operations, January–July 1941	73
3.5	Cargoes despatched from Italy and landed in Libya, January–July 1941	76
4.1	Numbers/tonnage of Axis shipping sunk, August–December 1941	94
4.2	Losses in anti-shipping operations, August–December 1941	97
4.3	Cargo tonnages despatched and landed in Libya, November–December 1941	100
4.4	Axis aviation fuel stocks in Libya, October–December 1941	104
5.1	Numbers/tonnage of Axis shipping sunk, January–August 1942	118
5.2	Losses in anti-shipping operations, January–August 1942	119
5.3	Cargo tonnages despatched and landed in Libya, January–August 1942	120
6.1	Numbers/tonnage of Axis shipping sunk, September–November 1942	136
6.2	Losses in anti-shipping operations, September–November 1942	137
6.3	Cargo tonnages despatched and landed in Libya, September 1942–January 1943	143
7.1	Numbers/tonnage of Axis shipping sunk, December 1942–May 1943	156
7.2	Losses in anti-shipping operations, December 1942–May 1943	157
7.3	Cargo tonnages despatched and landed in Tunisia, November 1942–May 1943	161
8.1	Numbers/tonnage of Axis shipping sunk, June–December 1943	183
8.2	Losses in anti-shipping operations, June–December 1943	184

Acknowledgements

This could be a book in and of itself! It is simply impossible to include all the people who assisted me in some manner during this long journey, so I should start with an open expression of gratitude to all those whom I cannot name individually. As for those that I can, I should start with Professor Richard Overy, Dr Christina Goulter and Dr Duncan Redford, who guided and encouraged me expertly when I was starting out in the world of historical research. Since then, numerous colleagues, both former and current, have offered vital aid in various ways, and I owe a general thanks to the professional services and academic staffs of the Social and Political Sciences Department at Brunel University and the Defence Studies Department of King's College London. In particular I must thank Professors Matthew Hughes, Matthew Seligmann and Niall Barr, Drs Jonathan Fennell, Christina Goulter (again), Aimée Fox, Tim Benbow and David Morgan-Owen for offering important advice and expertise and in some cases reading draft material. Any errors that remain, however, are my responsibility alone. I must also thank Professor Wyn Bowen for his invaluable advice and encouragement at an early stage of my career.

Beyond immediate colleagues, the international community of scholars has generally been very welcoming, and many have provided great help in dealing with archives and accessing material. Professor John Gooch, Dr Fabio De Ninno, Dr Marco Maria Aterrano and Dr Nicolò Da Lio have all helped me with the use of Italian archives and documents. Professor MacGregor Knox, Dr Brian Sullivan and the staff at the Imperial War Museum, Duxford, helped me with Axis source material available in the United States and here in the United Kingdom. I am grateful to Sebastian Cox for permission to quote from the Portal Papers.

Cambridge University Press has been a joy to work with, and I must thank in particular Michael Watson and Emily Sharp, who have guided me through the process from submission to publication, while the copy editors worked tirelessly to tighten the final manuscript. The Philip Nicholas Trust offered me vital financial support in the early stages, and further assistance has since been provided by both King's College London and Brunel University.

Some of the biggest thanks must go to my parents, Fiona and Jim. Without their constant encouragement, support and at times, frankly, baffling levels of patience, I would never even have embarked on this book. My sisters, Claire and Lucy also helped in this regard and were always willing to listen to me complain. Liz and Caroline kindly put me up in London on many occasions during the earlier stages of my research, helping me keep to a slim budget. The final word, though, must go to my wife, Joyce. She has lived and breathed this entire process with me and suffered through it all with incredible stoicism. Thanks Joyce; I don't know how I'd have done this, or indeed much of anything, without you.

A Note on Terminology: 'British' and 'Allied'

Throughout this book, references made to 'British' forces are frequently shorthand. The 'British' armed forces during the war were a huge, multinational conglomerate that consisted of people drawn from the entirety of the Empire and Commonwealth. That was very much the case in the Mediterranean theatre, where non-British manpower constituted a high proportion of the soldiers, sailors, airmen and other personnel who took part. Emblematic of this was the make-up of the 'British' personnel based in North Africa in October 1942 at the time of Operation 'Lightfoot'. Here, while nearly 400,000 personnel of all types from the United Kingdom were based in the desert, they were joined by over 100,000 from the Dominions of Australia, New Zealand and South Africa, almost 200,000 who were classified as 'other Imperial', and around 70,000 'Allied'.[1]

The 'Allied' figure given above is worth explaining. Beyond those servicemen from around the Empire and Commonwealth who formally served alongside the British, those of numerous other nationalities found themselves serving under a 'British' banner. Over the course of the war, service personnel of numerous different defeated nations who wished to continue the fight against the Axis wound up serving in units or warships that were under British operational control. In one Mediterranean-specific example, a total of sixty-seven non-British submarines, of six different nationalities, served under British operational control at some point during the war.[2]

While 'British' is therefore very broadly defined, the Mediterranean was very much a 'British' theatre from June 1940 to mid-1942. It is for that reason that Chapters 2–5 refer almost exclusively to a 'British' anti-shipping campaign. From summer 1942 onwards, however, there was increasing American involvement. This initially took the form of the transferal of large quantities of American equipment such as tanks and artillery, as well as American air units, to Egypt in the dark days of summer 1942.[3] The theatre became a truly Allied venture from November 1942, with the landing of Anglo-American forces in north-west

Africa. The American commitment to the anti-shipping campaign was important, although less diverse in terms of forces committed than that of the British. No American submarines operated in the theatre, while their surface warships took little part either. American air power, however, played an important role, through bombing ports in Italy and southern France, or through direct attack against shipping at sea. Therefore, from Chapter 6 onwards, this book refers more broadly to an 'Allied' anti-shipping campaign.

Abbreviations

AOC	Air Officer Commanding
AOC-in-C	Air Officer Commanding-in-Chief
ASV	Air to Surface Vessel Radar
ASW	Anti-Submarine Warfare
C-in-C	Commander-in-Chief
cbm	Cubic meters
CIGS	Chief of the Imperial General Staff
Comando Supremo	Italian Armed Forces High Command
COS	Chiefs of Staff (British)
CU	Consumption Unit
DAK	*Deutsches Afrika Korps*
FAA	Fleet Air Arm
GAF	German Air Force
IAF	Italian Air Force
JCOS	Joint Chiefs of Staff (American)
MT	Motor transport
OKH	*Oberkommando des Heeres* (German Army High Command)
OKW	*Oberkommando der Wehrmacht* (German Armed Forces High Command)
ORS	Operational Research Section
RAF	Royal Air Force
RDF	Radio Direction Finding (Radar)
S1	First Submarine Flotilla
S8	Eighth Submarine Flotilla
S10	Tenth Submarine Flotilla
SIGINT	Signals intelligence
Supermarina	Italian Navy High Command
USAAF	United States Army Air Force

Maps

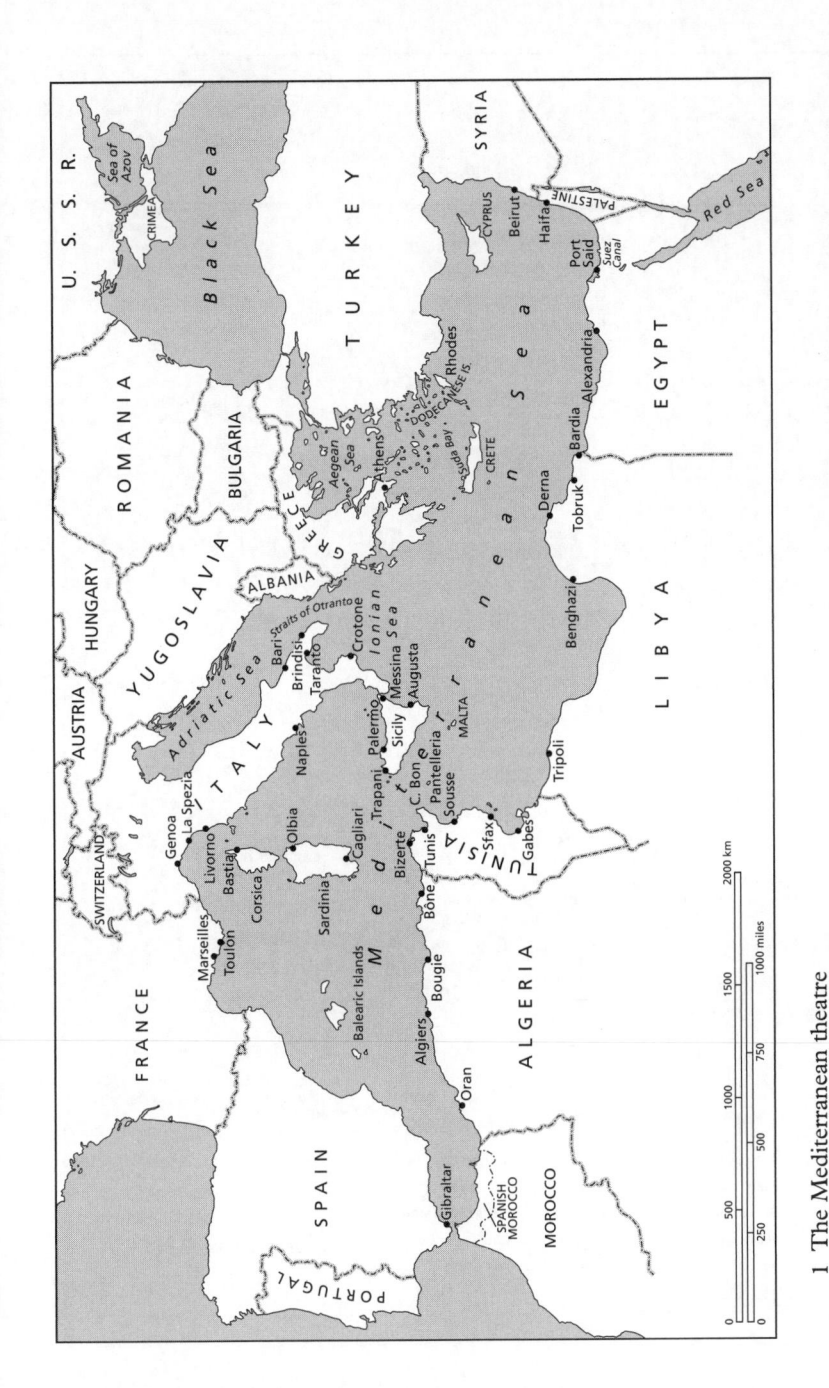

1 The Mediterranean theatre
Source: Adapted from I. S. O. Playfair et al., *The Mediterranean and Middle East, Vol. 1: The Early Successes against Italy* (London: HMSO, 1954), p. 9

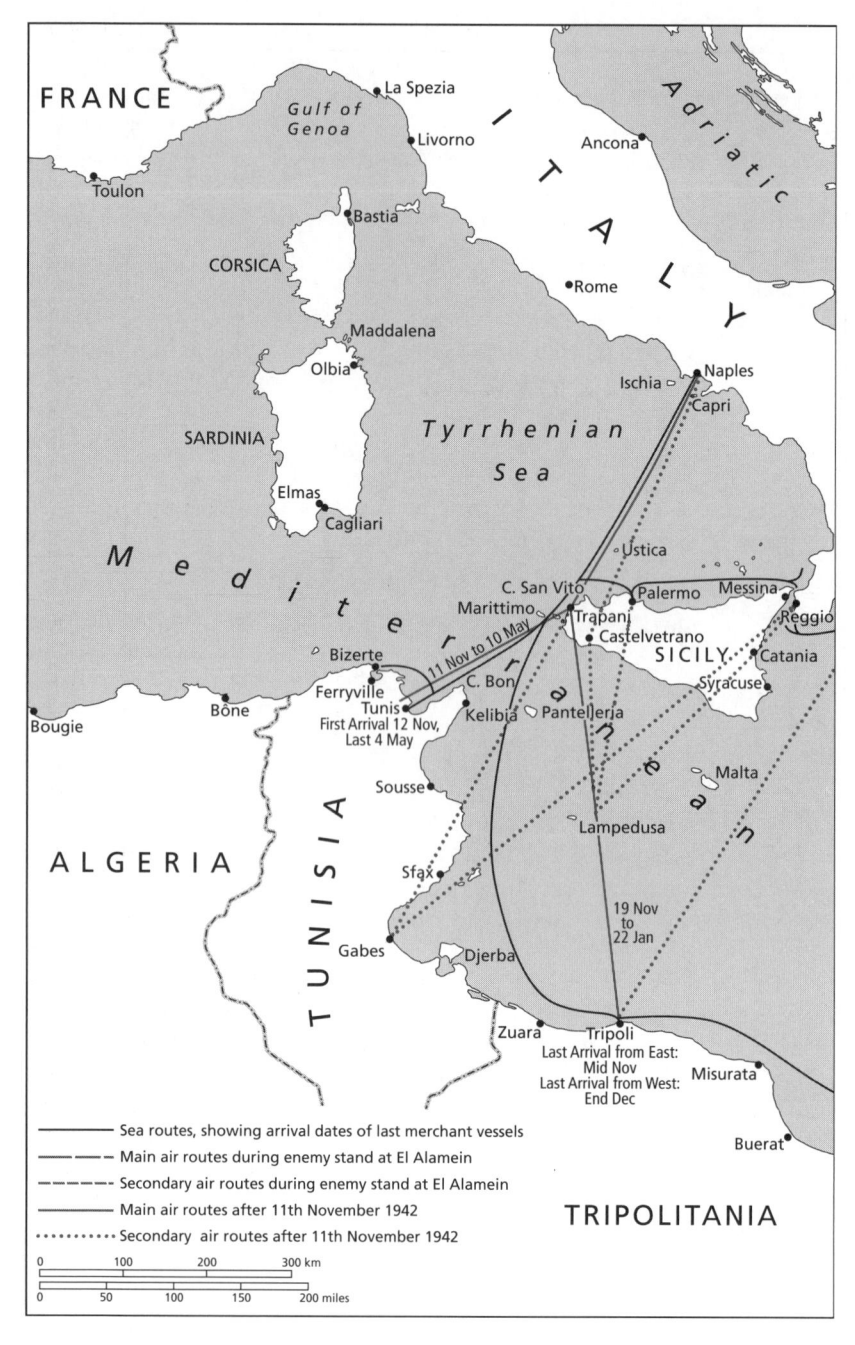

2 Axis sea and air transport routes to North Africa, October 1942–May 1943

Source: Adapted from I. S. O. Playfair et al., *The Mediterranean and Middle East, Vol. 4: The Destruction of the Axis Forces in Africa* (London: HMSO, 1966), p. 193

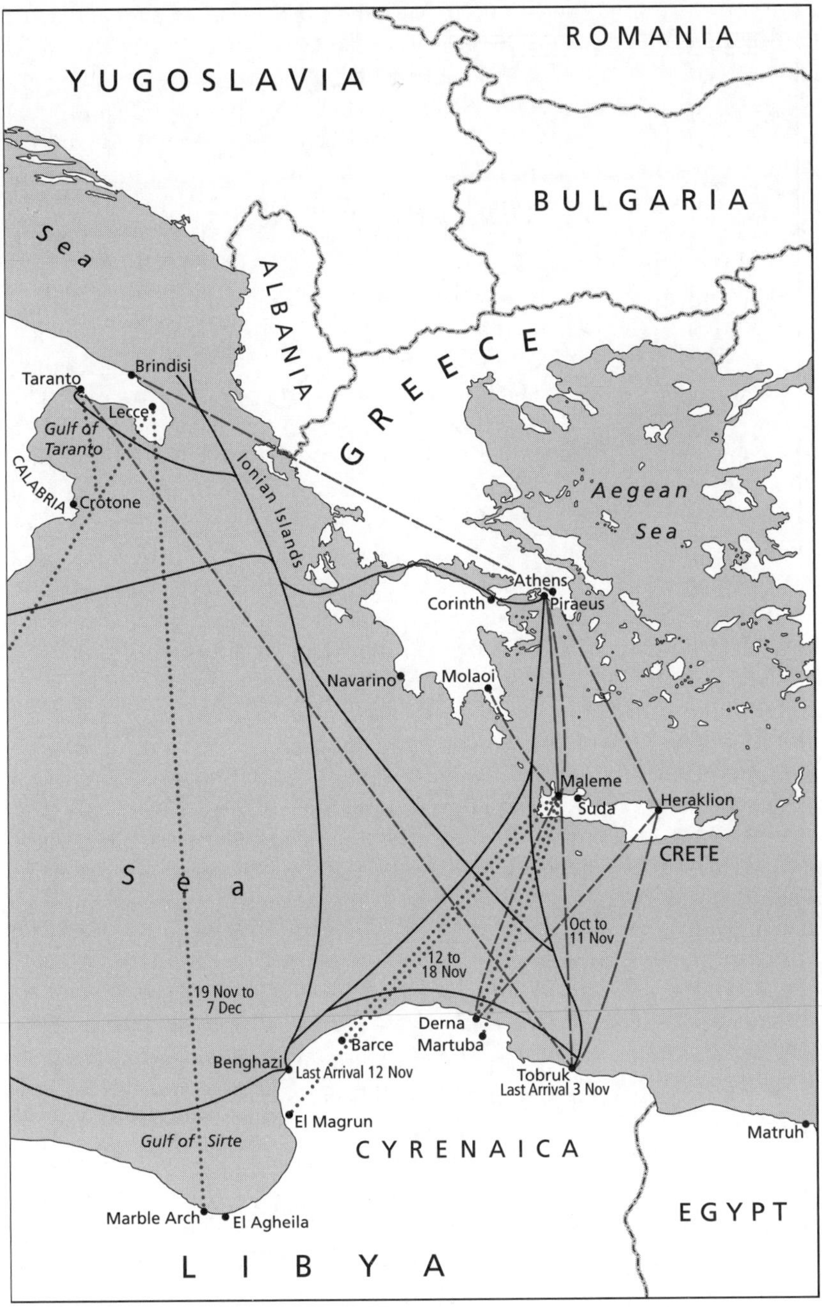

ROMANIA
YUGOSLAVIA
BULGARIA
ALBANIA
GREECE
Sea
Brindisi
Taranto
Lecce
Gulf of Taranto
CALABRIA
Crotone
Ionian Islands
Aegean Sea
Athens
Corinth
Piraeus
Navarino
Molaoi
Maleme
Suda
Heraklion
CRETE
Sea
Oct to 11 Nov
12 to 18 Nov
19 Nov to 7 Dec
Derna
Martuba
Barce
Benghazi
Last Arrival 12 Nov
Tobruk
Last Arrival 3 Nov
El Magrun
Matruh
Gulf of Sirte
CYRENAICA
EGYPT
Marble Arch
El Agheila
LIBYA

3 The central and eastern Mediterranean, including the Aegean islands
Source: Adapted from I. S. O. Playfair et al., *The Mediterranean and Middle East, Vol. 4: The Destruction of the Axis Forces in Africa* (London: HMSO, 1966), p. 193

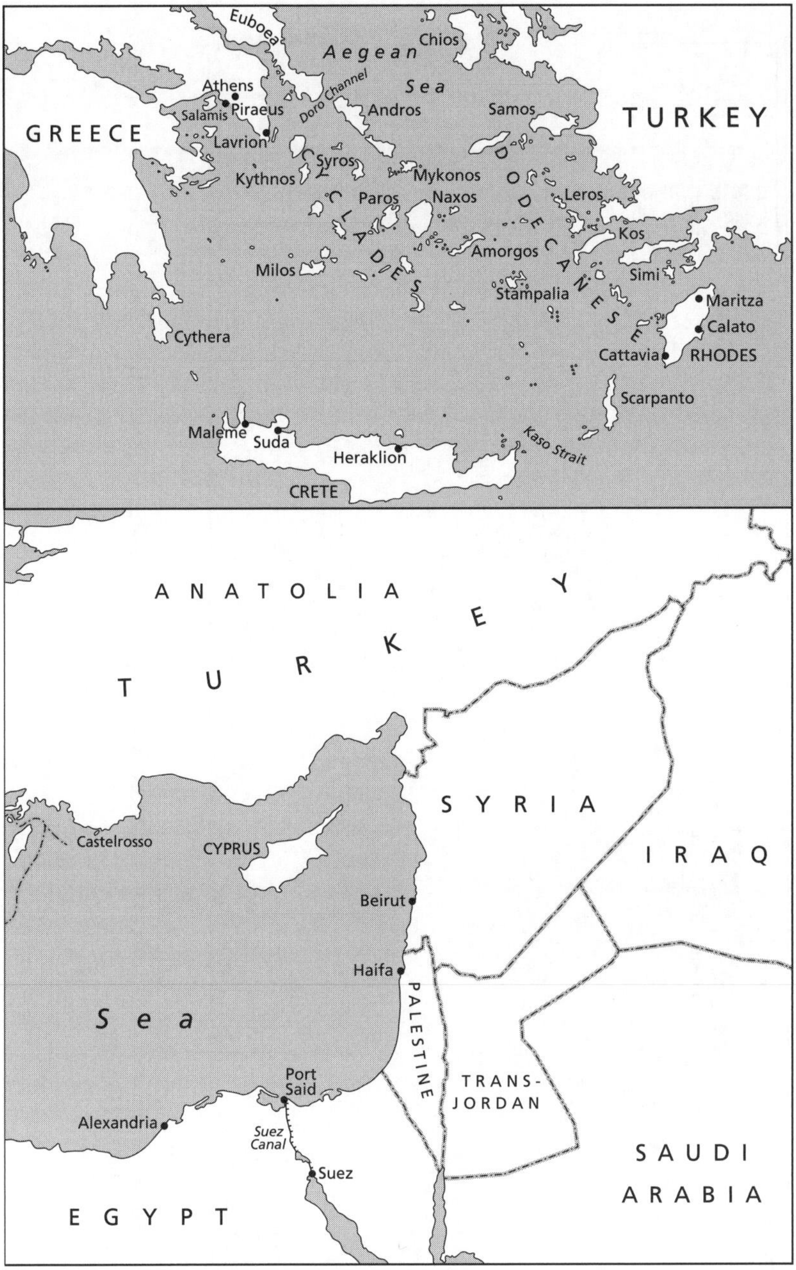
Euboea
Chios
Aegean
Sea
Doro Channel
Athens
Piraeus
Salamis
Andros
Samos
TURKEY
GREECE
Lavrion
Syros
CYCLADES
DODECANESE
Kythnos
Mykonos
Paros
Naxos
Leros
Kos
Amorgos
Milos
Simi
Stampalia
Maritza
Calato
Cythera
Cattavia
RHODES
Scarpanto
Maleme
Suda
Kaso Strait
Heraklion
CRETE
ANATOLIA
TURKEY
SYRIA
IRAQ
Castelrosso
CYPRUS
Beirut
Haifa
PALESTINE
Sea
TRANS-
JORDAN
Port
Said
Alexandria
Suez
Canal
Suez
SAUDI
ARABIA
EGYPT

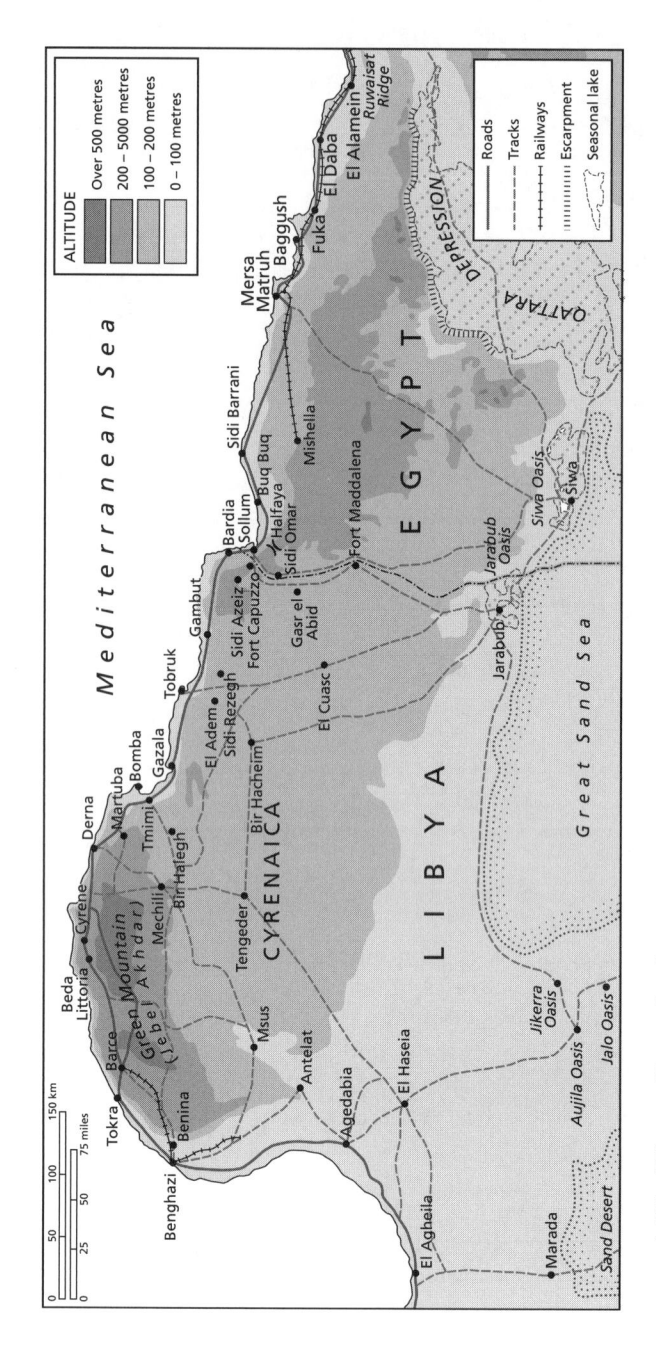

4 The Western Desert battle area
Source: www.asisbiz.com/il2/Fiat-G50/RA-151SA/images/Map-showing-the-Western-Desert-Battle-Area-Operation-Crusader-Relief-of-Tobruk-1941-0A.jpg

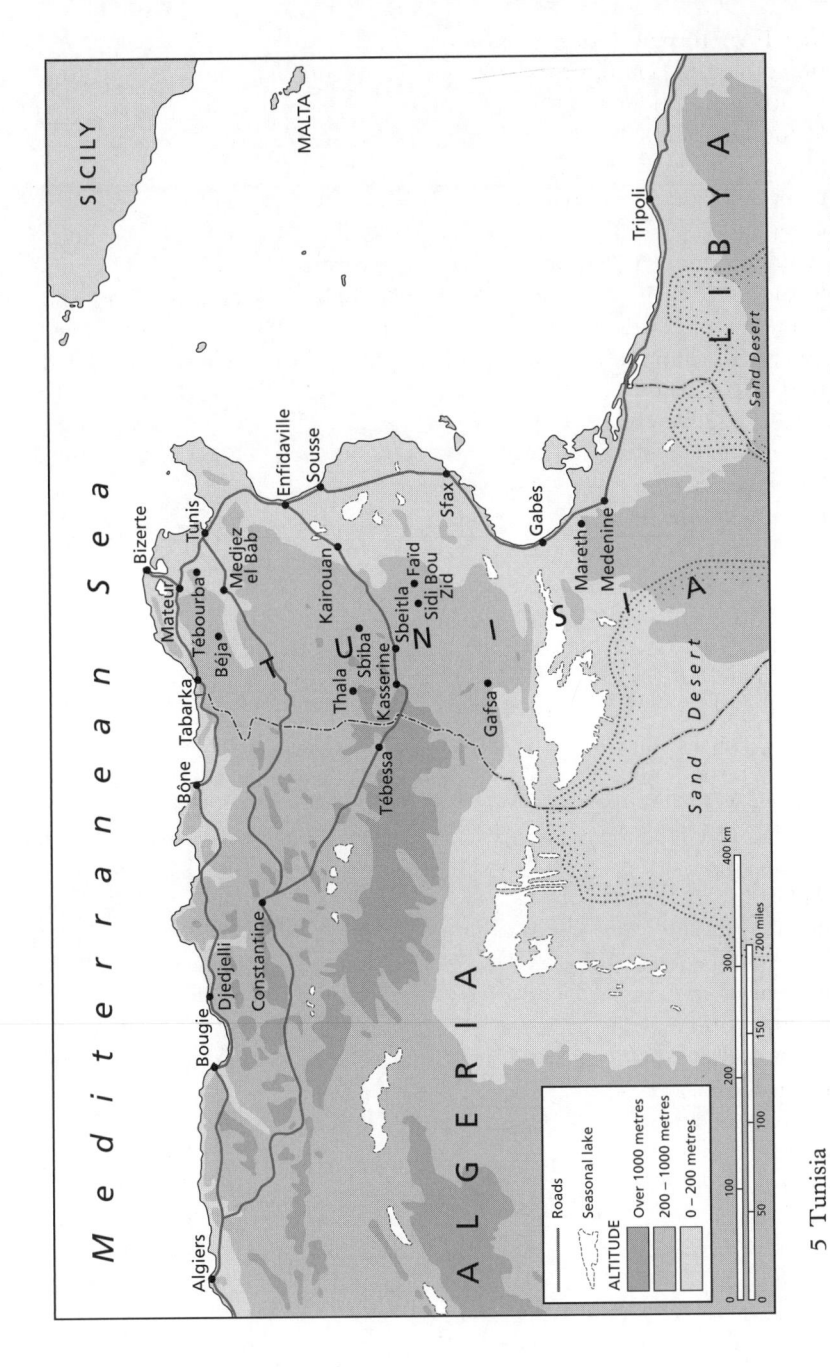

5 Tunisia
Source: www.asisbiz.com/il2/MC-200/MC-200-51S153G/pages/0-Map-Tunisia-Tunisia-Campaign-1942-43-0A.html

Introduction

On 10 June 1940, despite a distinct lack of enthusiasm from both the German and Italian military high commands, Benito Mussolini formally joined the war on the Axis side. That evening he gave a speech from the balcony of the Palazzo Venezia in Rome to an assembled crowd, informing them that their country was going to war to stop 'the plutocratic and reactionary democracies of the west'.[1] In reality, much of that 'stopping' had already been done by Germany: most of the British personnel had already been evacuated from the continent to a homeland faced with the prospect of invasion, while France would soon sign an armistice. What it did achieve was to transform the war by spreading it beyond the boundaries of Europe and igniting a long and bloody contest to control the Mediterranean. It was the ultimate ability of the Allies to prevail in controlling its waterways and thence strangle Axis communications at sea, which proved vital to securing victory. This forced the collapse of the Italo-German position across the broadly defined 'Mediterranean theatre', removed the threat to key British imperial possessions and ensured the defeat of Fascist Italy.

The Italian entry into the conflict was undertaken in order to deliver on Mussolini's long-held ambition of building a Mediterranean empire. With France now supine, realising this dream appeared to require one simple objective: to 'drive the British from the Eastern Mediterranean'.[2] Building and sustaining such an empire would require vast quantities of supplies, a requirement that would be exacerbated by the increased demands of expeditionary warfare. Given the geography of the Mediterranean, there was only one realistic method for the creation and sustainment of this new empire: to ship vast quantities of men, vehicles, munitions, fuel and supplies across the Mediterranean Sea. Axis shipping was in abundance across the Mediterranean, fulfilling multiple roles over the 1940–44 period in what became a sprawling maritime logistics network. Its best-known use was to transport vital stores and reinforcements from Italy to North Africa, to conduct and support the mobile land campaign that took place there for almost three years. Once these men and materiel had been transferred, they then had to be delivered to the frontline. This was achieved through a mixture of overland haulage and coastal shipping, which carried cargo from the main Libyan port of Tripoli to the advance Axis ports along the coast, such as Benghazi, Derna and Tobruk, when they were in Axis possession. Beyond North Africa, a seaborne system of supply was also vital to sustaining important Axis island territories from Sardinia to the Aegean. Finally, it was essential to the Italian war economy itself, as Italy was incapable of producing sufficient quantities of key resources such as oil, coal and iron domestically, and so relied on imports.[3]

The efforts of the Axis powers to develop a maritime supply chain to support their expansionist aims brought them into conflict with Britain, the dominant sea power in the region, which relied upon the Mediterranean for its own trade and supply.[4] Shipping was at the heart of this conflict and forms the central focus of this book. It shows that Allied efforts to curtail Axis shipping in the region were crucial to their ultimate victory in North Africa, the Middle East and southern Europe. This was so for two reasons: first the interdiction of supplies at sea decisively degraded Axis fighting capability on land, particularly in the campaigns in North Africa. Second, the overall attrition to Axis shipping resources fatally undermined their ability to sustain a wider Mediterranean position by depriving them of the means to support their various overseas territories.

This attrition to vital Axis shipping resources caused a fundamental collapse of their entire Mediterranean position due to the systematic isolation and debilitation of key logistical and air staging posts. Consequently, the retention of outposts in North Africa, Sardinia, Corsica, Sicily and in the Aegean all became completely untenable. The anti-shipping campaign thus played a central role in reversing the fortunes from a position of Axis dominance in mid-1942, when they exercised control of nearly the entire theatre, to one where they retained a hold over a fraction of the sea's northern shore by late 1944. The anti-shipping campaign was thus the fulcrum about which strategy in the theatre pivoted, and the vital enabling factor to ultimate Allied victory.

Sea Power and the Global Second World War

Whilst assessing the relative contribution of sea power to Allied victory in the First World War has proven problematic,[5] historians generally agree that maritime dominance exerted a crucial influence on the outcome of the Second World War. It received a dedicated chapter in Richard Overy's seminal *Why the Allies Won*, placing it as one among several key causal factors and emphasising the link between operations at sea and those on land. More recently Phillips Payson O'Brien's *How the War Was Won: Air-Sea Power and Allied Victory in World War II* went much further in making a case for its importance.[6] He minimised the role of the war on land compared to that from the air and at sea, positing that success in these environments had the greatest effect in terms of outstripping Axis production capacity. In a similar vein, Craig Symonds has since argued that while '"boots on the ground" were essential in this war (as they are in every war), it was supremacy at sea that eventually proved decisive'. For Symonds, while operational success at sea was an important factor, it was primarily the Allied ability to build vessels faster than the Axis ability to sink them that enabled this decisive role. Ultimately, the ability to build vast quantities of shipping and retain global sea communications within acceptable levels of loss was absolutely central to Allied victory in the war.[7]

These are key conceptual works that seek to place the importance of the war at sea within the multifaceted, global nature of the Second World War. In a separate strand of literature, historians have sought to determine the importance of the Mediterranean within this same global context and its position within different nations' grand strategy. Douglas Porch has argued forcefully that the Mediterranean was a pivotal theatre for the Allies, with victory there playing a central role in determining the overall outcome.[8] Simon Ball has taken a broader view of the position of the Mediterranean, assessing the changing dynamics of regional hegemony and the importance of the Mediterranean towards great power status, as well as identifying different themes of conflict ongoing in the theatre.[9] Sitting alongside these works are several studies that assess Anglo-American wartime strategy and the various frictions that developed over their disagreements regarding the place of the Mediterranean within it.[10]

The published works across these two strands of literature have delivered important analyses and new lenses through which to assess the outcome of the war. However, these two strands – assessing the paramountcy of sea power in the war and of the Mediterranean respectively – remain largely distinct. Discussions of sea power in the war generally focus on the Battle of the Atlantic and the war in the Pacific, while studies of the Mediterranean are either narrative histories of the engagements at sea or are dominated by the land campaigns around its periphery. This book reverses that trend by placing the anti-shipping campaign in the Mediterranean at the forefront of its analysis. Doing so enables us to see that success in the maritime war in the Mediterranean was crucial to ultimate Allied victory both in the basin itself, and more broadly.

After all, exerting any form of control over seas or oceans is not an end in itself. Rather, it is the benefits in terms of mobility that this allows the dominant power, or denies the opponent, that is important, a point recognised by key theorists of maritime warfare.[11] As Herbert Richmond succinctly put it immediately after the conflict, in wartime

> Sea power is that form of national strength which enables its possessor to send his armies and commerce across those stretches of sea and ocean which lie between his country or the country of his allies, and those territories to which he needs access in war; and to prevent his enemy from doing the same.[12]

In this sense, while the importance of shipping within the global context of war has received historical attention,[13] the impact within and importance of the Mediterranean has been underestimated. In other words, by understanding the shipping war in the Mediterranean, we simultaneously gain a fresh perspective on both an important theatre, and on the global Second World War.

Historians, Shipping and the Mediterranean War

Beyond the literature with a global scope, the war in the Mediterranean certainly does not lack in quantity of specialist studies, but this historiography is segmented and is missing a holistic approach. The question of how much the land and sea environments intertwined to deliver military victory is beyond the scope of the analysis offered in the numerous histories of the war at sea; both those covering the war as a whole,[14] and those dedicated specifically to the Mediterranean.[15] For a theatre where both military operations on land and the ongoing sustainment of territories relied so heavily on the lifeblood of shipping, these pieces of scholarship offer little coverage of the anti-shipping campaign and even less of the resultant effects. The narrative works tend to focus on fleet actions, with the anti-shipping campaign relegated to single chapters, footnotes and passing comment.

The official naval histories, while extensive, offer only a little more in this respect. Roskill's *War at Sea* outlines the conduct and results of anti-shipping operations and points to tabulated figures of shipping sunk as a sole indicator that they 'contributed greatly to the collapse in Africa', yet it does not actually assess the effect of those sinkings.[16] Italy has produced by far the most comprehensive of the official naval histories, with a series of nineteen volumes. These, along with a contemporaneous book by Giorgio Giorgerini, provide full statistical data regarding Axis shipping in the Mediterranean, as well as three volumes dedicated to the effort to safeguard their shipping for North Africa, and one volume that does the same for the Adriatic and Aegean.[17] The series gives valuable insight into the organisation, and frequently lack thereof, of Axis efforts to safeguard their shipping. This includes the priority assigned to the role and tactical and technical developments. However, these operational histories offer relatively little in the way of analysis as to the effects of the campaign. This is perhaps surprising when, by way of comparison, naval histories looking at British logistics and concerned with the siege of Malta offer rich analyses of the effects of supply losses on the island's sustainment.[18]

In contrast to the literature written from a maritime perspective, those from a land perspective have contributed a greater effort to integrate the issue of Axis supply losses with operational effect in North Africa. The multi-service British official history on *The Mediterranean and Middle East* gives a balanced study. Like Roskill, it also makes use of detailed tables of Axis shipping sunk, giving sinkings by cause and month in both number and tonnage. There is in addition some analysis of the development of the campaign, focusing particularly on the role of Malta within it and of the effects on Axis forces in North Africa.[19] Yet it does not delve deeply into how the actual repercussions on Axis fighting effectiveness manifested in North Africa, or the result of the loss of large quantities of shipping on the Axis war effort as a whole. The German official histories, while bringing useful new source material into an English-language publication, do not specialise on aspects of the war through the use of sub-series in the same way as their British counterparts. Therefore, they suffer from the same issues as the British series, to a greater degree, thanks to their brevity on this subject.[20] Numerous recent operational histories of the war in North Africa have also acknowledged the part played by Axis logistical difficulties, but their focus does not extend to examining a causal link between the war at sea and on land.[21]

Finally, there are a handful of specialised works that focus purely on the anti-shipping campaign and North Africa. Martin van Creveld, in *Supplying War: Logistics from Wallenstein to Patton*, limits himself solely to the period from spring 1941 to autumn 1942 and dismisses the campaign as irrelevant. He places the reason for Axis logistical difficulties squarely on overland routes and port capacities. In a similar vein, Brad Gladman has argued that the effects of the anti-shipping campaign paled in comparison to those of the aerial interdiction of motor transport. Alan Levine's *The War against Rommel's Supply Lines, 1942–1943* offers a more positive assessment of the impact of the campaign but is limited both temporally and in terms of material, relying almost entirely on Anglo-American sources for evidence.[22] Alongside these are several books focused solely on the role of Malta in the anti-shipping campaign. Of these, Douglas Austin's *Malta and British Strategic Policy, 1925–1943* is the most comprehensive, with the second half of the book offering both an operational analysis of the campaign and some exploration of the effects on the war in North Africa.[23]

What this survey of the current literature highlights is that the anti-shipping campaign in the Mediterranean lacks a dedicated and holistic study, incorporating the entirety of the theatre and the period after the fall of the Axis in North Africa.[24] What is more, no existing work has set out to ask the question of whether there were wider ramifications from the loss of large quantities of Axis shipping to their attempts to control the Mediterranean. This study rectifies both lacunae by taking such an approach. It examines the evolving place of the Mediterranean in Allied grand strategy, and the priority of the anti-shipping campaign within the theatre. It analyses the nature and number of forces of all types that were used within it, and their suitability, tactical development, efficacy, and the results they achieved in terms of sinkings. Finally, it assesses their effects on *both* the fighting effectiveness of Axis armies and air forces and on their broader ability to maintain a position across the Mediterranean theatre. Through the use of a unique mix of multinational source material, much of which has been underused to date, it demonstrates that the campaign fatally undermined the Axis in both of these respects. In total, source material from twelve archives across three different countries has been consulted during the research for this book.

***

This book opens with a discussion of the importance of the Mediterranean to the British Empire, highlighting its role as a 'vital artery' of communication between the eastern and western worlds. By examining the changing position of the Mediterranean in British strategic policy from the construction of the Suez Canal through to the Italian declaration of war in 1940, it shows how important the Mediterranean would be in the event of a major global war. However, British foreign policy in the late inter-war period included numerous efforts to keep Italy neutral, allowing the Mediterranean to be denuded of military assets in favour of their deployment against threats elsewhere. Consequently, these decisions led to a difficult context in which to plan realistically for war in the Mediterranean, and the subsequent paucity of British forces stationed there at the start of hostilities. It was this situation which set the foundation for early failures in the anti-shipping campaign.

This is followed by an examination of British war planning for the Mediterranean over the late 1930s, as relations with Italy soured. It highlights the argument between proponents of a 'knockout blow' and those who preferred the slow strangulation of Italy by cutting key communications at sea. The ultimate prevailing of the latter argument led to an appreciation of the importance of cutting Axis sea communications by 1940, even if they initially lacked the military power to do so and were restricted by legal criteria prohibiting attacks on merchant shipping in most cases, a situation that would soon alter under the demands of war. By contrast, the Italians and especially Germans neglected measures to protect and conserve shipping resources in order to maintain their ability to operate in the theatre – a neglect that was to come back to haunt them! Like the British, they too held some hopes to control the Mediterranean as a waterway not only for the safeguarding of their own sea communications, but to strangle those of their enemies. Yet a lack of appropriate planning and cohesion between the Axis powers ensured such hopes proved ill-founded.

After the Italian declaration of war came the period of their short-lived 'parallel war', where they attempted to fight independently of Germany in the theatre. Chapter 2 highlights the great numerical disparity between the scarce British and Commonwealth forces spread from the Middle East to Gibraltar versus those of Italy. Despite this lack of resources, theatre commanders recognised the need to make inroads into Italian sea communications, and they also received clear direction from Whitehall to pursue this objective. Consequently, the failure to do so was not for lack of will at any level of command, but a question of means. The scattered, incoherent efforts that were made are shown to have been completely ineffectual, with British success against the Italians in North Africa during 1940 instead being the product of a series of other factors. Nevertheless, this period set important foundations for an anti-shipping campaign in terms of the recognition of the vulnerability of Italian sea routes and the need for greater resources to prosecute it.

The failure of the 'parallel war' was followed by turmoil caused by a combination of German intervention in the theatre and the British decision to send aid to Greece. The shift in focus towards what would be a disastrous Greek expedition resulted in neglect of the Axis sea lanes with North Africa, and abortive efforts at interdiction were made in the Adriatic instead. Yet, as this chapter shows, there were also positive developments in the campaign. New types of more suitable equipment and weaponry were employed, accompanied by the beginnings of a learning process to develop new tactics and procedures and to incorporate new technologies. This offered the potential for greater efficiency in anti-shipping operations, but it was only from April onwards that significant attention was again paid to them. Sinking rates promptly increased and, although the overall required Axis supply quotas were generally met, the losses did cause logistical pressure in certain key areas. While anti-shipping operations had been relatively limited in terms of quantity and effect over the first year of the war in the Mediterranean, an important foundation was laid in terms of recognition of their importance, increasing priority and operational learning. This provided the platform for what would be become a decisive campaign.

Building on these progressive steps, Chapter 4 starts with the Mediterranean receiving a new level of recognition in British strategic priority during the August–December 1941 period, becoming the primary effort. Moreover, the anti-shipping campaign was promoted to a prime position in operational priority for the Navy and Air Force, with a corresponding dedication of forces to the task. Coupled with this was an increase in the pace of learning and the refinement of tactical procedures. This led to greatly increased levels of sinkings over August–December, which coincided with a new, major British offensive in North Africa: Operation 'Crusader'. These sinkings successfully denied Axis forces in Cyrenaica the necessary fuel and ammunition to either launch their own planned offensive or to resist the British advance, including the loss of 92 per cent of the fuel shipped in November. Furthermore, the increased levels of attrition meant that sinkings now greatly outstripped the Axis replenishment capability through new construction or other means. This was the first clear example of the dual effect of the anti-shipping campaign: one operational, affecting the war on land in North Africa, and one attritional, undermining the Axis ability to conduct any form of warfare in the Mediterranean. It caused serious concern among the Axis commands, leading to the adoption of new countermeasures, which were to have a major impact in the following year.

Despite the qualified successes of 'Crusader', Britain was faced with a disastrous turn of events in early 1942. The entry of Japan to the war had compelled a redistribution of force to the Far East, while some key British losses and new in-theatre German commitments had further redefined the Mediterranean balance of power. Chapter 5 outlines how the British were forced to adopt a defensive posture throughout the theatre, as their gains from 'Crusader' were rapidly reversed. As the Axis then advanced into Egypt, Malta was subjected to an intense aerial siege and came perilously close to being starved into submission. The difficulties in conducting anti-shipping operations during this period were numerous. Yet in a reversal of the thesis advanced by historians such as van Creveld and Gladman, the chapter demonstrates that significant sinkings (of over 300,000 tons) were achieved during this period. This continued attrition was greatly troubling for the Axis, contributing to a shipping shortage that was to reach crisis point later in the year.

Chapter 6 begins by illustrating the respective positions of each side by September 1942. It shows that while the Axis position can in retrospect be viewed as highly precarious, the British evinced real concern about a complete collapse in Egypt. It highlights the resurgent emphasis that was placed on the Mediterranean from Whitehall, and on anti-shipping operations by the theatre commanders. These were pursued with a ruthless prioritisation; even after clear evidence that some Axis vessels were carrying British prisoners of war, the Chiefs of Staff (COS) decreed that there should be 'no prohibition' on attacks under any circumstances.

This allowed anti-shipping operations to thrive, aided by the effective use of all-source intelligence to target the most critical cargoes of fuel and ammunition at sea, to the bafflement of the Axis powers. As a result, over the three-month period, ninety-five vessels of nearly 200,000 tons were sunk, with grave effects on the Axis. The chapter closes by showing how these sinkings helped curtail the final Axis offensive in Egypt and contributed to the vital British victory at El Alamein by depriving the Axis of essential fuel and ammunition. In contrast to arguments put forward by scholars such as van Creveld, Barnett and Gladman, the book uses a mix of Italian, German and British material to conclusively show that the supply shortages suffered by the Axis were primarily the result of seaborne sinkings.

While El Alamein represented an important defensive victory at the eastern fringe of the Mediterranean, joint Anglo-American landings in north-west Africa caused a transformation of the theatre. Chapter 7 begins with a discussion of this shift to a truly Allied venture, where the war in North Africa was fought on two fronts, with consequent effects on Axis supply requirements. Anti-shipping operations continued to receive high priority throughout this period, with senior American leaders in the theatre, such as General Dwight Eisenhower, also urging for ever greater efforts in this vein. These appeals immediately led to the transferral of additional aircraft from other theatres precisely for this purpose. This resulted in a devastating 477 vessels of over 700,000 tons being sunk in five months. The numerous emergency countermeasures introduced by the Axis powers were simply incapable of reversing the devastating scale of attrition. These sinkings had important effects across two different levels. First the interdiction of shipping had a drastic degrading effect on Axis fighting efficiency in Tunisia. The sinkings ensured that the minimum level of supplies required by the Axis forces were not received. In fact, the losses were so devastating that the

Axis came to lack the necessary vessels to even attempt to ship the required amounts in the first place.

Finally, the chapter offers a revolutionary new argument: that the period around October 1942 represented a tipping point towards collapse for the Axis position in the wider Mediterranean due to the sheer scale of attrition to their shipping. The question of a 'shipping crisis' has been dismissed by the few who have briefly considered it, yet by using new multinational source material this chapter demonstrates that one truly took place. By October the consistently high rates of sinkings had greatly eroded the base of available tonnage, and efforts to improve construction had failed. The attempts to fill the void with seized French tonnage were far less effective than some have claimed, and by early summer 1943 the Axis were acknowledging that maintaining positions such as Sardinia and Corsica was no longer possible, while retaining the Aegean islands and even Sicily were tenuous aims.

The final chapter opens with a discussion of the transformed nature of the war in the Mediterranean after the Axis surrender in Tunisia, where Axis maritime commitments had shrunk, yet remained substantial. The Allied focus on other in-theatre tasks, particularly the invasions of Sicily and mainland Italy, pushed anti-shipping operations into a peripheral role. Yet there were times when they received greater focus, including the Axis evacuation of Sicily, and in the Aegean during 1943–44. An account of anti-shipping operations over the period in question shows that there were in fact very high quantities of sinkings at certain stages of the period in question. These contributed yet further to the overall shipping crisis, forcing the Axis to expedite the withdrawal from Sardinia, Corsica and many of their Aegean possessions. By late 1944, most of the territories reliant on maritime supply had been abandoned, and the anti-shipping campaign had been a key element in ensuring Allied victory in the Mediterranean.

1   The Descent to War in the Mediterranean

The Mediterranean had been an essential constituent part of the British Empire long prior to the Second World War.[1] It was important as both a hub and a highway of communication, linking the homeland to key imperial possessions in the Middle and Far East and so making it a vital asset for trade and imperial defence. This is one factor that helps to explain why the British placed such a hefty strategic emphasis on it during the conflict, alongside the fact that the context in which they found themselves after the fall of France left it as one of their few options for offensive action.

The possibility for anti-shipping operations to play an important role in such offensive action was recognised by war planners well before conflict with Italy became a reality. The question of the role of such operations was tied up in a debate between advocates of their primacy as part of an effort to 'strangle' Italy into submission, and advocates of a short, powerful 'knockout blow' through naval attack and strategic bombing. The 'strangulation' school ultimately won out, and its proponents were acutely aware that control of the entrances at each end of the Mediterranean offered a unique environment for the success of their method. Likewise, the majority of the Italian military high command acknowledged that this situation made them highly vulnerable to such an approach. As the head of the Italian Navy, Admiral Domenico Cavagnari, put it, 'One fleet will station itself at Gibraltar and another at Suez, and we will suffocate inside the Mediterranean.'[2] Given the Italians' own military inadequacies for the task, they would require German aid to have any chance of breaking this imprisonment in the Mediterranean. Yet that prospect was to find little favour with Italy's German ally, which broadly regarded the region as a distraction from its continental European focus.

Capitalising on its geographic position would prove a tough task for the British, however. The combined economic constraints and multiple state threats across the globe in the inter-war years compelled them to denude the Mediterranean of much in the way of military forces. Consequently, although they held the Mediterranean in a position of great importance and came to embrace the opportunities of a 'strangulation' strategy, they initially had little with which to enable this. It is essential, therefore, to examine the pre-war period in order to understand why the anti-shipping campaign achieved so little in 1940 and early 1941.

Artery of Empire: The Mediterranean in British Imperial Policy and Grand Strategy

The Mediterranean held a prominent place in imperial defence strategy throughout the history of the British Empire, both in the day-to-day security of trade and during major conflicts. It reached new levels of importance after the opening of the Suez Canal in 1869, as this transformed it from an imperial end in and of itself into a hugely advantageous link to the wider Empire. From this point onwards, the British consistently viewed the 'Mediterranean' in its broadest sense, incorporating the Tyrrhenian, Ionian, Adriatic and Aegean seas, as a 'single geo-strategic unit'.[3] The ability to travel through the Mediterranean, rather than via the 'Cape route' passing south of Africa, slashed the transit time to the vital imperial possessions of the Far East, such as India, Ceylon, Singapore and Hong Kong. Crucial resources could be transferred between Britain and these possessions in record time, and in terms of defence, so could military and naval forces. Peter Dietz is certainly correct when he writes that by the late nineteenth century, 'the defence of the Suez Canal and the safeguarding of Egypt had become a cornerstone of British policy in the Mediterranean'.[4]

The First World War demonstrated just how essential this ability was to Britain for it to conduct a truly global conflict. Forces were transferred between theatres with relative ease, including the vast human resources of India that were so advantageous to the small island state of Britain. The discovery of large quantities of precious oil in the Middle East increased the importance of British hegemony in the region yet further, as the fates of the Mediterranean and Middle East came to be seen as intertwined by defence planners. By the late 1930s the region provided over a twelfth of Britain's normal oil, but more importantly offered sufficient amounts to sustain its entire military commitment in the region and an easy source through which to supply the wider Empire. These developments made defence of the area from threat essential in any time of major war, and proximity to vast oil supplies would later prove highly advantageous to the Allies during the war.[5] The central importance of the Mediterranean to the British Empire has been recognised by historians, who have variously termed it a 'vital artery', a 'strategic corridor', 'the strongest official interest in the British world-system' and a 'super-highway to the world wide web'.[6]

Victory in the Great War handed Britain the opportunity to exert control over vast swathes of territory in the Middle East. It seized this and established a patchwork of colonies, protectorates, mandates, treaties and other elements of a largely 'informal' empire. This afforded access to the increasingly important oil resources of the region, along with other trade links, and cemented control over the eastern Mediterranean and Suez Canal. While there were often problems with internal unrest, which was sometimes externally sponsored, there was no serious direct great power competition until the mid-1930s, allowing British regional pre-eminence.[7] All actions taken towards dealing with the often turbulent region were geared towards avoiding involvement of the other great powers, and the attention of the newly created League of Nations.[8] Providing defence and security across the whole Empire, though, was a complex task over the inter-war years.

Britain was faced with the problem of serious financial retrenchment after the First World War and the Royal Air Force (RAF) and Royal Navy were unable to avoid stringent treasury spending controls for long after the Armistice.[9] Although they fared better than the Army, the two services struggled to fulfil their global responsibilities when the rising powers that would later form the Axis began to offer a serious challenge in the 1930s, starting with Japan's aggressive expansion into Manchuria in 1931. This demonstrated Japanese ambitions and their potential threat to British territories in the Far East, as well as the impotence of the League of Nations and a lack of common ground between Britain and America to deter Tokyo. This crisis came at a time when the Chiefs of Staff (COS) claimed that the effects of retrenchment had left the Empire near-defenceless in the Far East.[10] The Cabinet yielded to pressure, but increased spending slowly and spread it thinly, forcing a brutal prioritisation of resources. As a result, when the Abyssinian crisis of 1935–36 raised the possibility of war with Italy, the Mediterranean languished low down the list of imperial priorities. The British were left in a quandary; although they opposed Italian imperialism, they did not want to risk precious naval units in a war with Italy, or 'drive them into the arms' of Germany and Japan. Ultimately, the conquest of modern-day Ethiopia was left unopposed beyond some limited economic sanctions imposed by the League.[11]

This appeasement continued throughout Italian involvement in the Spanish Civil War, when they sent large numbers of 'volunteers' to fight with Franco's Nationalists. The wish to keep Germany and Italy apart was one of the principal factors that underpinned the British policy of non-intervention during that conflict in spite of consistently escalating Italian provocation.[12] At best, the British hoped to retain Italy as an ally against future German expansion, in line with an agreement from the 1935 Stresa conference, but at the very least they felt it essential to avoid actions that would antagonise Italy and lead to Mussolini making common cause with Adolf Hitler.[13]

It was not that the British establishment viewed Italy as a major threat on its own, but if it were to side with Germany in a war, it would stretch British and French commitments unbearably. Meanwhile, Italian air and naval bases in the central Mediterranean would threaten the Allies' ability to use that route to transfer vital manpower and resources between the United Kingdom and the Far East. As the new Prime Minister Neville Chamberlain put it, 'If only we could get on terms with the Germans, I would not care a rap for Musso.'[14] Diplomatic efforts by Chamberlain to appease Italy while maintaining a wedge between it and Germany continued via both official and unorthodox channels. The efforts saw the signing of Anglo-Italian agreements in 1937 and 1938 and initially brought hope for Chamberlain. In reality, they had little import, and the 1938 'Easter Accords' have been termed by one historian as 'little more than an agreement to agree sometime in the future'.[15]

Despite these efforts, there was a broadly consistent strengthening of Italo-German ties. Mussolini had proclaimed a Rome–Berlin Axis in November 1936, and the bonds were further solidified when Italy joined the 'Anti-Comintern Pact' a year later. A lynchpin in Britain's position of keeping a wedge between the two states had been the 'Austrian question'. Italy had been fundamentally opposed to increased German influence in, and especially control of, Austria, to the point of active military deterrence after Austrian Nazis assassinated Chancellor Dollfuss.[16] Yet when the Germans marched over the border in 1938, they met with tacit approval from Mussolini. The British Ambassador in Rome gloomily noted that 'What happened in Austria had not weakened the Rome–Berlin axis. The two kindred regimes, Fascism and National Socialism would continue to march side by side.'[17] The two then concluded the 'Pact of Steel' in 1939, which set a formal agreement for military co-operation between them in the event of a European war.[18]

The implications seemed abundantly clear, yet all hope for keeping Italy neutral had not been lost and that remained so after the German invasion of Poland and subsequent British and French declarations of war. The Pact of Steel had been signed with the proviso that Italy would not enter a major war until at least 1942, giving time for the completion of key military projects underway, such as the construction of new battleships.[19] Despite his rampant bellicosity, Mussolini was beset by internal warnings that Italy was far from ready for war. His Foreign Minister, Galeazzo Ciano, had received repeated tales of military unpreparedness, including one general's confession that the armament situation was 'disastrous'. In August, Ciano managed to pull a vacillating Mussolini back from the brink of committing to any European war unless Germany could provide the essentials that Italy needed. An eye-watering list of requirements was sent to Berlin, which Ciano felt was 'enough to kill a bull, if a bull could read it'.[20] The Duce signalled that if these requirements went unfilled, Italy would have to remain out of any war stemming from an invasion of Poland. Unsurprisingly, Germany refused this outrageous demand.

Italy remained in a period of uncertain 'non-belligerency' until, after the initial German success in north-west Europe, Mussolini informed his service chiefs that war was unavoidable, and fixed early June as the moment to join it.[21] This period of Italian neutrality offered the Allies the ability to focus on Europe and not dilute the continental commitment too greatly with Mediterranean diversions. Keeping Italy out of the war was thus seen as being of prime importance. It was a potentially fruitful foreign policy, too, given the continuing deficiencies of the Italian armed forces and economy.[22] Indeed, as late as December 1939, the British COS told the Cabinet that 'Italy was slowly moving towards the Allied camp, and precipitate action on our part might drive her in the opposite direction'. This had some logic given that many senior voices in the Italian military advised against joining the war, even after the German breakthrough in France in May 1940.[23] Ultimately, of course, the policy would fail and Italy did indeed declare war. The 'wait and see' approach adopted by the Allies over 1935–40, along with the necessary focus on Germany, made for a difficult environment in which to plan for the possibility of war in the Mediterranean.

Planning for War in the Mediterranean

Britain had first seriously considered the possibility of war against Fascist Italy during the Abyssinian crisis and had developed plans accordingly before ultimately choosing to stand aside. Given the geography of the Mediterranean and the location of Abyssinia, it was likely that any war would be primarily aero-naval in its conduct. While land elements would be important for the defence of Egypt and possibly Malta, it was on the sea and in the air that Italy would have to challenge Britain first, and also where the most likely route to British victory lay. There was, however, significant disagreement within the planning process, particularly regarding the war at sea. Two distinct camps emerged: one advocated a hyper-aggressive approach aiming to end the war quickly with a 'knockout blow', while the other counselled a slow strangulation through blockade.[24] Ultimately, neither was pursued despite the confidence of the theatre commanders for all three services that Britain would easily triumph over Italy. The COS and Cabinet also expected victory in such a war but were concerned that losses would then hamper their ability to deter or fight Germany or Japan. It might even convince one or both of them to take opportunistic action and declare war.[25]

Nevertheless, the naval planning debate is noteworthy as it was one which would essentially be rerun during the Anglo-French staff talks which belatedly took place in 1939. The 1935–36 debate highlighted key issues that would underline the necessity of an anti-shipping campaign in any future Mediterranean war against Italy; it was deemed unlikely that a knockout blow could be delivered. Defeat of the Italian Navy would likely prove insufficient in and of itself to constitute such a blow, as would risky shore bombardments. The key targets on the Italian mainland were in its north-west industrial heartland, which could only be reached by air power, and the RAF lacked French approval for the necessary basing rights.[26] Economic warfare, while much slower, played on a key Italian vulnerability: sea communications.

There were two elements to this vulnerability. First, Italy was utterly dependent on imports for its supply of oil and essential raw materials like coal and pig iron. In peacetime the economy theoretically required 21–22 million tons of imports of all types to function properly; around half of that figure was coal, and a third of it was oil. From 1936 to 1940, 76 per cent of Italian imports arrived by sea, while 55 per cent of its exports were sent by that route. Of the seaborne imports, nearly 90 per cent came from outside of the Mediterranean, meaning they had to come through the British-controlled Straits of Gibraltar or Suez Canal.[27] Put simply, Britain was ideally positioned to close these entrances and starve Italy of the essential supplies that it needed to make war.

Second, if Mussolini was to make war in pursuit of his imperial ambitions, he would have to cross the sea to do so. The Italian Empire in Africa needed men and supplies sent from Italy just to subsist, let alone attack British possessions or defend itself. Italian war planning identified Libya as the biggest draw on seaborne supplies, and naval planners were quick to emphasise the scale and difficulty of the task. In a major 1938 study, codenamed 'DG 10/A2', the task was split into three sections:

a The transportation of 42,000 men, 5,600 vehicles and 12,000 tons of materiel before outbreak of hostilities.
b The establishment of an expeditionary force for an attack on Egypt, consisting of 136,000 men, 5,000 animals, 13,000 vehicles, 50,000 tons of supplies and 63 fighter aircraft.
c Monthly reinforcements of 6,500 men, 75 animals, 220 vehicles, 113,000 tons of materiel (45,000 of which was for the civilian population) and 40 fighter aircraft.

The study suggested that the first task would need fifteen days of uninterrupted continuous effort, while the expeditionary force would take at least sixty-five days to complete, but likely much more due to the effects of enemy action. The Navy was particularly pessimistic about the second and third tasks, given the vulnerability of regular, large and slow convoys following set routes and with a limited pool of escort vessels to draw on.[28]

Bizarrely, despite recognising the importance of seaborne supply routes, the Italian Navy was reluctant to incorporate their close protection as a key operational task in the event of war. The 'operational decision for the openings of hostility' set out in 1938 simply identified the need for local defence of the Sicilian channel, in order to divide the Anglo-French forces between the two basins and focus on the protection of southern Italy, Sicily, Sardinia, Pantellaria and the Pelagian islands. Outside of this area, offensive operations would only be conducted by light forces, special forces and submarines. There was no mention of sea communications whatsoever.[29] Only in May 1940 was the Navy's main operational plan finally updated to recognise directly the importance of protecting them, and even then only placed it ninth out of ten tasks:

1 A defensive orientation in the western and eastern basins and an offensive or counteroffensive posture in the central Mediterranean.
2 Impeding of the enemy's eastern and western forces by blockading the Sicilian channel.
3 The conduct of 'insidious' [surprise or special forces] attacks on enemy bases in conjunction with air raids.
4 The operation of insidious and light forces against the enemy's most important lines of communication.
5 The seizure and exploitation of every opportunity to fight under conditions of superior or equal strength.
6 To actively seek opportunities to co-ordinate surface forces with air and submarine assets.
7 To avoid confrontations with decisively superior enemy forces.

8 To employ, as soon as possible, the battle fleet against the enemy before his Mediterranean force could be reinforced and while battles can be fought closer to friendly bases than those of the enemy.
9 To protect communications with the islands, Libya and Albania.
10 To defend isolated territories with local resources.[30]

It would take over a month of war before the Navy reoriented its operational direction and placed 'Provide direct and indirect protection to military traffic for Libya' as its first task. Protection for traffic to and from Albania and the islands remained ninth of ten.[31]

Worse, muddled planning led to a proper system to administer the delivery of these men and materiel not being instituted in peacetime. Only after entering the war was something concrete created, but it was convoluted and poorly managed. By early 1941 supplies to North Africa flowed through five separate and often conflicting channels: Army, Navy,

Illustration 1.1 Benito Mussolini inspects an Italian warship and crew, behind him are the head of the Fascist Party, Achille Starace (left) and head of the Italian Navy, Admiral Domenico Cavagnari (right). The Italian Navy proved woefully unprepared for war with other major powers, something which Cavagnari frequently advised in the late 1930s.
Source: www.gettyimages.co.uk/detail/news-photo/italian-fascist-dictator-benito-mussolini-strolling-down-news-photo/50612248?adppopup=true
Credit: Time Life Pictures / PIX Inc. / The LIFE Collection via Getty Images

Air Force, the Ministry for Italian Africa and the Wehrmacht. It was not until far too late, in January 1943, that a much more streamlined, centrally co-ordinated organisation was achieved. This was in the form of the German naval command in Italy, which steered naval policy much more towards specifically German objectives.[32]

The other Italian possessions which sat at the end of various sea routes received less planning provision than Libya. The question of protecting Adriatic transit only became relevant after Italy's 1939 annexation of Albania, but a dedicated command was not organised until November 1940, after the loss of a whole convoy to a naval raid. The *'Comando Superiore del Traffico coll'Albania'* was then only kept in existence until victory in Greece, despite the fact that convoys continued to run for the rest of the war. It held control of a pool of naval assets, but had to request assistance from the Italian Air Force (IAF).[33] The Aegean does not seem to have received even that level of cursory organisation, being dismissed as a secondary sub-theatre that could be sustained through occasional convoys and submarine runs.[34]

While the Italian Navy vacillated, the 'knockout blow' once again proved seductive during the 1939 Anglo-French joint staff talks. These determined that 'The objective would be to secure their interests in the Mediterranean and Middle East, and to knock Italy out of the war as soon as possible.'[35] This would entail offensive air and naval action from the outset to compel Italy to seek terms and so allow a concentration of effort against Germany. Yet as it had during the Abyssinian crisis, the 'knockout school' soon ran into difficulties. The Chief of the Air Staff Cyril Newall poured cold water on the idea of such a blow coming from the air, citing a lack of means, a strong opposition and French agreement that it was unrealistic. Pressure could be exerted, but no knockout. The First Sea Lord Dudley Pound held the same view as regards sea power, complaining: 'I do not know who gave the politicians the idea that it could be done but it seems ... they are now undergoing the rather painful process of being undeceived.'[36]

The strangulation of Italy by cutting supply routes at sea was evidently the most plausible approach. It was well represented in the objectives laid down by the Admiralty in September 1939 for the Royal Navy in the Mediterranean, representing two of the three that were directly offensive in nature:

1 To bring enemy naval forces to action wherever they can be met.
2 To ensure the safe passage of reinforcements to our fleet and garrisons in the Mediterranean. These will, if possible, be sent before the outbreak of war.
3 To interrupt Italian sea communication with Libya.
4 To interrupt Italian sea communication with the Black Sea.

5 To obtain command of the sea in the Eastern basin, thereby preventing seaborne attacks on Egypt, Cyprus or Palestine.
6 To frustrate enemy seaborne attacks on Malta.
7 To ensure safe passage of seaborne supplies to our own forces and possessions in the Eastern and Central Mediterranean.[37]

What is more, Britain could boast an in-depth knowledge of the Italian usage of these routes thanks to some key intelligence breakthroughs. Since 1937, British signals intelligence (SIGINT) had cracked multiple Italian cyphers, including those of the Navy. They were able to read both the most secret and the general book of their cyphers, plus one of their two naval attaché codes. Intelligence from these and some human sources allowed them to build up an accurate picture of Italian naval and shipping sailings and movements up until mid-July 1940. Around this time, the Italian Navy became the last of their three services to introduce new codes and tables after the outbreak of war, and British SIGINT would spend around a year largely in the dark.[38]

Although Italy was still a non-belligerent in 1939, the Royal Navy's objectives remained in place through to Mussolini's declaration of war in June 1940. For their part the Air Ministry expected RAF Middle East to have only very limited resources available due to commitments in France and for home defence. As such, their planned objectives were focused on the defence of Egypt and the Suez Canal, with little scope for offensive operations. The basic joint strategy that was agreed gave responsibility for the western Mediterranean to the French, whereas the British took control of the east. The demarcation line ran through the straits of Messina, although it curved slightly to include Malta in the British zone. There would be no significant British naval forces stationed west of Alexandria, with Gibraltar hosting only a small escort force. The difficulties barring tactical co-ordination between the two Allies were expected to be insurmountable, but scope for operational and strategic co-ordination was identified. In particular, if the British drew Italian forces and attention eastwards, it would open greater opportunities for French exploitation in the western basin, and vice versa.[39]

By the time of the Italian declaration of war, this bare-bones strategy could no longer be implemented. Germany had already launched extraordinarily successful invasions of Norway, the Low Countries and France. Most of the British Expeditionary Force had been ejected from the continent and although bitter French resistance continued, it could only be a matter of time before their capitulation. The desperate situation necessitated a new Mediterranean strategy, conducted by the British and Commonwealth alone. Considerations for this new strategy were not actually the subject of a Cabinet meeting until 27 May. It concluded that the primary duty of the Navy was now the defence of the United Kingdom in home waters, despite acknowledging that an opportunistic Italy would likely attempt to 'overthrow' British positions in Egypt and the Middle East.[40] All control of the western Mediterranean was expected to be lost except for the possession of Gibraltar, which was contingent on continued Spanish neutrality. Malta, that key British possession in the central Mediterranean, was also thought to be in a parlous position, able to hold out against perhaps one sustained Italian assault at most.[41] The Mediterranean fleet was to hold the Eastern Basin, taking a very defensive strategy to ensure the safety of Egypt and the Suez Canal.[42] The prognosis was grim indeed.

However, the worst of the British fears were not borne out. Although the Italian Navy had flirted with grandiose strategic concepts for a 'breakout fleet' in the mid-1930s, these were frustrated by a lack of time, resource and building capacity.[43] As has been shown, they entered the war with very limited and generally defensive goals. They would seek to dominate the central Mediterranean, and keep the Allied forces divided across the two basins, cutting all communications between them. Meanwhile, they would support and supply the Army in North Africa in its drive on Egypt to take control of the Suez Canal. In order to facilitate these supply operations, Allied bases at Malta and Bizerte would have to be neutralised, or at least subdued.

The IAF entered the war with a similarly cautious remit. Having spent the latter half of the 1930s simultaneously developing plans for war both alongside and against Germany, they were only definitively told to opt for the former in 1939. Given this indecision, operational objectives were only disseminated to units at a very late stage. Plans for the bombing of Corsica, Tunisia and targets on the French coast were dropped. The bombing of Malta was to go ahead, but attacks on Alexandria were to be suspended for the time being. Worse, of the 1,569 bombers the IAF had for all purposes on 1 June 1940, only 783 were actually serviceable. They could offer an additional 204 maritime reconnaissance aircraft to help the Navy, but these were mostly antiquated Cant Z. 501 aircraft, described by the head of the IAF as an 'archaeological artefact'. Finally, the service was also suffering from a serious shortage of trained aircrew and engineers.[44] As such, while Malta received scattered bombing raids from the Italians after declaring war, an amphibious assault never materialised. Italy's pre-war proposal to eliminate it as a base for British forces was quickly altered to a policy of containment, opting instead to 'sterilize' the island through bombing, mining and a blockade by submarines and light forces.[45] Their limited bomber fleet soon proved it lacked the quantity and capability for such a task.

From Peace to War

Regarding the Mediterranean Sea, then, both Britain and Italy were formulating quite limited war plans that were largely defensive in nature, and both were doing so for reasons of strategic context. The Italian plans were merely to make a limited push for control of and security over their key north–south transit routes. Gaining a level of control of the central Mediterranean would simultaneously cut the British east–west route and force the isolation of Malta. Given its position as a 'prisoner' within the Mediterranean, this was the most they might hope to realistically achieve unless the 'walls' of the prison, Gibraltar and Suez, could be torn down.[46] Hamstrung by the inadequacies of their military power, there seemed little hope that Italy could achieve this alone. Yet for their new ally, the Mediterranean represented little more than a peripheral distraction from a continental European focus.

German policy from the 1920s onwards took very little consideration of the theatre at all. In 1925, war games were conducted under the assumption, for the first time, that Germany would benefit from the 'benevolent neutrality' of the Italians. This would aid Germany by forcing the French fleet to retain significant forces in the Mediterranean and delay the transportation of French troops and equipment to a western front from their North African territories. This stance changed little after the Nazi party came to power. German naval policy through to the mid-1930s remained the pursuance of a strategy based on Italian neutrality. They relied on Italy's ability to neutralise the French Mediterranean fleet by holding them in place, allowing the Germans to pursue their interests elsewhere.

By 1938, German strategy assumed that the Italian and German Navies would fight together in a 'parallel war', with the Italians taking responsibility for the Mediterranean, and the Germans for the Atlantic. In this respect it was a mirror of the Italian strategy of the late inter-war years, but where the two differed was how they each saw the nature of this 'parallel war'. For the Italians this would be a war fought equally between two allies in pursuit of both shared and individual interests. For Germany, however, this was an opportunity to have the Italians tie down enemy naval forces and hopefully 'close' the Mediterranean. Meanwhile they could wage war where their true interests lay: mainland Europe. As Admiral Cavagnari learnt to his horror, there were no proposals whatsoever to offer aid in the Italian struggle for the Mediterranean.[47] The upshot was that during 1940, whereas Britain would have to fight alone in the Mediterranean as its key ally had been defeated, Italy would do so because its key ally was uninterested.

In spite of their difficult situation, the Italians did manage to achieve one wartime objective before they even entered hostilities. The threat of their joining the war was enough to compel the British to activate contingency plans and close the Mediterranean to general mercantile traffic in May 1940.[48] The east-west route had thus been cut and Malta successfully isolated in-theatre. Yet due to Britain's vast shipping resources and numerous bases across the African coast, it could still fall back on the longer 'Cape route' to access the theatre via the Suez Canal or to reach the Far East. So long as the British retained control of the entrances to the Mediterranean, this, along with harrying efforts to supply Malta represented the limit of what the Axis could achieve in terms of strangling sea communications. Ultimately, due to reliance on them and a lack of credible alternatives, sea communications represented a far greater vulnerability for the Axis powers in the Mediterranean than they did for the British.

This limit to Italian power was borne out by the events of their brief 'parallel war' in 1940, when their threats to British possessions in the Mediterranean and Middle East remained muted. Their forces in North Africa did eventually advance eastwards into Egypt but were slow to do so, while initial clashes with the Italian fleet were largely indecisive, appearing to show that they were very cautious. In amongst the low ebb in British fortunes of 1940, some senior policy-makers, most notably Prime Minister Winston Churchill, sensed an opportunity. With no ability to bring the Germans into direct engagement at this stage, perhaps the Mediterranean provided the next best option. As well as defending imperial interests, the theatre might provide the victories so desperately needed by the British public and international opinion. Here was a chance to wage a 'war on the periphery'. Egypt was a place where the various forces of the British Commonwealth could be concentrated with relative ease, and victories over Italy on land and at sea could hamper Germany and favourably influence neutrals such as Turkey, Spain and Vichy France.[49] The defeat of Italy was seen by the British as a necessary precursor to the defeat of Germany, and this could only be achieved by offensive action in the Mediterranean. Reopening that sea would also free up much-needed shipping by greatly shortening routes through to the East, and this shipping could be used for the ultimate goal of landing in Europe. This strategy was reinforced by the fact that the Mediterranean was the only theatre in which the British could act offensively in all three environments (land, sea and air) over 1940–43.[50]

So it was that the broad outlines of a Mediterranean strategy, arrived at in such a piecemeal fashion, was vigorously pursued by the British. They exerted all their political expertise in coercing the often reluctant

Americans into joining the Mediterranean strategy, and progressed from North Africa to Sicily, Italy, the Aegean and southern France. Nested within this concept was cognisance of the fact that the ability of the Axis to wage war across this theatre was enabled more than anything else by one thing – shipping. A campaign against this lifeline for the Axis would be vital in securing victory. It was also seen as an important component of a wider general economic blockade on the European Axis powers, hampering the import of vital supplies for making war, particularly oil. It could contribute to the elimination of Italy from the war, and then exert major pressure on the primary enemy: Germany.[51]

Axis Shipping, Routes and Port Facilities

The Axis depended on a vast maritime logistics network to hold together their various territories across the Mediterranean theatre. Although it was the sea lanes between Italy and North Africa to supply the land war which lasted for almost three years that featured most heavily in both Axis and Allied considerations, these were not actually the most heavily used. Traffic to Albania, Greece and the Aegean was greater than that to North Africa in both the number of convoys and the quantity and tonnage of shipping, primarily due to the shorter distance. Between June 1940 and May 1943, 1,274 convoys consisting of a total of 3,067 merchant vessels sailings totalling 10,171,054 tons of shipping were run from Italy to North Africa. Albania, Greece and the Aegean received 4,762 convoys, with 7,055 sailings totalling 22,476,755 tons up to the Italian armistice, and German convoys continued to run some of these routes afterwards. The number of vessels plying other routes, such as to Axis-held islands, is incalculably large.[52] In addition to these routes, supplies also had to be shipped to the Axis-held islands of Sicily, Sardinia, Corsica and Pantellaria in the central Mediterranean. Finally, coastal shipping travelled along the various coasts of North Africa, southern France and every part of the Italian coast.

Table 1.1 contains a breakdown of the major trans-Mediterranean routes with their lengths, the period that they were in use by the Axis and their approximate transit time at eight knots. It does not include the shorter routes within the Aegean and it should be noted that the distances given represent the shortest routes between the ports with no delays en route. In reality, longer evasive passages were often taken instead, while slower vessels, Allied attack or mechanical failure at sea would frequently add further delays. What is clear is that even accounting for factors like evasive routing, Axis convoys spent relatively little time at sea. The times involved were certainly a fraction of the vast journeys of

Table 1.1 *Principal Axis convoy routes in the Mediterranean*

Route	Approx. route length (miles)	Period in use by Axis	Approx. minimum transit time (at 8 knots)
Naples–Tripoli	502	– Jan 1943	2 days, 15 hours
Messina–Tripoli	339	– Jan 1943	1 day, 19 hours
Tripoli–Benghazi	352	– Feb 1941, Apr–Dec 1941, Jan–Nov 1942	1 day, 20 hours
Brindisi–Benghazi	532	– Feb 1941, Apr–Dec 1941, Jan–Nov 1942	2 days, 19 hours
Athens–Benghazi	400	Jun–Dec 1941, Jan–Nov 1942	2 days, 2 hours
Athens–Tobruk	389	Jun–Nov 1942	2 days
Benghazi–Tobruk	255	– Jan 1941, Jun–Nov 1942	1 day, 8 hours
Naples–Bizerte	294	Nov 1942–May 1943	1 day, 12 hours
Naples–Tunis	304	Nov 1942–May 1943	1 day, 14 hours
Palermo–Bizerte	181	Nov 1942–May 1943	1 day
Palermo–Tunis	179	Nov 1942–May 1943	1 day
Brindisi–Athens	473	Jun 1941–Sept 1943	2 days, 8 hours
Brindisi–Valona	69	– Sept 1943	9 hours
Livorno–Bastia	61	Nov 1942–Oct 1943	8 hours
Naples–Cagliari	263	– Sept 1943	1 day, 9 hours

Note: The information for this table has been extrapolated from the United Kingdom Hydrographic Office NP 350, *Admiralty Distance Tables, Volume 2: The Mediterranean, Black and Red Seas*, 3rd edition, 1949.

Allied convoys across the Atlantic, and so the window of opportunity to attack them was small.

Axis convoys travelling to North Africa varied in size and composition, which depended heavily on their destination. Convoys to Tripoli between 1940 and 1942 generally consisted of between three and six merchant vessels or tankers, escorted by three to four warships, usually destroyers or large torpedo boats.[53] The other major Libyan ports of Benghazi and Tobruk received proportionately smaller convoys (between two and four vessels) due to their smaller capacities. The main Italian pre-war assessment; 'DG A2/10', gave the following capacities: Tripoli – five cargo ships and four troop transports, Benghazi – three cargo ships and two troop transports, Tobruk – three cargo ships and two troop transports. Naples, the main point of departure, could load fourteen ships at once, Bari and Brindisi five each.[54] The problem of these small capacities was exacerbated over the course of the campaign by damage from bombing raids and naval bombardments. Not only did such occurrences damage the port facilities and interrupt their working, they frequently scared away the local stevedores and other non-military personnel tasked with unloading merchant vessels.[55] The limitations of port capacity for North Africa have, however, been overstated by the Italian official histories and authors such as van Creveld. While they did impose difficulties, there were in fact occasions when the totals unloaded at individual ports exceeded their stated capacities. It has also been noted that they generally unloaded greater quantities of materiel when under British control, suggesting that Axis inefficiencies exacerbated the problem.[56]

The Italians were still in the process of hastily organising some aspects of the supply network to North Africa when they entered the war. They had gained some useful experience of successfully shipping large quantities of supplies across the Mediterranean during the Ethiopian war, but these efforts had been uncontested at sea.[57] In the lead-up to the Second World War, Italy had expected war with both France and Britain if it became involved, and thus transport of supplies across to North Africa would be extremely hazardous. In fact, the Navy had rather sensibly suggested building up the maximum possible supply surplus in North Africa before entering the war. The Army could then act in a largely self-sufficient manner, as naval planners believed transportation in the face of combined Anglo-French blockade would likely be impossible. Losses through internment of shipping in neutral ports and from the enemy at sea were expected to be in the region of 50 per cent.[58] It would not be possible for the Army to remain self-sufficient for a prolonged period of time, but the French armistice seemed to offer the Italians the possibility of a brief war for great gain. A convoy system was thus improvised at short notice, which lacked any real co-ordination between the three services.[59] Its unwieldy command structure meant it could not be easily adapted to new operational threats or strategic circumstances.

Coastal shipping off North Africa was much more irregularly sized and spasmodically run than the convoys travelling the major inter-continental routes. The vessels might be sailing in convoy or in unescorted small groups or individually. They consisted of vessels ranging from moderately sized and small merchant ships down to lighters, ferries, caiques and sailing vessels. Although considerably smaller than the shipping travelling the major routes from Italy to North Africa in both quantity and tonnage, a significant number of vessels plied these routes each month. The most common coastal shipping passage was from Tripoli to Benghazi, when the latter port was in Axis hands. Due to the small size of many of the vessels in use, though, some were also able to stop at the small harbours in Axis hands that were not suitable for taking larger vessels, such as Sollum and Bardia.

The Balkan supply route benefited from being much shorter than those to North Africa, and far less exposed to attack. Running supply convoys from the east coast of Italy across the Adriatic to Axis forces in Albania, Yugoslavia and Greece occupied around a quarter of Italy's merchant shipping in 1940–41 and continued to use a significant proportion even after the Axis conquest of the region. Convoys on this short route consisted usually of three to four merchantmen, initially with a small escort of one or two warships. Shipping to supply and finally evacuate the Italian island of Sardinia (and later occupied Corsica) from the west coast of Italy ran until the Allied occupation of the islands over September–October 1943. These convoys ran regularly and most commonly consisted of three merchantmen escorted by a single torpedo boat, although they would also receive an aerial escort.[60] The islands were also plied by much coastal shipping around and between them, with British intelligence identifying multiple schooners, yachts and other minor vessels of under 100 tons along with a few small merchant vessels of under 500 tons.[61] Some traffic also persisted between southern France and Corsica.

In the Aegean sea, the Italians held the numerous islands of the Dodecanese when they entered the war. This number was swelled by the addition of many more islands, most notably Crete in June 1941, after the successful Axis conquest of the Balkans. Comprehensive information on Axis shipping in the Aegean is hard to come by, but generally due to the short distances involved and the nature of the sea itself, smaller vessels were used than those on the major routes to North Africa, with minor vessels of various types frequently utilised.[62] There were some exchanges of Axis shipping between the Mediterranean and the Black Sea, which by necessity travelled through the Aegean. This traffic consisted, on average, of larger ships than those supplying the Aegean islands, and sizes ranged from a smallish 1,500 tons to a very substantial 6,000.[63]

In order to serve these wide-ranging and diverse requirements Italy could, as of 9 June 1940, dispose of 786 merchant vessels of over 500 tons, totalling 3,318,129 tons. Despite warnings from military chiefs and senior regime politicians about the consequences for the merchant marine, when Mussolini declared war the following day, 212 of these (1,216,637 tons) were left stranded outside of the Mediterranean. The overwhelming majority were captured or interned in enemy or neutral ports, while a small remnant continued to operate for Italy outside of the middle sea. A handful tried, generally unsuccessfully, to regain entrance. Of those within the Mediterranean, twenty-six of 352,051 tons had to be either immediately decommissioned due to impractical size, or converted to hospital ships. This meant Italy entered the war with 548 ships totalling a modest 1,749,441 tons, plus a variety of smaller vessels fit for use as coastal traffic.[64] Over the course of the war, new construction, purchases and especially seizures from enemy or neutral powers provided the Axis with new stock, but overall the total was consistently eroded by Allied action.

British Attitudes and Policy on Attacking Merchant Shipping

While seaborne supply may have been identified here as a critical vulnerability of the enemy in the Mediterranean, a key barrier stood in the way of exploiting it fully: international law. Even during a world war, merchant shipping might well be completely unarmed and crewed entirely by civilians, making an attack seem morally dubious. Britain had encountered first-hand the effects of so-called unrestricted submarine warfare on the Atlantic trade routes during the last two years of the Great War. The German U-boat campaign had severely hampered the British war effort and even threatened to choke Britain into a negotiated peace.[65] As well as the immediate wartime effects of the U-boat campaign, it helped to exacerbate the existent unpopularity of the submarine as a weapon of naval warfare, in the eyes of both the Admiralty and the British public.[66]

These effects were not just limited to submarine warfare, but rather to unrestricted anti-shipping warfare as a whole. Throughout the inter-war years, British policy regarding enemy merchant shipping was to stop the vessel(s) in question, board and search the ship before finally placing a 'prize crew' aboard to sail it back to a friendly port. Immediately after the First World War, the Admiralty stated that in times of peace all nations should have 'free and unfettered access to all seas' but that in times of war the privilege would have to be 'fought for by belligerent navies'. The Royal Navy retained the right to stop, search and capture even neutral ships.[67]

While such lengthy operations were possible for surface vessels, they were difficult for submarines and virtually impossible for aircraft. The Washington Naval Conference of 1921–22 decreed in one 'Root Resolution' that submarines would adhere to the same rules of 'stop and search' as surface vessels; unrestricted submarine warfare was considered illegal.[68] No ruling was given regarding air attack on shipping. There does not seem to have been any real consideration given to this until 1929, when differing international opinion on 'maritime belligerent rights' came to the fore, leading to their retention being raised at the London Naval Conference of 1930.[69] Although the complicated issue was in fact never raised, the British position was that aircraft should be treated according to the same rules as submarines. As submarines were likely to have to comply with 'stop and search', so would aircraft, no matter how impracticable.[70] By 1937 the issue was again under discussion but remained partially unresolved. The Admiralty wanted restriction to air attack on merchant shipping to be held in place, whereas the Air Ministry was less concerned and perhaps sensibly believed that it was very unlikely any international agreement would be reached on the subject.[71] As far as the Air Ministry was concerned, maritime air power was itself a lower priority with such scarce resources. The primary focus in the late inter-war years instead lay in areas such as the development of strategic bombing and fighter defence of the United Kingdom.[72]

So it was that when Britain declared war on Germany in September 1939, it retained the same 'stop and search' policy regarding merchant shipping. These rules extended even to aircraft, with the Air Ministry issuing instructions as late as February 1940 that only warships were to be attacked.[73] Other vessels could not even be challenged unless they were specifically being searched for under orders from the Ministry, in which case the highly impractical instructions were to divert the vessel from its destination. The instructions went so far as to state that aircraft should not act in a way that might provoke defensively armed merchant shipping into firing on them.[74] The rules for mine warfare had not changed since the Hague Convention of 1907, requiring that all minefields of any size must be declared before being laid.[75] The nine-month period of Italian non-belligerency saw more changes to British policy regarding attacks on merchant shipping than throughout the entire inter-war period, however.

Just prior to the start of the Second World War, the Rear Admiral (Submarines) had already rejected the use of 'stop and search' tactics in enemy waters due to the dangers involved with spending such an amount of time on the surface. Consideration had been given to attacks on enemy 'communications' at sea, meaning supply vessels of all types that were not necessarily warships. He made the suggestion of declaring areas of the sea as 'dangerous waters' to the enemy in August 1939. This initial suggestion of what would later be termed 'sink at sight zones' was rejected by the Admiralty.[76] By April 1940, however, during the German seaborne invasion of Norway and after the high-profile sinking of several merchant vessels by German U-boats, the British implemented 'sink at sight zones' in Norwegian, Danish and Dutch waters. This geographically limited form of partially restricted warfare applied to both submarines and aircraft, but came with the caveat that, rather than just any vessel, only 'naval auxiliaries' could be sunk without warning.[77]

Much had changed in British attitudes and policy on attacking merchant shipping over the course of the first nine months of war. Yet by June 1940, the Admiralty had not permitted the declaration of any 'sink at sight' zones in the Mediterranean. They stated that only declared minefields could be laid as regards anti-shipping warfare. The relaxation of this policy was actually spurred by Italian actions. The Italians declared large parts of the central Mediterranean 'dangerous' on 6 June and promptly sank a Norwegian tanker without warning three days after their declaration of war.[78] This caused the naval Commander-in-Chief (C-in-C) Mediterranean, Andrew Cunningham, to order in retaliation that Italian tankers could be sunk at sight in any location.[79] The order was quickly rescinded, as the Admiralty dictated that such a move would require a cabinet ruling. Nevertheless, the wheels had been set in motion for the relaxation of anti-shipping policy.

Cunningham made repeated calls for approval to attack enemy shipping, which he saw as essential if the Royal Navy were to pursue the war aims of attacking enemy communications in the Mediterranean.[80] On 14 July, the Admiralty approved attack on Italian shipping within thirty miles of the Libyan coast, by any means and without warning, following a decision reached by the Cabinet after much discussion.[81] This included allowing minefields to be laid without prior declaration to the enemy. Three days later, this policy was extended to allow attacks on Italian shipping within thirty miles of any Italian territory providing that this would not breach Turkish neutrality. In January 1941, the Admiralty belatedly realised this policy did not include German shipping off the coast of Italian territories, and quickly rectified the situation.[82] Strangely, air and naval bombardments of ports which the British were aware contained merchant shipping had already taken place on several occasions prior to these rulings. The Cabinet was aware of these sinkings of merchant vessels and regarded them as successes against 'military supply ships'.[83]

As will be demonstrated in later chapters, British policy regarding attacks on shipping would be rapidly relaxed over 1941 and early 1942 to the point of being almost entirely unrestricted. The British entered war in the Mediterranean with quite severe self-imposed restrictions, however, which was to be one of several factors limiting their ability to exploit the very vulnerability they had correctly identified.

2 Resisting *Mare Nostrum*
The Early Anti-shipping Campaign, June–December 1940

Early Priorities

When Italy finally declared war, Britain had little in the way of forces available in the Mediterranean, and France was on the verge of defeat. Even the relatively limited naval plans that had been proposed in 1938–39 were difficult to fulfil at this stage. On paper, the Mediterranean Fleet looked formidable, boasting four battleships, two aircraft carriers, nine cruisers, twenty-two destroyers, twelve submarines and a variety of auxiliary vessels.[1] However, with the French armistice clearly approaching, this fleet would be stretched across the whole theatre rather than focusing purely on the eastern basin. Worse, the naval balance of power in the theatre would be transformed by French capitulation. The Royal Navy would be roughly matched by the strength of the Italian Navy, which on

Illustration 2.1 The Italian battleship *Conte di Cavour* at Naples, with destroyers in the background, June 1940.
Source: www.gettyimages.co.uk/detail/news-photo/naples-italy-one-of-italys-capital-ships-the-conte-di-news-photo/515950838?adppopup=true
Credit: Bettman via Getty Images

10 June was four battleships, twenty-two cruisers, 128 destroyers and torpedo boats and a submarine fleet that numbered over a hundred.[2]

The paucity of British air power assets available to undertake the multitude of required tasks was even greater than that of sea power. In Egypt, RAF Middle East had just six medium bomber, three fighter and two flying boat squadrons, along with one general reconnaissance unit and a handful of support units and army co-operation aircraft. To this they could add a single squadron of flying boats at Gibraltar.[3] At this stage, there were no RAF squadrons based at Malta and what was to be their main operating airfield there, Luqa, was not actually made operational until 28 June. Prior to that date, only the seaplane base at Kalafrana was in a usable state, although No. 228 flying boat squadron had been transferred from Malta to Egypt prior to the Italian declaration of war.[4] The Fleet Air Arm (FAA) had about thirty Fairey Swordfish torpedo bombers split between the carriers *Eagle* and *Argus* plus a handful other Swordfish and reconnaissance floatplanes in shore stations or as catapult-launched aircraft on other warships.[5]

The British were at least relatively well positioned for conducting mine warfare against enemy merchant shipping and naval vessels. A pre-war assessment by the then C-in-C Mediterranean, Dudley Pound, advocated the development of two major mine depots at Malta and Haifa. He suggested that the former should initially have sufficient stocks to serve four minelaying submarines based at the island, which would serve as the primary base for offensive mining operations. Haifa was to act primarily as a base for defensive mining in the eastern basin, but in the event of an ongoing state of war, should then expand to facilitate offensive operations as well. Pound proposed that a fast surface minelayer be based there at first, with destroyers capable of minelaying to follow later.[6] By June 1940 the logistical preparations had proceeded well, with the mine depot at Malta fully stocked and the new depot at Haifa structurally complete.[7] Yet while the facilities were in place, the delivery systems were not. In readiness for Italian declaration of war alongside Germany in 1939, there had been four 'I' class destroyers fitted for minelaying operations along with the minelayer class submarines *Porpoise* and *Cachalot*. However, when it became clear that war was not imminent in the Mediterranean, these were recalled to the home theatre. By June 1940, only the submarines *Grampus* and *Rorqual* were in place at Malta, while none of the few available aircraft were fitted for minelaying.[8] With such a paucity in capability, Pound's pre-war proposal of aggressively instituting an immediate 'attritional' mining policy in the areas of the key Italian mainland and Sicilian ports, and the Libyan ports as far east as Benghazi, could not be carried out.[9]

The dearth of forces available and their wide range of tasks made the position of the anti-shipping campaign in British strategic priority a complex one. The British planning staffs and armed forces were fully cognisant prior to war of the crucial nature of the maritime supply network to Italy's positions across the theatre. Both the air and naval theatre commanders had given the interruption of enemy sea communications as key priorities prior to and at the outbreak of war. Cunningham had stated to Pound on 7 June that he would like the focus of his operations to be 'control of communications in the central and eastern Mediterranean'.[10] For his part, head of RAF Middle East Arthur Longmore recognised the 'vulnerabilities of her [Italy's] communication with Libya', and this is clear in points two and five of the aims he set out for RAF Middle East:

1 Offensive action against air bases.
2 Offensive action against ports, to destroy or damage submarines, shipping and facilities.
3 Destruction of resources in Italian East Africa, where it was anticipated no replacements can be made.
4 Full support of British armies.
5 Strategical reconnaissance for naval, army and air information.[11]

The Cabinet also quickly agreed to relax legal restrictions on attacking merchant shipping. In July, they approved 'sink at sight' zones that allowed attacks on any shipping within thirty miles of Italian territory.[12] Yet it was clear that, for the immediate future, attacks on the Italian supply network would have to take a back seat compared to other more immediate tasks. The Mediterranean Fleet was initially forced to be primarily defensive in nature, and its first operation on 11 June was a sortie designed to counter a potential Italian assault on Malta. The island had long been identified as the key base for surface forces if they were to regularly interfere with the traffic between Italy and Libya. However, the dangerous proximity to Italy and the delay in building up Malta's air defences resulted in policy dictating that no surface forces were based there. The fleet had to be based solely in Egypt, with a focus on the eastern basin and the interruption of Italian supplies to the Dodecanese islands. These were of secondary importance to those with North Africa but offered some opportunity for drawing the Italian fleet eastward where it would be more vulnerable, and to favourably influence Turkey. It was felt that the lack of a central Mediterranean base made attacking the North African routes impracticable.[13]

While Longmore had clearly demonstrated awareness of the importance of enemy logistics, his involvement in operations against them was hindered by several factors. The most overriding was his sheer lack of aircraft. With a huge area under his responsibility and a wide remit, finding the resources was a formidable challenge. Worse, the types of aircraft that he had were completely unsuited. The desperate need for aircraft in France and the United Kingdom meant that RAF Middle East was not only under strength in terms of quantity, but also of quality. The fighter squadrons in Egypt were all equipped with the ageing Gloster Gladiator biplane. The six medium bomber squadrons did at least have the modern Blenheim Mk I, but these lacked the range to interfere with Italian sea lanes and could only reach the closest Italian-held ports of Tobruk and Derna from bases in Egypt at that stage. The heavier Bombays and Wellesleys were obsolescent and in need of replacement, and Longmore immediately started to issue requests for more and better aircraft.[14] Finally, the Air Ministry had set out clear instructions as to the strategic priorities for RAF Middle East, and like the Royal Navy, these were primarily defensive, focusing on the keystone of Britain's imperial position:

> The primary role of forces under your command is the defence of Egypt and the Suez Canal, and the maintenance of communications with the Red Sea. This does not, however, preclude the possibility of air forces from your command being employed in the execution of such other plans as may be approved by the Chiefs of Staff from time to time.[15]

These instructions left minimal scope for involvement in an anti-shipping campaign, in spite of Longmore's wish that this would occupy 'a prominent place in the intentions of RAF Middle East'.[16] As a result, the only forces that could focus on anti-shipping operations in June were the dozen submarines of the First Flotilla (S1), and a dozen FAA Swordfish that were transferred to Malta on 19 June, and quickly renamed 830 Squadron, to reflect their transition from a training squadron to a front-line role.[17]

Both the low position of the anti-shipping campaign in British strategic priority, and the forces available to conduct it, were to improve gradually over 1940. The question of how best to conduct war with Italy was widely debated during this period. A COS committee meeting on 30 May had concluded that the most effective air action that could be taken against Italy was bombing the Milan–Turin–Genoa area to produce damaging economic effects, while even air and sea attacks on the Dodecanese would likely have an impact on Italian morale.[18] It was felt from the outset that Italian popular will for the war was fragile, and that the 'brittle' morale of the populace could be damaged through bombing Italian territory.[19] For this reason, both the RAF and the French Air Force attacked the northern cities in a series of small-scale raids up to the French armistice, resulting in little damage but some unrest and anxiety amongst the local Italian populace. It also exposed the complete lack of a prepared Italian metropolitan air defence system.[20]

The prospect of damaging Italian resolve and production capability through bombing was clearly an attractive one. Proposals were made in August by the new 'Ministerial Committee on Military Policy in the Middle East' to build up a bombing force at Malta to attack Italian cities. Italy was deemed to still be 'particularly sensitive' to such attacks, but the proposal was temporarily rejected for fear of inviting serious reprisals against the island, which was still not adequately organised or equipped for air defence. They did however recommend strengthening of the air defences to the COS, and that the island should be built up to operate as a bombing base in the future.[21] The Mediterranean theatre was certainly becoming a higher priority in terms of the allocation of aircraft, but the Air Ministry did not envision these being used to bomb Italian cities. The first aim was simply to re-equip squadrons where the aircraft in use were 'almost all obsolescent' with modern types. After this, the first requirements were more fighters to defend Alexandria and 'to provide bomber aircraft capable of attacking the principal and only effective Italian base for attack on Egypt, i.e. Benghazi'.[22] While this did not clearly specify attacking the port itself and attendant shipping, it does suggest greater freedom to do so.

August 1940 saw a renewed British focus on the Mediterranean, although it naturally came second to the home theatre, where the homeland itself was now under siege. An extensive Joint Planning Staff report on 'future strategy' stated that 'Although Italy is our declared enemy ... Germany is the mainspring of our effort. Whatever action it may be necessary to take against any other country must therefore be related to our *main object*, which is the *defeat of Germany*.'[23] Yet it went on to say that while homeland security must be the primary consideration, the Middle East was of the utmost importance to the strategy of defeating Germany through blockade. Reinforcing the position in the theatre was accordingly 'clearly a matter of the greatest urgency'. The report concluded that 'The elimination of Italy and the consequent removal of the threat to our control of the Eastern Mediterranean would be a strategic success of the first importance.'[24] The change in focus was reinforced by the belated, slow and seemingly reluctant Italian invasion of Egypt in September, after much badgering from Mussolini.[25]

The heightened priority was reflected by a flow of reinforcements to the theatre, including those that could take a direct role in an offensive against Italian shipping. The first three Martin Maryland aircraft arrived at Malta on 6 September; these were augmented by another six the following month. The Sunderlands of 228 Squadron were also transferred back to

Malta in October, where they would be better placed to provide essential reconnaissance services. These aircraft were immediately utilised to track Italian convoys between Italy and North Africa, as well as naval activity.[26] They were followed by the first four 'T' class submarines to arrive in the theatre, which conducted their first patrols from Gibraltar before heading to the island. These were part of a general increase in reinforcements to the Mediterranean submarine force, which reached twenty by the end of the year, representing a significant proportion of the Navy's total number.[27] Their exclusive role in the anti-shipping campaign was confirmed in October, when Cunningham decreed that the submarines would be employed 'in the interruption of Italian traffic to Libya to the exclusion of other operations'.[28]

As the threat of invasion of the United Kingdom was felt to have diminished considerably by late October, greater numbers of better suited aircraft began to reach RAF Middle East as well. This permitted some attacks on shipping, on the port of Benghazi and on Dodecanese harbours, but they were not arriving as fast as Longmore had hoped. When he protested to Chief of the Air Staff Charles Portal that most of his requests for reinforcements and permission for wider operations were frequently being rebuffed, Portal scribbled 'I am afraid the demands of Home Commands have to come first', in the margin of the paper. Early the following month, Longmore again complained that reinforcements through Malta were 'trickling in' slower than expected.[29] The issue of aircraft reinforcements was instead accelerated through Italian action.

Mussolini had long desired further expansion in the Balkans and informed his ministers of his plans for an invasion of Greece on 15 October, to a mixed reception. On 28 October, an Italian ultimatum was delivered to Greece accusing it of repeated violations of neutrality through collusion with British forces, and demanding concessions through allowing Italian forces to be stationed on Greek territory. As Ciano noted in his diary, 'Naturally it is a document that allows no way out: either accept occupation or be attacked.'[30] Unsurprisingly, the Greek Dictator General Metaxas refused the terms, and the Italians promptly invaded from Albania, where they had been massing forces. Previous British proposals to station forces in Greek territory had been refused by Metaxas to avoid provoking Italy, but he now requested air, naval and financial assistance. It was decided that efforts should be made to assist the Greeks, but that they would focus especially on the defence of Crete. This would secure a vital air and naval base in the eastern Mediterranean to allow greater attacks on Italian positions in the Aegean, and also deny the enemy a base from which to launch attacks against

Egypt. For their part, the Greeks saw Crete as being under little immediate threat, particularly after repulsing the initial Italian advance, and a small RAF contingent under Air Commodore D'Albiac was sent to mainland Greece. The Italian invasion also stoked the British appetite for further bombing of central and southern Italy, and proposals from Portal to base Wellingtons in Malta for this were accepted. Aircraft were slow to arrive and operated on an ad hoc basis at first, but 148 Squadron was formed on the island in mid-December. Portal also agreed to send more Wellingtons to Longmore in light of the developing Greek campaign and the commitment to assist in it.[31]

While Portal was more enthusiastic about bombing Italy directly, and the War Cabinet in general focused on securing Crete, the situation did allow opportunity for greater bombing of Italian-controlled ports on both sides of the Adriatic and for interdicting shipping crossing it. The directives outlined to D'Albiac included a comment that the intended use of Wellingtons based in Greece was to attack strategic targets in the Adriatic, and points of disembarkation on the Albanian coast were directly highlighted as a priority target. In spite of the legal restrictions that the British were still operating under at this stage, he also received permission to attack all enemy shipping, whether at sea or in port.[32] The Vice Admiral, Malta, and the Air Officer Commanding (AOC) Mediterranean (later retitled Air Vice Marshal, Malta) both requested information for prioritisation of targets from a naval point of view for their new bomber capability. They were informed that Naples, Brindisi and Bari were the primary port targets for the moment, with Sicilian ports being omitted for fear of increased reprisal bombings against Malta.[33] Given these instructions, Longmore related to the AOC Mediterranean, Foster Maynard:

Your present bombing policy is to be to dislocate Italian sea communications with Albania. Targets should therefore be shipping and port facilities at Brindisi and Bari when these can be reached under prevailing wind conditions.[34]

Submarine patrols in the Adriatic were increased and the first of the smaller 'U' class vessels started to arrive at Gibraltar in November and joined the forces at Malta after their first patrols, while Greek submarines also began to attack Italian shipping.[35]

Over the course of 1940, the place of anti-shipping operations in British strategic priority had increased notably. The desperate strategic situation and lack of forces available in June had led to it being almost completely ignored, with only the possibility of attacks by the dozen submarines then available. As time wore on, however, threats in the home theatre started to rescind, air and naval forces in the theatre increased in number and the question of attacks on Italian communications by sea started to return in British planning. A small FAA striking force was placed at Malta, while new submarines were regularly sent to the theatre, including newer and more efficient types, with orders to focus exclusively on the interruption of shipping routes. The Italian invasion of Greece brought a new level of escalation in the campaign, and an expansion into the Adriatic, where emphasis began to exceed that of interdiction on the Libyan routes. Reinforcements in bomber aircraft arrived with the intent to attack Italy directly, with Italian ports now receiving a much higher preference in targeting. The forces available for the campaign by the end of 1940 were still modest but they laid a foundation for the much greater efforts that were to come over the next three years. The operations that were conducted in 1940 were few though, and were fraught with difficulty, ultimately achieving little.

The Campaign in Earnest: Early Anti-shipping Operations

The paucity of forces available in June 1940 combined with the low position of anti-shipping operations within British strategic thinking to ensure that few took place in the early months of that year. What is more, the Italians did not actually run any convoys to North Africa immediately, only sending the first on the day of the French armistice. Instead, the first fortnight only small quantities of materiel were transferred by submarine and light warships.[36] The most immediate offensive potential was offered by British and French submarines and this was where the campaign started, and vessels from both nations were sent on offensive patrol immediately. The British *Rorqual* and *Grampus* both sailed on 10 June to lay minefields off Brindisi and Augusta respectively. Three French submarines (*Saphir*, *Le Nautilus* and *La Turquoise*) were despatched at the same time to lay offensive fields off Cagliari, Tripoli and Trapani. Between them, these five submarines laid 184 mines, the greatest single number for any one month in 1940.[37] Royal Navy submarines in general made a substantial early effort, with *Odin* and *Orpheus* both leaving Malta on 10 June, while patrols from *Proteus* and *Parthian* soon followed. These initial efforts turned out to be catastrophic, with *Grampus*, *Odin* and *Orpheus* all being lost in the space of three days.[38] Cunningham complained to Pound on 27 June that 'With one exception every submarine operating off an Italian port has been lost, and we don't know how, which is the worst part of it.'[39] This was the start of a submarine campaign that was beset by numerous problems in 1940, and went disastrously badly in the opening months.

The brief French involvement before the armistice also saw them bombard the port of Genoa on 14 June, while the battleship *Lorraine* took part in the bombardment of Bardia by the Mediterranean Fleet on 21 June. These attacks did not represent great commitment of the Anglo-French fleets to an anti-shipping campaign, however. The former occurred primarily as a show of defiance to the newly hostile Italians and targeted oil tanks and gas works rather than shipping and docks. Similarly, the attack on Bardia did not specifically list the damage of the port itself or of shipping within it as objectives.[40] French aircraft also made ten raids on Italian targets, nine of them cities or towns with ports, but only one of them (Cagliari, 16 June) listed the port itself as the objective.[41] Little was achieved by the powerful French submarine fleet in this brief window. There had been hopes that a number of the forty-six French submarines in the Mediterranean would look to fight on with the British after the armistice, yet only one did so. The *Narval* arrived at Malta on 26 June. The reason for this 'defection' from Vichy was given as the strong anti-fascist and pro-De Gaulle feelings of the commanding officer, François Drogou, and many of the crew. Drogou kept a private diary which, along with the correspondence with his wife, affirmed his strong desire to fight on for Free France.[42]

After the French armistice, the Mediterranean Fleet became even more constrained in its freedom of action, with a wider remit of tasks to undertake. The possibility of acting against Italian maritime supply thus became more remote, but Cunningham remained open to taking opportunities where possible. When, on 28 June, Sunderland aircraft from 228 Squadron spotted a group of three Italian destroyers that were carrying artillery units to Tobruk, it was decided to intercept them. A cruiser squadron was rerouted from escort duty to attack the Italian force. In an extended chase action, in fading light and obscured by Italian smokescreens, one of the Italian vessels was damaged, overhauled and finally sunk. The other two escaped safely to Tobruk with their cargoes. The action was far from a standout success; it used over 5,000 rounds of ammunition to sink a single old destroyer and caused such a shortage of shells that it hampered major operations for two weeks.[43] The shipping at Tobruk had to be dealt with by other means instead. On 5 July, nine Swordfish of 813 Squadron FAA flew from their base at Sidi Barrani while the RAF simultaneously attacked the nearby Italian airfields. This effort was far more successful, sinking the destroyer *Zeffiro* that had escaped the surface action, along with two merchant ships, while damaging a second destroyer and the 15,000-ton liner *Liguria*. For its part, the RAF kept Italian fighters from interfering with the Swordfish and damaged eight of them on the ground, in an early example of effective air co-ordination. A follow-up bombardment of the port by a force of cruisers and destroyers the next morning sank the coastal ship *Axum* and damaged another merchant vessel.[44]

While the surface action in June had exposed the limitations of naval forces when having to chase targets, the air strikes and bombardments in early July had demonstrated just how much could be achieved with minimal forces, but successes remained rare. Indeed, another bombardment of Bardia on 17 August was the only other involvement of the fleet with anti-shipping operations until November. Even then, shipping was not actually listed under the objectives for the bombardment, which was intended to hit Italian concentrations of troops, guns and stores and to damage morale. Vice Admiral Pridham-Wippell, was given the discretion to shift fire to any shipping in the harbour if he saw fit, but this was not done.[45]

The onus for anti-shipping operations instead fell on the few submarines and aircraft available. The submarine campaign continued but was still subject to restrictions in terms of what could be attacked and where, which greatly limited opportunity. They were hampered by inadequate numbers of reconnaissance aircraft and a paucity of intelligence. While the British retained an intermittent ability to read Italian low-grade codes and ciphers, SIGINT regarding Italian naval matters was very thin following tightened security measures. Italy's main naval book ciphers were in fact never read again, except for a brief period in June 1941 thanks to some captured documents.[46] The result was that rather than being directed against specific targets, the submarines could only be sent to patrol areas that were both likely to be heavily used and where they were allowed to make attacks, in the hope that they would happen to locate a target. Multiple patrols were made in July and August but only seven attacks were made on Italian merchant ships, resulting in just one damaged vessel and one sinking: the 1,968-ton steamer *Morea* on 15 August. There were also four attacks on warships by British submarines, resulting in the sinking of a French sloop, while *Rorqual* laid another fifty mines in each month, which sank two more steamers.[47] Not only were the submarines achieving little in terms of results, but losses continued to mount. The *Phoenix* was depth charged by a torpedo boat off the coast of Sicily on 16 July, and the *Oswald* was rammed by an Italian destroyer on 1 August.[48] These latest losses caused Cunningham to lament that

I am very much concerned about our [submarine] losses ... As soon as one sends an S/M off an Italian port, it seems only a matter of time before she is discovered and put under. At the moment, it is not a case of sending them where they will be useful, but where they will be safe.[49]

One former submariner has noted that the loss of the *Oswald* marked the nadir of the submarine campaign in the Mediterranean, as the number of operational vessels at this stage dropped to just five.[50]

If the submarine campaign was failing, the few FAA resources available were already achieving some impressive results. Nine Swordfish from HMS *Eagle* raided Augusta on 10 July, but rather than shipping, they were targeting a force of cruisers and destroyers located by aerial reconnaissance. They were disappointed to find on arrival that most had sailed, and only a destroyer and an oiler were in the port, but they successfully sank the former and received very little opposition from anti-aircraft fire.[51] A sub-flight of *Eagle*'s aircraft based in North Africa followed this up with a more impressive strike off the Libyan coast on 22 August, in which a submarine and its depot ship were sunk with just three torpedoes. Cunningham described it as a 'phenomenal result', but the attack, which was described as being 'against shipping' actually only affected Italian submarine operations. The commander of the *Eagle* later admitted that the nature and disposition of the targets were not known before the strike.[52]

While such strikes were impressive, they represented opportunistic efforts and were often not related to a concerted anti-shipping effort. Aircraft carriers were in high demand and not to be used for sustained anti-shipping operations, carrying out more attacks against Italian airfields than they did against shipping targets in 1940.[53] Squadrons and sub-flights operating from shore bases offered much greater opportunity, as demonstrated by 813 Squadron's attack in July. This squadron was primarily tasked with army co-operation duties however, and shipping strikes were rare. It was not until the night of 17 September that another attack was made, when nine Swordfish of 815 Squadron bombed shipping in Benghazi, while 819 Squadron laid mines. On 23 October, another ten FAA aircraft successfully laid mines in Tobruk harbour, while four others bombed air defences as a diversion.[54]

Over September and October, RAF bombers from Egypt increased attacks on the Italian Tenth Army, which had begun its desert offensive. These included frequent attacks on ports and the shipping, which were vital to sustaining the Italian advance. Five Wellingtons raided Benghazi on 19 September, with aircrew from one claiming that several ships were seen to be on fire after the bombing. The following day four more aircraft attacked shipping and the docks, although one failed to locate the target, and damage to the jetty was observed. These efforts brought a signal of congratulations from Longmore.[55] Repeated and increased attacks were made over the course of October against Benghazi and Tobruk, while attacks were also made against ports in the Dodecanese as part of the strategy to interrupt Aegean communications. Longmore claimed to Portal that a lot of damage had been done to the North African ports considering the limited resources that had been available, forcing them to rely more on Tripoli and less on the forward ports of Benghazi and Tobruk.[56] While the efforts by Wellington bombers were deemed to be causing damage, lower altitude raids by Blenheims were proving to be more problematic. Longmore felt that while dawn and dusk raids against Benghazi by low-flying Blenheim Mk IVs were 'just about possible', as they tended to avoid interception, daylight raids were taking losses from Italian fighters. In fact, only two aircraft appear to have been lost in such operations in October.[57] The bombing of the Albanian ports of Durazzo and Valona by aircraft from Greece proved to be much more dangerous, although raids against the former were few in number due to it being at the extreme range for Blenheims. Valona was attacked on seventeen occasions before the end of the year though, and six aircraft were lost in raids against the two ports in November and another eight in December.[58]

It was the Adriatic that witnessed the single biggest success in the fledgling anti-shipping campaign in 1940. The famous attack on the Italian fleet in its main base at Taranto took place on the night of 11–12 November. Simultaneously, a raid by three cruisers and two destroyers (Force X) was made into the straits of Otranto. It was intended to provide a diversion for the Taranto strike, show support for the Greeks and lift their morale, and demonstrate to the Italians that the fight could be carried into their own waters. Force X's commander, Henry Pridham-Wippell, made it clear to his officers that the immediate objective was to 'sink enemy transports and supply ships'.[59] The task force simply sailed into the busy shipping lane between Brindisi and Valona in the hope of detecting a convoy through Radio Direction Finding (RDF) equipment or sighting one visually, and one was duly found after fifteen minutes and promptly attacked. In an action lasting around twenty-five minutes and confused by the dark of night and Italian smokescreens, all four merchant ships of the convoy were sunk and one of the three escorts damaged. The force then safely withdrew after what had been a striking success, and Pridham-Wippell reported that there was great scope for future raids and patrols in the southern Adriatic. In fact, only a handful of small successive attempts were made by British and Greek surface forces over 1940 and 1941, and they all failed to make contact with enemy shipping.[60]

Up until late November, the vast majority of the limited anti-shipping operations had not come from Malta. The handful of submarines based there had conducted some patrols, but these were mostly unsuccessful.

The FAA strike force based on the island was highly inexperienced and spent much of its first month there on training flights, while the first offensive operations it conducted were not against shipping targets. In October and November, it did attempt some solo shipping searches around dawn (known as 'rat hunts'), but these were quickly discontinued due to being too risky. A lone Swordfish would be extremely vulnerable to Italian fighters, and the meagre resources available needed to be carefully husbanded.[61]

The stationing of bomber forces on the island at Portal's request in late October enabled a step up in offensive operations, and fifteen raids were made against Naples, Brindisi, Bari, Taranto and Crotone along with others against Tripoli. The question of command and control for this bombing force was a complex and often confused one. Longmore complained to Portal in early November that to date it was controlled partly by the Air Ministry, partly by RAF Middle East and the AOC Mediterranean with occasional input from C-in-C Mediterranean. The Air Ministry tried to simplify this by affirming that Longmore had overall control, with local control under Maynard. Operations were focused primarily on the ports themselves, although cities and airfields were also sometimes attacked.[62] Although patchy, aerial reconnaissance was being conducted almost daily by the few Sunderlands and Marylands at Malta, and they had located numerous build-ups of shipping at Naples for convoys to Libya in November and December. The Sunderlands of 228 Squadron had even flown some long-range reconnaissance in the Aegean and this was further bolstered by human intelligence passed along by the naval attaché in Athens of sailings in early December.[63] While the Wellington bombers could attack the shipping build-ups in port, Malta still lacked an effective air force for attacking shipping at sea. The commander of 228 Squadron complained in late December that: 'The personnel of 830 Squadron are not yet trained in torpedo dropping, so that although the frequent passage of large convoys is well known no attempt at interception and attack has yet been possible.'[64] He made several requests for permission for his Sunderlands to attack enemy convoys whenever the FAA aircraft were either unable to locate the target or to attack it. He proposed these attacks could be made at low level after a shallow dive for greater accuracy, and only take place at night to minimise risk. However, in view of the scarcity of reconnaissance aircraft, Maynard decided that Sunderlands could only attack surface targets if it appeared that their anti-aircraft armament was unthreatening, and the target had to be deemed sufficiently 'worthwhile'.[65]

As it was, virtually no ships were attacked at sea from Malta, despite knowledge of their sailing and on some occasions of their location at sea.

Comprehensive tactical doctrine for reconnaissance and strike efforts from shore-based aircraft would not start to be set down until the following January. The crews of 830 Squadron were only capable of bombing and minelaying operations at this stage, and they bombed ships in Tripoli on 10 December, and laid mines there on the 21st. The Wellingtons bombed Tripoli the following night and 830 Squadron returned to bomb it again the night after.

Developments in the submarine campaign began to offer some more promising results towards the end of the year. Increased numbers of reconnaissance aircraft and submarines, along with the introduction of more effective types and the opening of the Adriatic for attacks, combined to bring greater results. Eight merchant ships of 34,792 tons were sunk over November and December, a greater number and tonnage than the total in June–October. Operating completely independently of the British, Greek submarines scored some particularly high-profile sinkings, such as the 11,452-ton liner *Sardegna* on 29 December, with heavy loss of life among the Italian troops on-board. The early anti-shipping campaign ended on a depressing note though, as four more submarines were lost in December, including the Greek *Proteus* shortly after it sank the *Sardegna*.[66]

War on a Shoestring: Assessing the Early Campaign

In 1940, British forces were stretched thinly across the Mediterranean and Middle East and faced with an unenviable range of threats and tasks. The importance of cutting Italian maritime connections had been clearly identified prior to the war and was enshrined in the form of the Royal Navy's objectives in June 1940. Yet the greatly overtaxed surface fleet had virtually no input on this front during the year, with only the attack on the *Espero* convoy, the raid into the straits of Otranto and a few port bombardments acting as token contributions. Only the small submarine component, operating from Alexandria, Malta and later Gibraltar, could dedicate themselves to anti-shipping operations. Longmore certainly expressed his desire for the RAF to make a contribution, and significant efforts were made by air forces in Egypt and later Malta against enemy ports in Italy and Libya, which included attacking the facilities themselves and the shipping present. In this they were assisted by attached FAA squadrons, which made several opportunistic attacks with bombs, torpedoes and mines.

The Italian invasion of Greece had also spurred desire to attack ports on both sides of the Adriatic, to frustrate their new offensive in the Balkans, along with an increasing number of raids on the Italian mainland. There were no direct attacks on shipping at sea by the RAF, although as they lacked specialised aircraft, weaponry and aircrews for this, that was perhaps for the best. There were only a few opportunistic efforts by FAA aircraft from both carriers and shore bases, which were generally tactically successful but too few in number to have any notable effect. Finally, the same can be said of mining operations in 1940, which achieved a disproportionate level of success for the amount of effort expended, but were again too rare to have much of an impact. Post-war analysis based on the cross-referencing of British wartime claims, shipping lists and captured Axis documentation calculated sixty-six merchant ships of 168,821 tons sunk by Allied action in 1940. To this, a further thirty-eight of 84,631 tons were captured, scuttled, attributed to other causes or to causes unknown.[67] This was a slim return for a period of nearly seven months of war.

Apart from the sinking of the four merchant ships in the straits of Otranto in November, surface forces added only a handful of other sinkings through bombardment, but the Allies suffered no losses in any of these operations. Their involvement in the campaign would not truly begin until the next year. For the submarine fleet, it had been a very different story, and it is worth making an in-depth examination of their poor fortunes at this stage. Including the Greek *Proteus* and Free French *Narval*, eleven submarines were lost in 1940. In return the Allied forces sank just fifteen merchant ships of 55,776 tons by direct attacks, and a further six ships of 23,609 through minelaying. The early submarine campaign had proven to be extremely ineffective and costly, and caused great concern to Cunningham and other commanders. The reasons for such an unsuccessful start are numerous: the lack of available SIGINT and aerial reconnaissance in 1940, along with the restrictions on what could be attacked and where, have already been outlined.

Without the aid of detailed intelligence, submarines could only be sent to busy areas of shipping lanes in the hope of locating a target visually, as British submarines would not receive RDF equipment until November 1941.[68] This made sightings uncommon and converting those that occurred into attacks proved to be very difficult. A post-war analysis of British submarine attacks found that the most common reason given for no attack being made when a target was sighted was that it was simply too distant. The vast majority of successful attacks were made from under one and a half miles, with sharply decreasing returns as ranges increased.[69] British submarines had speeds of just 8–10 knots when submerged and so were unlikely to catch distant targets. Without intelligence to guide them into a position likely to result in a successful attack, they were faced with the choice between making an attack that was unlikely to hit, or none at all. When making an attack, they had only a few simple instruments to aid in fire control, which required highly accurate and speedy calculations to be completed by the crew.[70] Meanwhile, the standard British torpedo itself was an unintelligent point-and-shoot weapon; crews were unable to angle the gyros of their torpedoes electronically from the bridge but instead had to do it manually in the tubes or before loading. Put simply, British submarines did not aim their torpedo, they aimed their whole boat. They were also air-fuelled weapons, which while reliable, often left an identifiable trail on the surface of the water for the crews of potential targets to spot and hence give some warning to evade.[71]

British torpedoes were not just lacking in technical capability, but in number. At the start of the war Britain was producing just eighty torpedoes a month for all purposes. The majority of these were assigned to the surface navy, and only afterwards were aircraft and submarines considered. Production on the home front rose slowly in an overburdened and limited production capacity, reaching only 200 a month after two years of war. It was not until early 1942 that production exceeded requirement.[72] The shortage directly affected British submarine operations in 1940–41, forcing commanders to be sparing. Before taking over charge of the submarines based at Malta, Captain G. W. G. Simpson was told in December 1940:

The object of the Malta based flotilla was to deprive the Italian Army in Libya of supplies by sinking southbound shipping. Regarding northbound shipping this should not in general be attacked because of torpedo shortage, unless the target was a warship, a tanker or a large transport.[73]

While these issues go some way to explaining the lack of sinkings in 1940, they do not explain the heavy submarine losses. The most common explanations put forward relate to the ageing nature of the 'O', 'P' and 'R' class submarines and their unsuitability for operating in the Mediterranean. The clear waters of the sea are also frequently cited as making the sighting of submerged vessels easier, which made for a poor combination with the larger size of these older classes.[74] Cunningham was certainly concerned about these technical issues, and felt the crews were slow to adapt to the unique conditions of the Mediterranean from their previous service on the China station. He felt that the Italians must have had excellent direction finding and hydrophone equipment in order to sink the submarines.[75] The older submarine classes were certainly larger than the 'S', 'T' and 'U' classes that were to arrive later, being around 50 per cent longer than the 'U' class, for example.[76] They also suffered from very loud, poor-quality machinery, and could be unreliable. In one extreme example of equipment failure, the *Osiris* had two diesel breakdowns and a battery explosion in a single patrol in August 1941, requiring over a year in dock for repairs.[77] The external fuel tanks that they often used had a tendency to develop small leaks and so left a tell-tale trace of oil on the surface for anti-submarine vessels or aircraft to follow and locate the boat.[78]

These problems all tally with the historiographical claims regarding the poor quality and suitability of the older types, while the noisy machinery would seem to marry with Cunningham's suspicions of Italian hydrophone use. Nor was the problem of noisy machinery limited to the British submarines, as *Narval* had auxiliary machinery that 'had to be heard to be believed'.[79] However, they do not seem adequate to explain the very heavy losses of submarines in 1940, as the Italian Navy was not particularly advanced in the field of anti-submarine warfare (ASW). Despite progressive Italian experiments with radar in the inter-war years, sets were only ordered for their ships in mid-1941, and these were generally reserved for the larger warships that did not conduct close escort duties. They never produced adequate radar for their ASW forces and were only given a small number of sets by the Germans in 1942, which meant that detection of surfaced submarines was very difficult. In 1940, they relied solely on shore-based RDF stations, and sonar equipment only became available in late 1941 in the form of lower quality German technology.[80]

The technical issues were compounded by poor ASW weaponry and tactics. The depth charge was their only practical weapon for striking at a submerged submarine, and they lacked the other, more lethal, weapons that would be developed by their opponents.[81] Italian tactical development also left something to be desired. A common tactic was 'deterrent dropping' to discourage attacks, but what it often achieved was simply to highlight the position of the escort to the submarine and prove that the submarine's exact location was unknown. The poor tactical development in this area was likely a result of the fact that a dedicated ASW training school was not set up by the Italian Navy until August 1941.[82] For their part, the IAF had paid little attention to ASW in the inter-war years, and their involvement in this aspect in 1940 has been described by the Italian official naval history as 'absolutely insufficient'.[83] Up until January 1941, their only relevant operations were in reconnaissance and limited direct escort of shipping in the immediate vicinity of ports. In one stark example, a unit that was moved to Sicily on 5 June did not fly a single convoy escort mission in 1940 and made only a handful of maritime reconnaissance flights.[84] The IAF lacked detection equipment, did not carry depth charges, and operating procedures were rudimentary.

Some of the aircraft used were pressed into the role despite being highly unsuited to it; the SM 79, for example, lacked a good field of view for sightings, greatly exacerbating the problem of having no detection equipment. Worse, they could not co-ordinate with surface vessels due to lack of correct standardised radio equipment, and air–sea co-operation attempts were abandoned after two months of war.[85]

Given the huge difficulties faced by the Italians in terms of ASW in 1940, the explanations of the poor quality of the older British submarine classes and the unique conditions of the Mediterranean for their losses seem inadequate. What is known is that Italian SIGINT had cracked some low-level Navy and RAF ciphers. It thus seems likely that the Italian successes in breaking these lower level codes contributed to destruction of the British submarines in the early campaign. Surviving source material related to Italian SIGINT is extremely patchy in nature. From what remains, it is clear that the Italians had at least some knowledge of British submarine movements in 1940. Italian policy regarding action on such SIGINT later in the war would be to redirect convoys in order to avoid the potential attacker, but in 1940 they took a more aggressive approach.[86] In particular, the heavy submarine losses in June came before the Italians had instituted a major convoy system, leaving their light forces to be more flexible.

The minelaying efforts from submarines were much more successful than the direct attacks. A total of 467 mines were offensively laid in 1940, and all but twenty-five of these were by submarine. These, laid by just two Royal Navy submarines, three French submarines and a handful of FAA aircraft, sank sixteen vessels of 41,856 tons.[87] These efforts can be seen as having been rather successful compared to the other methods used in 1940, as the number of sinkings was roughly equal to that from direct submarine attacks and air power, but did not take similar losses. Only the submarine *Grampus* was lost, on its first mission while on patrol after having laid its payload of mines. Minelaying actually represents something of a missed opportunity for the British in 1940, as it could be conducted with limited forces, and the dangers were comparatively slight before combined Italo-German countermeasures were improved from 1941 onwards. The Italians lacked minesweeping capability in general and were unprepared for counter-mine work when they entered the war. As the volume of the Italian official history on minesweeping has noted, little attention appears to have been given to the issue by either the Chiefs of Staff or Naval High Command (called 'Supermarina'). The result was that 'in consequence no provision was made and no means prepared to parry the offenses of this new weapon'.[88] It had only thirty-nine dedicated minesweepers, plus another forty-four re-equipped naval vessels at the outbreak of war. To this could be added a total of 508 repurposed auxiliary vessels, of which 289 were small fishing vessels and coasters that could only work in close proximity to land. For the most part this force could only sweep the most basic types of contact mine and it had to cover the entirety of the Mediterranean theatre, while vessels from it were often reassigned to other duties as needed.[89]

Air power had also demonstrated its offensive capability in the limited operations that were conducted, sinking eighteen vessels of 52,370 tons. These were primarily the result of the few opportunistic attacks from FAA Swordfish based on land or from carriers. The bombing of ports in North Africa, Italy and Albania sank little at this stage, which is likely a result of both the small numbers of bombers available and the inadequate level of aerial reconnaissance to determine when ports were full of shipping. A total of twenty-seven aircraft were lost in these operations in 1940, twenty-five of them RAF bombers in port attacks where enemy opposition was greatest. Night attacks by FAA aircraft were proving themselves to be comparatively safe, as the IAF could not detect the incoming aircraft. The FAA bomb and torpedo attacks had focused against ships in harbour though, rather than attacking directly at sea, which was to become increasingly common from 1941 onwards.

Due to a low place in British strategic priority and a paucity of forces available, the number of anti-shipping operations in 1940 had been meagre, as had the results. The consequent impact on the Mediterranean war was thus equally minor. The Italian invasion of Egypt had ground to a halt at Sidi Barrani, less than sixty miles inside the border, having met virtually no resistance. The halt was due to a combination of the fact that Mussolini never actually assigned his rather reluctant C-in-C Italian North Africa any territorial objective for the offensive but rather to attack 'the British forces in front of you', and the realisation that the heavily under-motorised Tenth Army was not well prepared for the complex logistical difficulties of operating in the desert. Having stopped, they set about improving the sparse road network in the area, building up defensive positions and stockpiling supplies for a renewed offensive, which was repeatedly postponed.[90] While they dallied, the British prepared and then in December launched their own offensive, Operation 'Compass'. It met with immediate success, inflicting a crushing blow at Sidi Barrani that was rapidly followed by a drive into Libya and the fall of Bardia, Tobruk, Derna and Benghazi. The Tenth Army was pushed right back to El Agheila by February 1941, by a British and Commonwealth force totalling just 36,000 men. For fewer than 2,000 casualties, 'Compass' had forced the Italians not only out of Egypt but also out of Cyrenaica and captured 130,000 men, 180 tanks and over 2,000 guns.[91] Tenth Army had been practically destroyed.

This remarkable achievement did not owe anything to the scattered anti-shipping efforts in 1940, as only 2 per cent of the supplies sent to North Africa were successfully interdicted.[92] It was due instead to the Tenth Army being utterly unprepared for desert warfare and its consequent operational ineffectiveness. It was vastly under-motorised, a key concern for modern warfare, and utterly crucial in the desert. It also lacked both quality and quantity in tanks and artillery, while doctrine and technology for combined operations between infantry, armour and aircraft were limited, obsolescent or non-existent.[93] The defensive positions at Sidi Barrani were poorly co-ordinated and commanders appear to have overlooked warning signs of the coming British offensive.[94]

The parallel setbacks in Greece occurred for similar reasons. Poorly trained and equipped Italian units struggled to make headway in difficult terrain, and by early November had only managed to punch a few narrow salients into the opposing defensive lines. They were promptly compelled to withdraw by a Greek counteroffensive that, with some assistance from the RAF, pushed the Italians right back into Albania by the end of the year. Logistical problems were a headache for the Italians, but again this was not the result of anti-shipping efforts, as the 44,670 tons of shipping lost on this route in 1940 resulted in less than 1 per cent of supplies being prevented from arriving.[95] Instead, the Italians had simply underestimated the supply base required for what they falsely expected to be a very short campaign. A lack of assigned shipping and insufficient capacity in Albanian ports meant that the transfer of forces, equipment and other supplies was frequently delayed. The average daily unloading at Durazzo was just 1,000 tons of materiel plus fifty lorries over autumn 1940, while at Valona it was a paltry 250 tons. In a stark example of the effects of such limitations, the Trieste motorised division that had been scheduled for complete transfer to Albania by 15 November could in fact only muster the divisional headquarters and a few units of artillery by that date.[96] The issue was exacerbated by poor rail and road links between ports and the front, and even a decision to temporarily prioritise seaborne supply to Albania over North Africa had little impact.[97] None of this logistical failure was attributable to anti-shipping operations. The only tangible benefit of British and Greek efforts in the Adriatic was the Italian decision, in response to the highly effective raid by Force X in November, to double the number of escorts used per convoy. This drew away valuable escorts from the Italian Navy's limited stock, which they knew were already becoming dangerously overstretched.[98] These could have been used to help protect the more bitterly contested sea routes over the coming years.

There is no correlation between those few anti-shipping efforts in 1940 and the collapse of Italy's 'Parallel War'. However, the sinkings that were achieved were the first in a prolonged period of attrition to vital Axis shipping resources that was later to have serious ramifications for their war effort. The Italians were already recognising that their margin of available shipping versus their increasing commitments was very thin, and that protecting them would be their overriding focus. They also appreciated that losses on any one route would cause wider pressure on the entire shipping network, and therefore delivering on their pre-war aim of controlling the central Mediterranean was essential.[99] Similarly, the heads of all three Italian services quickly became aware of the completely inadequate quantity (and quality) of maritime aircraft available for both reconnaissance and convoy escort purposes.[100] Finally, the British had managed to use all four methods of attacking shipping, to varying levels, and had made some demonstration of what they could achieve. Surface forces had proven their capability to eradicate an entire convoy in a single night, and aircraft had shown the potential of attacks on ships in harbour, particularly through some highly successful FAA operations. Mining operations were few but had proven their lower-risk nature and caused some losses to shipping. For submarines, anti-shipping operations had featured highly in their priorities, but they had conversely endured the hardest time, suffering what would be their most intensive losses of the whole campaign. The campaign in earnest had provided important experience to the British, from which they could develop their procedures in the use of each method. In 1941, they would also start to be used in a more integrated manner, in one of a series of improvements that would be made alongside the priority accorded to the campaign, the forces available for it and the results achieved.

3 Enter Germany
January–July 1941

Gradual Increases in Campaign Priority and Inter-service Disputes

Despite the resounding success of 'Compass', the focus of British strategy in the New Year was pivoting away from North Africa towards Greece. While the operation was in full swing, discussions were already underway in Whitehall about sending further assistance to the Greeks. Initially, Churchill stated at a meeting of the COS in early January that 'The speedy destruction of Italian forces in North-East Africa must be our prime overseas objective in the opening months of 1941.' Yet the priority was for a limited advance to Tobruk or perhaps Benghazi in order to secure Cyrenaica for a strong forward defence of Egypt, and then to withdraw forces to reinforce the Greeks. He felt 'it would not be right for the sake of Benghazi to lose the chance of the Greeks taking Valona ... supporting Greece must have priority after the western flank of Egypt has been made secure'.[1]

The reason for such urgency in transferring forces was a build-up of intelligence that German forces were massing in Romania and were about to attack Greece. This was partially accurate, but the wider German intentions were misinterpreted by the British. It was thought that a German invasion would be their first act in a strategy of advancing to seize key British positions and sources of oil supply in the Middle East. While the German High Command had toyed with the idea of involvement in a dedicated Middle East offensive over 1940–41, it never got beyond the conceptual phase, and a renewed call from Rommel in the summer was similarly unsuccessful. In fact, the German intention was to avoid involvement unless required to eliminate any threat from Greek/British forces towards the vital Romanian oilfields and to secure their southern flank for a future invasion of the Soviet Union. A successful campaign in Greece would offer additional airfields from which to bomb British shipping, the Suez Canal and other positions in the Middle East, but ambitions went little further.[2] At a meeting of the Defence

Committee (Operations) on 8 January it was agreed that as a German attack seemed likely, Greece should receive the fullest possible support. Churchill informed Longmore that after taking Tobruk, that 'all operations in Libya are subordinated to aiding Greece'.[3] After receiving news of the unexpectedly rapid British advance, this remit was extended by the War Cabinet in late January to include the capture of Benghazi. Otherwise the policy of a forward defensive position in North Africa and subordination to Greece was unchanged.[4]

Not only did the British wish to counter a perceived German offensive on their position in the Middle East, but increased aid to Greece could also have other benefits. A continuing conflict there should force further Axis forces to be drawn in, as opposed to their being sent to North Africa, where they could threaten the Suez Canal. It would help secure continued access to vital naval bases on Crete for greater control of the Eastern Mediterranean and Aegean, along with air bases in Greece from which to attack Italy or the Romanian oilfields. Churchill also remained hopeful that it might still influence Turkey to enter the war on his side. Even if the question of German involvement is ignored, there were concerns amongst the British that Greece and Italy could conclude a separate negotiated peace and deny British access to Greek naval and air bases.[5] When Metaxas died in late January, the opportunity was taken to further pressurise the weakened Greek political opposition to allow serious British military involvement. The efforts were successful, and the Greeks submitted to full British assistance in late February. Army and further RAF units, including additional Blenheims, soon began to be transferred from North Africa and the UK to Greece, while 'Compass' culminated in February with the advance halted at El Agheila.[6] The decision denied the British Western Desert Force the required mass and permission to advance on Tripoli during a window of opportunity when its defences were critically weak.[7]

This new direction in British strategy had two important effects on the anti-shipping campaign. First, it further increased the range of commitments for British aero-naval forces that could compete with anti-shipping operations. In particular, convoys carrying the newly assigned forces to Greece would require protection against air and sea attack. Second, it caused a brief shift in priority from the North Africa sea routes to those in the Adriatic. The result was that relatively few new forces were made available for the campaign against the traffic to and from North Africa. The surface fleet focused on convoying men and supplies to Malta and Greece over March and April, while aircraft were broadly prioritised for Greece first, North Africa second and Malta third. Whereas requests from the Greek government for more aircraft to assist them during this period were met positively, similar requests for North Africa or Malta were less likely to be. In a meeting of the COS on 3 January, Portal stated that he could not make Beaufort torpedo bombers available for Malta even in light of the 'high priority' of Libyan supply lines, due to 'teething troubles' with their engines. Six Swordfish were transferred there by *Ark Royal*, but they were in such a poor state of repair that one could not be flown off and the rest required a week of repairs before becoming operational.[8] Even the increase in submarine forces that had taken place at the end of the previous year had slowed. There had been twenty in the theatre at the end of 1940, and there were still twenty at the end of March.[9] The problems for Malta's role in anti-shipping operations were further exacerbated by the arrival of the German air corps, Fliegerkorps X, in Sicily from December 1940. It was a mixed force of aircraft that had previously operated from Norway in a specialised anti-shipping role, and which would eventually number over 400 aircraft by March. It had originally been intended to operate purely against British shipping and naval targets, but this quickly expanded to include bombing Malta, convoy escort, reconnaissance and other operations in Libya.[10] Elements of the corps were transferred to Greece, the Dodecanese and Libya, but by March, the bombing raids on Malta had forced the temporary withdrawal of the Wellington squadron and the remaining Sunderlands.

Attacks on the Adriatic routes started to increase at the expense of those elsewhere, and the Cabinet duly approved extended 'sink at sight' zones in February that incorporated nearly all of that sea along with the entire central Mediterranean.[11] Longmore confirmed to Portal on 15 January that the Wellingtons sent to Greece via Malta had prioritised the Adriatic ports as their primary target, with only possible diversions for important naval targets.[12] In the meantime bombers in the Greek force targeted the Albanian ports in a concerted effort to disrupt supplies by damaging the port facilities on both sides of the sea, and blocking their entrances with sunken shipping. In March, Portal discussed the bombing of Italy with Churchill and the very recent shift to focus on the Adriatic ports. He assured the Prime Minister that he thought this was the best policy to disrupt reinforcements to Albania.[13] In reality the greater difficulty involved meant that the Italian Adriatic ports received very few raids, with Brindisi only being attacked twice during the Greek campaign. The more easily targeted Albanian ports came in for considerably more attention. Durazzo and especially Valona were regularly raided by bombers from Greece, while part of 815 Squadron FAA was sent from Crete to Paramythia aerodrome, just south of Albanian border, to operate against Adriatic shipping. Swordfish from this squadron were periodically flown in and out of Paramythia and Eleusis near Athens for these operations until they were withdrawn for good on 21 April.[14]

The division of British strategy and military power between Greece and North Africa quickly proved to be a grave error. In February, the first elements of the *Deutsches Afrikakorps* (DAK) began to arrive in Libya, along with their commander, Erwin Rommel. Although he had been sent there simply for the limited purpose of shoring up the tattered Italian position to ensure that they held Tripolitania, the headstrong Rommel was quick to launch attacks of his own.[15] On 30 March, these developed into a full Axis offensive that pushed the British and Commonwealth forces out of Cyrenaica within a month, apart from a garrison besieged at Tobruk. Meanwhile, the Germans invaded Greece and Yugoslavia on 6 April, and reached Athens by the 27th, while over 50,000 British, Commonwealth and Greek personnel were evacuated, mostly to Crete. That island was promptly assaulted on 20 May in the largest airborne operation that had ever been attempted. It fell after ten days of intense fighting, with the evacuation of over 17,000 men by the Royal Navy, which suffered grievous losses to its light warships.[16] A final layer was added to British woes when an anti-British uprising seized power in Iraq in April and threatened key positions. Iraqi appeals to Germany for increased assistance played directly to British fears over their oil supplies. German authorities exercised strong pressure on Vichy France to allow their aircraft to be routed through Syria to Iraq, which was accepted in May, although the Iraqi insurrection was quickly defeated that month, as German unpreparedness meant that their assistance barely materialised. The Vichy French involvement provided the British with a pretext to invade Syria in order to safeguard their oil supplies and Middle East possessions from a possible German attack. It led to a brief Anglo-Vichy conflict over June and July that resulted in British victory.[17]

By late March, North African sea routes were beginning to return to the fore in the minds of the military chiefs in Whitehall, and of those in the theatre. The Prime Minister and COS approved a decision to send additional submarines and aircraft to Malta in this respect. At the start of May the number of submarines had jumped to thirty-two, and Pound urged Cunningham to focus these submarines on shipping to Libya.[18] Portal allocated six Blenheims for Malta along with the experienced Hugh Lloyd to take over from Maynard. They had previously been operating against German shipping in the North Sea and, as Portal told Churchill, 'They will be able to take action against shipping with the special technique developed by that group.' This was to be the first major example of inter-theatre learning in the use of coastal air power during the war, and the start of a cyclical relationship in knowledge transfer between the home theatre and the Mediterranean.[19] Further Blenheims soon followed. Incremental increases to 'sink at sight' over April–June freed these forces and others for anti-shipping operations across the entire Aegean and routes to Cyrenaica.[20]

The transfer of the Blenheim aircraft at the expense of the metropolitan Air Force suggests that not only were the North African routes taking the higher priority within the theatre, but that the Mediterranean was becoming the primary theatre for the British.[21] After the withdrawal from Greece, the direction from Whitehall urged greater focus on the North Africa routes. The Chief of the Imperial General Staff (CIGS), John Dill, told the Air and Naval Chiefs that 'For the Air Force and Navy the primary desiderata are to cut the German communications to Libya and to Cyprus and Syria.'[22] This was met with general agreement, although it was felt that the Navy must first concentrate on the impending evacuation of Crete.

The priority and direction of the campaign over the first half of 1941 were largely determined by the events described above, but the period also saw significant and often acrimonious debate over conduct and responsibility. This debate was broadly built on service lines, and represented the latest dispute between the Air Force and Navy, each claiming the other should be doing more in the campaign and taking responsibility for its conduct. Initially, this did not take place in-theatre, as Cunningham and Longmore had a generally positive relationship. They worked together effectively, were willing to be flexible over contentious issues like the control of assets and made some impressive achievements in aero-naval co-operation in the face of very constrained resources.[23] Until June 1941, the dispute existed primarily between Cunningham on one side and Portal and Churchill on the other. Cunningham did often receive the support of Pound but could not always count upon it. Calls from Cunningham and Longmore for more aircraft often fell on deaf ears, particularly when related to aircraft that were to be used for maritime purposes. While Blenheims were received, the request for dedicated Beaufort torpedo bombers to be based at Malta, for instance, had already been refused or delayed multiple times by June. Although some appeared in North Africa in 1941, Malta did not receive any until 1942.[24]

The dispute can be viewed on two different conceptual levels. One is a more narrowly focused disagreement over how the anti-shipping campaign would best be conducted, and by whom. The other is a far broader debate that was taking place over the question of the quality of maritime aviation and the question of a dedicated maritime command for the theatre – an overseas equivalent of Coastal Command. Cunningham complained, with much justification, that insufficient training, numbers and suitable aircraft were leading to inadequate and poor-quality reconnaissance, ineffective convoy escort and highly inaccurate strike efforts. He noted the immediate superiority of the newly arrived German Air Force (GAF) in maritime operations of all kinds and claimed the only solution was 'more aircraft diverted to fleet co-operation and personnel that are trained in work over the sea and we shan't get those without ... a special organisation running in close touch with us'.[25] Perhaps unsurprisingly, Portal was opposed to the concept of placing RAF assets under naval control, as it represented a potential threat to the RAF's differing strategic priorities and concepts. Worse, it could even be perceived as a threat to the service's independence. Therefore, Portal, like most in the RAF, espoused the essential nature of the indivisibility of air power – the RAF must retain centralised control of all land-based assets. A similar dispute had also occurred over the operational control of the aircraft in Coastal Command, meaning that the RAF was seemingly under threat at home as well. Consequently, Portal told Churchill:

I notice that the C-in-C has once more suggested the formation of a Coastal Command in the Mediterranean as a cure for the present air situation. I cannot see how this would increase the forces available and I think it would certainly result in failure to apply our forces in the most economical way.[26]

As will be seen in the next chapter, some resolution to this aspect of the dispute was reached in the autumn that year, but the issue remained unchanged over spring and summer.

Aside from his pleas for a dedicated command, Cunningham vociferously complained that not enough was being done by the RAF in terms of maritime operations, due to a lack of forces and low priority. He felt that if greater emphasis were to be placed on Axis shipping then the RAF should play a greater part in attacking it. In particular, he claimed that it was 'essential' that large numbers of long-range bombers should be transferred 'immediately' to Egypt for the bombing of Tripoli. While the RAF could concentrate on bombing Axis ports of arrival and departure, the Navy would continue attacking shipping at sea with submarines and torpedo aircraft. Portal's response, via Pound, referenced 'teething troubles' and the lack of 'tropicalised' long-range bombers ready to be sent there. He suggested that bombardment, mining and even blocking operations against Tripoli should be considered instead.[27] For his part, Churchill was highly critical of Cunningham's rather brusquely worded calls for greater RAF participation. He informed Cunningham first that 'It is the duty of the Navy, assisted by the Air, to cut the communications

58 Enter Germany: January–July 1941

Illustration 3.1 A Consolidated B-24 Liberator Mark I bomber. The arrival of long-range aircraft such as these in the theatre greatly increased the range at which Axis ports could be attacked, and they played an important role both within RAF and later USAAF units, after the Americans committed to the theatre in late 1942.
Source: www.gettyimages.co.uk/detail/news-photo/american-aircraft-in-royal-air-force-service-1939-1945-news-photo/154421926?adppopup=true
Credit: B. J. Daventry / Imperial War Museums via Getty Images

between Italy and Tripoli.' He then went a step further on 14 April: 'the prime duty of the British Mediterranean Fleet ... to stop all seaborne traffic between Italy and Africa. Every convoy which gets through must be considered a serious naval failure. The reputation of the Royal Navy is engaged in stopping this traffic.'[28] The result of this was that the burden of the campaign remained almost entirely on the Navy at this stage. In spite of opposition from both Cunningham and Pound, light surface forces were to be based at Malta to attack shipping. Churchill also urged direct attack on Tripoli and Benghazi through naval bombardment, and even offered the highly fanciful suggestion of blocking Tripoli by sinking the ageing battleship *Centurion* in the approaches. Such was his conviction that he went so far as to say that the importance of blocking the port could even warrant the sacrifice of a battleship on the active list.[29] Cunningham was able to argue successfully against any blocking operation due to the huge risk and sacrifice involved, and that any blockage achieved could only ever be a temporary result. His compromise was that any battleships would take part in a bombardment, about which he also had reservations.[30] Four destroyers were consequently transferred to Malta to act as a specialised anti-shipping task force on 11 April, while the Mediterranean Fleet bombarded Tripoli ten days later, with the stated objective to 'relieve the pressure on our military forces operating in the western desert'.[31]

The operations of the Malta-based destroyers and the bombardment are described in the following section, but their apparent success during the brief period in April further fuelled the debate over the conduct of the campaign. The destroyers successfully eliminated one whole convoy, but in turn invited greater focus from Axis air forces against the docks at Valetta. Pound expressed continued concern over the safety of surface forces based at Malta, due to the threat of Italian warships rather than Axis air power. He felt that whatever cruisers might be based there, the Italians would be able to bring a superior force to bear, and so suggested the basing of a battleship at the island as well. Cunningham replied that he agreed in principle, but that this could not be done at that time due to the lack of air defences on the island and the threat of air attack.[32] This proved to be the right decision, as air attacks curtailed the destroyer operations and highlighted the continuing inadequacy of the fighter defences there. Despite brief reinforcement from other destroyers and the cruiser *Gloucester*, successes were limited and the last of the force was withdrawn in May to assist in the Crete evacuation. Nevertheless, the destruction of the convoy had seemingly exonerated Churchill's view of the Navy taking primary responsibility in the campaign and utilising dedicated surface forces at Malta.

As for the bombardment, Cunningham claimed that it was carried out without loss only because Axis air forces were committed elsewhere. However, Portal cited it as evidence that the Mediterranean Fleet was a more appropriate method to attack Tripoli than a dedicated force of heavy bombers. He produced a wealth of statistics for Churchill, showing that the fleet fired 530 tons into the port in forty-two minutes. He estimated that the equivalent weight of bombs could be dropped by one Wellington squadron from Malta in about ten and a half weeks, or one Stirling squadron from Egypt in about thirty weeks. He also claimed that every shell hit something important, and that this would not be the case with high-altitude bombing.[33] Churchill remained adamant that dedicated surface forces were the best method for attacking convoys at sea, and sided with his Chief of the Air Staff over the bombardment issue. He reiterated to Cunningham that 'There can be no departure from the principle that it is the primary responsibility of the Mediterranean Fleet to sever all communication between Italy and Africa.'[34]

The dispute was interrupted by the unfolding Balkan campaign. Cunningham was forced to focus the Mediterranean Fleet first on evacuating forces from Greece to Crete in late April, then on preventing a seaborne invasion of the island in May and finally evacuating it at the end of the month. The commitment of available naval resources was huge, while reconnaissance aircraft had to be focused towards watching the Italian Navy for potential interference or flying out particularly important personnel. Throughout May only submarines and disembarked FAA squadrons retained a high priority for anti-shipping operations. For the RAF bombers that remained in Egypt, though, denying the use of Benghazi as a forward supply base for the advancing Axis forces became one of the major objectives.[35]

The Crete debacle was disastrous for the Mediterranean Fleet, with its light forces suffering particularly painful losses. Three cruisers and eight destroyers had been sunk, and there were varying levels of damage to three battleships, an aircraft carrier, seven cruisers and nine destroyers.[36] This ensured that Royal Navy warships could take no significant further part in the campaign until the winter, and Cunningham had to concede in June that only submarines and aircraft could prosecute the campaign for the time being.[37] However, the end in Crete allowed for a renewed focus on the North African routes, with a secondary consideration over Syria, as Dill had urged. What is more, after butchering the fleet so effectively, elements of Fliegerkorps X in Greece and the Dodecanese were retained there to replace other units being withdrawn for the invasion of the Soviet Union. In fact, the remaining aircraft in Sicily were parcelled out between Greece, the Dodecanese and North Africa by early June, as the Germans put their faith in the IAF being able to hold Malta down in their absence. British intelligence made them fully aware of this development.[38]

Given the known lower quality of Italian air power, it was an opportunity for the offensive effort from Malta to be rebuilt, while aircraft and submarines from Egypt could concentrate against shipping to the forward ports like Benghazi and the Syrian supply lanes. This was an urgent concern not only to halt the Axis advance in North Africa, but because the British were hurriedly planning their own offensive to relieve Tobruk: Operation 'Battleaxe'. Having arrived in May, Hugh Lloyd set about following his instructions to 'sink Axis shipping sailing from Europe to Africa'. He immediately started streamlining the command and control systems and structures and improving the airfields and operating procedures on the island, as well as implementing the attack procedures that he had developed with No. 2 Group. He also started construction on new underground operations rooms to make them more resistant to air attack and set new dispersal procedures to help protect aircraft on the ground.[39]

Although Lloyd was busy setting the foundation for increased air operations, the actual increase in aircraft in Malta was very modest at first, but the increases in the theatre overall were more significant, as

Table 3.1 *Arrivals of RAF bomber reinforcements in the Middle East, January–July 1941*

	January	February	March	April	May	June	July
Beaufighter	0	0	0	0	16	5	0
Blenheim	12	38	35	37	39	55	115
Maryland	1	2	6	7	6	22	46
Wellington	2	2	16	27	15	11	31

Source: Adapted from Playfair et al., *Mediterranean and Middle East*, Vol. 2, appendix 7.

shown in Table 3.1. This was because they were sent to Egypt with a policy to focus on support for 'Battleaxe'.

This the RAF did partly through direct close air support and interdiction in the land war, but also against shipping routes to Benghazi, which they would not have been able to carry out effectively from Malta due to the long range. As the COS intimated in a telegram to Cunningham, 'Tripoli seems too distant to affect the immediate issue of Battleaxe.'[40] Portal signalled the new Commander of RAF Middle East, Arthur Tedder, criticising a decline in attacks on Benghazi and ordering him to increase his efforts. He expressed particular concern over intelligence indicating the recent arrival of tanks and vehicles. Anti-shipping attacks and port bombing from Egypt became increasingly common in response, and almost the entire heavy bomber effort from the RAF in June was directed against Benghazi.[41] Simultaneously, anti-shipping efforts in the Syrian campaign increased from mid-June, with RAF and FAA aircraft operating out of Palestine against Vichy shipping to Beirut and attacks on the port itself.[42]

'Battleaxe' quickly ended in failure, but the perceived need to attack the African routes remained firm with both in-theatre commanders and those in Whitehall. At a meeting four days after the end of the operation, the Vice Chief of the Naval Staff, Admiral Phillips, stressed the continuing importance of interdicting shipping to both Tripoli and Benghazi despite the failure of the latest desert offensive. He referenced the increased use of submarines for this purpose and urged a greater complementary effort from the RAF. His RAF counterpart, Wilfrid Freeman, replied that all possible action was already being taken from Malta, and that the question of range for aircraft in Egypt made this difficult, but promised that the Air Staff would investigate what more could be done. The meeting concluded that both staffs would make further efforts to intensify their anti-shipping work.[43]

Their agreement and the increases in aircraft conducting anti-shipping operations did not represent a thawing in the inter-service dispute though, which was instead becoming more heated. Angry over the failure of 'Battleaxe', Churchill sacked Longmore and replaced him with Tedder at the start of June. This exacerbated the inter-service dispute further, as while Cunningham had at least enjoyed cordial relations with Longmore, he and Tedder quickly developed an abrasive relationship. Tedder was not opposed to the use of RAF aircraft for maritime purposes, but in accordance with Portal, he was strongly opposed to losing complete ownership of RAF resources. Any prospect of a dedicated maritime command under naval control in the theatre was anathema to him. His appointment meant that the dispute was no longer purely between Cunningham and his opponents in London; it had also been brought to life in-theatre, too. Just days after Tedder's arrival, the two were already disagreeing over the issue of a dedicated maritime command and the extent to which RAF aircraft should be used for maritime purposes. Tedder did assure the other theatre commanders that he would attack the enemy's lines of communication with the 'maximum forces', but tensions only increased as time progressed.[44]

Malta was beginning to receive more aircraft for offensive purposes over June and July, but there were serious concerns over its ability to sustain these operations, as its air defences were so weak. Pound warned the other Chiefs in late July that unless the RAF in Malta was brought up to strength soon, their efforts to both interrupt sea lanes and defend the island would be seriously prejudiced.[45] The striking forces there were bolstered by the arrival of a further six Swordfish with experienced crews in July. These were the first aircraft on the island to be equipped with Air-Surface Vessel Radar (ASV) devices, able to detect shipping at range at night, and so of great aid to the anti-shipping campaign.[46] The island was able to become more active in general over the summer, as the Wellingtons had also returned by this time, while occasional Italian air raids were ineffectual at hampering operations.[47] After some disagreement in the War Cabinet over the use of the Wellingtons and the political considerations of bombing Italy, they were used to attack Naples, Sicilian ports and air bases.[48]

Broadly, the anti-shipping campaign had increased in British strategic priorities over the first seven months of 1941, with more direct focus on its necessity and more forces being made available for the purpose. The primary reason for this was the diminished threat of invasion to the United Kingdom, which allowed the Mediterranean and Middle East to become Britain's dominant theatre of war. There were of course a wide variety of other priorities in-theatre that drew on resources that could otherwise have been used for anti-shipping operations, especially the Balkan campaign and the subsequent evacuations. For the most part, though, the North Africa routes were the leading priority, particularly after the arrival of Rommel and the start of his first offensive, although those in the Adriatic and briefly the Vichy French lines to Syria also received attention. The increase in priority and forces for the campaign were accompanied by some important technical and tactical developments in the anti-shipping operations themselves.

Anti-shipping Operations and Tactical Developments, January–July 1941

On New Year's Day 1941, a conference was held at the RAF Headquarters on Malta between the Senior Air Staff Officer and the commanders of the different RAF and FAA squadrons. The subject of the event was 'The Interception and Attack of Enemy Convoys', and it aimed to improve procedures and ensure that the most was made from the limited resources available. In view of the limited quantity of reconnaissance aircraft, it was decided that the shadowing of vessels by Sunderlands on especially dark nights was useless. As there were no ASV-equipped aircraft at this stage, very dark nights greatly reduced the possibility of the Swordfish aircraft being able to locate the target and make an attack, and their low endurance afforded them little time to search. Risking the slow-moving and unescorted biplanes in daytime was also to be avoided. As such, rather than waste precious flying time from the few available aircraft, the Sunderland would instead make a sighting report and return to base. Hopefully, the targets would have been unaware that they had been located, and a new attempt at location and strike could be made at first light.[49] Tripoli and the Sicilian ports would need to be reconnoitred as frequently as was possible, and the more suitable Maryland aircraft were to be assigned to this role when available. It was agreed that everything should be done to determine the likely departure time of convoys, and shipping was to be attacked at sea at any possible opportunity, regardless of whether north- or southbound, loaded or empty. If attacks at sea could not occur, then they should be attacked in port as a second option, either by Swordfish or Wellington. The most important thing was to sink shipping of any type and purpose.[50]

As a result of the conference, new tactical procedures were set in place to simplify the reporting procedure for sightings and set the procedure for dropping flares by Sunderland to illuminate targets at night for attack by Swordfish. This was vital if successful torpedo attacks were to be made at night, and Cunningham had already complained to Pound in January that FAA torpedo bombers could not hit a fast-moving target. By this time, though, general efforts to improve maritime aviation training in the theatre were underway. Training of torpedo aircrews began to take place at the Operational Training Unit at Shallufa in Egypt, which was used for all maritime training purposes from late 1940.[51] Shortly after the conference, the command and control situation that Longmore had complained about the previous year was further simplified. The co-ordination and direction of all air efforts from Malta were to be made from the RAF HQ on the island. This would help to make the most of the island's limited potential, which offered just sixteen Wellingtons, twelve Swordfish, four Sunderlands and four Marylands, plus reserves, at the start of the year.[52]

The Malta air striking forces were further aided by the lifting of restrictions on attacking southern Italian targets, and Wellingtons raided Palermo twice and Naples and Messina once each in the first ten days of January, along with three raids on Tripoli.[53] The Swordfish were a little slower in starting their own attacks on shipping at sea, but soon there were increasing levels of attack in conjunction with reconnaissance from Sunderland aircraft, as per the procedures set out at the start of the month. On 27 January, they made their first direct strike on a convoy, after a sighting report from a Sunderland. The distance was sufficient that they had to be equipped with drop-tanks for extra fuel, but seven Swordfish attacked a convoy of two merchant vessels and an escort, successfully sinking one. Although this had been a daytime sortie, future attacks were conducted at night in order to safeguard the vulnerable aircraft.[54] The strike represented an early success and showed what the squadron was capable of. It was the first of ten torpedo strikes up to the end of July, while a further ten bombing and torpedo attacks were made on Tripoli and shipping present there. Some of these were combined with minelaying operations while wholly independent mining operations were also conducted.[55] The aircraft at Malta were the only air forces able to attack the North Africa routes in the first quarter of 1941, as those in Egypt lacked the range to reach Tripoli or were otherwise prioritised towards the land war.

Submarines continued to be active, with more of the superior types of craft becoming available, even if numbers overall did not appreciably increase until April. There were three patrols off Tunisia from the newly arrived 'U' class boats of the Maltese force in January, and other sorties from S1 at Alexandria, while Greek submarines operated in the Adriatic. *Rorqual* also laid fifty mines in two separate fields in the Adriatic, to hamper shipping to Albania. January was the most successful month of the submarine campaign to date, sinking six merchant vessels of

26,795 tons.[56] It was quickly determined that the smaller, shorter range 'U' class were ideal for patrols in the shallower waters off Tunisia to attack shipping taking a route west of Malta to Tripoli, while the other, larger classes could work in the deeper waters elsewhere.

In February, the naval contingent based at Gibraltar (Force H) made a rare input to the anti-shipping campaign in the bombardment of Genoa. The operation itself came about as intelligence had suggested the presence of Italian capital ships in the port, and these represented the main objective of four listed. The others were morale, the diversion of Italian naval and air resources and finally 'To damage war industries, shipping, supplies etc.'[57] The operation was thus linked to the anti-shipping campaign, albeit in a tangential manner. Force H was forced to operate rather 'blind' as there were no suitable long-range reconnaissance aircraft available at Malta, and the Italian naval units were ultimately not actually present. The bombardment went ahead, lasting for over thirty minutes, and Swordfish from *Ark Royal* simultaneously bombed the oil refinery at Livorno and four laid magnetic mines in the approaches to La Spezia. Significant damage was inflicted on the port and some to the city, while four freighters were sunk, although later raised.[58] The task force was able to withdraw safely without loss, after the Italians failed to find it, but the operation had represented a major risk for little reward.

The RAF involvement in anti-shipping operations had been very limited over January and February, but in March that gradually began to change. At the express wish of the Greek C-in-C, British bombers had been operating mainly in close support of the Greek Army, but on the 14th the weight of the bomber effort was switched to the airfields and ports.[59] Wellingtons and Blenheims continued to operate against the Albanian ports and shipping within them, with Wellingtons particularly targeting docks. Some efforts were also made against the port at Astropalia in the Aegean. All the raids were small-scale due to the few aircraft available, and Blenheim attacks were sometimes pinprick efforts by a single bomber combining the attack with a reconnaissance mission. Between 18 March and 6 April there were only sixteen sorties that specifically targeted ports and shipping in Durazzo and Astropalia. Anti-aircraft fire around the former was reported to be 'intense and accurate'.[60] Swordfish from 815 Squadron supplemented these efforts, operating from Greece against shipping in Valona, Durazzo and, on one occasion, Brindisi. When no shipping was found to be present in port, they would search for targets at sea, but this was generally unsuccessful due to a lack of reconnaissance, ASV equipment and the difficulties of visually locating vessels at night. Nearly all their operations were torpedo attacks, but two minelaying operations were completed as well.

The squadron flew nine missions before being withdrawn on 21 April, varying from one to six aircraft in each, and sank three merchantmen of 11,855 tons, as well as damaging others.[61]

As the focus from Whitehall shifted away from Greece and back to North Africa, attacks on Tripoli began to increase once more. Over the same 18 March to 6 April period discussed above, there were eleven missions against Tripoli involving thirty-nine aircraft. None of them were large in scale, with the biggest being a combined bombing/mining effort by nine Swordfish, but it represented the start of the return to focus on the Libyan routes.[62] The Secretary of State for Foreign Affairs approved of this increase, and urged greater Wellington reinforcement and bombing effort against Tripoli, which should be the main target of heavy bombers. For him, the port was 'the most important target of the war for us now and we should concentrate all we can against it by sea and air'. He noted a particular opportunity for operations from Malta, as Axis air forces on Sicily had recently been inactive.[63]

Operations against Tripoli were increased correspondingly, and the Axis recapture of Benghazi in April provided a new, more easily reached target for aircraft based in Egypt and eastern Cyrenaica. Over April and May, Tripoli was raided on six occasions by twenty-five aircraft from North Africa and a further ten times by forty-five aircraft from Malta. The Axis advance into Cyrenaica soon pushed Tripoli out of range for the air forces based in North Africa, meaning the important forward port of Benghazi quickly became a top priority. It was raided thirty-five times by 117 aircraft over April and May, and absorbed a greater effort than any other single target or type of mission from late April onwards.[64] As will be seen, this not only resulted in many sinkings and damage to shipping, but it also greatly damaged the port infrastructure itself and the associated workforce.[65]

Due to pressure from Churchill and others in Whitehall, surface forces of the Navy were also starting to take a greater role in the campaign, including the basing of destroyers at Malta in April. SIGINT successes against German sources had revealed that the German 15th Panzer Division had been assembling in Sicily for transport to Libya, but as the key Italian C38m naval cypher had not yet been broken, the dates and composition of the convoys were unknown. This, coupled with the persistent lack of reconnaissance aircraft, and Italian evasive routing based on their knowledge of the existence of the destroyer force resulted in the first two convoys slipping through undetected.[66] The third, known as the '*Tarigo* Convoy', was successfully located by aircraft and then intercepted by the destroyers. With the help of radar and a cleverly co-ordinated approach, they achieved complete surprise when they attacked, in spite of the convoy having been warned after Italian SIGINT intercepted the Maryland's sighting report. In a hectic action in the dark, the destroyers sank all five merchant vessels and two of the three escorts, heavily damaging the other. The price for this success was the loss of the destroyer *Mohawk*, sunk by torpedoes fired from the leading escort *Luca Tarigo* while itself in the act of sinking.[67]

The operations of the 14th Flotilla were followed by the bombardment of Tripoli by the Mediterranean Fleet on 21 April. Conducted at night, Cunningham was nevertheless surprised that there was no air attack on the fleet. The bombardment kicked up large amounts of dust that obscured the target, but he adjudged that a destroyer and three merchant vessels had been sunk and a further two damaged. In reality, only one vessel was destroyed and the damage to the port was moderate. He quickly made it clear that he felt that the operation was not worth the risk.[68] The surface forces were soon withdrawn for their role in the Greek calamity, but they did manage to fit in one FAA strike from the carrier *Formidable* when escorting a convoy in the Eastern Mediterranean in early May. When aircraft spotted a 'fuel convoy' on the Sicily–Benghazi route, four Swordfish were flown off to attack it. They got lost en route, missed the target entirely and one failed to return. The other three barely made it back to the carrier, the last of them completely empty of fuel.[69] It was a clear demonstration of the continuing difficulty of attacking convoys at sea with aircraft before sufficient reconnaissance capabilities and detection equipment were in place.

After evacuating the Greek expedition to Crete, the Mediterranean Fleet moved to the role of preventing a seaborne invasion of the island. It marked the first involvement of the fast minelayer class in the anti-shipping campaign, when HMS *Abdiel* laid 158 mines off Cephalonia to interfere with any shipping sent through the Corinth Canal to this end. In fact, it was highly successful against traffic going elsewhere, as a convoy carrying troops and equipment destined for Russia ran into the field. Two large steamers and two escorts were sunk.[70] The frequent patrols of the fleet to prevent any seaborne landings also bought success, but at a heavy price. Thanks to the work of one of the few available Marylands, a convoy of twenty-five caiques and small steamers carrying German troops and equipment was intercepted by a force of warships. The single escort – the torpedo boat *Lupo* – put up a gallant but desperate running defence using smokescreens. At the time it was believed that the entire convoy was sunk in the chaotic action, and Cunningham erroneously claimed 4,000 Germans were killed. In fact, while most of the vessels were sunk, fewer than 400 men were lost, the remainder escaping home along with the heavily damaged *Lupo* or being picked up later from the water. The following day another force intercepted a second convoy, sinking one of the stragglers and engaging its escort. The convoy turned back and successfully escaped, as the Royal Navy force was driven off by air attack that caused havoc.[71]

The subsequent evacuation of Crete and naval losses once again left the conduct of the campaign to aircraft and submarines alone. The Blenheims at Malta began attacking shipping in earnest in May, and both Lloyd and the aircrews brought with them the dramatic tactics that they had developed over the North Sea. They would fly in low at the target, at a height of just 50–100 feet, before pulling up at the last possible moment to pass just over the top of the ship, dropping their load of four bombs in quick succession. This was deemed to be the most likely method to hit a ship with unguided bombs, and for one or more to penetrate and explode within its superstructure.[72] These tactics made for much greater accuracy, as direct bombing from higher altitudes was haphazard, but the precision nature of the flying meant the operations had to be conducted in daytime. Achieving surprise during attacks was thus almost impossible in the frequently clear and cloudless skies over the Mediterranean, although the bombers regularly received fighter escort. There were frequent Blenheim attacks over their first three months of operation, restricted only by a lack of numbers and serviceability, as the nature of their attacks commonly led to damaged aircraft, while spares and sufficient ground crew were still being built up. Austin has claimed that by July, the average serviceability was just five out of twenty-one Blenheims.[73] The Blenheim attacks represented just one aspect of an increased air offensive from the island, as shown in Table 3.2. Clearly, the campaign was becoming sufficiently important to even warrant limited use of some of the precious Marylands in an attack role.

A major breakthrough in SIGINT offered increasing prospects of results to all forms of attack. In June, some document captures gave further high-grade Italian naval intelligence for a short time and this was quickly followed up by a breakthrough with the C38m cypher used by Supermarina. This cypher was introduced in December 1940 under pressure from the Germans over the perceived vulnerability of the existing Italian system, which in fact had been completely secured by code changes the previous July. With the information from C38m, details of almost every convoy and individual sailing became available. This included information consisting of the day and possibly time of departure, destination and make-up of the convoy. The first mercantile sinking based on this intelligence came the following month by the submarine *P33*.[74] The information provided through this breakthrough was not always made available in time to allow attacks. In mid-1941 the time-lag

Table 3.2 *Raids on ports and shipping by aircraft from Egypt and Malta, May–July 1941*

	From Egypt				
	Blenheim	Maryland	Swordfish	Wellington	Total
May	1 (2 aircraft)	0	0	25 (75)	26 (77)
June	0	0	0	33 (138)	33 (138)
July	0	0	0	43 (182)	43 (182)

	From Malta				
	Blenheim	Maryland	Swordfish	Wellington	Total
May	10 (39)	0	5 (19)	1 (4)	16 (62)
June	6 (34)	4 (14)	8 (42)	3 (14)	21 (104)
July	10 (41)	0	6 (28)	7 (45)	23 (114)

Notes: Calculated from TNA AIR 22/398, Fortnightly Operational Summaries Nos. 13–20, 21 April–10 August 1941.

from interception to decryption could be up to ten days; by the end of 1942 it was usually less than one. The information received was also sometimes open to misinterpretation.[75] Some streamlining to the process of receiving and decrypting SIGINT and disseminating it to the relevant personnel was implemented very quickly. In August, a Special Liaison Unit was created at Malta to allow information derived from SIGINT to be sent directly there, rather than via Egypt. This reduced the possibility of information arriving too late to be of use, but did not remove it completely.[76] The cracking of C38m did not, as at least one historian has suggested, offer the British a panacea.[77] However, this major breakthrough in SIGINT, assisted by a modest increase in reconnaissance aircraft in the theatre, provided a much more complete picture of Axis shipping to the British and sinkings rose accordingly over the remainder of the year. The British retained this vital source of SIGINT for the rest of the war with Italy.

For all the importance of Malta at this stage, air attacks against Axis shipping and ports from Egyptian bases were more numerous and substantially heavier. Almost the entire effort from Egypt was by Wellingtons, seeking to damage Benghazi and sink shipping in or near it to halt the Axis advance, and then support the 'Battleaxe' offensive. Concurrently, RAF and FAA aircraft from Egypt, Palestine and Cyprus also participated in a brief campaign over Syria. Beirut was frequently raided and Vichy French shipping was attacked at sea. Submarine patrols were intensified from S1 at Alexandria and S10 at Malta against shipping to Tripoli, Benghazi and Beirut, along with scattered attacks elsewhere: a total of 102 over May–July.[78] The period from January to July thus ended with a clearer focus for the campaign and the most intensive operations over the previous three months.

The Beginnings of Attrition: Assessing the Campaign, January–July 1941

As with 1940, anti-shipping operations in this period were generally conducted separately by the different arms of the campaign. Disjointery, rather than jointery, was the watchword. Submarines generally operated independently and without assistance, and still lacked the technical capability to co-ordinate directly with reconnaissance aircraft while at sea. Although sighting reports from submarines occasionally resulted in the despatch of aircraft to attack shipping at sea, this remained rare. They generally worked off information from other aircraft. Aerial mining operations were often co-ordinated with a bombing raid in order to shield the mining aircraft themselves and also to mask the use of the mines. Yet aircraft did not tend to work in conjunction with submarine or surface minelayers, which again operated autonomously. Only in the brief use of a surface task force from Malta was there some closer integration with air power. Although disjointed, the period did see a great increase in both anti-shipping operations and sinkings compared to 1940, as shown in Table 3.3.

Clearly, despite the increases in the numbers and use of aircraft, and the brief use of surface forces in a dedicated role, it was submarines that delivered by far the greatest results. Even then, apart from March, the first four months generally delivered poorly in spite of the influx of 'T' and 'U' class vessels. There were some problems with accuracy, notably

Table 3.3 *Numbers/tonnage of Axis shipping sunk, January–July 1941*

	Surface vessel	Submarine	Aircraft	Mine	Shared	Total
January	1/63	6/26,795	1/8,941	4/3,369	0/0	12/39,168
February	0/0	2/12,365	4/3,950	1/8,289	0/0	7/24,604
March	0/0	11/38,370	1/5,263	2/2,902	0/0	14/46,535
April	6/20,323	4/10,581	2/7,289	2/5,255	1/1,584	15/45,032
May	2/3,463	12/35,514	3/4,557	8/18,862	1/4,857	26/67,253
June	1/1,195	25/40,613	7/11,188	2/800	0/0	35/53,796
July	0/0	21/21,868	8/13,353	3/8,269	0/0	32/43,490

Source: Calculated from TNA AIR 20/9598, Table 3: 'Analysis of Enemy Merchant Shipping Sunk by all Causes, Scuttled, Captured or Surrendered in the Mediterranean'; Röhwer, *Allied Submarine Attacks*.

in February, but overall 53 per cent of torpedo attacks managed at least one hit over these three months. This is considerably below the 70 per cent achieved from May to July.[79] At the time, Cunningham ascribed this to the inexperience of the newly arrived 'U' class crews, and the Commander of submarines at Malta later stated in his autobiography that he was concerned over the abilities of the new crews arriving at the island in this period.[80] This factor should be coupled with the persisting lack of radar, SIGINT and reconnaissance ability, and the fact that a 'U' class still only had a twelve-pounder gun. This weapon was described by one submarine commander as 'useless against anything bigger than a rowboat' and hampered the submariners' ability to sink anything with gunfire. It was replaced by the more effective three-inch gun, which became the standard for the class in mid-1941.[81]

Torpedo problems continued to blight the submarine campaign as well. In March, the Flag Officer (Submarines) decreed that due to shortages, two of the older Mk IV torpedoes were to be included in every large salvo fired. Furthermore, First World War vintage Mk II torpedoes were to be loaded into the less frequently used stern tubes when necessary.[82] These actions were necessary to equip all submarines with at least some of the modern Mk VIII type. The older torpedoes had shorter ranges, were considerably slower and were less mechanically reliable weapons. Post-war analysis showed that the average salvo size in 1941 was smaller than in 1942–44, and suggested that in 1941, 60 per cent of all salvoes fired contained too few torpedoes, compared to just 1 per cent having too many. Evidently the torpedo shortage was having a detrimental effect.[83] At times, these shortages caused submarine commanders to take big risks. Having expended the small quota of modern weapons, *Parthian* was forced to use just two Mk II torpedoes when attacking a convoy of three small merchant vessels in June 1941 and had to supplement this by use of its gun in a dangerous surface action. It is unlikely that the riskier gun action would have had to be employed if the more modern weapons had been available. It stands as a testament to the skill of the commander and crew of *Parthian* that all three ships were sunk.[84]

In spite of these issues, the submarines reaped a steady toll of shipping from May onwards, including the 17,879-ton liner *Conte Rosso*. Sinkings generally came on the North African run, as it regained its position as the main focus of the campaign, and was the most easily accessible. Cunningham noted at the end of April that he felt that the new crews were now 'getting their hand in', while greater numbers of submarines, and important breakthroughs in SIGINT, greatly aided them.[85] Through these SIGINT developments, the British were finally getting a clearer, although far from complete, picture of the routes that were used between Italy and

Illustration 3.2 HMS *Taku* returns home after a successful tour in the Mediterranean. 'T' Class submarines such as this first started arriving in the Mediterranean in December 1940 and, along with 'S' and 'U' Class vessels, soon replaced the outdated and unsuited 'O', 'P' and 'R' classes.
Source: www.gettyimages.co.uk/detail/news-photo/the-royal-navy-during-the-second-world-war-hmsm-taku-news-photo/154418529?adppopup=true
Credit: Lt. C. Trusler / Imperial War Museums via Getty Images

North Africa.[86] Modest but increasing sinkings in the Aegean led Cunningham to claim in June that a wider campaign aimed at sinking larger quantities of shipping as opposed to focusing on specific routes could be of use. He told Pound that 'if we can sink enough shipping in the Mediterranean we shall impose severe limitations on the enemy operations'.[87] Although the British were slow to widely embrace the principle of pursuing the maximum possible sinkings regardless of positions, these comments, and decisions like those made at Malta in January to attack all targets regardless of direction and purpose, show that many were already using it as a guideline. It was also the case that whatever the specific intentions behind the anti-shipping operations, every ship sunk or damaged placed further pressure on the wider network.

Losses in the submarine campaign dropped rapidly from the high levels in 1940. It benefited from the influx of newer and more suitable vessels, other technical improvements and the continued inefficiency of

Table 3.4 *Losses in anti-shipping operations, January–July 1941*

	Surface vessels	Submarines	Aircraft
January	0	0	5
February	0	0	5
March	0	0	4
April	1	0	6
May	6	2	5
June	0	0	12
July	0	2	11

Italian countermeasures. Instead, losses in the anti-shipping campaign came primarily to surface vessels and aircraft, as shown in Table 3.4.

Surface vessels took relatively little part in the campaign, and so the lack of any losses in five of the seven months is not surprising. The brief existence of a dedicated anti-shipping task force in April resulted in the loss of the destroyer *Mohawk*, but it was during the battle for Crete that they suffered greatly. Attempts to intercept the two light convoys to the island resulted in either their destruction or turning back, but also in the GAF catching the Royal Navy vessels at sea. Four destroyers and two cruisers were lost in these actions, which succeeded in preventing seaborne reinforcements but failed to prevent the loss of the island. Further grievous losses followed in the evacuation operations.[88] For their part, aircraft suffered small but steady losses from January to May. The RAF losses in this period were all sustained during attacks against Axis ports and the shipping within them. The FAA operations continued to be relatively safe due to the cover of night. A few machines were lost over a combination of torpedo, bombing and mining operations.

The jump in losses in June reflects both the start of the daytime direct attacks on shipping by Blenheims from Malta and the increase in port bombing. The risky tactics employed made the aircraft easy targets even for the limited defensive armaments of Italian escorts. Under German direction, Italian merchant vessels were starting to have their own defensive armaments put in place, while aerial escort was also increased. The availability of German aircraft in Sicily and gradual operational integration between the Italian and German aircraft contributed greatly to the danger.[89] The head of the IAF, General Pricolo, set out new procedures for maritime reconnaissance and convoy escort in February. These called for daily reconnaissance flights and longer range strategic reconnaissance, shared duties and communication between Italian and German aircraft, increased convoy escort and ASW flights on the Naples–Tripoli route and the restriction of Italian submarine operating areas to avoid friendly fire.[90]

A report by one IAF unit demonstrates the change, detailing as it does greatly increased sea reconnaissance duties in 1941, and direct convoy escort and ASW roles since April. Having not flown any convoy escort missions the previous year, they had made 103 by the end of July. They had developed clear tactical doctrine for both types of operation, although as they had not sighted an attacking aircraft or attacked a submarine by the time of writing the report in August, it was admitted that the merits were unknown.[91] In fact, actual anti-submarine attacks were so rare that one 'Generale di Divisione Aerea' reprimanded his unit commanders for allowing crews awaiting calls to scramble for ASW attacks to become overly relaxed and thus sluggish if called upon.[92] The IAF was also starting to make more effective use of its reconnaissance aircraft by righting previous operational errors. For instance, in late July, the decision was made to provide fighter escorts for the aircraft and to stop making sea reconnaissance over identical routes. The previous procedure had led to many losses in aircraft due to predictability, and the variance both cut this down and made avoiding them more difficult for British units.

It should be noted, however, that most of these developments by the IAF were made without co-operation from the Navy, as the two services continued to vacillate between arguing and simply ignoring each other. It was not until October that a doctrinal framework for co-operation between the two services was created, in what has been described by one historian as 'a sort of treaty between two warring states'. Even after this, there was no joint centre or staff for aero-naval operations in the Mediterranean, while Italian bombers were not universally equipped with two-way radios until well into 1941 and it was not universal for their fighters until 1943. Prior to this some were even forced to rely on hand signals for communication.[93] For their part, German aircraft also operated separately of the Italian Navy, and so combined ASW and anti-surface operations remained unrealisable.

The German air contingent had certainly made an impact in early–mid 1941, but it would not be until 1942 that the Germans were able to dictate the course of the war in the Central Mediterranean. They were responsible for around 75 per cent of the 1,465 bombing attacks on Malta up to the end of May, which caused the Governor to state that aerial superiority had been lost.[94] However, after the fall of Crete, the majority of German aircraft, numbering around 450, were based either there or in Libya and offered little activity over the central Mediterranean. The decision to leave the suppression of Malta almost entirely to the Italians vastly reduced the pressure that was placed on the island, and so offensive sorties could increase. As the risky low-level Blenheim attacks at sea were only just starting, the main danger to British aircraft at this stage came in the increased bombing of ports, particularly

Benghazi. Anti-aircraft fire over these locations was frequently reported as being 'intense' and 'accurate'. German fighter commitment was more concentrated there than over the central Mediterranean, and included nearly all of their high-performance single-engine fighters. They were thus able to inflict some losses on RAF bombers, but were hampered by serviceability rates of 50–60 per cent and fatigue to aircrews after an intense period of operations. As such, British aircraft losses were still relatively low in the first half of 1941.[95]

Over the first seven months of 1941, the anti-shipping campaign had evidently improved in terms of operational effectiveness. The quantity of Axis shipping sunk had dramatically increased, accounting for 141 vessels of 319,878 tons. There were several factors behind this escalation in sinkings. An increase in priority of the campaign, in whatever part of the theatre it was taking place, meant more forces were devoted to it. There were also important developments in the types of submarines and aircraft employed, along with some tactical improvements. They were aided by important breakthroughs in intelligence and a small but significant increase in reconnaissance aircraft, while legal restraints were relaxed further.

The losses inflicted on Axis shipping had no great effect on the various land campaigns around the theatre, however. Successes in the Adriatic were very limited, and so failed to lead to any discernible results in Albania and Greece. Italy's unilateral war with Greece was plagued by the same problems over January to April as it had been the previous year. Low port capacities, poor road and rail links and a lack of motor transport and heavy equipment all continued to stymie the Italians, who were pinned back in Albania. Their withdrawal had at least shortened their own overland supply lines though, while the Greeks were left with increased lines of their own, and their own continual shortage of vehicles to bring up the necessary materiel meant that they could not deliver the coup de grâce. The result was a stalemate over the first quarter of 1941, marked by periodic but broadly insignificant offensives by each side.[96] The subsequent German invasion of Greece did not share the logistical problems suffered by the Italians. Rather than having to rely on supplies over the Adriatic and small ports, the Germans could make use of far superior rail and road infrastructure as they invaded via Bulgaria and later the newly conquered Yugoslavia. They had the full force of Fliegerkorps VIII to assist them from the air with preparatory strikes and close support, while the invasion forces were fully motorised and faced with less numerous opposition, due to the quantity of Greek forces that were tied down on the Albanian front. Despite fierce resistance from the Greek East Macedonia Army and supporting British units, the Germans were able to drive a wedge down the centre of the defensive line and divide them from those on the Albanian front. Several newly improvised defensive lines further south were quickly overturned by the rapid German advance. On 21 April, sixteen Greek divisions, cut off on the Albanian front, surrendered. The final Greek capitulation was agreed in Salonika two days later, while the following evacuation of British and a few Greek units to Crete meant that resistance on the mainland was over by 3 May.[97] A month later that island was in German hands too, as, although the Navy was successful in preventing any landings by sea, the Germans succeeded in capturing Crete using solely airborne assault.[98]

Although anti-shipping efforts in the Adriatic failed to have any effect on the war in Greece, they continued to cause disproportionate repercussions on the actions of the Italian Navy, drawing away escorts that were badly needed elsewhere. Admiral Riccardi, who had replaced Cavagnari as head of the Navy after the British strike at Taranto, complained in June about increasing losses to submarines in the Central Mediterranean and Tyrrhenian Sea. He stated that the recent loss of two steamers to gun actions by surfaced submarines was demonstrative of the 'grave consequences' of failing to provide adequate protection and 'the problem of the defence of maritime traffic is becoming a matter of capital importance for the nation'.[99] The proportion of Adriatic escorts was belatedly reduced shortly afterwards, freeing up a few precious warships for use elsewhere, although not enough to address a serious shortage that had been recognised as early as January.[100]

Sinkings on the North African routes were much more numerous than those in the Adriatic, but as Table 3.5 demonstrates, the impact on deliveries was limited.

Table 3.5 *Cargoes despatched from Italy and landed in Libya, January–July 1941*

	Ammunition		% Lost	Fuel		% Lost	Total sent	Total landed	% Lost
	Sent	Landed		Sent	Landed				
January	8,570	8,534	<1	3,097	2,897	6	50,505	49,084	3
February	6,438	6,255	3	11,642	10,682	8	80,357	79,183	1
March	3,766	2,224	41	4,059	4,059	0	101,800	92,753	9
April	1,151	1,151	0	27,128	23,676	13	88,597	81,472	8
May	2,692	2,692	0	20,027	20,027	0	75,367	69,331	8
June	8,843	8,784	<1	38,392	35,850	8	133,331	125,076	6
July	3,375	3,083	9	19,570	11,570	41	77,012	62,276	19

Source: Calculated from USMM, *LMI*, Vol. 1, *Dati Statistici*, Table LIVb, p. 125.

The Beginnings of Attrition

The totals landed in this period generally met the monthly requirements of the Axis forces in Libya. In June, the Chief of the German Armed Forces High Command (OKW), Field Marshal Keitel, placed the requirements of German forces in North Africa at 40–50,000 tons per month, including 30,000 for the DAK alone.[101] Estimates that include the requirements of those Italian forces that worked closely with the DAK at this time ranged variously between 70,000 and 100,000 tons per month, while the inclusion of Italian civilian requirements could boost this to as much as 120,000.[102] Whichever figure is used, there was no point when sinkings hampered the delivery of these requirements to Libya, with the partial exception of July. Nor were the key cargoes of ammunition and fuel notably affected, although the loss of nearly half of the fuel shipped in July likely contributed to the logistical problems described below.

The very arrival of the DAK in Libya, delivered with relative ease, also represents an undeniable failure by the British in this period. The Germans set up shipping offices at Brindisi, Naples and Tripoli under the overall command of a naval liaison officer at Rome (Admiral Eberhard Weichold) in order to expedite the crossings. By the end of April, the 5th Light Division (later renamed as 21st Panzer) had been fully transferred, using sixteen dedicated merchant vessels divided into four groups. It was followed by 15th Panzer, whose move started in mid-March and was completed by the middle of May, having used twenty-five convoys.[103] The only serious losses to these came with the wholesale destruction of the '*Tarigo* convoy', where 15th Panzer lost two regimental staffs, a signals platoon and some artillery.[104] The annihilation of a full convoy certainly caused great shock to Mussolini and his military chiefs, who promised an immediate response, including the use of cruiser groups as distant escorts. For their part, however, the Germans appear to have been relatively sanguine about the losses.[105] Ultimately, the price paid for the installation of the DAK in North Africa was small.

The Axis forces certainly were plagued by logistical problems in the desert. Rommel's first offensive that spring left the German High Command 'appalled' given the parlous supply situation that was in place after the arrival of the DAK and additional Italian troops. Neither this, nor later orders from both his Italian and German superiors to halt the advance, build a new supply base and bring newly arrived 15th Panzer units forward, stopped him.[106] The advance to the perimeter of Tobruk left the Axis forces dangling at the end of a perilously long overland supply route – over 1,150 kilometres from Tripoli, and more than 350 from Benghazi.[107] Supplies landed at either of these principal ports had to be bought forward either by coastal shipping or along the single coastal road by an increasingly overworked fleet of motor transport (MT) that numbered 3,667 vehicles at the start of April.[108] The strain quickly proved to be heavy, and within this context the sinkings were at times sufficiently concentrated to cause operational shortages at the front.

A leading formation reported its state as 'practically without fuel', having received no supplies for four days as of 6 April, in spite of the large quantities being delivered from Italy. There were also indications of acute shortage of aviation fuel in Cyrenaica, prompting requests from the GAF for fuel to be shipped direct to Benghazi rather than to Tripoli. Urgent calls for more MT to transport supplies to the front were coming in from numerous authorities by the end of the month, with the fuel situation becoming particularly serious.[109] Both sides recognised the importance of shipping directly to forward ports and the use of coastal transport to ease the overland strain, although Supermarina only approved direct sailings to Benghazi from Naples and Brindisi in June.[110] Benghazi was opened to coastal shipping almost immediately after it fell to the Axis on 4 April, while Rommel disregarded orders to halt in order to take the small port of Derna and made repeated assaults on Tobruk.[111] Benghazi received the *Citta di Bari* and its cargo of vital aviation fuel on 26 April, with over a hundred tons being unloaded a day. It was followed by the steamer *Rosa* with fuel, along with three coastal vessels three days later, which helped ease the situation. SIGINT informed the British that the sinking of *Verdika* by air attack on 1 May was 'hurtful', as it was carrying aviation fuel to Benghazi, while the war diary of the German Sea Transport Centre details the havoc wreaked by the subsequent explosion of the fuel-laden ship. The port's infrastructure, especially the east mole, suffered serious damage and the Italian–German–Arab workforce took numerous casualties from jagged metal splinters and burning fuel. The following day, 300 local labourers deserted. Despite these problems, the fuel losses were largely mitigated by the later arrival of *Silvas Baroni* with replacement loads, although the port was forced to work at lower capacity for some time.[112]

Evidently, not enough was being done to interdict fuel being shipped direct from Italy to Benghazi, but operations on the coastal route did have a demonstrable impact due to much-increased sinkings over May–July, resulting in a multitude of effects. Coastal shipping between Tripoli and the forward ports of Benghazi, Bardia and Derna totalled over 12,000 tons by May, a great increase on what had been a little more than 1,000 tons traversing a shorter route in February. Yet on multiple occasions in this period Rommel requested more be sent through the coastal route, and more shipping be provided for it.[113] The British were able to keep up pressure on this coastal route, including a bombardment of

The Beginnings of Attrition

Benghazi on 7 May that sank four vessels and damaged the port facilities. The DAK complained that the supply situation was

> Very serious, due to extremely successful pressure by British fleet and air force on rear communications via Benghazi and Tripoli. In the last 40 hours alone, 4 ships have been lost. Available land transport columns are inadequate. Request urgently that, apart from attacks on shipping round Tobruk, relief be provided by attacks on every British warship within reach.[114]

The Italians lacked large numbers of small auxiliary vessels to be used as escorts for this route, having also to cover commitments in the Adriatic and Aegean. It thus provided a rich hunting ground, especially for submarines that had the option to surface and use the gun against the smaller, poorly armed and weakly escorted targets. The DAK urged that 'energetic measures' should be taken against these submarines, while the C-in-C of the German Navy, Admiral Raeder, stated his intention to improve the organisation and quality of Italian ASW capabilities, but little was achieved in the short term.[115]

In late June, the Italians agreed to send 15,000 tons of supplies a month to Benghazi via the coastal route, using 7,500 tons of shipping. This was to be primarily delivered through a small set of essential merchant vessels along with numerous tiny auxiliaries, but three of the merchant vessels and numerous auxiliaries were sunk within days of the agreement. The available tonnage immediately dropped to 3,600.[116] Early in July, twenty-one small vessels of between 200 and 420 tons were sent to the route as replacements for losses, but the sinkings continued and a further nine had to be sent out before the end of that month alone.[117] Regular air raids had also sunk enough ships in the mouth of the harbour at Benghazi that its capacity was temporarily halved in June.[118] The German Army's liaison officer in Rome, Enno von Rintelen, admitted that due to the limitations of shipping caused by a combination of British action against the coastal route and the requirements for small shipping in the Aegean, it was not possible to build up enough in Cyrenaica through Benghazi alone.[119]

Martin van Creveld has claimed that the Axis capture of Benghazi in April 1941 did not appreciably relieve the troubled Axis supply situation, due to a lack of coastal shipping causing it to be underexploited.[120] Evidently, though, significant shipping resources were invested in the coastal route, but they suffered greatly from British interdiction efforts. The operational shortages suffered by the Axis during their advance and repeated assaults on Tobruk, while they endured Operation 'Battleaxe', were therefore clearly exacerbated by British sinkings on the coastal route. The British sank nineteen ships (28,064 tons) and seriously damaged twelve (11,362 tons), along with numerous other very small vessels, on this route.[121] In a signal to the head of the Wehrmacht, Keitel directly referenced the loss of shipping and the decreased capacity of Benghazi due to sunken vessels as being key factors in DAK's supply problem.[122] Losses to German-controlled shipping had been particularly severe, with 74 per cent of their available space lost by 31 July.[123]

The sinkings on the coastal route came at such a pace that they greatly outstripped any attempts to replace them, and this was indicative of a wider problem for the Axis. While the Italian Navy had broadly satisfied the supply requirements in North Africa, the increased rate of attrition was having a serious impact on the overall stock of shipping. The 141 vessels (319,878 tons) sunk from January to July were heaped on top of the 66 (168,821 tons) in 1940 and the 90 (140,610 tons) that were captured, scuttled or lost to other or unknown causes since June 1940. The Italian shipyards were completely incapable of balancing a total loss of 297 vessels (629,309 tons). Over the whole twenty-four months of 1940–41, they launched just 210,309 tons of new shipping. They were incapable of more as they were riddled with a range of problems, including the use of outdated methods, a lack of pre-war investment and standardisation in and across yards, low capacity, the paucity of raw materials and a bottleneck in skilled labour.[124] The issue was compounded by the large quantities of shipping that were damaged. Exact figures for damaged shipping are hard to determine, as there do not appear to be any that incorporate all shipping available to the Axis. Italian records documenting solely Italian-controlled vessels state that forty-five (212,222 tons) were damaged from June 1940 to July 1941.[125] The levels of damage to the vessels and how much additional German-controlled shipping was damaged remains unclear, but they placed yet further burden on the struggling shipyards. Repair duties were often assigned to the medium-sized, less efficient yards, essentially meaning they progressed slowly while those yards also had consequent slowdowns in their output of new construction.[126]

It was clear to the Axis powers that British anti-shipping operations were already starting to overwhelm their ability to cope, and threatening to undermine their ability to continue the war in the Mediterranean. Their primary response was to develop and institute a joint German–Italian emergency shipping production programme, but this would not come into force until the following year. Keitel recognised the immense difficulties of the intervening period: 'Losses in shipping space have hitherto been compensated by using Italian tonnage. In order to be certain in the future, the use of French shipping is suggested.'[127] The French were not, however, very forthcoming at this stage, and negotiations made little meaningful headway. The increased control over the central Mediterranean and the effects of corresponding attrition to Axis shipping resources were recognised by the British, too. At the end of July, Auchinleck told the COS

Our sustained and successful air and sea action in the central Mediterranean was having serious effects on the enemy supply position in North Africa. If we should continue to take heavy toll of the enemy supply ships, a situation might develop in which we could take early offensive action in Cyrenaica with good prospects of success.[128]

Although it would be a little longer until the British launched such an offensive, the foundations had indeed been laid.

4 Progress
August–December 1941

A New Emphasis in Priority

By August, Rommel's newly formed *Panzerarmee Afrika* was faced with a quandary. They had successfully retaken almost all of Cyrenaica, but had stalled short of the Egyptian border, while Tobruk still defied their siege. Another major offensive could end this stalemate and perhaps even the entire war in North Africa, but it would be predicated on the arrival of additional armoured and motorised units, air support, armaments and munitions, and fuel. Italy could only offer some of this, while German eyes were now focused on the Soviet Union. By the end of July, the German Army High Command (OKH) had concluded that they would not be able to launch a renewed attack on Tobruk until September at the earliest, while a major push into Egypt could not be attempted until the following year.[1]

In the meantime, successful conclusions to British campaigns in East Africa, Syria and Iraq had narrowed in-theatre commitments and freed up forces. This, coupled with German concentration on the Eastern Front, offered a new opportunity for another desert offensive. Churchill and the Defence Committee had been urging a new offensive, dubbed Operation 'Crusader', since July.[2] They suggested that it should take place no later than September, but Auchinleck was of a different opinion. He felt that his forces were still scattered and disorganised after their disparate involvements across the Middle East, while much of his armour was unsuited to fighting the now German-led opposition. He needed time to reinforce and train the new arrivals and was adamant that the offensive could not occur before November.[3] Auchinleck was to get his way in spite of consistent pressure to act sooner, which primarily came from Churchill.

British strategy had thus become centred on this new desert offensive. While their military strength was being built up and trained in preparation, there would have to be a simultaneous effort to stop the Axis from improving its own position. In a COS meeting in August, the importance of keeping up constant pressure against the North African sustainment was emphasised. What Churchill called the 'constant interruption of his sea communications' would both weaken the Axis ability to resist attacks and prevent them from being able to conduct their own pre-emptive offensive.[4] Not only had 'Crusader' become the focus of British strategy in the Mediterranean, but the anti-shipping campaign had gained a prime place in strategic priority.

Although this high priority was universally agreed by August, the best ways to pursue it were not. Worse, the ongoing inter-service dispute over maritime air power was yet to be resolved. The naval side, led by a vociferous Cunningham, continued to seek a dedicated maritime organisation for the Mediterranean. In a lengthy mid-August letter entitled 'Air Co-operation', he complained to Tedder that the existing system for air–sea co-operation was both 'cumbrous and inadequate'. He argued that it was only through closer and more effective co-ordination that they could continue to ensure both the safe arrival of adequate supplies for their own forces and limit those of the enemy. He brusquely informed Tedder that there could be 'no question' that the responsibility for and control of any operations against enemy ships or shipping should fall to the naval C-in-C. He ended with a demand for answers as to when a dedicated command would be created, what units it would control and who would be in command of it.[5]

The endeavour continued to run into opposition from both Tedder and the Air Ministry, particularly over the question of control of the resources. Tedder responded to Cunningham's communiqués of August and September by stating that the balance between air and naval needs could only be arbitrated by the Air Officer Commanding-in-Chief (AOC-in-C), in close conjunction with the naval and army theatre commanders. He did, however, agree that the situation needed improvement.[6] The situation finally reached a compromise solution early the following month, when RAF No. 201 (Naval Co-operation) Group was formed. The Group was based in Egypt, and contained all disembarked FAA units and RAF units with primarily maritime roles in North Africa. The RAF retained operational control, and it was not a theatre-wide command, covering only the eastern basin. Although the naval requests for overall control of a theatre-wide organisation were thwarted, the RN did not come away empty-handed. They received increased influence over the type and conduct of the Group's operations and training, along with a form of 'veto' over operations to which they were particularly opposed.[7] The problem was far from solved, but the compromise did provide greater levels of co-operation and go some way to dampening the flames of inter-service rivalry.

Meanwhile, Churchill had returned to agitating for another surface task force to be based at Malta. After repeated exhortation for greater efforts against the North Africa routes, he made the following request to Pound: 'Further to my minute about supplies reaching Tripoli from Italy, will you please consider the sending of a flotilla and, if possible, a cruiser or two to Malta, as soon as possible.'[8] He referenced the increased air defence of the island and withdrawal of GAF units from Sicily as evidence of a prime opportunity to assist the coming offensive in Libya. When informed of this by Pound, Cunningham replied that he broadly agreed that it should be done, and suggested a force of two light cruisers and four destroyers. He cautioned that while they might well 'bag a convoy' as the 14th Flotilla had, they would quickly revert to having only a deterrent effect, although this would still disrupt the flow of supplies. He also stressed that greater reconnaissance capability and long-range escort fighters would be needed.[9] Pound, however, was initially strongly opposed to the prospect of a task force in the face of a recovering Italian Navy and likely future return of Axis air forces. He told Churchill and the assembled COS that 'The Italians had shown themselves ready to escort their convoys by surface forces far more powerful than anything we could afford to base at Malta. Our small group of cruisers and destroyers could only exert a deterrent effect.'[10]

The issue was temporarily dropped, and two further Blenheim squadrons were sent to the island instead, as Lloyd's dispersal scheme and improvements to facilities meant that they could now be accommodated. It was agreed that four more submarines would also go, as they would be more usefully employed there than on their current task of watching German capital ships in Brest.[11] In fact, Pound informed Cunningham that he had decided to send 'every available submarine' to operate against the Libyan supply routes. Cunningham was unequivocal on the importance of the submarine's role, saying each was 'worth its weight in gold', but advocated an all-arms campaign. He highlighted a need for greater use of air power both in direct attacks and port bombing (including by Bomber Command), the use of submarine and surface forces and of minelaying from all methods.[12] The RAF's Director of Plans, William Dickson, chipped in to advise Portal that they should not be opposed to raids on northern Italian ports by Bomber Command. However, this could only take place in very favourable weather conditions, and thus could only ever be the result of 'snap decisions'. Ultimately, there were just two raids by Bomber Command on Genoa in the second half of 1941.[13]

Much of the dispute had so far concentrated specifically on Axis shipping between Italy and Tripoli, but from early September the

Benghazi route featured more heavily in the discussion. After much prodding from his superior to do more against the port, Tedder informed Portal on 5 September: 'There is no doubt that too much stuff is getting into Benghazi at the moment, against which from our present bases with our present aircraft it is very difficult to do anything.' SIGINT had already revealed first Axis intentions and then actions to make greater use of Benghazi and of the more easterly sea routes, including via the Aegean, to avoid forces based on Malta.[14] Attacks on Benghazi did increase during September, but not consistently enough to satisfy Portal. He questioned Tedder on a decline in raids on the port, and over the use of Wellingtons to attack shipping around the Corinth Canal and airbases on Greece and Crete. Tedder's response arguing the importance of these targets fell on deaf ears, and Portal stated in no uncertain terms: 'I have no doubt at all that bombs on the African ports are more important at the moment than bombs on Germany.'[15] Further reinforcements in aircraft continued to arrive in the theatre from August to October to aid in the campaign, although at a slower pace than over the summer. The pace of submarine reinforcements had also slowed, but the number in-theatre had reached thirty-six by the start of November, including Allied vessels under British operational control.[16] Although the quantity of reinforcements was slowing, there was some important qualitative progress. The first of the long-awaited Beauforts arrived in September, albeit to Egypt rather than Malta. That same month, three new Wellingtons arrived at Malta equipped with long-range ASV and a special device known as 'Rooster' capable of acting as a 'homing beacon' for ASV-equipped strike forces. In October, the first FAA Albacores landed in Malta, to offer increased range to torpedo strikes.[17] As will be seen, these forces were to be an integral part of important tactical developments in aerial anti-shipping operations of the period.

By October, the campaign had not just reached a new height in British strategic priority, it also had a sole focus on North Africa and could boast the greatest breadth and depth of available forces to date. Numbers of dedicated submarines and aircraft were at their highest, and later that month Pound yielded to renewed pressure from Churchill. On the 21st, a dedicated surface task force was once again stationed at Malta. On its arrival, it consisted of the light cruisers *Aurora* and *Penelope* and the destroyers *Lance* and *Lively*, and was designated Force K. The campaign against enemy North African sea communications in preparation for and support of 'Crusader' would remain the key focus for the rest of the year.

A full account of the operation itself is beyond the scope of this study, but in order to assess the effect of the anti-shipping campaign, a brief synopsis is required.[18] While logistical strife had blighted the Axis over the summer of 1941, the British had successfully built up significant mass for their new offensive. Combined with the Tobruk garrison, they outnumbered their opponents in the desert by 738 tanks to 390 and by roughly 550 combat-ready aircraft to 334, which included those on Crete. In spite of this impressive build-up, the implementation of 'Crusader' was still something of a rush thanks to political pressure from Churchill – much of the British and Commonwealth forces in place were new, and not fully acclimatised or trained for desert warfare. The plan was also a questionable one, involving a two-pronged thrust that hoped to draw the main Axis armoured forces into a pitched battle in a favourable location in the desert. After destroying the main Axis force, the northern thrust would push on to relieve Tobruk, while the southern would encircle those Axis forces remaining on the Egyptian frontier. In fact, after the initial British advances on 18 November, Rommel refused to believe that it was an offensive and retained his forces in place around Tobruk and the Sollum front, preparing for an assault on the former, and to maintain the latter.

Unsure of what to do next, a variety of piecemeal attacks on different positions were ordered by British commanders. Rommel now perceived this as an offensive, but still only an attempt to relieve Tobruk, as opposed to the British aim of retaking all Cyrenaica. He ordered the DAK commander (General Crüwell) to destroy the enemy before they could interfere with his cherished hope to retake the port. It was the contacts made by this force that finally convinced Rommel that a full-scale offensive was underway. As the DAK engaged the British around Sidi Rezegh, a breakout through the weakened encirclement was attempted by a division of the Tobruk garrison, but after a promising start it was rebuffed by the Italians. The fierce fighting around Sidi Rezegh over 21–23 November caused heavy losses to British armour, as their tanks were more vulnerable to German firepower. Knowing the British losses to have been great and disregarding his own losses and lack of supplies, Rommel made his infamous 'dash to the wire'. Taking personal command of the DAK and the attached Italian Ariete division, he hoped that a rapid advance through the confused battle areas would force the enemy to abandon their offensive, or even cut the newly renamed Eighth Army off from Egypt and allow them to be annihilated in the field. Only a weakened force would be left to hold the perimeter around Tobruk. It was a rash, poorly conceived move that had little realistic chance of working with the forces and supplies available, leading one historian to label it one of Rommel's worst mistakes of the whole North Africa campaign.[19] Although his advance forces did indeed reach the wire, it left his units hopelessly strung out – 21st Panzer division was scattered over a distance of seventy kilometres. The powerful British and Commonwealth forces in his rear were also able to take advantage of their lightened opposition. A combined infantry and armoured thrust westward towards Tobruk and a renewed breakout attempt by the garrison was successful, and the siege was partially lifted. On 27 November, too late to change the situation, Rommel ended his useless sojourn on the Sollum front and brought the DAK back west.

The Eighth Army, now under new command, as Auchinleck had replaced the exhausted Alan Cunningham with Neil Ritchie, had received sufficient respite to be reorganised. The ensuing battle around Sidi Rezegh was an immensely complicated, swirling mêlée, lasting for days. Confusion reigned in a series of engagements with thrust and counter-thrust, in which opposing units were frequently intermingled. Ultimately, although Tobruk was briefly cut off once more by the highly effective 15th Panzer division, the British succeeded in holding it before pushing the Axis back and inflicting heavy attrition. It came at the cost of even heavier losses to themselves, and a failure to stop the Axis forces regrouping from their two main fronts. On 5 December the DAK commander, Ludwig Crüwell, ordered the siege of Tobruk abandoned and a withdrawal to a new front around Gazala, to Rommel's undisguised rage. The siege was fully lifted on 10 December, and an Axis withdrawal from the Sollum front immediately followed. It was soon clear that the Gazala position was untenable, and ultimately a full withdrawal from Cyrenaica began on 22 December. By 6 January, the Axis front was once again formed at El Agheila, as it had been a year previously. The withdrawal had largely been successful, except for the cutting off and capitulation of one mixed Italo-German garrison at Bardia and another at Halfaya pass.

It was at this point that Operation 'Crusader' was terminated. It had seen the British save Tobruk and regain Cyrenaica, including the vital port of Benghazi and key airfields. They had also inflicted damaging losses on their opponents.[20] They had, however, suffered major loss themselves, and were in desperate need of rest, regrouping and reorganisation of their own logistics chain. Meanwhile, the Germans funnelled new aircraft and U-boats into the theatre to shore up the situation, and their arrival relieved much of the pressure that was being exerted on the Axis maritime supply network. The operation can therefore be seen as something of a qualified success for the British. What is clear, however, is that its course and outcome were influenced heavily by Axis supply difficulties, and that losses at sea were a primary reason for this.

Anti-shipping Operations prior to and during 'Crusader'

While the August–December period saw various developments in surface, submarine and air operations, they still followed a broadly similar methodology to what had come before. However, in terms of minelaying operations, the Royal Navy tried a radically new operation in August. The fast minelayer, HMS *Manxman*, was sent to the Mediterranean from the UK for a single, highly complex, minelaying operation. Based on a suggestion from Admiral Somerville, the head of Force H, the *Manxman* was to be disguised as the Vichy French light cruiser *Leopard*. This way, in the event of discovery by Axis forces, it would hopefully remain unmolested. The lay was to take place just south of Livorno and was designed to disrupt and sink shipping on the western coastal route of Italy. The audacious move relied on not being discovered and received further assistance to this end from a diversionary raid by Force H on Sardinia.[21] The operation went smoothly, and *Manxman* successfully laid 146 mines of various types just south of the port, before withdrawing without being discovered. Unfortunately, twenty-two of the mines failed to sink correctly and were spotted on the surface. The majority of the field was swept safely and it caused only minor disruption and a single casualty; an Italian minesweeper.[22] This was to be the only time that this style of offensive minelaying was conducted in the Mediterranean, but the ruse had been so successful that similar deception techniques were applied to a supply run by the *Welshman* to Malta the next year.[23]

The *Manxman*'s operation was also a rarity as it was not directly focused on the North African routes, which were the overriding priority in this period. Despite the intention to intensify attacks on these routes, the forces at Malta were hampered by a new practical issue. The conquest of Greece and Crete by the Axis meant that their shipping could now be routed via the Ionian Sea or even through the Corinth Canal and the Greek port of Piraeus. Increasing use of these routes started to be made from August onwards. This option was particularly helpful to the Axis for shipping supplies to Benghazi, but represented quite a long eastern detour for Tripoli. Cunningham expressed his concerns to the Admiralty that this could render the Swordfish aircraft at Malta useless, as they lacked the necessary range to attack this route. He again requested Beaufort torpedo bombers, or FAA Albacores fitted with drop tanks to rectify this issue.[24] Yet the Albacores were not to arrive until October, while Beauforts were only based in North Africa at this stage.

The result was that Malta could only harass shipping taking this new eastern route with submarines or briefly with Blenheims operating at extreme range. Otherwise, it was the domain of forces operating out of

Anti-shipping Operations

Egypt. Plenty of shipping remained using the routes to Tripoli though, and these bore the brunt of Malta's focus. Daylight attacks from the growing Blenheim contingent became an increasingly regular occurrence. There were eighty-seven sorties against shipping at sea or in harbour during August and ninety-eight in September.[25] September also saw the first attack by Beaufighter aircraft that were temporarily staged there. Night attacks by FAA aircraft from the island were gaining tempo. Swordfish aircraft managed forty-five sorties against shipping at sea or in port during August and fifty-three in September, plus the mining of Palermo by five aircraft and Tripoli by another six.[26] The arrival of special 'Rooster'-equipped Wellingtons in September heralded a new capability both in reconnaissance and in the translation of successful reconnaissance and shadowing into attacks. 'Rooster' acted as a beacon that could be used by reconnaissance aircraft that had located a target to accurately 'home in' on a strike force, as it sent out a signal that could be detected and tracked by ASV-equipped aircraft to their exact location from a range of up to sixty miles.[27] This ability was especially useful in aiding the FAA aircraft in locating targets at night, and as so few 'Rooster'-equipped aircraft were available at that stage, that was what they initially concentrated on. Updated tactical doctrine was soon developed to incorporate this new capability and to set out operating procedures to ensure the effective co-operation between reconnaissance and strike aircraft at night through the search, shadowing and strike phases of an operation. It incorporated not just the new technology, but new techniques in the use of flares and flame floats and of enemy evasive tactics, based on operational learning.[28]

In a constant, regimented barrage, Blenheims from Malta attacked shipping at sea by day, and Swordfish and Albacores by night, while Wellingtons continued to pound Tripoli in repeated raids. It was bombed on sixteen occasions in August using 120 aircraft, and thirteen times in September with fifty-seven.[29] Occasional raids were also made against Italian ports to disrupt the embarkation of supplies. Meanwhile, aircraft from Egypt kept up a regular stream of raids against Benghazi. It was attacked sixteen times in August using 113 aircraft and on twenty occasions, by a total of 132 aircraft, in September. They also raided the small harbours at Bardia and Derna several times over the two months, and made sporadic attacks on shipping at sea off Tobruk.[30]

As the aerial effort was intensifying over August and September, submarine operations maintained their already high tempo. Patrols were conducted regularly across the central and eastern Mediterranean, including in the Adriatic and Aegean, from Alexandria and Malta, along with a handful in the western basin from S8 at Gibraltar. The offensive patrols were only interrupted by occasional storing trips to Malta from Gibraltar and Alexandria. Four of these were carried out in August and another two in September, but they were mainly conducted by the larger and less operationally capable 'O' Class.[31] Operations over August and September continued the steady toll of Axis shipping that they had been exacting earlier in the year, but at an accelerated pace and with some notable individual successes. The Italians had started using large fast liners to ferry troops to Tripoli and on 20 August HMS *Unique* attacked a convoy of four of them, sinking the 11,400-ton *Esperia*. Yet the most stunning individual success was still to come. SIGINT revealed the sailing of another convoy of three liners which, coupled with effective aerial reconnaissance, aided in vectoring multiple 'U' Class submarines to intercept. Only the *Upholder*, under Britain's most successful submarine commander of the war, David Wanklyn, managed to make a successful attack. Despite firing at a range of over 3,000 yards and having equipment trouble, he hit the liners *Neptunia* and *Oceania* with one torpedo each. The former sank immediately, while he later closed with and sank the latter with another torpedo five hours later. The two liners totalled just under 39,000 tons combined, and were carrying 5,818 men, although thanks to quick rescue work from the escorts only 384 were killed.[32]

The steady successes of submarines and aircraft continued into October, each method sinking fourteen and eleven merchant vessels respectively, while another was sunk by a mine. However, the arrival of a surface force at Malta late in the month did not bring immediate results. Force K made its first sortie to intercept a convoy of destroyers carrying troops to Tripoli on the 25th, but failed to locate it after being despatched too late. The next attempt, on the night of 8/9 November, was a resounding success. With the aid of SIGINT, which noted that the convoy (nicknamed the *Duisberg* convoy) was carrying significant cargoes of vital fuel and ammunition, and aerial reconnaissance from an RAF Maryland, the task force was able to sortie and intercept it.[33] Using all the advantages of intelligence, radar, the cover of night and good fortune (the Wellington detailed to shadow had an ASV failure, but was ultimately not needed), they were able to launch a devastating surprise attack that sank all seven ships of the convoy and one of its escorts. The sheer level of surprise achieved allowed an incredibly accurate opening gun salvo that appears to have prevented the targets taking any evading action from the following torpedo fire. This resulted in two torpedo hits, while close range gunfire quickly finished off the rest. The attack procedure had been organised well in advance in conferences of senior officers of force and the Vice Admiral (Malta), and it helped to avoid return torpedo fire from the Italian escorts, as had sunk the *Mohawk* back in April. Given the top-secret nature of Ultra, the British report of the attack omitted the vital role of SIGINT. Instead it blamed the 'gross negligence of the Italian Navy' for their failure to put up a proper fight, as did the Germans.[34]

Force K followed this up with a series of other successes over late November and early December, focusing primarily on shipping to the vital forward port of Benghazi. It sailed on the night of 23 November to intercept an important convoy of two freighters (the *Procida* and *Maritza*) with two escorts. SIGINT had revealed the departure of this convoy, and that it carried a cargo that included vital fuel, from Piraeus to Benghazi.[35] A continuous, comprehensive stream of SIGINT and a sighting report from an aircraft of 201 Group helped direct the force onto the convoy, which intercepted it in the late afternoon of the 24th. As it was daytime, they came under attack from aircraft escorting the convoy, but these were ineffective types for such work and failed to do any notable damage. After a short engagement, the Italian destroyers disengaged, the merchant ships stopped and their crews abandoned ship. They were quickly sunk, and the force returned to Malta with no damage.[36] Soon afterwards, Force K was reinforced by a further two cruisers and two destroyers.

In a continuing run of success, similar fates befell the unescorted naval auxiliary *Adriatico* on the night of 30 November and the 10,540-ton tanker *Irido Mantovani* the following night, which had already been crippled by air attack and was under tow by its single escort. Ciano confided to his diary after the latter: 'I cannot deny it was a hard blow ... The battle – for the moment – has no new developments, but it is clear that the tempo works against us.'[37] These successes were not just aided by the usual SIGINT/aerial reconnaissance combination, but by the use of 'Rooster' from the Wellington aircraft to home *Aurora* directly onto the target, in an impressive new example of air–sea integration.[38] In the meantime, the Italians had responded to the increasing losses by putting an 'emergency transport plan' in place in late November, to try to ensure the arrival of the necessary cargoes to the hard-pressed forces in Cyrenaica. It included increased use of submarines, aircraft and dedicated supply runs by destroyers and light cruisers. While the standard convoys were having such serious problems, these efforts regularly completed successful deliveries, even if they were usually very small cargoes.[39] Yet the streak of successes by surface forces was extended further by the interception of two light cruisers operating as part of this very plan. SIGINT once again gave knowledge of the sailing of the *Da Barbiano* and *Di Giussano* for Tripoli, with their holds and decks each dangerously loaded with 950 tons of fuel. A group of destroyers that had been transferring from Force H to the Mediterranean Fleet was redirected to catch them, which they promptly did. Both cruisers were sunk in a short engagement, their highly combustible cargoes contributing to both the brevity of the fight and to the especially high level of casualties. Over 900 Italians were killed from gunfire or the ensuing infernos.[40]

From August to early December, the sinking rates of Axis shipping generally increased above, below and finally on the waves. The constant attrition to their merchant shipping had a clear effect on both German and Italian senior leadership. At a conference in mid-November, Raeder admitted to Hitler that 'Today the enemy has complete naval and air supremacy ... he is operating totally undisturbed in all parts of the Mediterranean.'[41] Three weeks later, Admiral Riccardi told the assembled Italian chiefs and German theatre commanders in Rome 'we can say that at this time the enemy has the aero-naval supremacy in the central basin of the Mediterranean ... It is therefore necessary to immediately make an effort to change this situation.'[42] The Germans vociferously and unanimously blamed the Italians for both incompetence and an unwillingness to risk their naval vessels. Accusations of cowardice were rather unfair given the incredible risks and ultimate sacrifices taken by many Italian sailors, as exemplified by the loss of the *Da Barbiano* and *Di Giussano*. Claims of Italian organisational inefficiency and overly constricting top-down control of naval units at sea were more grounded in reality, however. There were even claims from some on the German side that there were traitors in the upper echelons of the Italian military passing on details of sailings to the British. In fact, the increasing ability of the British not only to locate convoys but to intercept those with tankers or fuel-carrying cargo ships was primarily due to their increasingly effective use of top-secret SIGINT sources.[43] In the aftermath of such critical losses both nations acted to do more to safeguard shipping.

Apart from some sackings and court-martials of those involved in escort duties, the Italian solution, with much pressure from Germans, was to institute the so-called 'battleship convoys'. These were convoys with a close escort that was only slightly increased, but a distant covering force that was extremely powerful, and included Italian battleships. Faulty intelligence suggesting an attack from the Mediterranean Fleet meant the first two attempts at their use were failures, and turned back to Italy. The next attempt (Operation M.42) followed almost immediately, and was successful. A convoy of four merchant ships reached Tripoli, while the *Ankara* brought a vital load of tanks directly to Benghazi. The total escort for the operation consisted of no fewer than eight destroyers and torpedo boats in the close escort, and four battleships, five cruisers and thirteen escorts in the covering force![44] British warships from Alexandria and Malta were also at sea escorting the transport *Breconshire* to Malta, and a short indecisive engagement known as the First Battle of Sirte followed. After safely escorting the *Breconshire*, Force K sailed to intercept another convoy reported to be en route to Tripoli, but the sortie came too late and the target reached its destination. Instead, it ran into one of the enemy's defensive minefields, resulting in the loss of the cruiser *Neptune*, the destroyer *Kandahar* and heavy damage to the cruiser *Aurora*.[45] Force K had been crippled.

For their part, the Germans had already sent more U-boats to the Mediterranean, which announced their arrival with major success by sinking the carrier *Ark Royal* and battleship *Barham* in November and the cruiser *Galatea* in December, the latter during a sortie to intercept a convoy. They then once again transferred heavy air power resources to Sicily, the Balkans and North Africa. The objectives of all the available German air assets, amalgamated under the command of Albert Kesselring, were set as follows:

To secure mastery of the air and sea between southern Italy and North Africa in order to secure communications with Libya and Cyrenaica and, in particular, to keep Malta in subjection.

To co-operate with German and allied forces engaged in North Africa.

To paralyse enemy traffic through the Mediterranean and British supplies to Tobruk and Malta, in close co-operation with the German and Italian naval forces available for this task.[46]

The force transferred to the Mediterranean was of a different order of magnitude to what had arrived a year previously, with the hope that it would completely transform the conflict there. This time, an entire 'Air Fleet' (Luftflotte II) was sent, under the command of Albert Kesselring, who was also made Germany's theatre commander (C-in-C South). A full air corps from the fleet (Fliegerkorps II), was assigned specifically to 'the suppression of Malta'.[47] It began operating in late December and immediately made its presence felt with a massive raid on Malta on the 22nd, in a deadly portent of what was to come.

Operational Effects: Tobruk, 'Crusader' and the War at Sea

The August–December period witnessed a great increase in anti-shipping forces and efforts, with a clearer singular focus on the North African routes. A total of 124 merchant vessels and tankers of 350,771 tons was sunk in these five months, and it should be noted that this total does not include warships carrying supplies, such as the Italian cruisers sunk in December. At least a further forty-five vessels were damaged, although the exact number and their tonnage is unclear.[48] A detailed breakdown of the sinkings by cause is given in Table 4.1.

Table 4.1 *Numbers/tonnage of Axis shipping sunk, August–December 1941*

	Surface vessel	Submarine	Aircraft	Mine	Shared	Total
August	0/0	11/21,621	11/35,196	2/5,275	0/0	24/62,092
September	0/0	12/58,517	10/27,617	2/490	1/5,996	25/92,620
October	0/0	14/43,317	11/24,691	1/2,710	1/4,786	27/75,504
November	10/45,072	9/9,022	9/8,910	0/0	0/0	28/63,004
December	3/12,706	13/32,157	3/2,148	0/0	1/10,540	20/57,551

Source: Calculated from TNA AIR 20/9598, Table 3: 'Analysis of Enemy Merchant Shipping Sunk by all Causes, Scuttled, Captured or Surrendered in the Mediterranean'; Röhwer, *Allied Submarine Attacks*.

Submarines were still clearly providing the biggest returns in the campaign, and proving increasingly effective. Important SIGINT breakthroughs in the summer, along with some increase in the quantity and quality of aerial reconnaissance allowed them to be much more efficient. This was particularly useful for S10 based at Malta, whose small 'U' class boats with an average patrol time of just eleven days made speedy target location a priority.[49] This period also saw the first submarines being equipped with RDF in the theatre, and HMS *Proteus* became the first to detect a convoy using this apparatus on 9 November.[50] However, the RDF sets were generally found to be too weak for this work, with limited effective range on the surface and inoperative when submerged. Cunningham evidently saw potential in their continued use as he recommended to the Admiralty that sets with increased power should be fitted to submarines.[51] Yet successes involving RDF continued to be few. Dogged by the power problem as well as unreliability and poor serviceability issues, these sets often earned distrust from submarine commanders. There are only forty-three recorded incidents of RDF contacts made from British submarines from 1941 to 1944 in all theatres and not all of these led to attacks.[52]

Improvements had clearly been made in both the location of targets and in converting this into attacks. There had been no real improvement in accuracy though. Of the 136 attacks made by submarines, 82 (60 per cent) resulted in at least one hit, a similar ratio to the January–July period.[53] One reason for this is likely the fact that the torpedo problem had only been partially resolved; whereas 64 per cent of those fired by submarine in June had been the modern Mk VIII, it was 80 per cent in August. While an improvement, it meant that a fifth of those fired were still outdated types of lesser quality and reliability.[54] The increased successes from submarines seem related more to the numbers and types available, their greater activity and operational experience and improved reconnaissance and intelligence than to specific technical or tactical factors. The Germans recognised their

Illustration 4.1 Members of the crew of HMS *Utmost* pose with their 'Jolly Roger' success flag on their return from a year's service in the Mediterranean, February 1942. These small 'U' class submarines were designed for training purposes, but proved to be a highly effective component of the anti-shipping campaign operating at short range from Malta.
Source: www.gettyimages.co.uk/detail/news-photo/the-royal-navy-during-the-second-world-war-members-of-the-news-photo/154417291?adppopup=true
Credit: Lt. J. A. Hampton / Imperial War Museums via Getty Images

ongoing successes in the central Mediterranean, but also their increasing success in the Aegean. At a November conference with Hitler, Raeder noted that the transport situation there had 'greatly deteriorated' due to British submarine operations, and that the countermeasures in place there were completely inadequate.[55]

The much increased use of air power over this period, both in direct attacks and port bombing, also yielded greater results. In terms of both numbers and tonnage, sinkings reached new highs, as air power became an increasingly important method of attacking shipping. Increased numbers and priority for the campaign, better quality of aircraft, along with the breakthroughs in SIGINT, increased operational experience and technical and tactical developments all contributed to these results. ASV had been hugely helpful in increasing successful locations of targets. Operational research for the period from 1 October to 12 December found that ASV was utterly crucial to locating shipping at night. The Operational Research Section (ORS), itself a product of a newly formalised approach to development in-theatre, found that night searches were successful on 49 per cent of occasions in this period when ASV was utilised. Night searches without it had been practically abandoned, as they were near certain to fail. The report went on to note that ASV was almost never used in daylight reconnaissance sorties, and was used primarily when there was already a 'definite reason to suspect the presence of shipping'.[56] These limitations are likely due to the shortage of available sets rather than any other reason. However, the sets were not fool-proof: breakdowns occasionally occurred, while the FAA aircrews initially suffered from a lack of specialised personnel trained in its use. These problems were exacerbated in the case of 830 Squadron as it did not all have the radio equipment to communicate quickly until October. Nevertheless, the ORS concluded that ASV was vital for night attacks, and very helpful when used in daylight.

Malta had become the main base for the use of air power in a direct attack role. This was due both to its proximity to the sea lanes and to the ability to make the most of the limited reconnaissance resources available there. Cunningham felt that reconnaissance aircraft were still lacking by September, but that 'special intelligence' had helped maximise what they had. Although Lloyd believed another four Marylands were needed for Malta, Cunningham thought the theatre as a whole was still lacking. He noted the route between Greece and Cyrenaica was particularly weakly covered, as a result of the lack of long-range aircraft and of Axis possession of Cyrenaica.[57] Direct attacks from aircraft operating out of North Africa remained rare, for want of both reconnaissance and longer-range strike aircraft. Bombing raids on ports remained the best option. Cunningham also complained about the ability of RAF crews in a maritime strike role. In mid-August he claimed that so far, strikes on shipping at sea had been 'small and ineffective', except for the 'splendid efforts' of AOC Mediterranean. The ability to hit ships at sea 'commands no confidence', an issue he ascribed to the lack of proper maritime training in the RAF.[58] However, the belated creation of No. 201 Group, the increased training of RAF aircrews in maritime roles and the transfer of experienced FAA crews to this unit all helped to improve performance. By the end of the year, Cunningham was praising this progress, the work of the Group and its AOC.[59] Air power was thus becoming a method of growing importance in the campaign. It remained behind submarines as an individual method, and lacked the capability of surface vessels to wipe out whole convoys, but was sinking greater quantities and was clearly vital in aiding other methods in a joint approach.[60]

Table 4.2 *Losses in anti-shipping operations, August–December 1941*

	Surface vessels	Submarines	Aircraft
August	0	2	8
September	0	0	13
October	0	0	7
November	0	1	17
December	3	1	15

The total number of vessels sunk was actually a small decrease on the 141 sunk during January–July, but the tonnage total represents an increase of over 30,000, despite the period in question being two months shorter. This shows that larger targets, generally capable of carrying greater cargo, were being sunk. The average size of vessel sunk grew to 2,829 tons from 2,269 for the earlier period. The price of these sinkings came at the loss of a light cruiser, two destroyers, four submarines, and sixty aircraft, as detailed in Table 4.2.

The loss rate for submarines continued to be much lower than during 1940. The losses were split by cause between Italian surface vessels and mines. It is perhaps surprising that mines did not cause more losses, as the Italians immediately embarked on large-scale mining project when they entered the war. The Naval Staff History for the submarine campaign claims that a total of over 54,000 were laid by the Axis forces up to the Italian armistice, not including the Aegean.[61] It seems likely that effective use of intelligence to plan attack routes and patrol zones, equipment for mine detection and the poor quality of Italian mines all contributed to blunting the mine threat.[62] For their part, Italian warships still lacked radar and sonar equipment, while surviving intelligence documentation suggests that the ability to decipher submarine movements may have decreased by this stage.[63]

Aircraft might have achieved greater sinkings, but this came at the cost of noticeably heightened losses. Of the sixty aircraft lost, thirty-five were Blenheims, and all but five of those were lost in direct attacks from Malta on shipping at sea.[64] These rates of attrition quickly caused grave concern for Lloyd. He sent a terse telegram to Tedder on 18 August stating; 'Yesterdays convoy had six escort destroyers. Have noticed gradual building up of escort vessels. To launch Blenheims against such fire is sheer murder. Feel you should know this as it explains why Blenheims were not used.' He went on to say that he would look to concentrate Blenheim use against the Tripoli–Benghazi coastal route, where he felt anti-aircraft opposition would be less, and against single unescorted sailings or any 'lame ducks' left by the Swordfish.[65] The 'sheer murder' comment had brought a 'sharp rebuke' to Lloyd from Cunningham, who felt he was exaggerating, but losses continued to mount.

In October, at Tedder's request, Lloyd sent Portal a breakdown of the number and type of sorties conducted by Blenheims from 1 July to 9 October, and the number of losses incurred. No fewer than 284 sorties were made against shipping or ports, but losses were high at twenty-three aircraft. Lloyd defended his decisions on what to target, saying that he rarely went after heavily escorted convoys with low-level attacks, in spite of pressure from Cunningham. However, he felt that the anti-aircraft defence for coastal shipping on the Tripoli–Benghazi route had been greatly intensified. He described the flak from these targets as 'terrific' and postulated that the guns must have been manned by Germans. This last suggestion may well have had some truth to it, as the project instituted to increase defensive armaments to Italian merchant ships was German instigated and led.[66] Although Lloyd was more selective over which targets to attack, low-level daytime Blenheim attacks continued for the remainder of the year, as did the high rates of attrition. It is hardly surprising that losses remained high given the low-altitude exposure to enemy fire, while accidents such as flying into the sea or hitting the mast were not uncommon.[67]

The loss of two cruisers and a destroyer was doubtless the most painful to the British. The destruction of *Neptune* and *Kandahar*, along with the heavy damage to *Aurora*, tore the heart out of the previously dominant Force K. While surface vessels had demonstrated their ability to eliminate whole convoys and to deliver a sustained series of successes, the losses incurred in December could scarcely be afforded by an overstretched Navy, especially now that Japan had entered the war. The return of German air power to Sicily was not responsible for these losses, but suggested that continued use of surface task forces would be very difficult. The increased numbers of Axis aircraft were backed by improvements in technique and capability. The Italians retained the main responsibility for reconnaissance duties, and made an important doctrinal development in August. By order of General Marzucco, of the Sicilian Air Fleet, reconnaissance aircraft would, when sighting enemy surface forces without an aircraft carrier, keep out of sight and shadow, transmitting regular reports and meteorological data.[68] This, along with a greater focus on reconnaissance, appears to have resulted in improved methods and results, including successful tracking of many British naval movements. Fliegerkorps II would also grow to contain a higher proportion of high-performance, single-engine fighters, in order to help gain initial dominance in the skies over Malta.[69]

Overall, the August–December period had been the most successful to date for the anti-shipping campaign. Although the total number of vessels sunk was lower than that of the longer January–July period, it was proportionately higher, and the higher tonnage total suggests that more important targets were being sunk, while the destruction of store-carrying warships was also important. The higher priority placed on the anti-shipping campaign, along with a near-total focus on the North Africa routes allowed for a greater concentration of force and effect. Perhaps the most important development in the campaign during this period was in terms of jointery. This period represented the first true use of a combined arms offensive – surface vessels, submarines and aircraft in significant use, frequently working in tandem. An ORS report concluded that co-ordination of reconnaissance aircraft with surface vessels had been so successful that similar methods should be employed between aircraft and submarines, and suggested fitting Rooster sets to the latter. It also suggested that air attacks were starting to have important effects, and that they should increase the use of torpedo bombers in particular, which were found to have the greatest lethality.[70]

The sinkings had a demonstrable effect on the war in North Africa, and especially on 'Crusader'. The attrition over January–July had continued, with serious ramifications for the hopes of the Axis for a renewed attack on Tobruk. The total available to the Germans by September for the North Africa routes, including that ordered from Vichy France and chartered from Spain, was twenty-nine vessels of 65,700 tons. Of these thirteen (11,600 tons) were being used for coastal traffic. This was considered just about sufficient to maintain their position but no more, and reserves were dangerously thin. Elsewhere in the theatre, eleven ships of 31,000 tons were engaged in ore traffic, and taking them away from this would weaken the Axis's overall economic situation. Seven ships of 15,000 tons were engaged in the Aegean and Black Sea 'where they are almost indispensable'. At a joint conference with Mussolini and his Chief of the General Staff (Ugo Cavallero), Keitel and his staff demanded more use of Italian shipping space, which still had 120 ships of over 2,000 tons totalling 552,000 tons, and 114 under 2,000 tons totalling 122,000 tons, along with forty-two passenger ships and nineteen tankers. Angry claims were made that the Italians were holding back their tonnage for post-war use, and that a German director of war transport should have control of shipping. Clearly, new construction was urgently required, and the Germans insisted that it must be produced in-theatre by Italian yards and labour, noting that, 'Of first importance is the construction of tankers.' In response, Cavallero assured them that 'Ship-building has first place in the Italian war economy. Extensive building contracts have been given, but there is a shortage of raw materials.' Keitel responded that Germany could help with raw materials, and that German plans for the construction of small vessels and tankers would be placed at Italian disposal.[71] There is evidence that awareness of the dangers of attrition was even penetrating down to the level of the average Italian citizen. Reports from the security services in Naples in September noted widespread concern in the city that 'as a result of the deficiency of our merchant navy, it will prove impossible to reinforce and supply our troops in North Africa'.[72]

Yet while the negative construction-to-attrition ratio represented a serious concern in the longer term, the immediate Axis problem was transporting the necessary supplies to the front for a renewed assault on Tobruk. In order to expedite this, the best possible option was to send the maximum possible quantity of supplies to the forward ports, notably Benghazi but also the smaller harbours such as Bardia and Derna. The need for shipping direct to Cyrenaica whenever possible was recognised at all levels of the Axis hierarchy, from Hitler and Mussolini down to operational commanders.[73] Table 4.3 shows that despite regular shipping losses, large quantities of supplies were still consistently landed in North Africa over August–October.

What it does not show is a breakdown of where the supplies were landed. The overwhelming majority was unloaded at Tripoli, as efforts to supply Cyrenaica suffered from a lack of port capacity there, losses at sea and the rerouting from Benghazi to Tripoli while at sea, due to perceived danger.

Although British forces reaped a steady toll of shipping over August–October, Malta-based strike forces attacking convoys on the Tripoli route achieved the majority of this success. In October, for example,

Table 4.3 *Cargo tonnages despatched and landed in Libya, November–December 1941*

	Ammunition			Fuel			Total cargo sent	Total cargo landed	
	Sent	Landed	% Lost	Sent	Landed	% Lost			% Lost
August	6,322	4,968	21	37,705	37,201	1	96,021	83,956	13
September	7,078	5,850	17	17,759	13,408	25	94,115	67,513	28
October	7,143	6,163	14	15,113	11,951	21	92,449	73,614	20
November	3,331	1,503	55	31,788	2,471	92	79,208	29,843	62
December	2,345	2,074	12	7,606	7,223	5	47,680	39,092	18

Source: Calculated from USMM, *LMI*, Vol. 1, *Dati Statistici*, Table LIVb, p. 125.

only 12 per cent of the tonnage sent from Italy to Benghazi (either direct or via Greece) was sunk en route.[74] Losses inflicted on the crucial Tripoli–Benghazi coastal route continued to mount, however, and Keitel was informed that its use was 'particularly dangerous', as fourteen vessels had been sunk on it from 11 July–31 August alone. The continued sinkings here were identified as causing a 'supply crisis' in Cyrenaica.[75] By 22 September, losses on the North African coastal route had left the Germans with only two vessels for the Tripoli–Benghazi route, having briefly been reduced to just a single freighter.[76] Losses at sea over August and early September had also meant 332 motor vehicles badly needed for overland supply had not arrived, placing further pressure on the coastal route to deliver.[77]

It was not an auspicious situation in which to build up for a new assault on Tobruk, let alone a full offensive, yet failure to take the port was just as problematic. Not only was the Axis being denied an important forward port for supply, but bypassing it lengthened the overland supply route, with further depreciation to the vehicles, a subsequent delay in the arrival of supplies, and an increase in the expenditure of fuel to deliver them. In July, OKH had estimated that if 20,000 tons of supplies could be transferred solely to the armoured and motorised units of *Panzerarmee*, then it would be able to launch the long-awaited attack in mid-September, so long as it was not part of a wider offensive.[78] As the supply situation in Cyrenaica worsened incrementally, Rommel had claimed that 30,000 tons of supplies would need to be sent directly to Benghazi in September and October to allow for a new assault, and that the amount of supplies travelling to Cyrenaica by sea desperately needed to be increased, either by shipping directly there from Italy, or via the coastal route from Tripoli.

This hope was thwarted by a combination of British sinkings and the fact that Benghazi could only berth two ships at any one time, and thus could not unload any more than twelve ships a month at this stage. It also had limited storage capability for fuel until new storage tanks with a capacity of 5,000 tons were completed in early December, meaning unloading was slowed down.[79] *Panzerarmee* as a whole required 60,000 tons of supplies in October, but only 8,937 had arrived in the Benghazi area, while only about a third of the artillery needed for a new assault had reached the Tobruk front.[80] The anti-shipping campaign had thus played a central role in frustrating the Axis hope to take Tobruk in 1941. On 26 October, Rommel finally ordered the new attack, setting it to take place on 15–16 November despite the parlous logistical situation. He also insisted that no British offensive was coming despite both Italian warnings and OKH providing him with clear evidence to the contrary.[81]

Instead, regardless of such opposition, he gained the support of OKW and Hitler, who gave the go-ahead in early November. Approval alone was not enough; Rommel still needed the supplies, and he did not get them. The Italian C-in-C North Africa, Ettore Bastico, noted on 27 October that a new attack on Tobruk was not currently possible. He urged that 'To improve the situation, it is however indispensable that the sending of units, arms, and vehicles already required ... will flow with urgency from the motherland.'[82] Yet Just 700 cubic metres (cbm) of fuel and 5,765 tons of ammunition had been stockpiled at Benghazi by the start of Operation 'Crusader' on 18 November, as opposed to 5,300 cbm and 20,636 tons respectively at Tripoli.[83] By 11 November Bastico was complaining of 'the insufficient capacity of transport to satisfy even the normal demands of life and activities of units existing here'.[84] The necessary build-up had still not been achieved by the planned start date, and it was promptly undermined further by the launching of 'Crusader'.

The link between the anti-shipping campaign and the progress and outcome of 'Crusader' is even more explicit than that for the Axis failure to assault Tobruk. Sinkings rocketed over the last two months of 1941, including a great increase on the Italy–Benghazi route. Whereas just 12 per cent of the tonnage on this route was sunk in October, it reached 45 per cent from 1 November to 20 December. Seven of the nineteen vessels plying this route were sent to the bottom.[85] This was exacerbated by instances of convoys scheduled for Benghazi being redirected while at sea, either to proceed instead to Tripoli or to return home, in a desperate effort to preserve vessels. In the light of increasing sinkings and legitimate concerns over information security, the Italians decreed in August that the departure times, routes and destinations of convoys should only be revealed at the last possible moment. Even then they would only be made known to the convoy itself and relevant air and naval units involved in escort duties. Even authorities at the intended unloading port were often left unaware. Radio messages to and from the convoy while at sea were also to be limited, further increasing the confusion.[86] The result was that Axis forces in Cyrenaica often expected supplies to be landed at a comparatively nearby port, only to learn much later that they had been redirected to Tripoli. Axis attempts to reinforce the coastal route with additional vessels briefly gave some relief, but quickly led to further losses.[87]

The proportion of cargo that failed to arrive in North Africa during November represented a new high in the anti-shipping campaign. The loss of 62 per cent of all supplies shipped was hugely damaging, but the loss of 92 per cent of the fuel shipped was devastating. Most of what did arrive was sent to Tripoli rather than to the forward ports, despite the need for it there. On 6 November, 250 tons of cargo shipped from Tripoli and 492 tons from Italy were unloaded at Benghazi, along with a further 408 tons for civilian purposes only. However, no new fuel arrived in the whole of North Africa from the opening of Operation 'Crusader' on 18 November through to the end of the first phase of the battle. What little came to the front during this period was brought overland and by coastal shipping from the Tripoli depot.[88] What is more, the destruction wreaked by Force K in November prompted the Italians to temporarily suspend all merchant shipping on the Tripoli route, leaving only Benghazi open until December.[89]

The Axis armoured and motorised divisions relied on receiving sufficient fuel to practise the mobile operations on which they thrived, and there is clear evidence showing that the loss of fuel at sea over November and early December had a restricting effect on them. From as early as 21 November, units of the DAK had been ordered to limit their actions in the defensive around the Tobruk front, due to fuel shortages. Later, during Rommel's cavalier 'dash to the wire', 15th Panzer reported a 'desperate shortage of fuel' that curtailed its offensive action.[90] Losses to ammunition shipments also degraded the fighting power of Axis units at the front, particularly during December, when stocks for both small arms and especially artillery neared exhaustion.[91] It was a combination of attrition to their own forces, knowledge that there were no immediately pending reinforcements, fear of encirclement, the lack of fuel and ammunition and British aerial dominance that ultimately convinced the Axis forces to withdraw first to the Gazala line, and then from Cyrenaica entirely.[92]

More pivotal even than the loss of fuel and ammunition to Axis armoured and motorised units was the crippling lack of aviation fuel received by Axis aircraft. In the desert war, both sides were reliant on air power for vital reconnaissance, close support, interdiction and transport roles, as well as contesting aerial superiority. Table 4.4 displays the rapid decline of stocks of both types of aviation fuel (B4 and the much less commonly used C3) in Libya over the October–December period.

As Table 4.4 clearly demonstrates, aviation fuel stocks fell drastically, especially in the operational area of Cyrenaica where it was most needed. There were repeated urgent calls for more fuel from Rommel, from the Commander of GAF contingent in North Africa and from numerous other senior GAF and Italian personnel in both North Africa and Italy.[93] The GAF supply staffs had set out on 23 October that a minimum stock of 4,000 tons of fuel was needed, so the totals actually available were completely inadequate. The lack of fuel was so severe by late November

Table 4.4 *Axis aviation fuel stocks in Libya, October–December 1941*

	Tonnage in Tripolitania		Tonnage in Cyrenaica		
Date	B4	C3	B4	C3	Total
11 October	850	160	2,350	370	3,730
22 October	680	110	2,200	400	3,390
1 November	550	190	1,720	250	2,710
11 November	430	130	1,460	390	2,410
23 November	250	450	870	240	1,810
30 November	0	0	284	282	566
14 December	Unknown	Unknown	103	110	213

Note: The figures in this table are taken from various reports given in TNA DEFE 3/690; DEFE 3/745 and DEFE 3/746.

that Axis air operations over both land and sea were being 'greatly endangered', and by 10 December there was sufficient fuel for just one day of operations in Cyrenaica 'due to lack of arrival of supplies by sea'. Axis fighter resistance to bombing of their positions and overland and sea supply lines soon became 'negligible'.[94]

There is a clear causal link between the targeted sinking of shipping and the shortage of aviation fuel at the front. Fliegerkorps X and Fliegerkorps Afrika both made repeated statements about the urgency of fuel being transported direct to the Benghazi area, something not happening fast enough supposedly due to shipping shortages. It had been hoped that *Procida* and *Maritza* would alleviate the problem by taking 2,200 cbm of it to Benghazi via Piraeus, followed by another 2,000 in the *Rondine*.[95] The targeted destruction of the first two by Force K ruined this plan, while the *Rondine* repeatedly had its departure delayed and was ultimately sent to Tripoli after 'Crusader' had finished.[96] The sinking of the *Procida* and *Maritza* by Force K caused the loss of 1,700 tons of aviation fuel alone, which would have almost doubled the total stocks in North Africa at that time if they had been landed.[97]

The anti-shipping campaign had played a vital role in halting the Axis advance, preventing the planned attack on Tobruk and in aiding the success of Operation 'Crusader'. The British and Commonwealth forces cleared the Axis forces from all of Cyrenaica, recovering Benghazi on Christmas Eve, along with numerous small harbours and important airfields. Even van Creveld, one of the staunchest critics of the anti-shipping campaign, grudgingly admits that it had some effect during the November–December period.[98] Nevertheless, he still claims there was significant fuel in Tripolitania at that time, which could not be utilised due to a paucity of land transport and coastal shipping capabilities. This claim is evidently not true of aviation fuel, stocks of which consistently dropped throughout all of Libya, as the Axis were unable to ship enough across to replenish them. It was clearly losses at sea that were preventing Axis air involvement from hampering 'Crusader', and allowing the British and Commonwealth forces to exploit the resulting asymmetric advantage. As for the paucity of coastal shipping, this was precisely due to British anti-shipping operations, which effectively cut the coastal route in this period and inflicted damaging rates of attrition on the available stock of coastal shipping. Although significant quantities of material were transported successfully to North Africa in December, it arrived far too late in the month to have any effect on 'Crusader', as the Axis forces were already in the process of withdrawal. The supplies would only be of use for operations the following year.[99]

For all the success at sea in influencing the war on land, and the quantitative advantage in men, tanks, aircraft and artillery, 'Crusader' was not a comprehensive victory for the British and Commonwealth forces. The Axis were ultimately able to stabilise in a strong position around El Agheila, while the attrition suffered by the Eighth Army was enough to halt ambitions for further advance. The primary reason for this was the disparity in fighting quality that still existed between the two sides. Although the British numerical advantage in tanks was large, they were generally qualitatively inferior to their German, if not Italian, counterparts. The main armament of most British tanks struggled to penetrate the front armour of German tanks except at close range, while the Axis forces had developed a highly successful method for mixed defences using both tanks and anti-tanks guns, that frequently blunted British armoured attacks with heavy losses. The Germans in particular also operated with much more devolved power to units at the tactical level, allowing for greater initiative. The British, meanwhile, still lacked a proper, integrated doctrine for combining infantry, armour artillery and air power in the offensive. This issue was exacerbated by the rather rushed nature of the 'Crusader' offensive and a propensity to make piecemeal attacks as opposed to the German preference for concentrating effort on a 'Schwerpunkt'. These factors, along with the comparative inexperience of many of the newly arrived Eighth Army units and some instances of poor leadership, meant that the advantages conferred by Axis logistical difficulties, numerical superiority and the rash actions of Rommel could not be translated into greater success.[100]

For all the achievements of late 1941, the year also ended on a very sour note. After the setback to Force K, the torpedoing of *Barham*, *Ark Royal* and *Galatea* and the arrival of Fliegerkorps II, there was to be one more blow to the heart of the Royal Navy. In late December, six Italian frogmen stealthily entered Alexandria harbour using manned torpedoes. They fixed charges to the battleships *Queen Elizabeth* and *Valiant*, along with a tanker. Although the frogmen were apprehended, the charges detonated successfully, and the two battleships were heavily damaged, as were the tanker and a nearby destroyer. The battleships would each be out of action for over a year. Cunningham lamented that 'The striking power of the fleet was thus seriously reduced just at the time when we had at last reached a position to operate offensively in the Central Mediterranean.'[101] The British official history for the Mediterranean and Middle East states that at the close of 1941, 'The outlook at sea ... could hardly be called encouraging.'[102] This was something of an understatement, as the events of early to mid-1942 would demonstrate.

5 Axis Ascendency
January–August 1942

Shifting Priorities

The New Year started with mixed fortunes for the British. Although they had been rocked by naval losses and the catastrophe in the Far East after the Japanese entry to the war, they had also gained the USA as a formal ally, and their situation in North Africa still seemed relatively positive. The advance from Operation 'Crusader' might have ended, but it had succeeded in driving the Axis forces completely from Cyrenaica. The hope of Churchill and of the War Cabinet in general was that a continued advance on to Tripoli would still be feasible and indeed imminent.[1] Significant air reinforcements for maritime purposes were set out to Cunningham by the Admiralty on Christmas Eve 1941 to help expedite this effort. This included a promise of three Beaufort squadrons, to make a total of four in the theatre, with the caveat that this would only be reached once sufficient construction could replace the removal of squadrons from Coastal Command. Further reconnaissance aircraft, heavy bombers and Beaufighters were also offered, in a clear indication of the continued commitment to the anti-shipping campaign. The stick that accompanied this carrot was that no aircraft carriers could be provided, as *Illustrious*, *Formidable* and *Indomitable* would all be destined for the Far East due to the Japanese threat. The Mediterranean Fleet would thus have to make do with a limited number of heavy warships for some time, and it was hoped that land-based aircraft could fill the maritime void and help retain control over the central Mediterranean.[2]

Despite this will to aid a renewed offensive, a new attack on the Axis position at El Agheila was not yet possible. Axis resistance had become increasingly determined, as its forces had reorganised to hold a more stabilised front, coupled with improved logistics thanks to shortened overland supply lines. For their part, the British advance had led to serious logistical difficulties at the front.[3] Instead, their overstretched and somewhat surprised advanced units were quickly pushed back by a new Axis offensive, starting on 21 January. The speed with which

Rommel organised his forces and struck was as impressive as it was unexpected, as SIGINT had not given advance warning of such a move. It also took both the Italian and German high commands by surprise, as Rommel had not consulted either of them.[4] By the end of the month, after swift defeats around Agedabia, the British and Commonwealth forces had to withdraw rapidly from Benghazi, which fell once again into Axis hands, and retire to a new position around Gazala. They promptly stabilised their front around the new 'Gazala line', and focused on rebuilding the power of the Eighth Army there, but the damage to the British position in the theatre was severe. The Axis advance itself halted just east of Benghazi, paralyzed by the unsolved logistical strain and high-level arguments about the priority of the North African campaign versus the eastern front in Europe.[5] OKH certainly favoured the latter, and *Panzerarmee* was in no position to advance further over spring.

Nevertheless, the damage to Britain's position in the theatre was clear. The loss of Benghazi was a blow to its logistics and boon to those of the Axis, while the loss of the vital Cyrenaican airfields would put both Malta and maritime operations at greater risk. It also placed Tripoli out of range of aircraft in Egypt except for the few long-range Liberators that were available.[6] The advance had greatly increased the Axis ability to control the Mediterranean as a waterway for the transfer of supplies, allowing them to supply their armies and territories with much greater security. It also correspondingly harmed the British ability to do so, hampering the anti-shipping campaign and the supply of Malta.

Many in Whitehall, especially Churchill, wanted a resumption of offensive action as soon as possible, and the Joint Planning Staff recommended as much in early April.[7] Commanders in the theatre were pessimistic about the possibility, though, most notably Auchinleck, who felt it would not be possible until June at the earliest. The reason for such urgency in Whitehall was to guarantee the security of Malta. A successful offensive would once again deny Cyrenaican airfields to the enemy, while also claiming them for defensive coverage of the sea passages that were vital to sustaining the island.[8] After examining an appreciation by the Middle East Defence Committee, the COS agreed with Auchinleck and recommended that no offensive should take place until June or July. It would thus coincide with the next planned major Malta supply convoy, and the offensive would aim to secure the airfields required to safeguard it. The minutes of the meeting even suggested that the offensive could be referred to as the 'Battle for Malta'.[9] Evidently, protection of the island had become the greatest strategic priority in this period, followed by the interlinked priority of building up forces and preparing for the new Libyan offensive. The anti-shipping campaign, for all the possibilities it offered in terms of weakening Axis resistance to any offensive, had slipped down the pecking order. This was not a direct neglect of the campaign per se but reflected the perception that defending Malta should come first, and with that achieved the focus could then return to 're-exerting a throttling effect on the Axis supply line to North Africa'.[10] In the meantime, it was expected that little would be done to interrupt Axis supplies. As the First Lord of the Admiralty confided to the Defence Committee in late March, the enemy 'would be able to run large reinforcements across to North Africa in the next few months, which we shall be unable to prevent'.[11]

Little mention appears to have been made in Whitehall around this time of the possibility of attacking Axis North African seaborne cargoes with forces based in Egypt or of attacking their wider network across the Mediterranean. A rare exception was the Leader of the House of Commons, Sir Stafford Cripps, who urged Churchill to send more heavy bombers to the theatre for the bombing of Tripoli and Benghazi.[12] Cripps's appeal was not acted on, as in fact reinforcements for RAF Middle East were being threatened by the demands of the Far East. While Portal resisted suggestions that Liberator aircraft destined for Tedder's command should be reassigned, he did approve the sending of twenty non-ASV Wellingtons from the Middle East to India during April.[13] Worse, the transfer of the Liberators was then further delayed. While Portal noted their importance for the ability to attack Tripoli, it was decided that the first eight of the intended twenty-two Liberators would instead go to Coastal Command, where they were desperately needed over the Atlantic. The remainder would only be transferred to the Middle East once Coastal Command had increased its own complement of Catalina aircraft to forty-five.[14] There were simply not enough aircraft to cover all the requirements in different theatres, and Portal confessed to Churchill that without the Liberators, there was nothing available with the range to bomb Tripoli or the Italian embarkation ports.[15]

It was not just aerial assets that were suffering. As a new offensive in Cyrenaica was not currently possible, Axis focus in the theatre returned to the subjugation of Malta. It became 'the most bombed place on earth' over the spring, with grave effects on the ability to operate a submarine flotilla from it. On 26 April, the commander of S10 reluctantly took the decision to withdraw the flotilla to Alexandria.[16] There was even discussion in Whitehall over the possibility of sending S1 to the Far East, rather than have two flotillas in the eastern Mediterranean. The decision was placed on hold as it was felt that US submarine assistance in the Far East could be forthcoming. At the end of April, it was agreed that S1 would remain in the theatre, as the suppression of Malta and limited ability of air forces in Egypt to intervene would leave it as one of the only effective offensive forces in the meantime.[17] It was later relocated to Haifa and then to the better facilities at Beirut instead. The turmoil did not just impact on attempts to interdict the North African shipping, but also those elsewhere in the theatre. There were hopes to sever the less travelled, yet still important, sea communications in the Aegean. It was noted by the Ministry for Economic Warfare that during early 1942 the Axis had rejuvenated their use of the Istanbul–Trieste route to bring in important supplies for their war industries. These had been effectively cut over 1941 by a combination of Turkish restrictions and sinkings by a small number of submarines. It was thought that the sinking of just two or three vessels on this route in quick succession could cause its resuspension, yet although emphasis was placed by both the Ministry and the Royal Navy on doing so, even the small number of submarines required was not currently available thanks to the upheaval.[18]

Over the spring and early summer, Malta came perilously close to being starved into submission due to the pressure on its supply convoys,

Illustration 5.1 Photograph from an Italian bomber dropping bombs on Hal Far airbase, Malta. Axis air raids on the island would frequently target the air and naval bases, in an attempt to neutralise its offensive capability.
Source: www.gettyimages.co.uk/detail/news-photo/north-africa-mediterranean-theatre-of-warair-war-italian-news-photo/543822619?adppopup=true
Credit: ullstein bild via Getty Images

but remained resilient in punishing conditions and managed to inflict notable losses on the Axis air forces. It was sustained only by the sacrifice of the Royal and Merchant Navies, along with RAF support. However, the island was ultimately 'saved' by the Eastern Front, as the demands for resources there became so great that Fliegerkorps X was transferred out of the Mediterranean in May. Renewed Axis plans for an invasion of the island ultimately came to nought.[19] By the summer, British strategy remained a defensive one. It resulted in offensive forces that could have been utilised in the campaign being used instead to help defend Malta and its supply convoys. Beaufort torpedo bombers that were being sent to the Far East in May were retained at Egypt en route, but to defend the upcoming Malta convoy from the Italian Navy rather than to be used against Axis shipping.[20] Tedder ordered Lloyd in early June to switch the efforts of the Wellingtons on Malta from bombing important supply ports in Italy and Libya to locating and bombing the Italian fleet, which remained an extant threat. He assured the new C-in-C Mediterranean, Admiral Henry Harwood, that he was trying to secure some Liberator aircraft for the island and that these would be used against the fleet as well.[21] The poor strategic situation had been exacerbated greatly by a new Axis offensive.

Rommel successfully managed to initiate a new attack around eastern Cyrenaica, which he falsely justified to his superiors as a response to British probing attacks. He managed to gain agreement from both Cavallero and Rintelen that he could advance as far as the Egyptian border, and finally take Tobruk in the process. In doing this, he hoped that large parts of the Eighth Army would be destroyed around Tobruk, Gazala and Bir Hakeim. It was an audacious plan considering the strength of the British defensive line, yet the offensive achieved impressive success despite British superiority in numbers, their recent receipt of much higher quality tanks and anti-tank guns, and much improved intelligence that gave Cairo a good indication of Rommel's intentions.[22] Rommel's basic plan involved a feint to the north using the Italian infantry divisions and a few German units, while the armoured divisions delivered an outflanking 'southern hook' past the strongpoint of Bir Hakeim. The resulting series of fast-paced and frequently confusing engagements saw heavy losses to both sides, with particularly bitter resistance coming from a Free French brigade around the key position at Bir Hakeim. The initial result was stalemate, with tactical surprise and an early advance achieved by the Axis before being checked by counterattacks.

Despite the setback, Rommel stubbornly continued with the offensive in what was becoming an extremely perilous situation for him. With great difficulty, the Axis managed to gain victory in a large battle around the area north of Bir Hakeim dubbed 'the cauldron', which saw particularly heavy losses amongst British armour. He was aided by the poor decision making of General Ritchie, head of the Eighth Army, and several of his subordinates, who used their reserves in a piecemeal and uncoordinated manner. There was also additional, unintentional help from the chief US liaison officer to the Eighth Army, Bonner Fellers. His reports back to Washington on its state and dispositions fed valuable intelligence to the Axis, as the Italian intelligence service had broken the relevant US cypher. The fortress at Bir Hakeim finally fell on 10 June, meaning Rommel had inflicted a disastrous defeat on the British and Commonwealth forces. The battered Eighth Army withdrew with its morale in tatters, and the victorious Axis forces quickly followed up with the capture of Tobruk on 21 June.[23] The loss caused shockwaves in the British establishment, and even led to a vote of no-confidence in Churchill, albeit an utterly unsuccessful one. The premier later characterised it as one of the lowest points of the whole war.[24]

This success cemented the Axis strategy for the theatre: that there should be an immediate 'push for Suez' to gain definitive victory in North Africa, which must take precedence over any attempt to take Malta. The question of which strategy to adopt had been the source of much debate. Some, such as the German Naval Operations Staff, even suggested that a full-scale pincer attack on the Middle East via both North Africa and the Caucasus could be possible. Others, including very senior officials such as the head of OKH, thought it a complete fantasy and responded accordingly.[25] Rommel himself told Rome on 22 June that he had captured enough supplies at the Gazala Line and Tobruk to advance 'deep into Egypt' and asked for Mussolini to 'remove all restrictions on the freedom of movement'. He claimed it would be possible thanks to a combination of captured stocks and a boost in morale from the victory.[26] This argument managed to persuade both Hitler and Mussolini on the issue, while the Malta operation itself was the victim of continued scepticism on the part of some, and claims of inadequate resources from others.[27] As such, despite protestations from the likes of Cavallero and Kesselring that Malta should come first, or that caution should be exercised, the advance did not stop there.[28] Rommel was granted permission to push into Egypt itself, capturing the small harbour of Mersa Matruh on 29 June.

With the seemingly unstoppable advance rolling closer, panic reigned in Cairo. In an episode dubbed 'the flap', vast quantities of official documents were burned, preparations to abandon Egypt were hastily finalised and the Mediterranean Fleet was withdrawn from Alexandria and split across bases at Port Said, Haifa and Beirut.[29] Auchinleck sacked Ritchie and stepped in personally to take command of Eighth Army,

Shifting Priorities

a move which resolved one problem of leadership, but also created another by confusing the chain of command between the operational and strategic levels. There was a pervasive concern in Whitehall that North Africa might now be lost, while Fellers's report to Washington, the last to be read by the Axis before the British finally staunched this leak, was similarly bleak.[30] In fact, the Axis forces were finally halted at the First Battle of El Alamein, which began on 1 July. Multiple attempts to break the Eighth Army's defensive line on a narrow front all failed, as did several British counterattacks. The battle ground to a halt on the 27th, with the Axis advance arrested, the British unable to turn them back, and the overall situation still in the balance.[31]

Although the advance had been stalled, the Axis remained in Egypt, and thus a major threat to the survival of the British position in North Africa. Increased attacks against Axis shipping could degrade their ability to launch another successful offensive or to resist a British one. Meanwhile, although the situation in the theatre remained difficult, preparations for an Anglo-American landing in north-west Africa were well underway. Increased anti-shipping efforts relating to Libya and Egypt would not only aid the British position, but simultaneously focus Axis attention and resources there and away from the proposed 'western front'. The anti-shipping campaign would thus return to a prime position in strategic priority.

With Malta still only capable of limited operations, the burden remained on British forces based in North Africa. As their operational bases were further from the Axis sea routes themselves, this meant a focus on the Axis ports of Benghazi, Tobruk and Mersa Matruh. The influential South African Prime Minister Field Marshal Smuts even suggested to Churchill that significant forces be withdrawn from the strategic bombing of Germany to aid in this:

> In view of gravity of position in Egypt, idea has been mooted that RAF, instead of bombing German towns should concentrate maximum of its bombing force against Rommel and pound his army and African ports to pieces. I would suggest that we fly as many long-range bombers as possible in great numbers to Egypt for this purpose ... RAF could now play most important part in Egypt in delaying his advance and enabling us to assemble our forces and material for his final destruction.[32]

Portal's response to this was to point out that a few very heavy bombers were going to the theatre and that they and other aircraft were already being used to the fullest possible extent against Axis forces and ports. However, transferring significant forces from the strategic bombing campaign would be too lengthy a process to be worth it.[33] Ultimately, while preserving the strategic bombing campaign, Churchill agreed that efforts against Axis ports should increase. He emphasised this in a brief minute in July, stating:

> It is vital that the use of Benghazi and Tobruk as supply ports should be denied to the enemy. They must be subjected to heavy and continuous bombing on the largest scale. Please let me know the resources Tedder will have available, and the use he intends to make of them. He should be informed of the great importance we attach to the destruction of these ports.[34]

They became the primary target of RAF Middle East's bombers over July and August, assisted by newly arrived American aircraft in one of their first acts of direct involvement in the theatre.[35]

As stalemate reigned in North Africa, efforts to succour Malta reached their peak in August with the famous Operation 'Pedestal'. With the island near the brink of starvation, a huge effort involving three aircraft carriers, two battleships, seven cruisers, twenty-four destroyers and around a hundred aircraft was made to deliver a supply convoy. Further protection was offered from the island itself by aircraft and S10, which had been reinstalled there in late July.[36] Nine of the fourteen ships of the convoy were lost, along with an aircraft carrier, two cruisers, a destroyer and over thirty aircraft. Yet the five vessels that reached the island delivered an essential 32,000 tons of supplies and 15,000 of fuel. It was enough to keep Malta in the war, albeit with severe rationing and heavy restrictions on most activities. The strike forces on the island were allowed some greater freedom to operate and, given the critical situation in North Africa, the COS ordered that 'supreme importance should be attached to [strike] operations and that considerations of economy in petrol would not justify limiting these operations' over the rest of August.[37] Late summer had thus seen the anti-shipping campaign come full-circle, and retake a high position in strategic priority.

Weathering the Storm: Anti-shipping Operations

The losses to the Royal Navy and subsequent resurgence of its Italian counterpart at the end of 1941, along with the increased bombing of Malta and the loss of Cyrenaican airfields, all contributed to a rapid curtailing of the use of the island as a base for surface vessels. By late January what remained of Force K was being ordered not to intercept convoys due to their increased escort being far too strong to overcome even with the aid of darkness and intelligence.[38] The excessive escort efforts by the Italians could not be sustained forever, but the intense aerial siege of Malta effectively neutralised it as a threat. There were 2,299 German and 791 Italian bombing sorties in February alone, while new levels of intensity were reached from late March. A peak in bombs dropped was reached in

Weathering the Storm: Anti-shipping Operations

Illustration 5.2 A heavily damaged HMS *Penelope* after narrowly escaping from Malta in April 1942. The extent of the damage gave it the nickname 'HMS Pepperpot'. Prior to this the cruiser had taken part in multiple highly successful actions against Axis shipping as part of Force K in late 1941.
Source: www.gettyimages.co.uk/detail/news-photo/royal-navy-sailors-line-the-deck-of-their-splintered-news-photo/613513696?adppopup=true
Credit: Hulton-Deutsch Collection / Corbis Historical via Getty Images

April, at no fewer than 6,700 tons.[39] It led to the complete suspension of surface operations from the island, and the withdrawal of Force K began in March. The final vessel, the heavily damaged *Penelope*, was towed away on 8 April. It was so riddled with shrapnel holes that it had earned the nickname 'HMS Pepperpot'.[40] The only notable action that Force K had taken part in during this period was a defensive one, aiding in the escort of a convoy to Malta in March, including involvement in a delaying engagement with the Italian fleet at the Second Battle of Sirte.[41]

Interdiction efforts by surface forces from Alexandria were attempted as a substitute for Malta, but were both fruitless and expensive. On 10 March a force of cruisers and destroyers sailed to intercept a convoy but failed to make contact, and the cruiser *Naiad* was sunk by a German U-boat on return. Two months later an attempt by four destroyers was turned back by concentrated Axis air power, which sank three of them. They had not even gotten close to the target convoy.[42] Several bombardments attempted in this period were more successful, if only marginally. Three destroyers shelled the harbour at Rhodes and the shipping within it in March, while Mersa Matruh was attacked on five separate nights in mid–late July. Along with damage to facilities, the latter attacks claimed at least one victim sunk.[43]

The withdrawal of Force K left Malta as a base only for aircraft and submarines once more. These had been more active in anti-shipping roles from the start of the year, and achieved some success. Cunningham felt able to record at the end of January that 'The outstanding features of the month were the magnificent efforts of our submarines, FAA and RAF aircraft. Hardly a day passed without some loss to the enemy which must have complicated his problem of supplying North Africa.'[44]

Yet these efforts were to suffer in a similar manner to those of the surface forces. First, even the submarines were sucked into the desperate struggle to supply the island. This year saw the most intensive use of submarines to bring in additional supplies to the island, in what was nicknamed the 'magic carpet' service. The smaller 'U' class vessels could avoid this role as they simply had no storage capacity, but larger submarines based out of the island, as well as Gibraltar and Egypt, were engaged heavily in it. This reached a peak with the conversion of the *Clyde*, one of the few large 'River' class vessels to serve in the theatre, being converted specifically for the purpose. In return for an additional 120 tons storage space, almost its entire offensive capability was removed, with only a single torpedo tube left functioning.[45] Far more problematic for British submarines was the aerial siege, however, which was quick to stifle their operations.

Submarine patrols dropped steadily from December 1941 through to the withdrawal of S10 in April. There had been nineteen vessels at sea at the start of December, but by March they numbered in single figures. The decline continued after the withdrawal and affected both S10 and S1, as the bases at Beirut and Haifa were not fully prepared, and the loss of the S1's depot ship *Medway* to a U-boat caused an additional strain. The depot ship took over a hundred of the standard British Mk VIII torpedoes to the bottom with it, along with around thirty others, including irreplaceable Greek and Yugoslav models. Although forty-seven were later salvaged, many of them were too corroded to be of use.[46] Nevertheless, submarines continued to exact a steady toll of enemy shipping, primarily thanks to the efforts of 'T' class vessels from S1, as Alexandria was not subjected to such heavy bombing.

They were aided by an important technical development – their fitting with 'Rooster' sets began in May. New operating procedures were quickly developed for ASV-equipped reconnaissance aircraft to home those submarines onto their targets. An ORS report suggested that this was the most successful form of target location for submarines, and would be particularly useful at a time when strike aircraft were few, but reconnaissance machines were relatively plentiful, allowing submarines to continue taking the lead in the campaign.[47] They sank a total of sixty-seven vessels of 135,539 tons from January to June, the only serious drop in successes coming in July, which yielded just 792 tons. The re-establishment of S10 at Malta that month allowed for a resurgence in efforts in August, while operations by S1 were significantly increased. The result was a greatly increased number of both attacks and results, with over 50,000 tons sunk.[48] Not all of these came from the North African routes, with S1 sinking several vessels across the Adriatic and Aegean, demonstrating that even during a crucial period in North Africa, the campaign still had a wider perspective.[49]

The aerial interdiction campaign suffered even more heavily under Axis pressure. Two large vessels were sunk in January, including the 13,098-ton liner *Victoria*, in a well-executed FAA night attack making effective use of ASV.[50] Yet successes soon dried up, as the aircraft on Malta were particularly vulnerable to the increased Axis bombing. The comparative fragility of aircraft, the difficulty of truly effective dispersal and camouflage on a small island and the logical tendency of the Axis to target airfields first all contributed to the rapid curtailment. Attempts to set up 'dummy' dispersal pens with unserviceable aircraft attracted some attention from the attacking bombers, but never enough.[51] Lloyd withdrew his Blenheims, which had already been taking heavy losses prior to the renewed siege, as early as mid-February. The Wellingtons continued a little longer, with some success against shipping in Sicilian and North African ports, but were withdrawn in March.[52] Only the diminished and beleaguered FAA squadrons remained, conducting missions with a few aircraft, or sometimes only one. Whereas they flew eleven offensive missions in January, this dropped to nine in February, seven in March and just two in April. By the end of that month, only two Swordfish and two Albacores remained serviceable on the island.[53] No. 201 Group failed to significantly augment these efforts for technical reasons, especially the long ranges involved.

Table 5.1 shows this drop in sinkings by air power, along with the successes by other methods. Evidently, Kesselring was justified to inform Hitler and OKH in April that bombing had 'eliminated Malta as a naval base', and that the airfields and their equipment had suffered 'heavy damage'.[54] With Malta's role rapidly reducing, the scale of effort from aircraft based in North Africa was increased to compensate. Units of 201 Group conducted 110 anti-shipping sweep sorties in the central Mediterranean in March, along with sixty-two sorties for shadowing or

Table 5.1 *Numbers/tonnage of Axis shipping sunk, January–August 1942*

	Surface vessel	Submarine	Aircraft	Mine	Shared	Total
January	0/0	7/20,941	2/18,839	0/0	0/0	9/39,780
February	2/1,650	9/26,171	1/145	1/1,334	2/10,257	18/39,557
March	0/0	13/22,584	4/13,192	2/6,008	1/1,778	20/43,562
April	0/0	14/32,030	0/0	1/199	0/0	15/32,229
May	0/0	10/19,347	1/6,836	1/288	0/0	12/26,471
June	0/0	14/14,466	3/16,701	1/750	0/0	18/31,917
July	1/2,480	4/792	3/11,923	0/0	0/0	15/15,195
August	0/0	17/51,831	10/12,020	2/5,358	1/8,326	23/77,535

Source: Calculated from TNA AIR 20/9598, Table 3: 'Analysis of Enemy Merchant Shipping Sunk by all Causes, Scuttled, Captured or Surrendered in the Mediterranean'; Röhwer, *Allied Submarine Attacks*.

attacking convoys. Yet these aircraft were having to operate at extreme range and were often not equipped with ASV. Consequently, of the sixty-two aircraft sent out to attack targets found by reconnaissance, only seventeen located them, of which thirteen made attacks. This netted four sinkings of 13,192 tons, along with damage to two warships, including some of the first uses of torpedo-armed Wellington bombers.[55] As Table 5.1 shows, this led to a brief increase in successes in March, but they were still quite modest and a brief anomaly in the period. Aerial efforts in April and May were significant, but results much weaker still. The Group managed seventy-five sorties in April, but this translated to just twelve attacks and no results. The sixty-six sorties and thirteen attacks managed in May sank just a single vessel. Around 600 sorties were made against Axis ports, but while there was some damage to facilities and losses to personnel, there were few sinkings.[56] Those in June–August came primarily from attacks on the forward ports of Benghazi, Tobruk and Mersa Matruh. The one notable positive from this period was the development of new tactics, often based on operational research, regarding best practices in height of approach to achieve surprise, aircraft formations, flare-dropping techniques for night attacks, use of location and homing aids and the use of 'flak suppression' escort aircraft. These were to become so successful that they caught the eye of Coastal Command, and became an inspiration for their development of 'Strike Wings'.[57]

The 130 vessels of 306,246 tons sunk over these eight months compares a little unfavourably to the 124 of 350,771 tons sunk over the last five months of 1941. It still represented a substantial total, however, and was accompanied by damage to around 89,900 tons of shipping. In terms of sinkings alone, it seems a far cry from the 'Annus Horribilis' of the campaign presented by some scholars.[58]

Table 5.2 *Losses in anti-shipping operations, January–August 1942*

	Surface vessels	Submarines	Aircraft
January	0	1	6
February	0	2	9
March	1	0	10
April	0	2	13
May	3	1	7
June	0	0	13
July	0	0	44
August	0	1	39

The cost of anti-shipping operations, as shown in Table 5.2, came to four surface vessels, seven submarines and 141 aircraft.[59] This compares well with the surface and submarine losses in late 1941, but represents a massive increase in aircraft lost, over half of which came in July and August. This was the result of a series of massive raids on Tobruk, after the loss of the port, from aircraft in Egypt. A total of 380 aircraft attacked it in late July alone, while Benghazi and Mersa Matruh also received attention. This was part of a wider herculean effort by air power over late spring–early summer to try and reverse the Axis tide through interdiction at sea and on land, through fighter sweeps and by dislocating attacks on local Axis HQs among other sorties.[60]

For all the scale of effort, and the continued attrition of shipping in this period, though, its operational effect was rather limited.

Attrition versus Operational Effect

When Rommel launched his offensive in January, immediately after the termination of 'Crusader', he angered numerous superiors on two counts. First because they were not consulted, and second because they had planned for a longer pause at El Agheila to build up a stronger logistic base. The result of his headstrong decision was that the supply situation quickly returned to being critical. The Quartermaster General of *Panzerarmee* noted in February that his organisation alone required 25,000 tons a month for normal requirements, rising to 45,000 during an offensive. The extant transport capacity, thanks to the retaking of Benghazi, was felt to be sufficient for the smaller figure, but inadequate for the higher one.[61] A halt before the Gazala line thus represented a realistic position for the Axis to hold, as supplies were pouring into Tripoli almost unhindered, thanks to the neutralisation of Malta.

Table 5.3 *Cargo tonnages despatched and landed in Libya, January–August 1942*

	Ammunition			Fuel			Total cargo sent	Total cargo landed	% Lost
	Sent	Landed	% Lost	Sent	Landed	% Lost			
January	5,475	5,475	0	22,842	22,842	0	66,214	66,170	<1
February	3,805	3,303	13	24,458	24,458	0	59,468	58,965	1
March	3,109	1,257	60	16,415	15,105	8	57,541	47,588	17
April	12,067	11,908	1	48,696	48,031	1	151,578	150,389	<1
May	13,256	11,028	17	19,069	18,581	3	93,188	86,439	7
June	4,368	3,178	27	6,760	5,568	18	41,519	32,327	22
July	12,108	12,108	0	26,870	23,901	11	97,794	91,491	6
August	4,743	3,628	24	38,384	22,500	41	77,134	51,655	33

Source: Calculated from USMM, *LMI*, Vol. 1, *Dati Statistici*, Table LIVc, p. 126.

Table 5.3 demonstrates the British failure to interdict Axis supplies to Libya over the first seven months of 1942. The sinking of the *Victoria* was the only notable success on this route in January, which caused the Italians to abandon the use of large liners for troop transport in favour of aerial transport as much as possible, or failing that by warship.[62] Otherwise, effects were very limited. Only during March and June was any kind of limited inroad managed into the supplies sent in the first six months, whereas the quantities landed almost every month were vast, including a record 150,000 tons in April. The problem for the *Panzerarmee* was that most of these supplies were landed at Tripoli, and were thus a long way from the frontline where they were most needed. The increased sinking in August, however, saw a parallel increase in losses of supply, worsening conditions in Cyrenaica significantly.

The *Panzerarmee*'s fuel situation in Cyrenaica remained poor over 1942. This is best illustrated by their recording of Consumption Units (CUs), where one CU was defined as the amount of fuel required for a division over 100 kilometres. The German armoured units had just 3.7 CUs overall by early April, of which only 1.6 were in Cyrenaica; this was an insufficient amount for any kind of mobile operations in the region. Similar problems beset their air support, as Fliegerführer Afrika was down to 500 cbm, enough for around 10–15 days of operations. Although British sinkings were limited, the Axis stocks were already sufficiently low that even a handful of losses in the right places could have an effect. The destruction of the *Cuma* and *Achaia* in March, both having been loaded with fuel assigned to German units, was highlighted by the *Panzerarmee* as a key factor in the ongoing shortage. Italian efforts to supplement shipping with the use of large submarines for store-carrying on the coastal route suffered too, as all but one of them were sunk by April. Some relief came on 4 April, when six transports carrying 2.2 CUs among them, along with other supplies, arrived in Tripoli. Numerous other ships were loaded with fuel and waiting in Italian ports, but the Italians regularly postponed sailing due to a dearth of escorts.[63] The totals available were still below the logistical requirements outlined by Rommel for a new offensive; he stated it would be conditional on the supply of twenty-five CUs of fuel, five ammunition consignments and supplies for thirty days. Of these, fifteen CUs, three issues of ammunition and fifteen days' supplies would need to be stored in battle area. The air forces needed fuel supplies for twenty days' operations.[64]

In April, SIGINT revealed with considerable accuracy the daily intake of stores by Axis forces that were in the broadly defined area of the frontline in North Africa. The daily averages were:

- By sea, Italy–Benghazi: 240 tons
- By sea, Tripoli–Benghazi: 240 tons
- By sea, Tripoli–Derna: 50 tons
- By road, Tripoli–Cyrenaica: 620 tons
- By air to Cyrenaica: 35 tons
- Total: 1,185 tons.[65]

The total of around 35,000 tons per month reaching Cyrenaica was notably below the estimated requirements for an offensive outlined by *Panzerarmee*'s Quartermaster, despite the large quantities reaching Tripoli. It was clear that increased shipments to their 'forward ports' was the only possible solution for the Axis. As the British report noted:

Owing to the shortage of motor transport, the enemy would find it most difficult to make up for any reduction in the tonnages reaching Benghazi by sea. By sinking a high proportion of ships either making for or in Benghazi, the enemy would be forced to withdraw vehicles from the forward area or formations, in order to augment road transport to Cyrenaica. This would partially immobilise formations and possibly deprive them of the power of offense.

Given the difficulty in attacking convoys to Tripoli at that time, and the identified importance of the Cyrenaican routes, the report strongly suggested that the latter should became the primary, if not sole focus. Submarines were to be concentrated in the Gulf of Sirte and north of Benghazi, while air attacks on shipping in this area, as well as on Cyrenaican ports, should increase.[66] As has been seen, this was the broad policy that was followed, albeit with great difficulty.

The Axis also recognised the need to ship more to these forward ports. Two ships that had previously been sunk in Benghazi harbour were converted into jetties after it had been retaken, while a joint German–Italian conference on 10 March agreed that it must be brought to an unloading capacity of 3,000 tons a day; a notable increase on anything managed to date in either British or Axis hands. Although there were immediate increases, the greatest daily tonnage unloaded over March was 775 tons, and the daily average was 416. By May, however, regular sailings along the coastal route and direct sailings from Italy had been increased sufficiently that unloading broke the 2,000 ton mark.[67] There was also broad agreement that the German divisions would receive an increased proportion of all arriving supplies, artillery and vehicles. This process had begun as early as January, but by the time of the Gazala offensive a specific 60:40 ratio of available shipping space dedicated to the operation would be used for the transfer of German supplies to Benghazi. There would also be increased efforts to provide protection from air attack to shipping on the eastern routes.[68]

Although Italian authorities retained concerns over the security of the eastern sea lanes, the increased Axis focus on using and protecting them was broadly successful in permitting a modest build-up of men and materiel, assisted by the work of trucks and coastal shipping bringing stores forward from Tripoli. By 25 May, the Axis had amassed a force of around 90,000 men, 565 tanks and 542 aircraft, along with moderate quantities of fuel and munitions. They also believed (incorrectly) that they held numerical superiority in terms of men and most types of artillery and that their deficit in tanks was only small, whereas the actual difference was 284.[69] Given his willingness to court great risks, Rommel went ahead with the offensive despite the narrow logistical margins. It is unsurprising, therefore, that throughout the Gazala Line battles, Axis army and air units repeatedly complained of a lack of supplies, especially of fuel.[70] They were, however, aided by two key factors. First, they captured large quantities of British stores after overrunning supply dumps on several occasions. These helped sustain both the first and second phases of the offensive. Second, British operational shortcomings, most notably in the realms of senior leadership and combined operations, greatly hampered their ability to resist.[71] Despite some serious setbacks during the offensive, Rommel was thus able to win an astonishing victory in the face of major logistical difficulties. The capture of Tobruk and Mersa Matruh brought a further boon in the form of a huge haul of British supplies: over 1,400 tons of fuel, vast quantities of ammunition, 5,000 tons of provisions, 2,000 serviceable vehicles and various artillery pieces. The loot was so big it prompted Rommel to assert to OKW that 'pursuit into the heart of Egypt' was immediately possible.[72]

Although the advance had moved the Axis forces yet further from Tripoli, it had bought them the new supply port of Tobruk, as well as useful small harbours at Derna, Bardia and Mersa Matruh. British intelligence judged Benghazi capable of bringing in enough supplies alone to sustain the Axis position, but not any major offensive action. The capture of Tobruk could help the Axis supply an offensive primarily through shipping direct to Cyrenaica, with the smaller harbours allowing further forward distribution from there, via light coastal shipping. This in turn would ease congestion on the overland routes and the overworked MT, which was suffering increasingly at the hands of aerial interdiction efforts.[73] Yet in the immediate aftermath of its capture, Tobruk could only unload 5–800 tons a day, meaning that even more emphasis would have to be placed on Benghazi as the main supply port.[74]

The problem for the Axis was that while the newly acquired ports relieved pressure on the over-taxed land supply route, they were also more vulnerable to Allied attack, especially from air power. As the pessimistic Cavallero warned Ettore Bastico, the Italian Supreme Commander in North Africa, a resurgent effort from British air power meant that 'the routes for Tripoli are considered, for the moment, precluded, and those for the ports of Cyrenaica dangerous'. He assured Bastico that every effort would be made to use the forward ports more, coupled with increased aerial transport of supplies and the use of submarines to carry fuel where possible. Greater aerial escort would have to be provided for them from both Southern Europe and North Africa.[75] In separate correspondence with Keitel, Cavallero also drew attention to the fact that there was a serious deficit between Italy's allotted proportion of imported oil, and consumption by the Navy and Merchant Navy. For the previous nine months, they had received 23–32,000 tons monthly, while usage for naval purposes stood at 65,000. The impact on sailing and escorting convoys was perilous.[76]

The number of sinkings on the eastern route over June and July was moderate, but important. Of greater effect were the sinkings on the coastal route from Tripoli to Benghazi, or from Benghazi to the newly acquired ports. These routes were targeted very deliberately, with the aid of intelligence. As these carried supplies which had already arrived in North Africa, they are not recorded in Table 5.3. Losses over June and July, such as the *Reginaldo Giuliani*, *Regulus*, *Brook*, *Sturla*, *Città di Agrigento* and the *Maria Gabriella*, caused great damage to Rommel's fragile supply base. As he complained in late July:

The supply situation is tense owing to continual and partially successful attacks by enemy naval and air forces on German supply at Tobruk and Matruh. Quick relief is hardly possible owing to distance from supply bases [Tripoli and Benghazi]. Formation of supply bases in the area of operations has not yet met with success owing to shipping losses. Relief depends on the continuous arrival and unloading of coastal and Italian vessels, on the employment of more barges, on the arrival of locomotives and on using the railway.[77]

Added to the cost of these losses was the deterrent effect exercised over the Italians regarding the use of their dwindling reserves of shipping on such dangerous routes. Direct and coastal sailing to the forward ports was regularly postponed, rerouted or cancelled. For some individual convoys this was a repeat occurrence; the starkest example was the *Bixio*, which as part of various planned convoys suffered seven 'false starts' in the attempt to travel from Italy to Benghazi during June, including a full convoy being turned back while at sea. It finally arrived in early July, over three weeks late.[78]

As his inability to break the Eighth Army's defensive line at El Alamein became clear, Rommel sent an 'Estimate of the situation and of the condition of *Panzerarmee*' back to OKW explaining his shift to a more defensive posture. It was written in a broadly optimistic style, reaffirming that the major offensive to break the deadlock and drive on Cairo would come soon, but it made several key admissions about the woeful supply deficit of his force. Losses during the fighting at Alamein, combined with the limited number of reinforcements arriving by sea or land, had reduced his combat mass far below the estimated requirements of major operations. His German units had 30 per cent of the required men, just 15 per cent of the tanks, 70 per cent of the artillery, 40 per cent anti-tank artillery and 50 per cent of the heavy anti-aircraft guns. It was even worse for the Italian units: 30 per cent of the men, 15 per cent of the tanks, artillery at only 25 per cent, and anti-aircraft guns of all types at just 20 per cent. He expressed confidence that he would be back at strength in a month, 'provided that no further actions occasion more losses and that the sea transport is carried out punctually as planned'. His admission that the RAF had gained aerial superiority over both land and sea supply routes, as well as at the front, belied his otherwise belligerent tone. Fuel stocks near the front were sufficient for his operational pause, but not for a renewed offensive or major defensive work. Weapons, ammunition and vehicles were similarly adequate for limited action, thanks mainly to captured British stocks. He ended the report with a list of supply demands and a reminder that 'Supply in advance for an offensive, however, depends on seaborne supply to Tobruk and on increased seaborne supply to Matruh.'[79]

If Rommel's decision to attack the Gazala Line had been risky, the attack on Alamein was little short of reckless. While the treasure trove of British supplies captured in June offered some relief to his logistical situation, he lacked the combat power for a final push. Coupled with this, the well-chosen, narrow defensive site at El Alamein deprived the *Panzerarmee* of much of the room for one of its greatest strengths – manoeuvre – while also mitigating the effects of the inappropriate defensive 'box' structure used by Eighth Army. The anti-shipping campaign had achieved proportionately fewer sinkings over January–July than it had during late 1941, but given the already strained nature of Axis logistics, these were sufficient to have an operational effect. This was particularly true of those vessels sunk on direct sailings to Cyrenaica and on the coastal route from May onwards. Furthermore, the growing number of damaged vessels increased the strain on the Axis even further, with manpower shortages leading to lengthening repair times and a complete inability to keep pace with demand.[80] As a result, continued shipping losses, damage and deterrence over the use of forward ports were a contributing factor to Axis failure at the first battle of El Alamein. Supply shortages were a powerful restraining factor on *Panzerarmee* during the engagement, as units regularly complained of being hampered by a lack of resources, especially fuel. Required reinforcements also failed to arrive in sufficient numbers to restore an effective offensive.[81]

In August, while both sides observed a pause in major combat operations in Egypt, sinkings spiked and supply deliveries dropped correspondingly. Over 41 per cent of the fuel shipped that month failed to arrive in North Africa, let alone what was then lost on coastal routes to intensive British air and submarine activity. British all-source intelligence allowed them to target vessels carrying the most important cargoes of fuel, ammunition and reinforcements to Cyrenaica. The *Ogaden, Lerici, Istria, Dielpi* and *Manfredo Campiero* were all victims of this in August alone, as were the tankers *Pozarica* and *Sanandrea*, and their vital cargoes of fuel.[82] By focusing their efforts, the Axis still managed to unload a record 1,661 tons at Tobruk on 30 July – much higher than the maximum daily capacity that had been given at the time and repeated by historians since. Yet consistent attacks on the port and the shipping travelling to it quickly set the daily totals on a generally downward trajectory over August; from the 11th to the 15th they unloaded 955, 1,069, 1,007, 750 and 540 tons respectively. Figures fluctuated greatly as shipping continued to arrive, including a new high of 1,838 tons on 26 August, but much of that arriving could not be immediately unloaded, causing congestion and making the vessels easier targets for attack.[83] The traffic of very small coastal vessels bringing supplies onward from Tobruk and other forward ports also suffered very heavily over July and August. On 24 August, there were seventy-nine 'A-lighters' in North Africa for this purpose, split between Italian and German control. Of these, thirty were under repair, twenty-one were completely unserviceable, one was conditionally serviceable and just twenty-seven were fit for use.[84]

Shortages had impeded Rommel at Alamein in July, and subsequently prevented him from resuming the offensive over most of August. Sheer determination from the Axis meant that they managed to feed significant reinforcements to the *Panzerarmee* over late July and into August, such as the German 164th and Italian Folgore divisions. These were significant, but still failed to reach the required mass in men, tanks, artillery and other heavy weapons required for a new offensive. Instead, German and Italian units held 40–85 per cent of the requirements in each of these categories, while the fuel and ammunition shortages remained critical.[85]

In this utterly unsuitable situation, Rommel made his last throw of the dice, launching a new offensive towards the key terrain of Alam Halfa ridge on 30 August. He hoped to crack the Eighth Army once and for all, and to do so quickly, before large quantities of reinforcements and supplies could arrive. It appears that misinterpreted intelligence that underestimated Eighth Army's tank strength helped influence the decision, but it was in any case a forlorn hope to launch an offensive in such conditions.[86] Consistent interdiction of their shipping since the previous year had progressively undermined the Axis ability to sustain an expeditionary force in North Africa, and it would continue to affect their operating ability during the final battles in Egypt. They had reached their high watermark in North Africa; the period of Axis ascendancy was over.

6 The End of the Beginning
Alam Halfa and El Alamein

Return from the Nadir

In retrospect, the Axis situation in Egypt might be viewed as being highly precarious by September 1942, as Rommel's exhausted force dangled at the end of an extended supply line. The front at Alamein was 375 miles from Tobruk, 800 from Benghazi and 1,300 from Tripoli.[1] Yet key British figures were evidently concerned about the possibility of impending disaster. After all, the Eighth Army had been pushed back to its point of last resistance by a series of seemingly miraculous defeats from an enemy that was always outnumbered. An intelligence summary at the start of first battle of Alamein had gone so far as to proclaim after Rommel's initial thrust that 'With this success vanished the last military hope of saving Alexandria.'[2] Even after the last-ditch defence prevailed in that engagement, the existential dread was not extinguished, and views of a desperate last stand remained prevalent. This is what Auchinleck continued to plan for with his staff in August before being sacked from both his roles by Churchill. His replacement at the head of Eighth Army, Bernard Montgomery, shared this perspective, stating in a speech in Cairo on 13 August that: 'If we can't stay here alive, then let us stay here dead.'[3]

It had been recognised by both theatre commanders and those in Whitehall that the defence of Egypt must become Britain's main effort, and that the 'attack on Axis shipping by all possible weapons' would play a central role in tipping the balance.[4] Consequently, requests for more submarines in the eastern Mediterranean, and more aircraft capable of effective anti-shipping operations were all approved. By the start of September, there were thirty-two submarines across the theatre, with the vast majority of them concentrated in the eastern basin and clear instruction to focus on enemy shipping. Air efforts were bolstered by the arrival of further RAF and US units.[5] Similarly, pre-existing plans to remove aircraft from the theatre for work elsewhere were promptly cancelled. In one example, two shore-based Albacore squadrons engaged in this role had been earmarked to form the air fleet for a carrier in

September. The new C-in-C Middle East, General Harold Alexander, felt that this was a sufficiently important issue to appeal to the COS directly to urge retention of the Albacores in the theatre. Both Portal and Pound agreed that these aircraft were doing essential work at a critical time, and must remain in place until the battle for Egypt was decided. These decisions stand as clear indications of the widespread agreement both in the Mediterranean and in London on the pivotal place of the anti-shipping campaign within strategic policy.[6]

In spite of British concerns, their position in North Africa, in the wider Mediterranean and indeed in the war as a whole, was vastly improved from earlier in the year. Over July and August they had managed to send more than 150,000 tons of supplies to Egypt via the Cape route, along with new infantry and armoured divisions. They also received new and better-quality tanks, artillery and aircraft. Morale in the Eighth Army was on the increase from its dire low-point at Gazala, while Malta had been partially relieved and Axis aerial dominance of the central and eastern Mediterranean removed.[7] Anglo-American plans for a landing in north-west Africa were progressing after initial disagreement, and elsewhere the American entry to the war was being more forcefully felt. Thus, while the Allied strategic picture brightened and their material superiority in Egypt increased, interdiction at sea would help deepen this disparity into a chasm and ensure ultimate Axis failure. In these circumstances, Rommel's new offensive on 30 August was to be his last in North Africa. The plan was to bypass the main defensive line of Eighth Army to the south and attack the key rear position at Alam Halfa Ridge. The subsequent battle, varyingly labelled as the 2nd Battle of El Alamein, the Battle of Alam Halfa or the 'Six days' race', lasted under a week. There were vague hopes that another crushing victory here might either force a final capitulation from the Eighth Army or allow a breakthrough that would open a path to drive on Cairo and Suez, although few Axis officers seem to have thought this likely.[8]

Fighting another set-piece defensive battle played greatly to the strengths of the Eighth Army, which was well prepared for such a thrust. It allowed immediate and significant loss to be inflicted on the *Panzerarmee* by unmarked minefields, artillery fire and the RAF as it drove around the southern flank. Once the minefields were bypassed, the Axis managed a quick advance to Alam Halfa ridge itself, but were promptly halted by well-positioned artillery and anti-tank guns. With his forces almost immobilised through lack of fuel, Rommel decided to withdraw on 2 September, specifically mentioning the shortage in his orders. Yet thanks to these very shortages, the withdrawal had to take place incrementally over three days before they finally established themselves in a coherent defensive position. In the meantime, they suffered the full force of British firepower, although there was no serious counterattack. Instead, the situation returned to a lull, with both sides aiming to build up their strength for the next bout.

For Rommel, this was a particularly difficult prospect given the complex logistical chain that he sat at the end of. Believing that administrative inefficiency was one of the biggest problems, he travelled to Rome to try and personally re-energise efforts to supply North Africa. He frequently blamed disorganisation, inefficiency and reticence from the authorities there for setbacks in the desert war, and continued to do so right up to his death. He personally impressed on Mussolini that unless the supply situation improved, they would be 'chucked out of North Africa'. Later, in Berlin, he outlined the supplies and reinforcements that he felt were required to continue fighting in North Africa. They were eye-watering; 5,200 men, 2,000 trucks and 70 guns for the Italians; and 6,000 men, 1,080 trucks and 120 tanks for the Germans. In addition to these there should be enough men to bring understrength units up to strength and to replace the 17,000 Germans who had fought in North Africa for more than a year. The frontline units would also need 30,000 tons of supplies in September, and 35,000 in October.[9]

Montgomery, meanwhile, saw the ranks of the Eighth Army swell with newly arrived units and replacements, and he worked hard to ensure that they underwent sufficient training. They also received the latest equipment, including an influx of new American tanks and aircraft.[10] Although both OKH and OKW were not expecting a British offensive until 1943, Montgomery's orders from Alexander were to launch one at the earliest possible moment. A familiar debate ensued in which many in Whitehall, and especially Churchill, favoured near-immediate action, while those on the spot requested more time to prepare. Montgomery argued forcefully that the necessary preparations would preclude an offensive in late September or early October, and suggested late October instead. Alexander supported him, and 23 October was selected as the key date to launch what had been christened Operation 'Lightfoot'.[11]

Anti-shipping operations were a key element of the preparation for 'Lightfoot'. While the build-up of the Eighth Army continued, offensive action remained the preserve of the RAF, FAA and the Navy, which were tasked with continuing to degrade Rommel's army by attacking its communications on land and at sea. The emphasis on these efforts was to be placed as much as possible on interdicting supplies sent to the forwardmost Axis ports and harbours. Portal was quick to instruct Tedder as such, as he did 'not think that what goes into Tripoli is likely to affect the issue of any battle in the near future'.[12] Churchill was in agreement, announcing to the War Cabinet in late September that:

> [The] Emergency in the Boniface shows the increasing dependence of the enemy on Tobruk as against Benghazi. It seems to me astonishing that the whole of the air forces which we and the Americans have in Egypt are not able to bring the work of this port, which lies so near to them, to an end.[13]

Anti-shipping operations thus retained a prime place in British priorities, and submarines and aircraft from Egypt and Malta were dedicated to this task wherever possible, only being held back by a lack of fuel at the latter.[14]

Montgomery and his staff had initially planned to pin down and then destroy the Axis forces facing the Eighth Army through a simultaneous assault by two corps, one to the north and one to the south. A third corps would then exploit successes from the heavier northern blow by executing a powerful armoured thrust through breaches in the Axis position in order to deposit tanks and guns 'on the ground of its own choosing astride the enemy supply routes'. This would then coerce an Axis counterattack, allowing for their encirclement and destruction or capture. It was nothing less than a plan to end the war in North Africa, but it was quickly altered to something less grandiose after intelligence received in October indicated that Rommel's defensive positions were stronger than had been assumed. A revised, more cautious plan opted for a simultaneous assault by all three corps, breaking into, rather than through, the Axis line. The weight of mass and firepower would then 'crumble' the Axis resistance, draw in their reserves and instead inflict a decisive defeat on them through attrition, in advance of an Anglo-American landing in north-west Africa.[15]

Operation 'Lightfoot' was launched on the night of 23 October, with a huge preliminary artillery barrage, followed by the RAF, which dropped 125 tons of bombs on enemy positions in the northern sector alone.[16] The barrage shocked the Axis defenders and caused great disruption, but progress in the advance and break-in was patchy in the face of strong resistance and troublesome minefields. While the crucial Miteiriya ridge was taken, concentrated Axis anti-tank and artillery fire ensured it proved immensely difficult to advance beyond it. The battle essentially became an attritional slog at this point, with the Eighth Army and the RAF making full use of their available firepower but suffering heavy casualties themselves, especially amongst the infantry.[17] The German defences had been partially broken into, but not truly breached or 'crumbled', and Axis armoured reserves were not fully committing as hoped. Faced with such heavy going in the war on land, the COS responded by making further decisions on force allocation to sustain anti-shipping efforts and so ease the Eighth Army's task. In one example, Portal agreed to cancel the transfer of thirteen Beaufighters equipped for maritime work that were destined for India, and have them remain in the Middle East instead, for the sole purpose of contributing to the anti-shipping campaign. The number of submarines also crept up, reaching thirty-five by the start of November.[18]

As the attritional battle continued, a new breakthrough plan was improvised at the end of October: Operation 'Supercharge'. This was essentially another set-piece operation, with another preparatory bombardment closely followed by an infantry advance to hold key ground before the armoured thrust. The operation was launched on the morning of 2 November and deepened the breach of enemy lines and inflicted great destruction but failed to break through, while suffering heavy losses to infantry and armour. A subsequent Axis counterattack suffered a similar fate, with the 15th and 21st Panzer divisions risking elimination, and the battle devolved into a series of localised attacks and counterattacks.[19] In the face of such relentless pressure and attrition, Rommel made and started to implement the decision to withdraw from his untenable position, before being shocked by an unequivocal 'stand and fight' order from Hitler. It promised large numbers of fictional reinforcements, stated that the Axis would triumph at El Alamein so long as they demonstrated the greater will, and ended by urging Rommel to pursue 'victory or death'. As Rommel later wrote, it was an order that 'demanded the impossible'.[20] On 4 November, a desperate Rommel was assured by the visiting Kesselring that a resumption of the withdrawal was permissible, and the order was reissued to most of the *Panzerarmee*. He jumped at the opportunity, leaving a rearguard consisting primarily of remnants of the Italian Ariete, Littorio and Trieste divisions, along with the German 90th Light division. British armour finally managed a difficult breakout against this force, practically wiping out most of the stubborn Italian units in the process, which bought enough time for the remainder of the *Panzerarmee* to escape, albeit under aerial harassment.[21]

The pursuit began on the next day, but the now disorganised Eighth Army failed to catch the bulk of the *Panzerarmee*. They were hampered by serious congestion on their lines of advance, minefields, the remains of the rearguard and some ill-timed heavy rainfall, although some substantial splinters 'fell into the bag', totalling over 30,000 prisoners.[22] Tobruk was recaptured on 13 November, and Benghazi was reached a week later. Much to his chagrin, and despite his multiple protests, Rommel was forced by political pressure to put up a stand at the Mersa

Al Brega line, just east of El Agheila, after advance elements of the Eighth Army pushed the Axis rearguard out of Agedabia on 22 November.[23] He had just forty-five German tanks, plus a handful of Italian machines, whereas the British could muster around 420, along with 300 armoured cars and large quantities of artillery and aircraft. He was hugely outnumbered in terms of men and materiel, yet Kesselring and Cavallero continued to refuse to countenance a withdrawal from Libya. This opportunity did not prevent a typically methodical preparation from Montgomery for the next push, which gave the *Panzerarmee* a full seventeen days' respite before the assault, during which time Rommel personally visited both Hitler and Mussolini to plead for permission to retire further west. Hitler was doggedly opposed but Mussolini eventually agreed to a withdrawal to western Libya, from where Rommel was supposed to build up for a renewed offensive.[24] In spite of the decisive nature of the defeat and Allied landings in north-west Africa, Hitler still referred to the loss of Cyrenaica as 'temporary' in a meeting on 18 December.[25]

While Hitler continued to hope for fantastical reversals of fortune, the Allies were facing a changed picture in North Africa, with consequent repercussions for the priority of anti-shipping operations. The ejection of the *Panzerarmee* from Cyrenaica had removed the vulnerable sea routes to Benghazi and Tobruk from play, leaving the *Panzerarmee* to rely solely on Tripoli once again. Throughout the period of the withdrawal there was widespread agreement across British higher and theatre command that pressure must be maintained against the Axis seaborne supply, as an essential tool to preventing Rommel's escape. There was ongoing agreement among the COS, for instance, that despite the very limited fuel reserves on Malta, all available stocks should continue to be used for striking at enemy communications.[26] Churchill and the COS were also adamant that enemy shipping should be attacked no matter the circumstances. After it came to light that one merchant vessel that was successfully torpedoed had in fact been carrying British and Commonwealth prisoners of war the issue was briefly discussed by the War Cabinet. The decision was quickly reached that, 'in view of the extreme importance of attacking enemy shipping and of the relatively small number of casualties to prisoners of war so caused, no prohibition should be placed at present on the attack of north-bound enemy ships in the Mediterranean'.[27] It was through this sheer bloody-mindedness and focus that the campaign retained such a high priority prior to, during and following the victory at El Alamein. This allowed for large quantities of increasingly effective anti-shipping operations to take place, with demonstrable and decisive effects.

From Desperation to Optimism: Anti-shipping Operations, September–November 1942

As the Eighth Army warded off Rommel's final offensive in Egypt, and prepared for its own, the most powerful asset the British had to interdict the Axis supplies was air power. The very advance of the Axis forces bought their forward coastal shipping well into range of Egypt-based aircraft, but the main focus of effort was Tobruk. This was partly due to the explicit instruction that had come down the RAF command chain from Portal via Tedder to focus on the forward ports, but also because at that stage only those few Liberator aircraft available in Egypt possessed the ability to reach Benghazi.[28] Huge efforts were made by air power against Axis forward ports during September; Tobruk alone was raided by over 700 allied aircraft between 30 August and 4 October. This was coupled with increased efforts by No. 201 Group to attack shipping at sea from bases in Egypt which, along with some diminished efforts from Malta, saw more than 300 of these sorties being flown over the same period. These direct attacks reached a peak at the time of El Alamein, with 207 sorties over just two weeks from 25 October to 8 November.[29] During the preparation for 'Lightfoot', these attacks were weighted overwhelmingly against shipping to the vital Cyrenaican ports, rather than that headed to Tripoli. These were partly a product of the range of the aircraft involved, but were also a deliberate attempt to maximise the effect of shipping losses by interdicting supplies heading to ports that were closer to the Axis frontline. In October, the ratio of attacks on the Cyrenaican routes and forward coastal shipping versus that to Tripoli stood at a stark 85:15 per cent, but these quickly rebalanced in November, as the *Panzerarmee* began its long withdrawal. Instead, November saw 65 per cent of direct attacks targeting shipping on the western routes to Tripoli, Tunisia and Sardinia, with the remainder against that to other parts of Libya and a handful of attacks into the Aegean.[30]

Supported by accurate and effectively implemented intelligence, aircraft from No. 201 Group could target key vessels carrying fuel for the *Panzerarmee*. They continued to utilise and further refine the new tactics that had been developed through comprehensive operational research in the theatre, including the use of 'flak suppression' aircraft to escort those torpedo aircraft carrying out the strike. Not only were these tactics more effective than the previous ad hoc approach, but with a greater number of aircraft available larger forces could be concentrated in a single shipping strike, rather than being parcelled out. Attacking such crucial convoys and independent sailings resulted in these aircraft often taking heavy casualties due to the scale of Axis aerial escort and anti-aircraft defence, but they succeeded in sinking numerous important vessels with significant operational effects.[31] Efficiency in strike operations was very important, as shipping sent to Tobruk first went through the Corinth Canal, keeping it largely out of the range of Beaufort and Beaufighter aircraft. It could only easily be attacked between Crete and Tobruk, which offered a window of opportunity of around one and a half days at sea.[32]

A highly efficient and well-rehearsed routine was quickly developed for night-time attacks on convoys between Crete and Tobruk. Based on intelligence, an ASV-equipped Wellington would search the most likely area to find a target. On doing so, it would transmit signals to a strike force, often of torpedo-equipped Wellingtons, with aircrews specially trained in the torpedo attack role. They would be accompanied by flare-dropping aircraft to first illuminate the targets, before the attack went in. Given that it was a night-time attack, there was minimal danger from enemy fighters and the effectiveness of anti-aircraft fire was reduced.[33] It was not simply a story of unbridled success, however. One notable issue was that it took time for newly arrived aircrews to familiarise themselves with the role and gain valuable experience. This was especially the case for newly arrived American aircraft, and the first forty sorties by American-manned Liberators in a direct attack role sank just a single vessel.[34]

New methods were also developed to attack Axis coastal shipping around Mersa Matruh and Tobruk, as new types of German-built coastal craft such as the F-lighter and Siebel Ferry were proving more difficult to sink than their predecessors. Bomb- and cannon-armed Beaufighters had proven to be largely unsuccessful against them, and after experimentation a solution was hit upon. It was found that ASV-equipped Hudson aircraft, which were normally preserved solely for ASW, were actually well suited, and armed with 100-pound anti-submarine bombs (a weapon that had proven completely useless in its originally intended purpose) were highly effective at both locating and sinking these troublesome vessels.[35]

These efforts from Egypt-based aircraft were supported where possible by attacks from those at Malta, although these were greatly hampered by the fuel supply crisis on the island. Indeed, it was only Rommel's attack on Alam Halfa that convinced the COS to extend the allowance for strike operations from the island up to 10 September despite the fuel shortages. Following this, however, instructions were given that the use of aviation fuel on the island was to be restricted to 150 tons per week, but the decision was reversed again in November, accepting the importance of anti-shipping operations above everything else and counting on future successful convoys to the island.[36] Given the difficulties, sorties were few – the FAA managed just three attacks on shipping in September, using nine aircraft. This improved slightly in October, to six using fifteen aircraft. These attacks used flights of two to four aircraft, generally involving an ASV-equipped Swordfish leading the newer Albacore biplanes onto the target.[37] Despite using much older machines, the FAA continued to outperform the RAF, and later also the increasingly active US Army Air Force (USAAF), in terms of accuracy and efficiency in obtaining results in direct attacks at sea. During the October–December period, Swordfish and Albacore aircraft in the eastern basin maintained an impressive 42 per cent hit rate with their torpedo drops, compared to just 23 per cent for Beaufort aircraft and 28 per cent for torpedo-armed Wellingtons.[38] Malta-based aircraft were able to increase their levels of operation significantly after the arrival of two more supply convoys in late November and early December.

Having recently returned to Malta, the submarines of S10 had been quick to reassert their influence in August and modest successes came in September. A handful of patrols by S8 from Gibraltar into the western-central Mediterranean also brought some limited success off the Sardinian coast. Perhaps surprisingly, though, given their relocation to a less favourable base and the recent loss of their depot ship, S1 managed the greatest achievements that month. T-Class submarines patrolling off Cyrenaica quickly brought sinkings such as the 1,590-ton *Padenna* on 4 September and the 1,245-ton *Albachiara* the next day. It seems that part of the reason for this disparity was excessive caution from S10 due to their knowledge of improved echo-detection equipment on some Italian escorts, which made them reluctant to patrol off well-defended areas of the Italian coast, such as Taranto. During September, the British submarines also followed a policy of very dispersed patrolling, which succeeded in further straining Italian escort efforts, but seems to have diluted their successes.[39] They rectified this dispersion the following month when, thanks to intelligence and aerial reconnaissance, S10 were able to concentrate five submarines over 18–20 October against a single four-vessel Naples–Tripoli convoy, and in conjunction with the FAA successfully sank two merchant ships and a tanker.[40] This was the most prominent incident from what was a generally successful month for British submarines.

Their success was aided by new levels of integration with air power in many of their operations, enabled by the use 'Rooster' radio location and homing technology. In a newly developed tactic, ASV-equipped Wellingtons would highlight convoys beyond the reach of shorter-range strike aircraft in order to allow their interception by submarine. The co-operation and sorties were organised through close inter-service integration in command and control. S1 had withdrawn from Egypt at this

Table 6.1 *Numbers/tonnage of Axis shipping sunk, September–November 1942*

	Surface vessel	Submarine	Aircraft	Mine	Shared	Total
September	0/0	15/18,682	8/21,071	0/0	2/2,737	25/42,490
October	0/0	23/29,650	11/20,085	0/0	1/5,397	35/55,132
November	0/0	9/41,046	24/44,805	2/5,784	0/0	35/91,635

Source: Calculated from TNA AIR 20/9598, Table 3: 'Analysis of Enemy Merchant Shipping Sunk by all Causes, Scuttled, Captured or Surrendered in the Mediterranean'; Röhwer, *Allied Submarine Attacks.*

stage, a liaison officer was embedded at the 201 Group HQ in Alexandria to advise RAF personnel on submarine matters and to help co-ordinate these attacks, which proved to be highly effective, as demonstrated by the increased submarine success rate in this period.[41] The much lower number of sinkings by submarine in November, despite numerous attacks, appears to have been the result of a combination of poor weather and submarine crews getting used to the different patrolling conditions off Tunisia. Yet as the sinking achieved in November included some very large vessels like the 10,534-ton *Giulio Giordani*, the tonnage for that month was still impressive.[42]

As Table 6.1 demonstrates, submarines and aircraft delivered all the sinkings in September and October. November was a very similar story, although the first minelaying operations against the Tunisian routes, including the laying of 156 mines by HMS *Manxman* and another 35 by aircraft, sank two vessels.[43]

The ninety-five vessels of 189,257 tons were a continuance of the success achieved in August, and demonstrates that the campaign had improved notably after the low of January–July 1942. This was the result of a combination of ruthless prioritising of anti-shipping operations over other maritime tasks, with appropriate dedication of forces, an ongoing improvement of techniques and the degradation of Axis countermeasures. That is not to say that Axis countermeasures were themselves completely ineffective, as they did prevent sinkings from increasing to the even greater levels that would occur during the Tunisian campaign. They also inflicted significant loss on allied aircraft in particular, as illustrated in Table 6.2.

The losses to aircraft were a direct result of concerted Axis efforts to counter their threat to shipping, which they perceived to be greater than any other method. On 16 September 1942, the Italians had belatedly created the new Comitato per la organizzazione e la protezione dei trasporti per l'Africa to examine the task of improving the organisation

Table 6.2 *Losses in anti-shipping operations, September–November 1942*

	Surface vessels	Submarines	Aircraft
September	0	1	28
October	0	0	19
November	0	1	10

and escort of convoys and coastal shipping, and to co-ordinate both Italian and German naval and air units to this purpose. To aid this integration, the committee was headed by the Deputy Chief of the Italian Navy and composed of senior representatives from both nations' navies and air forces. A mixed 'special office' to undertake the necessary research was also instituted.[44] The move was a positive step towards alleviating some of the problems already discovered by Italian research into the causes of shipping losses: an incoherent command structure between the air and naval elements and the two allies, lack of sufficient escorts and the difficulties caused by constant changes in sailing timetables. Further problems recognised included incorrect procedures being followed by merchant crews and inadequate protection of the destination ports. Other than the creation of what became the Comitato and the suggestion that merchant crews should be treated and trained in exactly the same way as military ones, the rest of the recommendations were familiar: greater escort efforts, more building and repair work to be focused on merchant shipping, greater aerial subjugation of Malta and Egyptian air bases and increased use of aerial transport. Accordingly, modest aerial reinforcements had been sent to Sicily to participate in the bombing of Malta, while efforts were made to increase the anti-aircraft firepower of both merchant ships and escorts.[45]

The increased anti-aircraft armament was most notable on the numerous new small coastal vessels that were increasingly being employed by the Axis powers. The two most prevalent of these were the Siebel Ferry and the Marinefährprahm, which was commonly referred to as an 'F-lighter' by the Allies. Siebel ferries consisted of two pontoons lashed together into a catamaran of around 150 tons, and they usually boasted three powerful 88mm guns plus two 37mm or 20mm weapons, all of which could be used for anti-aircraft purposes. F-lighters were generally larger, heavier and could hold more cargo but boasted a smaller armament. They were still impressive, however, with two 20mm, one 37mm and a 75mm or 88mm gun. Both types had a very shallow draft, making them near-immune to torpedo attack, while their small size and thick armour made bombing and strafing with cannon a difficult prospect.[46]

Convoys of these small vessels were thus able to put up a barrage of anti-aircraft fire that was described by aircrews as 'intense', while they also operated within range of single-engine fighter cover, offering further opposition.[47] Elsewhere, the new armaments fitted to merchant vessels and the attempts to increase the air defences of Italian escort vessels were more limited in their success. The efforts suffered from an overall lack of weapons, a lack of effective fire control equipment and the poor quality of Italian-manufactured weaponry. Better results were achieved when German weaponry was fitted, but these were mainly concentrated on the new German-controlled coastal vessels.[48] Overall, the result of increased armament was to allow convoys to be able to put up powerful barrages against daylight attacks, although these were partly mitigated through the use of 'flak suppression' aircraft to escort torpedo bombers. The Axis, and especially the Italians, lacked the technology to be so accurate at night, where barrages proved to be 'spectacular rather than lethal'.[49]

Overall, the effect of the increased efforts was tangible, accounting for seventeen Allied aircraft undertaking direct attacks at sea over the three-month period. Of the fifty-seven aircraft lost on anti-shipping tasks, the majority came in bombing attacks against ports, however, and forty were destroyed either by anti-aircraft fire or fighter defence.[50] Other, more passive forms of defence also caused problems for the use of air power in an anti-shipping role. The jamming of ASV signals was a nuisance, although the Axis lacked any well-sighted beacons to cover the eastern basin, rendering aircraft operating from Egypt largely immune. More effective was the use of smokescreens by merchant vessels and their escorts. Although not a new defensive tactic, it was used more frequently in this period, and when done correctly could really hamper attacking aircraft. As one report put it: 'The effectiveness of the smoke was that under favourable conditions it rendered flares for night attacks more or less useless as an aid to torpedo dropping. Equally the use of smoke screens at times rendered bombing ineffective.'[51] The range of countermeasures and techniques being used goes to show just how far the Axis considered this to be a problem. Allied losses of aircraft had been significantly higher than in January–June, although lower than the spike that occurred in July and August.

By contrast, submarine losses had been consistent throughout 1942, averaging a little under one per month, and September–November was no exception. A T-class vessel from S1 was sunk by an Italian torpedo boat in September off the west coast of Italy, and a U-class of S10 was mined in the Sicilian channel in November.[52] The ongoing lack of effective anti-submarine countermeasures and paucity of escort vessels continued to hamper the Axis powers at this stage, as did the dispersal of Axis sea routes and thus potentially fruitful submarine operating areas. The latter issue would be largely removed during the Tunisian campaign, with consequently higher submarine casualties. Instead the Axis powers had to rely on more passive measures, including some effective use of low-level SIGINT to reroute convoys away from known submarine patrols.[53]

The losses to anti-shipping forces in the air and under the sea had been notable but did not represent any great increase on previous efforts. They were well within the parameters of what theatre commanders considered acceptable given the situation prevailing in Egypt, while the result of nearly 200,000 tons of shipping sunk in three months had a disastrous effect on the Axis ability to wage effective war in North Africa.

'Screaming for Fuel': Operational Effect from Alam Halfa to the Axis Withdrawal from El Alamein

From Alam Halfa through to the Axis withdrawal from Egypt and across Libya, anti-shipping operations had a constant and important detrimental effect on the fighting efficiency of the Axis forces. This was achieved by consistently harassing the seaborne supplies on which they remained utterly reliant, without any realistic alternative. Indeed, as the Axis prepared to assault Alam Halfa ridge, it had been agreed between Comando Supremo and the IAF that airlifted supplies could never be enough to substitute for sealift capacity unless a vastly increased number of aircraft could be used. Such quantities of aircraft were simply never available to the Italians, who lacked the ability to construct them on that scale. For his part, Kesselring initially promised 500 tons of fuel per day to be delivered by the GAF for the attack on Alam Halfa, and assigned additional aircraft to the task, but this ultimately proved completely unachievable, and the actual deliveries were minimal.[54]

The concentration of anti-shipping efforts from August onwards against tankers and merchant vessels carrying crucial fuel was essential in weakening the Axis offensive. It was enabled by the effective use of multi-source intelligence that frequently allowed a deliberate and selective targeting of these vessels and their cargoes. The urgent need to get these cargoes through, ideally to forward ports, was recognised by key Axis figures. The situation was so grave in late August that Cavallero stated of one tanker: 'It will have to be sent, if need be, with all the fighters in Sicily ... The *Pozarica* must arrive at any cost.' Yet the 7,751-ton *Pozarica* was first damaged by a submarine before being sunk by aircraft near Corfu while en route to Benghazi. This was followed by the sinking of the Tobruk-bound *Sanandrea* at the end of the month, causing the head of the IAF to concede that it was now clear that fuel-carrying vessels were being deliberately targeted. He immediately requested the expediting of eight ships that were loading in Italy to all be sent to forward ports in the hope of keeping the offensive alive. He feared it might be too late, as Rommel was not yet aware of the loss of *Sanandrea* and was desperate for supplies. He concluded by emphasising that 'We cannot lose ships and fuel in this way.'[55] Yet the reality was that these last-gasp efforts were too late to save the offensive. The loss of the *Sanandrea* alone had cost the *Panzerarmee* and the GAF a combined 5,000 tons of fuel for their offensive, and Mussolini himself later conceded that the British focus on tankers and fuel transports had 'achieved something remarkable'.[56]

The absence of fuel and a strong defence combined to prevent the continuation of Rommel's attack after it cut through to Alam Halfa ridge itself. The impact of these supply losses was articulated in *Panzerarmee*'s report on 1 September, stating that they would have to shift to a defensive posture, as 'the POL [petrol, oil and lubricant] promised for 1 September has not arrived and the *Abruzzi* is still at sea'. The language in the Quartermaster's War Diary for 1 September was much blunter, warning that 'Troops screaming for fuel; they have only 0.5 Consumption Units left.' Rommel was informed of the losses of the *Pozarica* and *Sanandrea* the next day, while the *Abruzzi* was bombed at sea and forced to beach with heavy damage, failing to reach Tobruk.[57]

The *Panzerarmee* outlined the dire fuel situation to Rome on 3 September: there were just three CUs between the unloading ports and the front and supply of units at a maximum rate of one CU per day could thus only be ensured until 5 September. Over the preceding week, 2,610 tons of fuel (5.5 CUs) and 443 tons of ammunition assigned for the *Panzerarmee* had been sunk. By comparison, only 2,352 tons of fuel (4.2 CUs) plus 350 tons of munitions had arrived in the same period. The loss of over half of the fuel shipped specifically for German units in the run-up to and during the offensive stifled their movement. The fuel situation for Italian units at the front was even worse thanks to the sinking of the tanker *Picci Fassio* with 1,100 tons of fuel on 2 September. The arrival of two ships at Tobruk on 3 September was only enough to ensure that units would get one CU per day for three days, and even that would only be from 7 September as it took three days to unload at the bomb-damaged Tobruk and then transport the fuel to units. Losses off Tobruk and Derna continued to mount, as another three ships laden with petrol and ammunition were sent to the bottom over 4–5 September. The next day, the decision to move temporarily to the defensive had become a permanent one.[58]

The *Panzerarmee*'s report explaining the initial move to a defensive posture did not solely blame the issue of supply, but counted it as one of several factors. It also admitted that the offensive had been held up by stronger than expected fixed defences in the southern area, losing the element of surprise which had been deemed essential for success. British aerial superiority and constant day and night air attacks before and during the offensive had also caused problematic losses.[59] It is difficult to disagree with this assessment, placing the supply factor as one of many contributors, although the importance of SIGINT revealing much of the Axis plan to the British and aerial reconnaissance tracking initial Axis movements should be added to the list.[60]

In fact, the main achievement of the anti-shipping campaign at this point was to curtail the offensive almost before it began by preventing the delivery of the minimum level of supplies needed to maintain mobility within the *Panzerarmee*. Rommel had specified in mid-August that for it to have a chance of success, 6,000 tons of fuel and 2,500 tons of ammunition would have to be delivered to the front over 25–30 August, followed by ongoing deliveries into September. Efforts to achieve this were made, with over 10,000 tons of fuel despatched to forward ports for the land and air forces combined. By 29 August, only 1,500 tons had arrived, yet Rommel still decided to gamble on striking for decisive victory rather than staying in his increasingly unsustainable position. Sinkings around the forward ports continued for the duration of the offensive, preventing it from being logistically 'rescued', and it had to be abandoned. The wisdom of pressing ahead with the attack has been questioned, both at the time and in the historiography, but it is evident that anti-shipping operations made an important contribution to its swift defeat.[61] Rommel had conjured victories from seemingly impossible tactical situation on several prior occasions, but it did not come close to happening at Alam Halfa.

Not only had the offensive failed, it had consumed much of the minimal supply reserves held at the front, meaning the new defensive position itself was in jeopardy unless significant quantities could be delivered. Even the previously satisfactory food supply was becoming constricted, and bread rations were halved, contributing to a rise in sickness rates. Rommel made an urgent appeal for 30,000 tons of supplies in September and 35,000 in October. This was to include eight issues of ammunition, thirty CUs of fuel and thirty days' supplies. He also pleaded for the shipment of 11,200 men, 3,200 vehicles and 70 field guns currently awaiting transfer from Italy to be expedited.[62] The current fuel supplies that were available were projected to last only until 19 September, and while there were over 4,300 tons of ammunition and around thirty days' supplies available in Tripolitania, there was nowhere near enough fuel there either.

This lack of fuel refutes the notion of authors such as van Creveld and Barnett that anti-shipping operations were ineffectual in 1942, and that the deciding factor was overland distances. Elsewhere, Gladman has argued that it was the aerial interdiction campaign overland that strangled the *Panzerarmee* rather than efforts over the sea. While overland interdiction was no doubt important given the destruction of such large quantities of MT, Gladman offers little evidence of its effect in the July–September period and thus on Alam Halfa and the subsequent shift to a defensive posture. Indeed, it had been agreed by the Axis High Commands that the most effective method for bringing supplies forward would be coastal shipping (which itself then suffered heavy attrition) rather than MT. Finally, it is worth noting that efforts to move supplies overland were themselves dependent on successful sealift, and 30 per cent of the MT and related equipment sent to North Africa in September was lost at sea, rising to 46 per cent in October.[63]

In spite of the difficult situation, however, a note of cautious optimism was sounded from OKW. There were, as of 14 September, 7,138 cbm of fuel, 1,421 tons of food, 2,290 tons of ammunition and 1,109 tons of miscellaneous supplies at sea and heading to North Africa. A further 2,080 cbm fuel, 2,410 tons of ammunition and 2,910 tons of food were being loaded in Italy. As Warlimont put it: 'If losses are not heavy and shipping circulation is not seriously held up by enemy fleet movements, and if no priority troop movements are ordered, the *Panzerarmee* ammunition and food supplies can be maintained or slightly improved, in the case of fuel the rate can be maintained.'[64] Such optimism was quickly proven to be unfounded, as sixty vessels of nearly 100,000 tons were sunk over September and October. Table 6.3 demonstrates just how damaging these losses were in terms of key deliveries, including the loss at sea of over half the fuel shipped in October.

The hope among the *Panzerarmee* leadership was that a renewed offensive could be mounted, but General Georg Stumme, temporarily replacing a convalescing Rommel, admitted to Cavallero in early October that supply losses were making this impossible. He instead reiterated the call for intensified supply efforts, but this was ignorant of the sheer scale of attrition to shipping, which was rendering such attempts impossible.[65] Germany's newly appointed Reich Commissioner for Shipping, Karl Kaufmann, recognised this problem, confessing that:

Table 6.3 *Cargo tonnages despatched and landed in Libya, September 1942–January 1943*

	Motor transport		% Lost	Fuel		% Lost	Total sent	Total landed	% Lost
	Sent	Landed		Sent	Landed				
September	9,433	6,591	30	40,200	31,061	23	96,903	77,526	20
October	5,884	3,201	46	25,771	12,308	52	83,695	46,698	44
November	7,061	5,551	21	39,928	21,731	46	85,970	63,736	26
December	108	50	54	7,950	2,058	74	12,981	6,151	53
January	0	0	–	48	24	50	487	152	69

Source: Calculated from USMM, *LMI*, Vol. 1, *Dati Statistici*, Table LIV, p. 126.

At the present moment, however, the prevailing losses in shipping, especially in the Mediterranean, are causing me great anxiety, and at the present, apart from the drive for surrender of neutral and French shipping, they cannot be replaced. According to my information, the shipping losses German/Italian tonnage in the supply service to Africa have again risen in the last weeks to such an extent that, should those losses continue, the time can be calculated when it will no longer be possible to provide the shipping space for supplies to Africa.[66]

In this situation, the best that could be hoped for was to hold and check any British offensive.

On returning to take direct command of the *Panzerarmee*, Rommel was quick to decide that his only chance of stymying any attack by the Eighth Army was to withdraw from fixed positions and fight a battle of manoeuvre in the open. This would mitigate the Eighth Army advantages in artillery and air power and allow the *Panzerarmee* to play to its strengths, but the hope was dashed by the utterly inadequate levels of available fuel. Instead, Rommel was forced into the battle of attrition that he so desperately wanted to avoid.[67] As of 6 October, the *Panzerarmee* could call on 8.5 CUs of fuel throughout all of North Africa – enough for seventeen days at their low usage of that time, but insufficient for major combat operations, while much of it was not at the front. For ammunition, there were 3.5 units of most types throughout North Africa, but there were greater deficiencies among certain types, especially 50mm and 75mm tank rounds. Comando Supremo committed to delivering sufficient fuel and ammunition by 20 October to ensure overall increases of at least two units of each, in order to mount a successful defence against any coming offensive. They reiterated that the best way to assure this was increased coastal shipping and direct deliveries to Tobruk and Mersa Matruh.[68]

As a direct response to these needs, Comando Supremo set out an intensive programme of sailings over a week, carrying cargoes deemed most important in North Africa. A convoy of the *Monginevro, Foscolo* and *D'Annunzio* would arrive at Benghazi on 12 October. *Tergestea* and *Petrarca*, with cargoes of ammunition and some fuel, were to arrive at Tobruk on the 16th. The *Giulia* and the tanker *Ankara* were destined for Benghazi on the 18th, with their cargoes to be taken forward both overland and via coastal shipping. The tanker *Portofino* and the steamer *Gualdi* would dock at either Tobruk or Benghazi on the 18th. Their meeting on the subject ended on a very gloomy note, however, emphasising both the extreme danger of the eastern route, and the lack of sufficient coastal shipping thanks to recent losses.[69]

This intricate supply plan unravelled almost immediately in the face of organisational difficulties and concerted British aero-naval aggression. Planned departure times and unloading dates quickly and repeatedly slipped backwards due to slow loadings, heavy loads and a lack of available escorts.[70] Although the *Monginevro* and *D'Annunzio* arrived at Benghazi three days late and the *Ankara* reached Tobruk, the rest were heavily delayed or did not sail at all. Worse, the *Kreta* and the *Dandolo*, steamers that were already on the coastal route to Tobruk during the formation of the programme, were sunk by submarine and aircraft respectively on 8 and 10 October. A hurriedly devised replacement schedule assigned the *Petrarca, Tergestea, Prosperina* and *Luisiana* to all reach Tobruk with cargoes of fuel before the end of the month.[71] *Petrarca* was promptly damaged first by air and then submarine attack. Aircraft of No. 201 Group then struck a devastating blow by sinking both the *Prosperina* and *Tergestea* on 26 October followed by the *Luisiana* two days later. They followed this up by sinking two more ships carrying fuel and ammunition on the Benghazi–Tobruk coastal route at the end of the month.[72]

The damage to both the Axis's ability to supply the *Panzerarmee* and that force's delicate situation was palpable. Cavallero had admitted at a meeting with Kesselring and von Rintelen that the losses of tankers were seriously harming the ability to supply the *Panzerarmee* with fuel, and stressed the importance of the arrival of the *Proserpina* and *Luisiana* to help alleviate the crisis.[73] In fact, the Quartermaster of *Panzerarmee* noted that the *Ankara* was the only serviceable ship remaining capable of carrying 1,000 cbm of fuel at a time. Losses to the Italian tanker fleet at this time were also coming on the Tripoli route (such as the *Panuco*) and even in the Aegean (such as the *Arca*). They had been so heavy that the situation was considered critical and efforts were even made to loan small Spanish merchant ships to carry barrels of fuel secured to their decks.[74] A *Panzerarmee* report of 24 October warned that 'if the tanker due to arrive on the 26th [*Proserpina*] fails to arrive there will be a serious crisis. The Italian fuel situation is already very precarious.'[75]

'Screaming for Fuel' 145

It was not just the Italian Army suffering from this dearth of fuel, but also the Air Force, where stocks were so depleted that by the withdrawal in early November personnel were forced to beg for handouts from their German counterparts in order to operate at all. Given this situation, it is hardly surprising that Rommel described receiving the news of the loss of *Louisiana* as 'shattering'.[76] He had hoped to build up stocks of 19,000 tons of fuel (equivalent to thirty-two CUs) and 32,000 tons of ammunition by the end of October in order to resume the offensive. Instead, the *Panzerarmee* was down to just three CUs by 20 October, as only a little over 12,000 tons was landed at all that month, with 52 per cent of stocks shipped lost en route, and then more with coastal shipping. The losses had been greatest on the routes to forward ports, and especially to Tobruk. While some, notably van Creveld, have criticised reliance on Tobruk for its lack of capacity, it should be noted that it was capable of unloading over 1,800 tons in a single day during August.[77] Such performance demonstrates that it was potentially capable of handling sufficient supplies for Rommel's stated supply needs, but failed to do so because of the impact of successful anti-shipping operations.

Instead, Operation 'Lightfoot' began with the Axis forces so denuded of fuel as to deprive them of their greatest strength, mobility, while ammunition was also low. Whereas the need to preserve mobility had been viewed as paramount, major movements by motorised and armoured units were having to be curtailed, hampering an effective defensive deployment. Ammunition stocks were low enough to necessitate 'the utmost economy' in their use, and rendered it impossible for their artillery to conduct counter-battery missions, further exacerbating the Eighth Army advantage in this area. There was also not enough available shipping to send tanks to replace losses as all cargo space available was being used for fuel and other supplies.[78] Accounts of the battle agree that these supply difficulties greatly impinged Axis fighting effectiveness at Alamein, and indeed afterwards. When Rommel gained permission to withdraw, the lack of fuel in 15th and 21st Panzer Division was so acute that a stalling counterattack was cancelled and numerous tanks had to be abandoned and sabotaged rather than taken along.[79] By 8 November, there was enough fuel for just 4–5 days of non-intensive operations, as attempts to send more to Benghazi had proven largely abortive. Similar problems were occurring with stores of ammunition, with only a single issue available around Tobruk, half an issue in the Benghazi zone, and one more at Tripoli.[80]

The *Panzerarmee* was forced to conduct a withdrawal in an immensely difficult situation, with less than the minimum supply requirement.

Illustration 6.1 Sunken wrecks of Axis shipping strewn across Benghazi harbour. The largest supply port in Cyrenaica, this was a key point of forward disembarkation for Axis forces advancing across eastern Libya and into Egypt. Consequently, it and the shipping bound for it became a focus for attack by aircraft and submarines based in Egypt.
Source: www.gettyimages.co.uk/detail/news-photo/wrecked-axis-ships-pounded-from-the-air-and-sea-littered-news-photo/499295867?adppopup=true
Credit: Toronto Star Archives via Getty Images

Along with the air force, it ideally required 47,000 tons a month, but while substantial quantities of supplies did arrive in November, nearly all went to Tunisia or Tripoli. Attempts to supply precious fuel further forward to aid retreating units generally failed, as was the case with the *Hans Arp*: the last tanker sent to Benghazi before its evacuation was quickly sunk on the coastal route. By 17 November, Rommel admitted that his German units were 'currently immobilised' at Marsa al Brega due to lack of fuel, and most had less than a single issue of ammunition.[81] Rommel was forced to complete a withdrawal from a temporary position around El Agheila on 12 December thanks to fuel deficiencies that made any prospective defence realistically impossible. He had hoped to begin the withdrawal on the night of 5 December, but the lack of fuel was so severe that even a straight withdrawal was impossible at that point. Instead, a phased retirement began with Italian infantry units on the 7th. In spite of the extreme vulnerability during this withdrawal, which had to be conducted in a piecemeal nature, Montgomery's pursuit was ultra-cautious, failing to prevent the escape of the *Panzerarmee*.[82]

'Screaming for Fuel'

Although the Eighth Army failed to eliminate the retreating Axis forces, the anti-shipping campaign had helped ensure that it was untenable for them to remain in Libya. On 15 December, Fifth Panzer Army command in Tunisia admitted:

> Our ships are being sunk either outside the harbour or inside by submarine and air attack ... It cannot yet be estimated whether sufficient coastal shipping will be available to ensure the carriage of supplies to Rommel once the use of large ships, railways and roads is no longer possible. A similar situation prevails in Tunisia, where with the present resources it will take several months to assemble the necessary resources.[83]

By the end of the month both Italian and German authorities had definitively conceded that all forces must withdraw into southern Tunisia to a front that was more defensible with their limited resources.[84]

Although the last Axis units did not cross into Tunisia until February 1943, the war in Egypt and Libya was effectively over. The anti-shipping campaign had made a decisive contribution to the defeat of Rommel's assault on Alam Halfa and to subsequent victory at Alamein by depriving them of key resources. Not only that, but the sheer scale of attrition to Axis shipping resources was leading to an impending crisis, as the Axis struggled to sustain any kind of position across the Mediterranean through seaborne supply. In 1943, this would lead to a collapse first in Tunisia, and then beyond.

7 The End in North Africa and the Shipping Crisis
December 1942–May 1943

The Road to Tunis

While Rommel was extricating his battered forces from Alamein, the Allies launched Operation 'Torch'. The full-scale invasion of north-west Africa began on 8 November with landings at three points along the Moroccan and Algerian coasts, around Casablanca, Oran and Algiers. The venture had a long and troubled birth, marred by Anglo-American differences over the priority of the Mediterranean in Allied grand strategy. Many senior US strategy-makers, including the Joint Chiefs of Staff (JCOS), questioned why they should be dragged into the Mediterranean war at all. Yet crucially, President Franklin Roosevelt agreed with the venture and his subordinates fell into line.[1] The landings transformed the war in the Mediterranean into a truly allied venture as American men and materiel poured into the theatre, and the war in North Africa morphed into a conflagration fought on not one, but two fronts.

The Axis response to this new situation was swift, acting to deny any other unoccupied French territories in the Mediterranean to the Allies. Operation 'Anton' was launched on 11 November, and involved the seizure of Tunisia, Corsica and southern France, including the vital port of Toulon, where the bulk of the French Navy was stationed. Although most of the French ships there were defiantly scuttled, the occupations were otherwise a great success; the French offered no resistance and Corsica was taken by the Italians on the 12th, while southern France was fully under control by the 14th. German airborne forces started arriving in Tunisia on the night of the 11th to secure key airfields and the port of Tunis, and were soon joined by other units sent by sea and air.[2]

The changed strategic situation now raised a new question for Axis strategy: was the aim in Tunisia to secure a bridgehead through which to allow evacuation of their forces from Africa back to Italy over the shortest route, or to use it as a position from which to hold on to a permanent place in North Africa? There were senior proponents on both sides; Rommel felt by this stage that keeping any kind of permanent position in North Africa was no longer possible and requested preparations for evacuation, much to Hitler's fury. General Jodl, Chief of OKW's Operations Staff, favoured holding a strong bridgehead, stating that 'North Africa, being the approach to Europe, must be held at all costs', a view that was echoed by Mussolini in his instructions to Rommel. For his part, Hitler held the fantastical view that the build-up in Tunisia offered a base from which to launch a decisive westward offensive to drive the Allies back into the sea, before then focusing on the Eighth Army once more.[3] Ultimately Axis strategy crystallised around a rather vaguely defined aim of holding a position in Tunisia, and the ideas of either a breakout or evacuation seem to have received no serious consideration. General Walter Nehring was initially given command of Axis units in Tunisia in November, and early in December, they were given the rather grandiose title of Fifth Panzer Army. His orders from Kesselring were to expand the bridgehead and delay the Allies by conducting an 'active defence'. Kesselring later relieved him of command on 8 December, replacing him with Hans von Arnim, whose task remained the same.[4]

Whereas previously anti-shipping operations had been given a prominent position in British priorities in order to degrade the *Panzerarmee* and aid the war in Libya and Egypt, now new sea lanes were opened up between Italy and Tunisia. As the Eighth Army reclaimed Cyrenaica, the need to refocus on the Tunisian routes was recognised at both the strategic and operational level, and, given the westward shift in focus, Malta was once again the best-positioned base for such forces. After a brief diversion of some aircraft to cover the Malta convoy of Operation 'Stoneage', the COS were in complete agreement that all Malta-based aircraft, now replenished with supplies, should focus their efforts solely on attacking shipping to Tunisia.[5] They communicated this view to the theatre-commanders on 22 November: 'It is evident that if the First and Eighth Armies are to achieve speedy and decisive victory, the objective of prime importance at the present time must be the stoppage of sea borne supplies to Tunisia and Tripolitania.' Tedder was clear that Malta must be exploited fully for this purpose, something which the theatre commanders assured him they were in the process of implementing, albeit with some difficulty.[6]

Churchill was also quick to urge Portal to dedicate greater air power resources to the task, by transferring more medium and heavy bombers to the theatre to attack the primary destination ports at Tunis and Bizerte. In addition, he advocated sending more torpedo aircraft to attack the shipping directly at sea. Portal concurred, as did Pound.[7] Discussions in Whitehall on the issue of torpedo aircraft had been ignited after Cunningham complained directly to Pound about the need for a more powerful air striking force to interdict the Tunisian routes.[8] As a result, twelve additional Wellington bombers, capable of either port bombing or direct attacks, were sent to Malta in late November, while Churchill also approved the relocation of two more Wellington squadrons from Bomber Command to north-west Africa in early December. Space was made at the island's facilities for these new arrivals by the transfer of Beaufort torpedo bombers to airfields near Bône in north-east Algeria. From here, the shorter-range Beauforts would be better placed to attack the Tunisian routes, while additional Beaufighters were also sent there from the UK.[9] A 'sink at sight' zone was also approved in November that declared the whole western basin an 'operational zone' for Allied submarines. This included the waters off southern France, Corsica and near Spain, so long as Spanish territorial waters were not infringed. The move allowed the use of submarines to disrupt Axis sea communications in a broad sense – with Tunisia, with Corsica and to discourage Spanish trade with Italy.[10] Finally, Force K was re-established at Malta in late November after renewed pressure from Churchill, boasting three cruisers and four destroyers with the express aim of hunting down convoys. Another task force, Force Q, was based at Bône with the same purpose and a similar strength.[11]

These changes were due to both Allied recognition of the growing importance of the Tunisian routes, and also intelligence that indicated the rate of Axis build-up in Tunisia during November. A report by the Joint Intelligence Committee suggested that a daily average of 1,000 men and 100 vehicles had been bought across by air and sea, although they were in a disorganised state and likely only capable of limited offensive action. On hearing this, Churchill expressed irritation that it had been allowed to happen.[12] British intelligence also correctly identified at the end of November that Tunis and Bizerte had become the main Axis destination ports, with Tripoli only receiving very restricted service. They expected, correctly, that use of Tripoli would only decrease further over time. Based on this information, the decision was made to focus all efforts on the Tunisian routes.[13]

After this recognition, the Tunisian routes overtook those to Tripoli in Allied targeting priority in December. This was a shift in focus that was soon mirrored in changes by the Axis. On 24 December, they declared Tripoli was closed to direct shipping from Italy, meaning all trans-Mediterranean shipping had to go to Tunisia. Tripoli could only receive whatever was sent from Tunisia by coastal shipping and submarine.[14] This decision reflected the realities of the Axis position, as they undertook a complete withdrawal from Libya. Rommel had been forced to retire from his temporary position around El Agheila on 12 December thanks to a lack of fuel making any prospective defence realistically impossible. He had hoped to begin a full-scale withdrawal on the night of 5 December, but the lack of fuel was so severe that it was impossible at that point. Instead, a phased retirement began with Italian infantry units on the 7th. By 19 December the first units were back at the temporary defensive line at Buerat in Tripolitania. They had crossed the central region of Libya in a week with minimal fuel, and narrowly avoided encirclement from the vanguard of the Eighth Army with the help of local counterattacks and a liberal sprinkling of mines. By 29 December, the entirety of the *Panzerarmee* was behind the Buerat line as Montgomery, now at the end of his own elongated supply chain, once again embarked on a programme of methodical build-up and preparation.

It was only on 2 January that Rommel was finally given the permission that he had so desperately sought: to fall back (albeit slowly) to the much more defensible terrain of south-eastern Tunisia, around Gabes. After implementing a phased withdrawal, Tripoli was abandoned on 22 January in the face of a two-pronged British advance. The *Panzerarmee* took whatever supplies they could with them and left the port with demolitions only partially completed. By 26 January, most of the slower-moving Italian and German infantry units were already in Tunisia at the now-reinforced 'Mareth Line', the site of old French frontier defences. Rommel's few remaining Italian and German tanks, supported by small numbers of other armoured vehicles and motorised infantry, continued to act as a rearguard, and the last remnants of 15th Panzer only left Libya on 15 February. Battered, shorn of supplies and very low on tanks and vehicles, the *Panzerarmee* had nevertheless escaped. Rommel's reward for this remarkable feat was to be informed that he would be placed in command of 'Army Group Africa', the new unified command for all Axis forces in Tunisia.[15] He was replaced as head of the *Panzerarmee*, later renamed First Italian Army, by the Italian General Giovanni Messe. Reorganisation at operational-level command took place among the Allies as well. American General Dwight Eisenhower was installed as the Supreme Allied Commander in North Africa, at the head of the newly created Allied Forces Headquarters.

By 1943, the war in North Africa was thus solely confined to Tunisia, as Army Group Africa sought to conduct its 'active defence' on two fronts, against General Kenneth Anderson's Anglo-American First Army in the west, and Montgomery's Eighth Army in the south-east. The Axis 'active defence' had begun almost immediately after 'Torch', with Nehring quick to launch a counterattack westward against the advancing Allies. It succeeded in first halting the most advanced elements twelve miles from the vital city of Tunis on 27 November, before forcing them back to a more stable position further west on the night of 10 December. First Army spent the remainder of the year attempting poorly coordinated ineffectual attacks, and stalemate reigned in the north as the rainy season set in.[16] To the south-east, Rommel looked to conduct his own 'active defence', but was struggling to organise it in the manner that he wished.

As the remainder of the *Panzerarmee* withdrew to the Mareth Line, Rommel first launched attacks into central Tunisia against the First Army, combining elements of both the *Panzerarmee* and Fifth Panzer Army. The results were the Axis seizing the Fäid Pass on 30 January, and delivering a bloody nose to the Allies at Sidi Bou Zid and the Kasserine Pass in February. Although the Axis powers themselves had suffered unwelcome losses, these efforts had unified their front, halted the possibility of an Allied breakthrough in central Tunisia and bought time. At the end of February, Rommel asked his two army commanders, von Arnim and Messe, for their appreciations of the situation. Both agreed that it was hopeless to try and defend a front of 625 kilometres with just 120,000 men and 150 panzers in the face of 210,000 Allied troops and over 1,200 tanks. Getting sufficient supplies to sustain more than 350,000 men over such a widely dispersed area would be impossible. Rommel agreed, and saw withdrawal to a much shorter front as essential, yet this represented something of a deadly Catch-22. Shortening the front would ease the overland supply difficulty but would simultaneously remove all depth from their defensive position, cede important airfields to the enemy and expose them to increased air attack. Rommel maintained that withdrawal was the best and indeed only option. His repeated requests, however, were rebuffed by both Kesselring and Hitler.[17]

On 9 March, Rommel flew out of Tunisia to try and personally persuade Hitler to reconsider. Little did he know that Hitler, Mussolini and Keitel had just agreed that Tunisian territory should be held for as long as possible as a buffer while the defences in Italy were strengthened in preparation for the next Allied move. Despite the degrading situation on the ground, both Hitler and Mussolini continued to agree on the need to hold as much Tunisian ground as possible in March. Hitler even made the nonsensical claim that keeping the Axis forces there supplied by sea should be easy, citing a highly unfair comparison with the German campaign in Norway in 1940. He felt it only required greater efforts to be made by the Italian Navy and Merchant Marine, and streamlining of the supply organisation. Accordingly, he sent the new C-in-C of the German Navy, Karl Dönitz, to Italy in an attempt to 'fix' this problem.[18] Clearly, although there were still differences among the senior Axis leadership, overall perceptions of Tunisia had shifted towards those of near-inevitable final defeat. In spite of this, the Allies were finding the campaign there a very hard slog, and recognised the need to intensify anti-shipping efforts to aid the war on land.

The Allied political leaders and their military staffs had convened at a major conference at Casablanca in January, to discuss future strategy. One of the outcomes of the conference was an agreement, including grudging acceptance from the American JCOS, was for an Allied landing on Sicily, following completion of the Tunisian campaign.[19] As planning staffs prepared for Operation 'Husky' and earmarked resources, Eisenhower sounded a note of caution to Churchill in February regarding problems of training and sufficient landing craft. He also warned that the clearance of Tunisia required a 'major operation', and an expedited build-up of force and supplies but that the Tunisian campaign could not be rushed. Bringing forward an attack by the Eighth Army on the Mareth Line to a date earlier than 15 March would not be possible, and overall, he felt the destruction of Army Group Africa would not be achievable before the end of April.[20] He was to be proven right.

Eisenhower's telegram drew an immediate reaction of anger from Churchill over what he perceived as pessimism, but it also persuaded the Allies to expedite reinforcements for the fight in Tunisia, not just those to prepare for Husky.[21] It also led to a further intensification of focus on the Tunisian routes. Eisenhower had already warned in January that the volume of supplies and reinforcements reaching the enemy was 'a matter of grave concern. Unless this can be materially and immediately reduced, the situation both here and in Eighth Army area will deteriorate without doubt.' He urged yet more reinforcement of reconnaissance and torpedo aircraft, which should be based in north-east Algeria.[22] The combined COS agreed that it would be 'worth heavy air losses if a substantial proportion of the merchant shipping can be sunk', and a fresh squadron of FAA Albacores was ferried to Algeria by aircraft carrier as a first step.[23]

In order to foster a more co-ordinated use of Allied air power, a new theatre-level combined Mediterranean Air Command was created, with the experienced Tedder at its head. This organisation would sit atop both RAF Middle East and the newly created Northwest African Air Force. Allied airmen, including many in north-west Africa who were new to the theatre, were made aware of the importance of the anti-shipping role when Tedder set out a list of six objectives for Allied air power. Number three outlined the importance of attacking enemy shipping at sea and in port, as well as bombing both ports of departure and arrival.[24] Similarly, Bomber Command agreed to increase the number of raids against targets in northern Italy, including the port of La Spezia, which housed important shipbuilding and repair yards, as well as having become the main base for Italian capital ships. Overall, with an influx of new resources and new airfields available, 1943 saw a great increase in the bombing of southern European ports compared to 1942.[25]

As Allied aircraft, submarines and surface forces descended on the Tunisian sea lanes in an ever more concentrated effort into early spring, the offensive on land also restarted. The Germans had launched their last notable offensives, Operation 'Ochsenkopf' and 'Capri', in late February and early March. The former was an attempt to mount a spoiling attack in the north-west against Anderson's First Army and involved sending much of their best remaining armour, along with infantry and air support, against a natural defensive position in the mountainous terrain around Sidi Nsir. Although it succeeded in taking ground and pushing the frontline further away from Tunis and Bizerte, it fizzled out in early March a long way short of its stated objective at Beja. The losses suffered by the Axis were intolerable, amounting to 90 per cent of the tanks used, including some of the new heavy Tigers. The ground lost was promptly retaken by the Allies in early April. 'Capri' was an abortive frontal assault from the Mareth Line against an Eighth Army forewarned by intelligence, which ran into massed firepower and included the loss of fifty-five tanks for no gain, instead hastening the end of the Mareth Line position.[26] These efforts marked the end of any proactive Axis activity in Tunisia and were followed by the final Allied offensives to end the campaign.

Von Arnim had received orders from Comando Supremo that the Mareth Line must be held 'to the last', despite the vastly overstretched front. Yet in his orders to Messe, von Arnim stressed the importance of the defence, but also that a withdrawal would be allowed under his express orders.[27] After a week of preparatory air attacks on the line, the Eighth Army's assault began on the night of 16 March with Operation 'Pugilist'. Combining a frontal assault with a 'left hook' to flank the line, this successfully broke into the enemy positions before stalling. The follow-up Operation 'Supercharge II' was launched on 25 March and quickly took key heights and broke through the line in several places. With the position now completely untenable, Messe ordered a withdrawal on 28 March, which saw a retreat forty miles north to Wadi Akarit, the last natural defensive barrier against access to the coastal plain of Tunisia from the south.[28]

The Axis withdrawal had left them with a much-constricted foothold in northern Tunisia and allowed the two Allied armies to link up in a continuous front for the first time. The Allied emphasis was now on concluding the Tunisian campaign as quickly and effectively as possible, by securing victory on land and ensuring that there was no escape by the Axis forces back to mainland Europe.[29] All available means were to be used for interdiction of shipping to ensure there was no let-up in Army Group Africa's logistical crisis. As the Allies prepared for their final offensives, the Northwest African Air Force was issued with four key priorities, two of which were 'To disrupt the enemy's supply lines by air and sea' and 'To use every available aircraft to attack shipping or air transport if the enemy attempted a Dunkirk.' It was with this support that the Eighth Army launched its new assault on Wadi Akarit on 6 April, pushing the Axis back to Enfidaville, even further north. From 22 April, as part of Operation 'Vulcan', Anderson's First Army attacked all along its front. Although it met with fierce resistance in places, Axis positions were soon breached under the weight of superior land and air power. With the campaign clearly drawing to a close, some of the Allied anti-shipping efforts were in fact redirected against supplies to Sicily and Sardinia in late April, which represented potential future targets for invasion.[30] British troops entered Tunis, and American forces Bizerte, on 7 May, depriving the Axis of their two main ports. At the same time, Admiral Cunningham ordered the commencement of Operation 'Retribution', a series of intensified naval and air patrols in the straits to catch any attempted evacuation. He did so with the now famous Nelsonian line, 'Sink, burn, destroy. Let nothing pass.'[31]

Over 12–13 May, the remaining Axis forces bottled up in the Cape Bon peninsula surrendered. Accounts of the final number of prisoners vary but the most commonly cited total is around 250,000–275,000. The vast number is even larger than those who finally laid down their arms at Stalingrad earlier in the year, earning the moment the moniker 'Tunisgrad'.[32] The war in North Africa had finally ended.

'La rotta della morte': Anti-shipping Operations, December 1942–May 1943

From December onwards, the contribution to sinkings was shared much more between the different arms, as demonstrated by Table 7.1. Aircraft and submarines continued to be the main protagonists but there was a much-increased role for surface vessels, and a small but consistent contribution through mining. Having been formed at Bône in late November, Force Q quickly managed a spectacular success. On the night of 1–2 December, guided by intelligence and reconnaissance aircraft that illuminated the target convoys with flares, it struck a convoy of four merchant ships and three escorts. In a short but frantic night action, all four merchant ships, totalling 7,800 tons, were sent to the bottom along with

Table 7.1 *Numbers/tonnage of Axis shipping sunk, December 1942–May 1943*

	Surface vessel	Submarine	Aircraft	Mine	Shared	Total
December	5/8,382	16/37,198	21/29,846	5/10,350	3/10,761	50/96,537
January	13/15,223	30/39,873	13/41,605	3/14,383	1/6,107	60/117,191
February	0/0	29/52,259	28/44,433	3/1,734	0/0	60/98,426
March	2/6,912	43/49,873	46/68,776	2/145	0/0	93/125,706
April	5/9,944	32/53,630	53/63,020	3/664	3/11,904	96/139,162
May	4/5,344	19/14,129	94/101,086	1/3,099	0/0	118/123,658

Source: Calculated from TNA AIR 20/9598, Table 3: 'Analysis of Enemy Merchant Shipping Sunk by all Causes, Scuttled, Captured or Surrendered in the Mediterranean'; Röhwer, *Allied Submarine Attacks*.

an escorting destroyer. The success was greatly aided by the advantage of SIGINT and RDF, but also by superior night-fighting tactics and clever use of flash-less munitions to extend the confusion for the Italian escorts once battle was joined.[33]

The ships of Force Q suffered no damage whatsoever during the attack, although the destroyer *Quentin* was sunk by a torpedo bomber on the route home. The Axis response to such a devastating attack was to temporarily curtail lightly escorted night-time sailing and substitute daytime convoys with the maximum possible air escort. The decision wrested the initiative from the surface striking forces, but handed the advantage again to submarines and aircraft. The change was only brief however, while the Axis laid defensive minefields around the flanks of the Tunisian routes to hamper intervention from warships. Once this was completed, the emphasis returned to night-time sailings.[34]

The spectacular success of Force Q coincided with the decisive shift in focus to interdicting Tunisian, rather than Libyan, routes. Similar results from Forces K and Q were not immediately forthcoming, however. A combination of bad weather hampering reconnaissance aircraft and effective use of defensive mining by the Italians frustrated such hopes, and instead they were often sent out in a series of piecemeal 'sweeps' involving two to three warships each. Rather than targeting a specific and important convoy, these smaller operations generally consisted of destroyers being sent to patrol a busy shipping lane or area in the likelihood of encountering some easy targets. For example, two destroyers of the reformed Force K were repeatedly detached and sent to conduct antishipping sweeps in the target-rich area off the Tunisian and Tripolitanian coast throughout December and January.[35] The operations were simple – a sortie from Malta to the relevant coastal area where a two-hour sweep

Table 7.2 *Losses in anti-shipping operations, December 1942–May 1943*

	Surface vessels	Submarines	Aircraft
December	1	3	25
January	0	1	27
February	0	0	25
March	1	3	19
April	2	3	20
May	3	0	38

was conducted before returning. While rather haphazard, these could be very efficient operations when targets were located, achieving multiple sinkings of relatively small vessels for no loss in such a short time at sea. For example, one such sweep by HMS *Kelvin* and *Javelin* on the night of 19/20 January 1943 reported sinking two schooners, four small naval auxiliaries, a motor launch, one small merchant ship and three unidentified small steamships.[36]

The inclement weather and the need to adapt to completely new routes and conditions initially had detrimental effects on all forms of attack as they were switched to the Tunisian routes. Submarine patrols proved difficult, especially at first, as the waters were narrow and often difficult to navigate. This was coupled with the multiple defensive minefields laid by the Axis to cover the routes to Tunis and Bizerte, which hampered submarines just as much as surface forces. Finally, Italian ASW techniques had shown some notable improvement. Consequently, one submarine Captain called it 'quite the nastiest patrol area I have ever endured', while another admitted he hit a 'bad patch' in the period after 'Torch'.[37] These factors help explain the loss of three submarines in December, as shown in Table 7.2. Their scoring remained strong, however, quickly recovering from the difficulties of November, and was helped by the relocation of S8 from Gibraltar to Algiers in January, giving the flotilla easier access to the sea communication routes and a sole focus on the Mediterranean rather than its previous split remit with the Atlantic.

Having definitively switched to targeting Tunisian routes and ports of arrival in December, air power was wielded against them with increasing weight. In the first week of December alone, 128 aircraft bombed Bizerte, thirty-five attacked Tunis and twenty-four USAAF bombers hit Naples, all while eighty-two aircraft made direct attacks at sea.[38] Smaller Tunisian ports like Sfax and Sousse also started to receive attention that month, as Axis coastal shipping was passed down to them from the main ports, as did Palermo, which was regularly used as a stop during passage from Naples to Tunisia. Tunisian ports received 789 attacks in January, while 340 sorties were made against shipping at sea, and others against Italian ports. Although another 340 were made against shipping at sea in February, attacks on Tunisian ports declined to 185.[39]

Part of the reason for this decline was the fact that both senior leaders and aircrews operating out of north-west Africa lacked experience in the co-ordination and conduct of anti-shipping operations. This was evident in the initial decision to use some lumbering heavy USAAF bombers against shipping at sea rather than against ports, and the resulting failure to deliver results thanks to their lack of manoeuvrability. They were later reassigned to port bombing when it was recognised that they were much more suited to that role. It was also belatedly discovered that FAA Swordfish operating from Bône lacked the necessary range to cover most of the sea lanes, and time was lost while replacement Albacores were brought in.[40] Finally, the ongoing bad weather remained a factor over January and February. It was directly blamed by Tedder, and this was later repeated by Portal in response to a query from Churchill about the comparative lack of results despite such huge efforts by air power.[41] An improvement in the weather was certainly one factor behind the improved results from March onwards, as was the arrival of Wellingtons equipped with the new ASV Mk III set to overcome ASV jamming. The Axis had been able to concentrate their ASV jamming efforts more successfully over the Tunisian routes as they were closer to the jamming stations, hampering efforts in January and February.[42]

Portal himself expressed concerns about the augmented air defence of Axis convoys, stating that this was the greatest cause of loss of aircraft, a claim subsequently supported by operational research. This reflects increased Axis efforts to counter the threat of aircraft that had been instituted by the 'Comitato per la organizzazione e la protezione dei trasporti per l'Africa' since its creation in September.[43] By early 1943, convoys thus generally exhibited greater anti-aircraft firepower. At this stage, much of the new building taking place were of smaller Siebel Ferries and F-Lighters that possessed powerful armaments of German built guns ranging from 20mm to 88mm, and were often crewed by German specialists. In part this dated from the ongoing efforts spurred by the Comitato, but also from increased pressure from senior German voices into 1943, including Hitler, Dönitz and the Reich Commissioner for Shipping, Karl Kaufmann.[44] Operational research records indicate that over January and February this was indeed the greatest cause of loss among strike aircraft, and Table 7.2 demonstrates a small monthly increase over those two months compared to late 1942.[45]

The Axis also benefited from the constriction of the area of operation in North Africa, as it allowed them to concentrate their remaining air power assets and hold an advantage or rough parity in the air over northern Tunisia and the straits through to late January.[46] For some on the Allied side, this very intensification of air defence was itself a marker of success and the subsequent Axis desperation, despite the problems it caused. In Tedder's words:

> The degree of air protection now being given by the enemy to his shipping both at sea and in port is clear indication of the crippling effect of our successful shipping strikes on his land operations in Tunisia. Our pressure, if maintained, will prove decisive, but we have now been forced almost entirely off day strikes.[47]

From late December, a concerted effort was made by the Allied Air Forces in north-west Africa to wrest aerial superiority from their opponents, by attacking enemy airfields in greater strength and conducting aggressive fighter sweeps. By February the Axis were at a 3:1 disadvantage in aircraft and also had to contend with dwindling fuel stocks, meaning they had definitively ceded a contest that they recognised as vital to ensuring the supply situation.[48] In this context, monthly Allied losses in anti-shipping operations dropped over March and April, and while they ballooned to thirty-eight in May, many of these came from more dangerous operations in the straits of Messina or around Sardinia, as some aircraft were switched to this role in late April.[49] There were also aerial attacks on shipping in the Aegean by No. 201 Group over March–May, which one operational research report claimed were a 'blow ... aimed at enemy morale'. In fact, it seems likely that they were intended as part of the deception operations to suggest an impending Allied landing in Greece, rather than Sicily. Beaufighters, Wellingtons and Baltimores were all used to attack traffic in Aegean and off the west coast of Greece. The report estimated at least 2,340 tons of shipping was sunk plus another 3,385 damaged and that by mid-June day sailings in these areas had almost ceased. It therefore concluded that the effect on morale on the islands was 'probably considerable', although it offered no clear evidence of this.[50]

Along with aircraft, concerns dogged the Axis about British submarine operations, and similar efforts were made to counter these. Mussolini outlined the need for more escorts and Kaufmann ordered the conversion of some seized French vessels into submarine chasers in January, but urged that more of the building capacity was given to the creation of specialised ASW vessels. Concurrently, a report for the Italian high command stressed the 'capital importance' of defending sea communications and the need for more ASW vessels and increased anti-submarine minelaying.[51] These increased countermeasures had an effect, with six submarines lost over March and April: four of them to ASW vessels and the other two mined.[52] Yet this was not nearly enough to stem the tide of shipping losses. Axis production, especially from Italian shipyards, was very slow. The conversions from French vessels were of relatively low quality, and the escorts themselves suffered grievously. In the first six weeks of 1943 alone, fifteen were either sunk or put out of action for the remainder of the Tunisian campaign.[53] British submarines were thus able to inflict their heaviest losses of the war to date over March and April, although their opportunities were rather more restricted in May after the Axis surrender.

During March and April, with such overwhelming air and naval superiority, the Allies descended on the Tunisian routes in an orgy of destruction. Aircraft and submarines were again the primary contributors, although surface forces and mining also contributed. Over those two months alone, 189 vessels of 264,868 tons were sunk, almost exclusively on the Tunisian routes. May eclipsed all other months to that point or to follow, however, with 118 sinkings totalling 123,658 tons, although many of these came after the surrender in Tunisia. Given these devastating losses, it is hardly surprising that Italian sailors nicknamed the Tunisian route 'La rotta della morte': 'The route of death.'[54]

'Supplies Disastrous': Operational Effects during the Tunisian Campaign

Withdrawal to Tunisia meant that the Axis now relied on fewer and shorter sea approaches, while the overland distances they were faced with were nothing like those suffered previously across Libya and Egypt. Nevertheless, Allied superiority in the air and at sea enabled their ability to interdict them, especially from March onwards, and the supply needs remained great. In mid-January, Kesselring claimed that 60,000 tons a month reaching Tunisia would be enough to defend the region, while Hitler promised a highly improbable monthly delivery of 150,000.[55] Other estimates differed. Rommel later retrospectively claimed that 140,000 tons of supplies would have been required per month to defend the position in Tunisia from a major combined offensive from both sides. Admiral Riccardi made a similar claim at the end of January 1943, saying that 132,000 tons (including 35,000 of fuel) were required at that stage, but did not expressly state that was a requirement for each month. He also went on to claim that the Navy could only transport a maximum of 70,000.[56] Warlimont claimed in February that a minimum of 70,000 tons a month could sustain the forces and proposed offensive actions on the south-eastern front so long as it was strictly used for military purposes. He, von Arnim and the new chief of the Italian armed forces General Ambrosio all agreed that 80–90,000 tons would be a much more

Table 7.3 *Cargo tonnages despatched and landed in Tunisia, November 1942–May 1943*

	Ammunition		%	Fuel		%	Total	Total	%
	Sent	Landed	Lost	Sent	Landed	Lost	sent	landed	Lost
November	5,166	5,166	0	11,947	11,947	0	34,339	34,339	0
December	13,993	8,278	41	23,911	14,838	38	84,804	60,619	29
January	15,139	11,268	26	29,522	25,580	13	88,933	70,193	21
February	14,802	12,406	16	25,598	14,798	42	77,781	60,038	23
March	18,661	12,010	36	22,912	16,634	27	77,193	49,361	36
April	15,877	11,481	28	17,678	10,052	43	48,703	28,623	41
May	8,511	2,197	74	954	623	35	14,416	3,359	77

Source: Calculated from USMM, *LMI*, Vol. 1, *Dati Statistici*, Table LX, p. 135.

comfortable total for this though, while up to 150,000 would be required if civilian populations were included.[57]

As Table 7.3 demonstrates, while there was no effect in November, Allied efforts prevented 20–30 per cent of supplies arriving in Tunisia each month from December to February. Although these were significant proportions, the question of whether they prevented the Axis from receiving their required supplies depends on which set of requirement figures is used. The 60,000 per month specified by Kesselring for Fifth Panzer Army was met in each of these months, albeit just barely. The Axis clearly attempted to ship enough to meet Warlimont's minimal 70,000 or preferred 80–90,000 tons per month over December–March. Yet sinkings at sea prevented the minimum of 70,000 from actually arriving in Tunisia in every month except January, when that mark was narrowly achieved. As for any of the higher figures of over 100,000, no month ever saw that amount being attempted in the first place. If the immediate effect of losses at sea at these times is a little ambiguous, what is clear is that the total losses of shipping were impacting on the ability to send the required resources in the first place. By December, only 140,000 tons of shipping was immediately serviceable for the Tunisian route thanks to the losses to date and the extremely high proportion of vessels under repair; as much as 53 per cent of all shipping space in the Italian area, according to some sources.[58]

While this situation was partly relieved by the acquisition of French shipping (initially 450,000 tons, later over 700,000) from late November onwards, this was a slow process. Less than half of the tonnage was 'even remotely seaworthy' according to Kaufmann, and most of that which was seaworthy still needed work first, slowing its introduction. Some were

Illustration 7.1 Sunken vessels litter Bizerte Harbour, May 1943. Anti-shipping operations reached their peak intensity during the Tunisian campaign, while the major destination ports there received repeated bombing raids. The losses suffered during the period led Italian sailors to christen the journey 'le rotte delle morte', or 'the route of death'.
Source: www.gettyimages.co.uk/detail/news-photo/bombed-out-buildings-sunken-vessels-in-lagoon-after-allied-news-photo/50864420?adppopup=true
Credit: Margaret Bourke-White / The LIFE Picture Collection via Getty Images

also large liners, which were unsuited or unable to be used for the task at hand, while others were required for use in the Adriatic or Aegean.[59] Ultimately, only a small proportion of this seized tonnage, possibly even below 100,000 tons, was ever used on Tunisian routes.[60] Given that the combined maximum capacity of the five largest Tunisian ports was 225,000 tons per month when unmolested, it is clear that the total shipping losses had a major impact, as rarely more than a third of this quantity was attempted in any one month. This stands in stark contrast to claims made by the Italian Official History, among others, that the quantities delivered to North Africa were only significantly limited by the maximum capacity of the ports.[61]

As has been noted, the impact of this failure to receive the required supplies did not translate into immediate Allied success in Tunisia, as progress on both fronts was slow over the winter. On Tunisia's western front, this was due to a number of factors. The fact the Allies landed so far to the west for Operation 'Torch' (over 600 miles from Tunis) gave Nehring and his successor von Arnim vital time to prepare an active defence, while the Anglo-American build-up and concentration was also slow. First Army also attempted the first major combination of Anglo-American forces in the field, and they approached this new task by integrating units right down to the battalion level. This led to chaos thanks to differing British and American (and later French) equipment, doctrine and styles of command, along with frictions at all levels. The results in terms of combat effectiveness were so poor that it was never tried again. Furthermore, it was by necessity led by inexperienced commanders and consisted of largely green troops who struggled to integrate tanks and infantry, in comparison to their more experienced opponents who were also able to concentrate their limited air power resources at first to gain a degree of parity. Finally, torrential rains in December put paid to offensive hopes for several months.[62] To the south-east, the issue was simpler. Montgomery's Eighth Army was far more experienced and lacked the immediate complexities of large-scale alliance warfare, but in line with the slow pursuit after El Alamein, the advance into Tunisia was gradual and methodical. Given that a significant defensive position would have to be dealt with, Montgomery continued his preferred method of waiting for a major build-up of forces and supplies, hampered by his own long logistical chain.[63]

The Axis did suffer from supply shortages over December–February, notably of fuel, but these were not enough to prevent them from exploiting their superior fighting effectiveness over the First Army in particular. They achieved a series of tactical successes in these months, most notably at Longstop Hill, Sidi Bou Zid and the Kasserine Pass.[64] While these frustrated the Allies, they were far from decisive victories for the Axis, which failed to build the necessary supplies or requested reinforcements, thanks to the paucity of remaining operational shipping. By early February, von Arnim complained to Kesselring that 'The Army could not fight with shells which were at the bottom of the Mediterranean' and was forced to notify Warlimont that this and the lack of fuel meant that Fifth Panzer Army was no longer fit for major operations. Kesselring recommended that von Arnim's force needed at least two more major mobile formations, ideally divisions, as soon as possible. While efforts were made, the lack of shipping ensured they never fully arrived, elements instead gradually appeared piecemeal and often under-strength over January–April. By the end of January, there were just 74,000 Germans and 26,000 Italians in northern Tunisia, plus 30,000 and 48,000 respectively in the south-east. In 1943 efforts to increase the transport of manpower by using fast destroyers and aircraft allowed quicker and in some cases safer transit for a time, but could not solve the problem of vital tanks, vehicles and heavy equipment, which still had to come via slow, vulnerable merchant ships.[65]

The lack of sufficient supplies and combat mass meant that the Axis victories achieved up to February were of a limited nature, even their famous success at Kasserine Pass, and contributed only to stalemate in Tunisia. From then onwards, the ongoing supply problem became completely unsustainable and the tide shifted inexorably towards their ultimate defeat. As Warlimont himself put it in a visit to Tunisia, the logistical situation would soon lead the entire position to collapse 'like a house of cards', before hinting that an evacuation should be mounted.[66] When the Axis spoiling operations 'Ochsenkopf' and 'Capri' were launched in late February and early March, it was without sufficient forces and supplies thanks to shipping losses on both the main routes, and along the Tunisian coast to the smaller ports of Sfax, Sousse and Gabes. These latter ports were effectively neutralised by February, thanks to Allied bombing and coastal interdiction by aircraft and submarines.[67] The operations quickly resulted in costly failures and only hastened the end in Tunisia.

The botched 'Capri' was Rommel's last direct involvement in North Africa, and he was not present for the subsequent Battle of the Mareth Line in late March, which the Axis had to face while suffering from critical shortages. Reports from 10th Panzer division highlighted the 'gravest concern' regarding these shortages which were forcing them to be extremely conservative with what they had. The entire First Italian Army was down to less than one issue for all types of ammunition, with stocks for armoured and anti-aircraft units especially low at 0.5 and 0.6 issues respectively.[68] The fuel situation was little better. Diesel supplies for the Italian units were felt to be 'urgently necessary', as stocks were almost depleted, and aviation fuel was desperately short. The Army did have a slightly better fuel supply overall by 26 March, but it was still just 1.6 CUs.[69]

The fuel situation quickly worsened, and the loss of tanks, vehicles and spares at sea was adding to the Axis losses in the land war itself, greatly hampering serviceability among armoured and motorised units. On 27 March, the Panzer Grenadier Afrika formation reported it was down to just 0.8 CUs of fuel and its last two serviceable vehicles. Nothing was available to be sent from elsewhere in Tunisia to address this crisis; all depot stocks in Tunisia were empty of ammunition for 20mm weapons and medium field howitzers, while stocks for the infantry and anti-tank units were just 0.4 and 0.3 issues respectively. Anti-aircraft and heavier artillery stocks were little better. Von Arnim made an urgent appeal for additional fuel, artillery ammunition and mines to be sent across the Mediterranean, but even if there had been the shipping to do this, it was too late.[70] The last major defensive position on the south-eastern front was lost by the end of the month.

Von Arnim kept up his futile efforts after the battle, complaining directly to OKW 'Supplies disastrous. Ammunition for 1–2 days, nothing left in the depot for heavy artillery. Petrol similar, major movements no longer permitted. No ships for several days. Supplies and provisions only for one week.'[71] Yet fewer than 50,000 tons of all types had reached Tunisia in March, followed by just 28,623 in April. Armoured and motorised units soon lacked the fuel to conduct anything other than basic movement, and later not even that. The regiments of 21st Panzer division, for example, were variously down to between 0.2 and 0.5 CUs of fuel. This meant they did not even have the necessary fuel to bring up supplies, vehicles and artillery from rear areas, let alone conduct effective combat operations.[72] By 1 April, German Naval Command Tunisia confessed that due to lack of fuel for MT, any ammunition that did arrive from Italy could no longer even be delivered to the nearby forces of the Fifth Panzer Army.[73] Given that nearly half of the fuel sent that month was lost at sea, and little more than 10,000 tons of fuel and 11,000 of ammunition were successfully shipped, only miniscule amounts were distributed by various improvised means. Increasingly desperate pleas thus came from frontline units; 10th Panzer division had less than one CU of fuel and reported that some munition types were completely exhausted and others nearing it, 15th Panzer 'urgently' requested medium artillery shells, but over a third of the ammunition shipped in March had been sunk.[74]

Despite the arrival of some fuel supplies early in April, thanks largely to a special effort to ensure the arrival of the tanker *Regina*, by the night of the 7th, the German divisions in Tunisia still only each held between 0.4 and 0.8 CUs. The remaining Italian armoured and motorised units were soon reduced to acting in static defence roles while the mobility of the German armoured divisions was felt to have been 'crippled'. Von Arnim advised Kesselring that only short movements were possible for the better-supplied units, but most units were being forced to move on foot.[75] By the middle of April the Axis forces were crippled by the lack of fuel, ammunition and transport as anything other than token shipping efforts virtually ceased. The Chief Quartermaster of Army Group Africa reported at the end of April that all units were down to just 0.2 CUs, while depots were virtually empty. By 2 May, all divisions except 10th Panzer had run out of fuel entirely. Five days later, the last remaining serviceable Axis aircraft in Tunisia were ordered to evacuate under the cover of darkness, while the last Italian aircraft left on the 12th.[76]

In light of these crippling shortages, the Allied offensives on both fronts brought quick success despite certain instances of bitter Axis resistance where the terrain favoured static defence. The resource-starved Axis forces eroded under constant pressure from the massive Allied superiority in all arms, and there were occasions when the Allies were able to exploit greater manoeuvrability alongside their greater firepower.[77] As the end approached, Operation 'Retribution' was launched to prevent any evacuation by sea, alongside Operation 'Flax' to stymie any efforts by air. The question of a full-scale evacuation had been discussed by various Axis political and military leaders at several points over spring, and was urged by some, including Rommel, but was never very seriously considered. Both Hitler and Mussolini seem to have clung to the hope that Tunisia could have been held right up to May, probably encouraged by overly optimistic reports from some quarters. Hitler then issued one of his characteristic 'fight to the last round' orders, officially precluding any attempt.[78]

It is highly unlikely that a different policy would have mattered, however, as even ignoring Allied control of the air and sea, they simply lacked the shipping to pull off an 'Axis Dunkirk'. Kesselring had admitted as much to Messe on 16 April, noting they lacked anything like the means required to remove nearly 300,000 men. By late April, the Italians could offer only around 70,000 tons of shipping for Tunisia, with nothing additional immediately forthcoming from the French tonnage.[79] Other, more realistic options were considered, such as evacuating only selected German units or senior staff, but this proved impossible.[80] Even von Arnim's hope to ship 7,000 sick, wounded and civilians fell apart, as the three ships he had assigned to the task were all damaged or sunk by air attack before loading had even started. Orders for a limited evacuation of German headquarters personnel on 7 May suffered a similar fate.[81] Ultimately, evacuation never got further than a few scattered, very small-scale attempts at improvised endeavour. Men tried to slip past the naval cordon in the darkness in a variety of small craft and even rowboats, and around 800 were captured in groups ranging in size from a handful to over 100. Some other vessels were sunk or rounded up by patrolling coastal forces. Efforts at airlift suffered even worse, as 'Flax' accounted for the destruction of more than 400 Axis transport aircraft. Only a few succeeded in escaping by air and sea, with sources giving totals ranging from 600 to 800.[82]

The anti-shipping campaign, now pursued with the aid of American air power, had clearly positively influenced the war in Tunisia for the Allies and prevented any Axis escape, but the ramifications of attrition to Axis shipping were actually much wider.

For Want of a Ship: Shipping Losses and the Collapse of the Axis Position

By the end of September 1942, it was clear to the Axis that they were approaching a shipping crisis in the Mediterranean. They had lost a total of 486 ships totalling 1,188,206 tons to enemy action since June 1940, to which must be added the losses by other or unknown causes, and the large quantity of shipping under repair. By contrast, the Italians only launched 295,303 tons of newly constructed shipping over the whole of 1940–42, supplemented by those vessels they purchased, those constructed or transferred to the theatre by the Germans and those seized from defeated nations.[83]

In an attempt to stem the impact of shipping losses, a renewed programme of construction for the Italian Merchant Marine was announced in September, to be accompanied by an increased focus on escort units in naval production. It planned for 129 ships of 577,210 tons made from steel, plus thirty ships of 54,000 tons constructed from reinforced concrete. The highly ambitious project (which was ultimately unrealised) required a vast input of additional material, notably 25,000 tons of steel over October–December 1942 alone, which only Germany could provide. Even if that was provided, and the full quota of 11,000 workers assigned to the merchant marine focused solely on the project, it could not be completed before February 1944 at the earliest. It was thought that the addition of 3,000 more workers would expedite this to November 1943, but it was not clear where this skilled manpower could be found.[84] The emergency construction programme was planned to run alongside the construction already scheduled for 1943, pushing the timetable back further to August 1944 and exacerbating Italy's perennial problem of paucity in raw and semi-finished materials. It also retained an imbalance in the assignment of skilled shipyard workers. Of the 48,242 shipyard workers as of 1 August, 25,650 were assigned to new military construction and just 10,932 to mercantile construction. In an indication of just how much damage had been inflicted during the anti-shipping campaign and against the Navy, the remaining 11,660 were dedicated to repair work.[85]

The emergency programme, therefore, did not seem likely to fix the immediate problem of shipping requirements for North Africa, let alone across the whole Mediterranean. As Mussolini pointed out at a high-level conference on 1 October:

Remember that in addition to supplying the ongoing war we must supply Sardinia and Sicily, Dalmatia, Albania and Greece, not to mention the coastal shipping which must continue to take place, albeit in small scale. The problem which the Merchant Marine has therefore been faced with is that related to the different armed forces, because it is closely connected to them.

It was admitted that in order for the programme to be realised there would need to be a great increase in raw materials, expanded plants and machinery, sufficient workers, and most of all help from Germany.[86]

Taking the floor at the meeting, Italy's Minister of Communications, Giovanni Host-Venturi, emphasised that leaving aside new construction, there was a deficit of 167,000 tons of merchant shipping for the minimum needs across the theatre and at home. Increasing traffic to somewhere like Tunisia would further degrade the situation elsewhere, as 'Any additional demand for ships for military needs affects transport for food and of those for the war industry.' He warned against the temptation to reduce transport for non-military purposes as doing so would then impact the import of raw materials, which were needed for the construction of new shipping, among other things. It was a vicious cycle that seemed to lack any quick solution. Host-Venturi could not even say whether the new construction would actually result in an overall increase in shipping or form only a replacement of losses, as it depended on whether enemy action continued in terms of scale and efficacy. Mussolini's mournful, and rather belated, response to Italy's myriad problems was simply that they should not have entered the war until 1942![87]

Similar concerns were expressed by the Germans around this time, with Kaufmann warning in October that with the current rate of loss, the time would soon arrive when there was simply not enough shipping to keep North Africa supplied. The OKW was clear that plenty of materiel was sitting in Italy awaiting transit to keep the Axis forces supplied, but the question of actually transporting it was vexing.[88] The solution to the crisis seemed to lie in the form of French tonnage, and many were initially confident that seizing what was available after the occupation of Vichy territories would rectify the shortage of capacity. Kaufmann boasted to Hitler in December that the process of seizing, readying and utilising it would be quick and easy. Kesselring offered his Führer similar assurances and the more cautious Host-Venturi, although bemoaning in January the loss of six ships for every new one being built, noted that 'we can look with some serenity to the situation due to the availability of 400,000 tons of French shipping'. The reality proved extremely different. It soon became apparent that not all the vessels were in a seaworthy condition, while the vast majority were incapable of carrying the tanks and heavy equipment that was needed in Tunisia.[89]

By early February, Kaufmann reported a total of 742,037 tons as having been 'procured', yet only 107 vessels of 356,610 tons were actually seaworthy and had been transferred to Italian ports. The rest needed further refit, or more serious repair, while some were considered too damaged or unseaworthy to be worth the effort. The vessels were split roughly 60:40 between Italian and German control, although some were still not ready for full service, while others were earmarked for the Aegean and the Black Sea. Given the increasing losses on the Tunisian route, Kaufmann was also forced to repurpose fifteen of the smaller vessels to be used as makeshift escorts. He warned that despite the increase in tonnage, the current rate of loss would make it 'impossible to ensure the necessary supplies for Tunis'. Kesselring also recognised that the French tonnage did not represent a panacea and made a similar admission, much to Hitler's fury.[90] Numerous efforts were made to reinvigorate emergency building programmes, stimulate the repair of damaged shipping, to improve the management and administration of shipyards (generally by increasing German control), or to bring the parts to construct small vessels from Germany to southern France and Italy by rail or inland waterways. Hitler even urged the abandonment of all safety regulations in ship design in order to speed construction, as 'life jackets were much easier to make than bulkheads'.[91]

It was too late to save the situation in the central Mediterranean, however. By mid-April a total of 132 former French or neutral merchant vessels of 464,000 tons had been taken over and made serviceable. Of these, 34/145,000 were heavily damaged and in long–term repair, and 37/118,000 had been sunk. A further 18/49,000 were sent to the Adriatic and Aegean and 2/4,000 to Black sea, leaving just 41/148,000 for the Tunisian route, Sardinia, Corsica, Sicily and coastal shipping combined.[92] Although this could be supplemented by some of the remaining original Italian tonnage and the efforts to concentrate very small vessels in the theatre, it was clearly insufficient for Axis needs and the ramifications were great, reaching beyond the shores of Tunisia.

The combined impact of sheer attrition to shipping and the Axis focus on Tunisia with what was available led to dire shortages elsewhere. These were perhaps most evident in the case of Sardinia, despite the fact that only limited attempts had been made to attack its supply routes directly. The heavy losses sustained by Axis shipping meant they were forced to economise on shipping space to Sardinia in order to free up more vessels for North Africa, particularly from October 1942 onwards.[93] The squeeze on supplies quickly made itself felt on the island, and as the greatest Axis need in North Africa was fuel, it was this resource that saw the greatest economisation. By late November, German authorities in Sardinia were complaining that the fuel situation had become 'very strained'.[94]

This was problematic for the Axis powers, as Sardinia remained an important air base from which to menace Allied convoys through the western basin to Algeria or to Malta. The former was particularly crucial if there was to be a serious attempt to retain a long-term foothold in

Tunisia. Sinking ships carrying supplies to the Allied First Army would have a detrimental effect on their ability to mount major offensives, and thus aid the Axis defence. In March 1943, Kesselring thus emphasised the 'importance to smash Allied seaborne supplies' as 'Every ship destroyed gives most effective support to the defensive battle.'[95] The dearth of incoming supplies, however, greatly hampered the ability to prosecute such efforts. Much of this was simply the result of a lack of shipping due to losses and commitments elsewhere, but it was exacerbated by several major bombing raids. The key Sardinian port of Cagliari was attacked multiple times from February to May. Ten large vessels were sunk in the harbour, along with an unknown number of auxiliaries. After a raid on 28 February, it was concluded that greater use would have to be made of the port of Olbia in the north due to damage an obstruction by wrecks. By the aftermath of the raid of 13 May, the majority of quays and moles were unserviceable, and the cumulative damage had rendered the port 'almost completely useless'.[96]

By late March, fuel stocks were sufficiently low to significantly hamper air operations. Not only that, but insufficient spares were arriving in order to keep the aircraft serviceable. Of the sixty-two German aircraft on the island on 7 April, only thirty-three were in a serviceable state.[97] The situation continued to worsen, with an appreciation on 5 May showing that for all but one of the airbases on the island, stocks of aviation fuel were very low, and in one case held just two tons. Olbia, the one exception, had 193 tons, but the central tank depot for the island was completely empty. Daily consumption even for restricted operations was placed at 29 tons, meaning stocks at Olbia would have to be shared around in order to keep some of the airfields operational at all.[98] During November 1942, the Allies did lose over 100,000 tons of shipping to a variety of causes including air attack, but due to this strangulation of Axis supplies and to Allied air raids on airfields, this threat quickly diminished the following spring. While forty-five Allied merchant ships were lost over January–March 1943 the tonnages were much lower, and just nineteen were lost in the following three months.[99] While unwelcome, these losses were well within the Allied capacity to cope and much lower than some of the early concerns about potential loss rates, particularly from the American JCOS. The Allies were comfortably able to meet and exceed their supply demands by sea to the Algerian ports for the First Army and attached air forces.[100]

Similar issues were felt in Corsica, although as its supply routes with Italy were shorter and more distant from Allied air and naval bases, supplying it was a safer prospect. Even Sicily was feeling great strain, partly due to the attrition to shipping, and partly to Italy's general lack of raw material and the exportation of so much war materiel out of the country. Weichold claimed that in February, 'there were days in which, throughout the whole of Sicily, there was not even a ton of fuel to be found'.[101] Just after the Axis surrender in Tunisia, Admiral Dönitz estimated the monthly supply requirements of Sardinia at 80,000 tons and Corsica 20,000. He felt that the period of 'relative calm' after the fall of Tunisia should be used to build up stocks of supplies in Sicily, Sardinia and Corsica. However, he also appreciated that due to heavy losses, there was not sufficient shipping available in the Mediterranean to do this, and greater efforts should be made to increase the amount available.[102]

This was problematic given that the ramifications of the shipping crisis stretched as far as the Aegean, where the shortage of tankers was especially felt. By August 1942 aviation fuel on Crete was sufficiently low that air transport to Africa had to be suspended, which had further exacerbated the supply problem for Rommel. The situation quickly worsened, and intercepted GAF signals demonstrated that they laid the blame on the breakdown of the tanker service in the Aegean.[103] From September to November, a crucial period of the war in North Africa, the fuel situation in Crete was 'in crisis', greatly curtailing the operation of transport aircraft.[104] In such a situation, even the small number of sinkings in the Aegean could have a direct effect. The torpedoing of the tanker *Arca* in October further worsened the situation and forced another tanker to be transferred there.[105] Not only were transport flights suffering, but the lack of fuel being delivered to Aegean territories affected the ability to fly convoy escort sorties there and in the eastern basin.

While they remained small, sinkings in the Aegean did increase in 1943, as aircraft from No. 201 Group and submarines of S1 intensified their attacks from March onwards. While attacks did increase, the potential threat to shipping was often considered worse by Axis authorities than the actual results. The paucity of escort forces available meant that a handful of attacks in a concentrated area often caused the suspension of shipping, even on very short routes. This was further exacerbated by the increased mining efforts; while still limited, they resulted in further Axis shipping suspension due to a lack of minesweepers. The sinkings and shipping suspensions worsened the supply situation on the islands, and by early April the Axis naval commander in the Aegean warned that ASW operations were being curtailed and would soon have to cease due to lack of fuel.[106]

The reverses on land in North Africa had been highly damaging to the Axis, but the attrition to shipping was precipitating a collapse of the broader Axis position in the Mediterranean. As will be shown in the next chapter, hopes to sustain Sardinia and Corsica after the loss of North Africa proved impossible, and the seeds for their abandonment were already being sewn. The Axis position in the central Mediterranean was soon to collapse entirely.

8 After North Africa

A Theatre Transformed

By late May 1943, the Mediterranean was a theatre transformed. The Axis had been expelled from Africa and the Allies held a unified position across its northern coast. The vital west–east through-route had been restored to the Allies, although shipping traversing it still remained under threat from Axis air power, U-boats and the remainder of the Italian surface fleet. In the immediate aftermath of the Tunisian campaign, there was something of a lull in the theatre, as both sides prepared for their next moves. The Allies remained committed to a landing on Sicily, as agreed at Casablanca in January although the Mediterranean strategy remained a notable bone of Anglo-American tension.

It was the question of what to do after Sicily which greatly vexed the alliance, due to fundamental national differences in preferred strategies. The potential avenues for follow-up Mediterranean operations seemed numerous and highly attractive to both Churchill and his COS. Landing on mainland Italy would likely knock the Italians out of the war for good, and provide a southern route into Europe via what Churchill called the 'soft underbelly'. Alternatively, an operation to take Sardinia and Corsica would provide useful air bases for intensifying bombing raids. These could be used as a means to force Italian capitulation without a costly mainland invasion, and to pin German forces down in southern France. Another option, the personal preference of Churchill, was an Aegean offensive. Success there might fulfil his ambition of bringing Turkey into the war on the Allied side, a possibility that had been supported by the British planning staff prior to 'Torch'.[1] This would also have the benefits of cutting an Axis seaborne oil supply route from Romania and providing a base for a possible landing in south-east Europe. British planners produced a raft of studies into each of these options and their relative merits while a British delegation travelled to Washington in May for the 'Trident' Allied conference.[2]

Unfortunately for Churchill, the Americans were near-unanimous in their opposition to all these ideas. The JCOS produced a memorandum, coinciding with the Axis surrender in Tunisia, that heartily extolled a 'Germany first' approach. Yet it conflicted directly with the British hopes for a Mediterranean strategy by stating that 'from our standpoint the concept of defeating Germany first involves a determined attack against Germany on the continent at the earliest practicable date; we consider that all proposed operations in Europe should be judged primarily on their contribution to that end'.[3] The debate on this issue was frequently robust, and sometimes bordered on hostile, as the Americans argued their case much more coherently than they had done at Casablanca. The broadly held American perspective was that any attempt to strike at Germany overland via a southern route would be hampered by difficult terrain and logistical issues. The best approach was therefore to focus the main effort on a cross-channel attack; any major Mediterranean diversions of manpower and resources would simply delay this for what would probably only be marginal gains. American planners were, however, prepared to consider more limited post-'Husky' exploitation in order to ensure Italian defeat, draw German resources away from the eastern front and north-west Europe, and to provide useful air bases for the combined bomber offensive. The upshot was a compromise outcome from the conference; both sides agreed that a cross-channel assault was ultimately the way to defeat Germany, but in the meantime exploitation could take place in the Mediterranean and further planning for this could begin immediately.[4]

One objective that linked all the planned and proposed targets for future Allied attack in-theatre was the desire for 'maximum removal of the threat to Allied sea communications in the Mediterranean'.[5] These continued to be threatened after the fall of North Africa, primarily by Axis aircraft operating from bases in Sardinia, Sicily, southern Italy and Crete. Allied and neutral merchant ships continued to suffer considerable losses over the second half of 1943.[6] The need to remove this threat left a clear role for continued anti-shipping operations in the Mediterranean. As the Joint Planning Staff noted earlier in the year when considering an assault on Sardinia: 'It will be necessary to take the maximum offensive action through the whole operation against enemy reinforcements attempting to reach the island. Submarine patrols and air attacks on shipping will be required to the maximum intensity.' Not only would such operations restrict reinforcements to island territories during a fight for its control, but it would continue the effect already achieved of hampering the ability of air forces to operate from them for lack of fuel and munitions. While the use of surface vessels to this end was considered unlikely, due to the risk from air attack and coastal batteries, two highly experienced FAA torpedo bomber squadrons were reassigned to attack Sicilian and Sardinian traffic even before the Tunisian campaign had culminated. Submarines from S8 were also frequently directed to patrol the lanes from Italy to Sardinia and Corsica for enemy shipping.[7]

By contrast, Kesselring's immediate focus at the time of the Tunisian surrender was to use the subsequent lull in major operations to build up forces and stores in Sardinia, Sicily and southern Italy as much as possible. This would enable them to continue attacks on Allied shipping and to resist amphibious assault. Doenitz emphasised the necessity of safeguarding sea communications as an essential duty in order to achieve this, and even suggested increased use of submarines and cruisers for supply-carrying purposes. Doenitz and Kesselring were in agreement that the issue of maritime supply continued to be a vital one, and that the greatest possible advantage should be taken of the relative lull in the Mediterranean war to supply the islands. Doenitz was adamant that while shipping losses to date had been damaging, there was sufficient tonnage remaining to achieve the required supply rates – a view shared by Kaufmann.[8]

The lull in the Mediterranean did not last long, however. The Allied preparations for 'Husky' continued apace, albeit with frictions, and were masked by a series of deception efforts that had been ongoing since the New Year but were now increased. These were to persuade the Axis powers that rather than Sicily, the next target would be Sardinia, Greece, Crete or other islands in the Aegean. The most famous of these was Operation 'Mincemeat', and the planting of false plans on the body of the 'man that never was', but this was just one amongst many. Dummy forces in North Africa, misleading signals and double agents all contributed to this end, as did the use of force. Bombing raids and anti-shipping operations by aircraft and submarines were also used in the Aegean and Adriatic to give the appearance of shaping operations in those areas. Overall, the numerous deception efforts achieved some success, helping, alongside other factors, to limit the German presence on the island when 'Husky' took place.[9]

On the morning of 10 July units of the US Seventh Army and the Anglo-Canadian Eighth Army landed in southern Sicily, having been preceded by airborne drops the night before. Battle was thus joined in what would prove to be an arduous campaign with sluggish progress. Initial gains were easy, as the Allies were opposed largely by Italian coastal divisions and poor-quality fixed defences. These reserve formations were very poorly equipped and trained, and often quick to surrender in a war for which they had little appetite.[10] This led to severe criticism of their efforts by Mussolini, especially at Augusta, 'where there wasn't resistance worthy of the name'. He also recognised, as did others, the dangers of the 'shocking' Allied superiority in the air and at sea. This led him to suggest that the straits of Messina needed greater levels of anti-aircraft defence, as the main reinforcement route for the island.[11]

The Allies recognised the benefits of interdicting these reinforcements, with Eisenhower ascribing a critical status to it during the planning of the operation.[12] Naval and air forces were allocated to this task accordingly, although roles in directly supporting the land forces or protecting the coasts consistently consumed greater quantities of resources. The air plan for 'Husky' had been split into three phases; the first of these was the degradation of Axis air forces through the targeting of airfields and production capabilities in the theatre, which had been ongoing since the Tunisian campaign. The second, which spanned the week prior to invasion, focused more narrowly on destroying Axis air power on the island itself, as well as disrupting both sea and land lines of communication. Finally, from the landings onward, air power would directly support the land forces, in the form of both close air support and interdiction.[13] The naval element of the plan had a similar remit. Their main task involved ensuring the safe passage of convoys through the western Mediterranean during the build-up of forces for the invasion. This was then followed by the primary need to protect the landing of the assault forces themselves, and to shield Allied shipping carrying men and materiel during the campaign.[14] Offensive support for the land forces frequently took the form of naval gunfire support, but also of anti-shipping operations. Having been focused on guarding against a sortie of the Italian fleet against the invasion fleet, or acting in support of the landings in a variety of ways, submarines were later allotted to the interdiction of shipping north of the island.[15] Additionally, on 21 July, a nightly patrol of coastal forces was instigated from captured Sicilian ports, to prowl the straits of Messina each night until the end of the campaign.[16]

After the initial success of the landings themselves, the Allies soon found the going much tougher in the face of strengthened Axis resistance, led by German formations on the island. Two weeks into the Sicilian campaign, however, a big step was taken towards the Allied strategic aim of knocking Italy out of the war. On 25 July, the Fascist Grand Council ousted Mussolini from his position and had him imprisoned. Although his successor, Badoglio, vowed to continue the war with the Axis, there was little belief in the veracity of this on either side, and in fact secret peace feelers to the Allies were soon extended.

Progress on the island itself remained slow, as the Allies battled stout resistance from the Axis positions around Mount Etna followed by a well-co-ordinated phased withdrawal. The bitter Axis defensive effort there bought time for them to attempt to evacuate their remaining forces from the island.

The day after the deposition of Mussolini, Hitler ordered Kesslering to make preparations for the evacuation of German troops from Sicily, and the withdrawal of excess materiel began almost immediately. High-level authorisation for the actual evacuation of troops was slow in coming, however, and so the German operational commander on the island (General Hube) took the initiative. On 4 August he authorised the shipping of units that were not essential for combat across the straits. This was the beginning of the German evacuation, Operation 'Lehrgang', and full-scale withdrawal took place from 11 to 17 August. The Italians ran their own evacuation beginning on 3 August, entirely independently of the Germans and with relatively little co-operation, given that they ran side by side.[17]

The Allies had become aware of the Axis evacuation by 4 August through a combination of human intelligence, SIGINT and aerial reconnaissance.[18] The discovery gave them renewed impetus for conducting anti-shipping operations, along with a recognition that these efforts would primarily need to be delivered through air power. While submarine and coastal forces continued their own operations, it was never possible for them to commit in any great scale, while the straits were considered far too dangerous to risk naval warships in the face of powerful shore batteries. Both British and American senior naval officers agreed warships could be used only if the shore batteries were somehow neutralised by other means. The one exception to this rule came when Force Q was authorised to conduct a sweep and bombard the Calabrian reception port of Vibo Valentia on the night of 16 August.[19] Unfortunately, no plans had been prepared for the use of air power against evacuation shipping in the straits. Authorisation for the use of the tactical branch of the Northwest African Air Forces against this traffic came first, followed by its strategic arm, with their heavy bombers, on 5 August. Despite this, both Tedder and 'Hap' Arnold (the head of the USAAF), had espoused the view that the main purpose of the available heavy bombers was to bomb the strategic targets of Rome, the Ploesti oilfields and German airfields in southern France. These were ultimately given the higher priority, and received attacks by a combined total of over 450 Allied aircraft during the period of the evacuation.[20] By 17 August the evacuation had been completed, and Sicily was wholly in Allied hands.

The loss of the island, along with the fall of Mussolini, persuaded the Germans to expedite their planning for an Italian exit from the war, and hardened their expectation of an armistice to near-certainty. Planning for this had been under consideration since the late stages of the Tunisian campaign, but Operation 'Achse' only emerged shortly after Mussolini's deposal.[21] It called for the occupation of all territories under Italian control, the disarming of the Italian armed forces, the seizure of heavy weaponry and equipment and the withdrawal of German forces from Sardinia to Corsica and thence to mainland Italy. While the initial plan earmarked Corsica purely as a staging post to be abandoned along with Sardinia, many in both OKW and the German naval command in Rome felt that the island could be held alongside northern and perhaps central Italy. After brief consideration, it was ultimately decided four days after the Italian armistice that the island would have to be evacuated.[22] In August, OKW issued directives to the German Naval staff on their measures as part of Operation Achse:

> To execute the evacuation from Sicily and Sardinia and provide transport from non-French ports. To establish coastal traffic along the Italian coast as required by the land operations. To assume control of Toulon. To assume the naval duties of coast defence ... and take over Italian naval vessels and merchantmen and prevent them from going over to the enemy.[23]

The announcement of the Italian armistice, when it finally came on 8 September to coincide with Allied landings in southern Italy, was botched. In the reverse of the German approach, the Italian armed forces were completely unprepared, and units were left with few or no orders as the political and military leadership looked to escape. Much of the Italian Army and remnants of their air forces were rounded up with ease, leaving only some to resist bloodily on isolated islands or to join up with the Allies in southern Italy. Only the Navy successfully escaped, reaching Malta almost entirely intact.[24] A new Italian 'co-belligerent' government was created in southern Italy under Badoglio to bring the remnants of the Italian forces onto the Allied side in October.

While the turmoil of 'Achse' unfolded on the mainland, a protracted argument developed between Hitler and his military commanders over how the operation should manifest in the Aegean. Hitler had unequivocally expressed his desire to retain a presence there, to secure the maritime link with the Black Sea for Romanian oil and to deter Turkey from bowing to Allied pressure to join them in the war. Despite clear and near-unanimous opposition from his military chiefs, German strategy crystallised in October around a directive to hold not only a line south of Rome but also the entirety of the Balkans and the Ionian and Aegean islands.[25]

While the evacuation of Sardinia and Corsica offered an opportunity for anti-shipping operations to interdict German forces bound for Italy, it was only brief, and the withdrawal was completed by early October, narrowly ahead of Allied forces which had been landed. Thanks to Hitler, the corresponding opportunity in the Aegean was longer-term, and it linked into much bolder ambitions held by Churchill. He had long coveted the idea of an Aegean offensive, where he believed success could seduce Turkey to enter the war on the Allied side as well as open up a new route for supplies to the Soviet Union, close the ring around Germany more tightly and offer further opportunities for an offensive into south-eastern Europe.[26] The Italian armistice seemed to offer a golden opportunity to secure the Aegean with minimal use of force, as there was little German presence on the islands other than Crete and Rhodes. Furthermore, it was hoped that the disillusioned Italians would actively assist arriving British forces and fight the Germans.[27]

The Aegean venture found no support from the Americans, who still viewed the Mediterranean as a subsidiary theatre where the only effort should be on the Italian mainland. This prevented forces under the command of Allied Forces Headquarters from taking part in it without express permission from Eisenhower, leaving only the limited British forces of Middle East Command to take part. Consequently, they lacked sufficient available combat mass to attempt to crack the strongly held Rhodes (Operation 'Accolade') immediately, and hopes of an Italian-led coup-de-main were foiled by swift German action to disarm the garrison.[28] Nevertheless, the British persevered by landing a small task force on the Dodecanese islands of Kos, Leros and Samos, with the aim of building up sufficient force in the future to tackle Rhodes and its key airfields. Their arrival initially caused panic amongst the Germans, and one of the responses considered was a full evacuation of the Aegean, although worries abounded that a scarcity of shipping space would make this a very slow or even impossible process. The Fuehrer admitted the situation was highly precarious but was adamant that evacuation could not take place due to the likely political ramifications; that Turkey could join the Allies.[29]

The German decision to remain in the Aegean launched a race with the British, as both sides attempted to build up their own forces while preventing the other from doing so. Accordingly, warships from the Navy's Levant force were issued two tasks: building up British forces on newly acquired islands and intercepting Axis shipping from Piraeus to the Dodecanese. Anti-shipping operations thus became one of their primary duties, and they were frequently directed to sweep the area for enemy shipping. The policy for S1 during the Dodecanese campaign was even more focused around anti-shipping operations: their priorities were to prevent enemy troops landing on British-held islands and to interdict German supplies to their own islands.[30] The Germans were able, however, to assault and retake Kos over 3–4 October and deprive the British of their only airstrip in the Aegean.

Given the German decision to contest the region and the paucity of available British forces, those in Middle East Command felt that they would have to secure American backing to sustain the venture. During a meeting in October, they agreed that the benefits of 'Accolade' had to be extolled persuasively to Eisenhower at an upcoming theatre-level Allied conference at La Marsa in Tunisia. Their case was two-fold: first it would divert German forces away from other theatres, and second it would provide excellent bases for naval and air striking forces in the Aegean. The latter of these two perceived benefits was therefore at least partially an argument for the concerted extension of anti-shipping efforts into the Aegean. It was not an argument that Eisenhower or his staff found convincing, and they categorically rejected the argument at La Marsa. 'Accolade' was suspended once more and only the brief loan of some USAAF long-range fighters was secured.[31] The fallout was brutal for the Dodecanese campaign. The Germans assaulted Leros on 12 November, landing by air and sea, and after bitter close-quarters fighting the garrison surrendered on the 16th. The campaign closed two days later with the evacuation of Samos.

Even after the abject failure of the Dodecanese campaign, the British nursed ambitions to bring Turkey into the war on the Allied side. They also had other reasons for continuing to contest German control of the Aegean: those of tightening the ring and forcing the Germans to spread their resources more thinly. For the Middle East C-in-Cs, the greatest immediate operational boon would be that it could allow the stationing of forces in Turkish territory for which 'The primary object ... was the offensive object of attacking enemy sea and air communications in the Aegean.'[32] Even without the ability to do this, there remained an incentive for attacking these communications as 'an energetic air and naval campaign against enemy communications in the Aegean, begun early in the New Year, might achieve its object of rendering the Dodecanese untenable to the Germans before the earliest date at which the assault on Rhodes could be staged.'[33] The Aegean thus offered an opportunity for the anti-shipping campaign to retain a role into 1944, as did the continued coastal shipping in the Adriatic and along the west coast of Italy. Coastal shipping offered the Germans a potential route to alleviating the burden on their road and rail networks in Italy, while successful interdiction would deny them this opportunity. Such efforts reached a peak in spring 1944 as part of the wider Operation 'Strangle'. This was a concerted effort to interdict German logistics using air power and starve their forces defending the powerful Gustav Line of vital supplies in preparation for the next offensive against it. Although primarily focused on road and rail traffic, coastal convoys were fully incorporated within the planning and prosecution of 'Strangle'.[34]

Although anti-shipping operations were accorded a much-decreased priority over 1944, and numerous warships, aircraft and submarines were withdrawn for service in other theatres, it was only late in that year that the campaign ceased to have any continued role. By September the Allies had advanced beyond the Pisa–Florence–Rimini line, and while the Italian campaign remained an attritional slog on land, the potential for coastal convoys to play a role had virtually vanished. The Soviets were making fast progress to the east, however. In the face of repeated requests from OKW, Hitler authorised evacuation of the Aegean in September, after Bulgaria declared war on Germany. This was followed by approval to evacuate Greece, southern Albania, southern Macedonia and the Dalmatian islands in early October. By the end of that month seaborne withdrawal ceased, and although a small number of troops remained on a few islands, the reason for any further Allied anti-shipping operations was removed.[35]

Anti-shipping Operations through to the End of the Campaign

From the completion of the Tunisian campaign through to the end of July, supplies heading to Sicily from mainland Italy were the primary target of anti-shipping operations. The Sicilian ports of Palermo and Messina had been on the receiving end of increasingly powerful bombing raids since January, as had those in southern mainland Italy. The planning for 'Husky' had mandated the need to interrupt shipping as part of the preparatory measures, in order to erode resistance to the landings, and it was felt that attacking the key departure and arrival ports was the best way to do this.[36] These ports were raided by a total of 3,872 aircraft over the three-month period, while another 270 attacked key ports in August up to the completion of the evacuation.[37] The drop in port attacks over the first half of August did not represent a cessation of air power's involvement in the maritime element of the Sicilian campaign, but rather a shift to direct attacks in an attempt to halt the evacuation shipping. In June and July combined, there were a total of 419 direct attacks against shipping across the whole theatre, not just around Sicily. Over the evacuation period of 1–17 August, there were 2,753 direct attacks solely against shipping from

U. 288   Air Force Strike, Messina Sicily, June 18, 1943. Direct hits on ferry ships and   26 YI
          and administration buildings were made in this raid.

Illustration 8.1 Image from an Allied bombing raid, Messina, Sicily, June 1943. Direct hits on ferry ships and administration buildings were made in this raid and many others, but ultimately the Axis forces were able to successfully evacuate in August.
Source: www.gettyimages.co.uk/detail/news-photo/air-force-strike-messina-sicily-june-18-1943-direct-hits-on-news-photo/540446126?adppopup=true
Credit: George Rinhart / Corbis Historical via Getty Images

Sicily, with the intensity at its greatest during the same period that the evacuation reached its peak – 11–17 August. Here, Wellington bombers were switched to attacking the shipping itself rather than focusing on ports, while some days saw more than 200 fighter bombers swarm over the routes.[38] The air attacks generally took place at night, even after Hube switched the evacuation shipping largely to daytime sailings in response to the damage taken.[39]

Air power was by a large margin the greatest weapon the Allies could wield against the Sicilian traffic. From early in the 'Husky' planning process, it had been assumed that the heavy coastal battery defences and mining of the straits of Messina would keep it closed to Allied surface warships and submarines.[40] The creation of a dedicated coastal forces patrol on 21 July did alter this slightly, but with little impact. According to the local German artillery commander, Axis batteries around the Messina straits had 'daily engagements' since the 12th with Allied light naval forces. Yet after opening fire on them, even at 'great ranges', the ships would simply put down smoke and disengage.[41] On one occasion, an attempted sortie by four British motor torpedo boats met the Italian light cruiser *Scipione Africano*, and they promptly withdrew after it sank one of their number and damaged another two.[42] The sole involvement of heavier warships came on the night of 16 August, when Force Q ventured into the straits to search for shipping and bombard Vibo Valentia. They sank only a single Italian barge and the damage they caused in the bombardment was to have little effect as the evacuation was almost completed.[43] Submarines were positioned in cordons over July, both to protect Allied shipping from any sortie by the Italian fleet and to interdict any supply shipping. Yet the former never emerged and the latter proved extremely difficult. 'A disappointing lack of [large] targets' appeared north or east of Sicily after the landings, and the multitude of very small vessels often had a draught that was too shallow for a successful torpedo attack. The ideal solution to this was to surface and attack with the gun, but this was highly dangerous in such close proximity to the enemy-held coastlines. While eight very small vessels were successfully sunk in gun attacks, several submarines were damaged in the process.[44]

As demonstrated in Table 8.1, aircraft managed to sink seventy-four vessels of 105,975 tons over the June–August period. Not all of these sinkings were related to Sicily, as some came from the routes to Sardinia

Table 8.1 *Numbers/tonnage of Axis shipping sunk, June–December 1943*

	Surface vessel	Submarine	Aircraft	Mine	Shared	Total
June	2/5,041	24/43,468	19/31,418	2/1,463	0/0	47/81,390
July	2/12,657	40/28,736	27/36,228	3/2,436	0/0	72/80,057
August	2/1,949	8/12,007	28/38,329	1/1,416	0/0	39/53,701
September	4/8,526	27/30,664	8/15,433	7/11,085	0/0	46/65,708
October	7/16,314	15/28,777	6/13,646	2/1,496	0/0	30/60,233
November	0/0	26/9,721	9/10,463	1/253	0/0	36/20,437
December	1/1,200	21/34,713	9/9,970	2/676	0/0	33/46,559

Source: Calculated from TNA AIR 20/9598, Table 3: 'Analysis of Enemy Merchant Shipping Sunk by all Causes, Scuttled, Captured or Surrendered in the Mediterranean'; Röhwer, *Allied Submarine Attacks*.

and Corsica, and a small number of others from the Aegean or off the west coast of Greece. Given both their heavy involvement with other duties related to the Sicilian campaign and the dangers of interdiction within range of powerful shore batteries, the contribution of surface vessels in this period was very small. Submarines sank almost as many vessels as the aircraft: seventy-two totalling 84,211 tons. Few of these, however, were part of the Sicilian traffic as they enjoyed much greater success in the waters around Corsica during this time.[45]

The success achieved by aircraft can be seen as relatively small when viewed in comparison to their scale of effort, and their operation over the straits was hampered by several factors. First, the shipping used there by the Axis consisted of a ferry service supplemented by a plethora of barges, Siebel ferries and other minor craft.[46] These small craft were very difficult to target at sea accurately, and this was exacerbated by the intensity of defensive flak, which forced attacking aircraft to drop payloads from altitudes of between 500 and 2,000 metres and so reduced accuracy further.[47] This flak also inflicted substantial losses on the attackers.

Recognising its importance, the Axis had managed to concentrate a series of powerful anti-aircraft guns on both sides of the straits of Messina. Allied intelligence noted that 'The importance with which the Axis powers regard the maintenance of the ferry service is reflected in the countermeasures taken against our bombing attacks.' They estimated that there had been a 50 per cent increase in heavy guns over the first half of 1943.[48] There are conflicting reports of the precise number of guns, but sources generally agree on a total of over 250 distributed across both sides of the straits, and perhaps as many as 500 of all types when dual-purpose weapons are included. Whatever the actual total, it was the heaviest concentration in such a small area faced throughout the war in the Mediterranean, and was considered by some aircrew to be worse than that over the Ruhr.[49] Over the June–August period, seventy aircraft were lost during anti-shipping attacks or while port bombing, with well above half of these losses coming over the straits of Messina and associated ports.[50]

Table 8.2 *Losses in anti-shipping operations, June–December 1943*

	Surface vessels	Submarines	Aircraft
June	2	0	24
July	2	0	22
August	1	2	24
September	0	1	15
October	4	2	8
November	3	1	9
December	0	0	6

As Table 8.2 demonstrates, the scale of losses dropped dramatically after the conclusion of the Sicilian campaign. By contrast the losses to the other arms over the same period were small, with just five coastal forces and two submarines, and neither of the latter were lost near Sicily.[51]

As the Sicilian campaign drew to a close, air sweeps from Malta for shipping around the western Mediterranean and off the coast of Greece were still frequent.[52] Sardinia and later Corsica remained common targets, and numerous Allied bombing raids took place to sink shipping and damage ports. Seventy bombers raided the port of Olbia in June, utterly destroying one steamer and damaging three others, along with the port facilities. Another raid on Livorno, the key departure port, caused substantial damage to six of the warships and merchant vessels present and significant casualties among the workers due to a surprising lack of air raid facilities. Livorno was hit again in September by a total of eighty-two Wellingtons, as evacuation efforts were reaching their peak.[53]

At the time of their evacuation, submarines were moderately active in the region, and sank several small vessels through a mix of torpedo and gunfire. The most notable success was the sinking of the 9,946-ton steamer *Champagne* off Bastia. This was attacked on at least three separate occasions between 24 and 27 September, first being badly damaged, and then rendered a constructive loss. Significant air attack also occurred on the Corsica–Livorno route, which led to the loss of the *Tiberiade* and a variety of minor vessels, causing consternation for the German naval staff in the theatre.[54] There was no interference with the evacuation traffic from Allied surface warships, however. Most were busy with other tasks, but a group of French destroyers which had landed troops on Corsica were available in the vicinity. The reasons for their lack of engagement with the lightly defended minor vessels remain unclear, although Axis air cover remained a threat at this stage.[55]

The conquests of Sicily, Sardinia and Corsica removed the majority of shipping targets from the western and central Mediterranean, with only coastal shipping and those plying the short trans-Adriatic route remaining. These routes were still targeted, notably during the aerial interdiction of Operation 'Strangle' in spring 1944, but the areas generally remained fairly quiet. Impetus remained for the Aegean though, as the British embarked on their ill-fated adventure there. The Aegean remained the one area of the broadly defined Mediterranean theatre where the Germans retained aerial superiority. They boasted airfields in the immediate vicinity, on Rhodes and Crete and in mainland Greece where they were thought to have concentrated a combined total of 350 fighters. By contrast, the nearest Allied airfield was 270 miles away in Cyprus, while it was 350 miles to Gambut, the nearest airfield in North

Africa. This meant that Germany could cover the Aegean with regular sweeps from high-performance single-engine fighters, while the Allies were right at the extreme limit of range for lower-performance twin-engine fighters.[56]

The danger of German air power had been recognised in the lead-up to the Dodecanese campaign. Rhodes was considered a key target for the very reason of it containing major airfields, while the Mediterranean Air Command made the decision to allocate 100 B25s in southern Italy to bomb Greek airfields as a preparatory measure. It was the view of the head of RAF Middle East that this would degrade the Axis ability to operate aircraft over the Aegean. He even suggested that they could put off appealing to the Americans for the loan of four Lightning squadrons if this proved to be accurate.[57] Ultimately it proved to be inaccurate, and the Germans were able to exercise air power with freedom, causing havoc amongst both the assault and occupation forces and those assigned to anti-shipping operations.

Aircraft, surface vessels and submarines were all used in an attempt to sever German communications in the Aegean and prevent their re-conquest of Kos and Leros. Baltimore aircraft were regularly used for shipping searches, with aerial strike forces of Beaufighters and Marauders sent out based on their reports, along with those of photographic reconnaissance aircraft and of SIGINT. These reports were patchy, however, as searching aircraft frequently failed to locate targets, or the information was out of date once strike forces reached the area. The distances involved for aircraft magnified this problem, and gave little scope for aircraft to fulfil both search and strike roles, while further problems were caused by the 'skilful concealment policy' operated by the Germans for their shipping. SIGINT and HUMINT (human intelligence) were unable to satisfactorily fill this void, as they also gave patchy and incomplete returns.[58] From the British occupation of the islands through to the evacuation of Samos, they mounted a total of sixty-four attacks on shipping and German harbours across the Aegean, using a total of 360 aircraft.[59]

Submarines were intended to play an important role in the campaign, and additional boats were transferred to S1 from S8 and S10 in recognition of this. They initially concentrated on traffic supplying Rhodes during September, before switching to the interdiction of assault shipping to attack Kos and Leros in October. After the fall of Leros their task was simply converted to the general sinking of shipping in the area where possible.[60] Their greatest individual success, however, came outside of the Aegean; the Polish *Sokol* managed to sink the 7,094-ton *Eridania* in the Adriatic in early October while on passage to the area. Some modest sinkings were achieved, such as the 1,925-ton *Kari* in October, which was carrying 500 German troops, and the 1,855-ton *Trapani* in November. Yet most of their contribution in the Aegean came in the form of more than twenty very small vessels such as caiques and lighters being sunk with the gun, or on occasion boarded and sunk with a demolition charge after the crew's surrender. The prevalence of these very small craft and the lack of large targets negated their most powerful weapon, the torpedo, and restricted their ability to cause much overall damage despite regular patrolling.[61]

Finally, warships were frequently tasked with running sweeps of the Aegean to catch Axis convoys and prevent them retaking the islands occupied by the British. Following the loss of Kos, the 12th Cruiser Squadron along with five destroyers from Malta were allocated to the Aegean and immediately began night-time patrols. On the night of 6–7 October, they successfully intercepted a key German convoy. Known as the *Olympus* convoy after its lead escort, eight of the nine vessels were sunk and around 400 Germans were killed. Similar patrols took place over the next two nights but failed to find substantial targets, while the latter was caught by the GAF in daylight on the return leg. HMS *Panther* was sunk and the *Carlisle* badly damaged. The ongoing threat from aircraft soon persuaded the Royal Navy to alter the policy to prevent cruisers from entering the Aegean and to act solely as cover on the approach to and from the area, leaving only a weakened force of destroyers to contest the sea routes.[62]

From this point onwards, the destroyer force laid up in Turkish territorial waters by day for protection, venturing into the battle zone only at night in the hope of preventing an assault on Leros that intelligence suggested was imminent. The distance from Alexandria, the brief night-time window available for sweeps and patchy intelligence made interceptions very difficult. One sweep on the night of 15 October chased a convoy but failed to catch it before being heavily bombed without loss. Another on the next night had more luck, finding a small merchant ship off Kos along with two auxiliary craft, which it promptly sank. Several bombardments of German ports and harbours on nearby islands also took place, sinking the occasional vessel, but none of the sweeps after 5 October succeeded in delivering a truly serious blow to German sea communications. There were, however, further losses to air attack, including the use of new remotely controlled glider bombs that heavily damaged the destroyer *Rockwood* and sank the *Dulverton*. After the landings on Leros, Royal Navy warships were switched to evacuating Samos and then Leros itself, and although a few landing craft filled with German troops for Leros were opportunistically sunk, anti-shipping operations during the Dodecanese campaign had effectively ended.[63] During the campaign, nine German merchant vessels of around 18,000 tons were sunk, alongside a large number of very small vessels that is difficult to precisely calculate, but was likely around forty vessels of 50–100 tons each. For this the Navy lost four destroyers, two submarines and several coastal vessels, and received significant damage to four cruisers and six destroyers.[64]

The conclusion of the evacuation of Corsica and the Dodecanese campaign did not end anti-shipping operations, although they were scaled back even further. Continued shipping in the Aegean to supply the island territories Hitler was desperate to hold formed an ongoing target. So did that across the Adriatic, intended to compensate for poor overland communications when supplying forces in Greece, and that along the coast of Italy. Anti-shipping operations thus continued, with notable effect, immediately after the completion of the Corsica evacuation and Dodecanese campaign, as evidenced by the sinking of nearly 50,000 tons in December. Some of these actions are worthy of special mention, such as the submarine *Sokol* ambushing a convoy of five caiques on the surface in the Aegean and sinking four of them in a hectic mid-December night action. Elsewhere that month, destroyers exploited what was now a rare opportunity in the western basin to sink a 5,000-ton supply ship and a 4,000-ton tanker off the Tuscany coast while the submarine *Uproar* torpedoed the 11,702-ton liner *Veriglio*. Bombers flew nearly 1,500 sorties against Italian, Yugoslavian and French ports over November and December, resulting in the sinking of six vessels of over 500 tons, the largest of which was the 8,446-ton *Mar Bianco*.[65]

Clearly anti-shipping operations continued through to the end of 1943 with both significant effort and result, and in fact they persisted throughout 1944, albeit in decreasing scale thanks to lower priority, decreasing numbers of available forces and fewer targets. Over the course of the year, direct attacks by aircraft against shipping at sea represented a miniscule proportion of the overall effort of the newly restructured Mediterranean Allied Air Forces. In any one month they never reached as much as 4 per cent of the overall type of sorties conducted and they averaged less than 2 per cent for the whole year. Yet this still reached a substantial total of 1,148 sorties over twelve months and demonstrated that efforts to interdict German shipping by air power were also ongoing.[66] Confronted with a multitude of very small targets, the aircraft involved were frequently equipped with appropriate weaponry like the cannon and the newly introduced rocket projectile. This had already been in use by Coastal Command for some time, and was first introduced to the Mediterranean in 1943. By 1944 it had seen wide-scale distribution and was incorporated successfully thanks to the effective inter-theatre transfer of knowledge.[67] While this aided them in sinking large numbers of small craft, there were some larger victims, the most famous of which was the 51,062-ton liner *Rex*. After setting sail on a mission to be used as a blockship in September 1944 it was attacked by a total of twenty-eight aircraft and destroyed in a deluge of cannon and rocket fire.[68] Through a mixture of direct attacks and port bombing, aircraft sank a total of 225 vessels of 321,589 tons in 1944; this was the most successful method by far.[69]

It was not the only method utilised, as surface vessels and submarines each contributed to varying degrees. The combined issues of lack of numbers, other priorities and remaining threats from German countermeasures limited the involvement of larger warships, although occasional destroyer sweeps were still made with some success. The main involvement on the surface instead came from coastal forces, which were more suited to engaging the smaller types of target that had become prominent. These gained some success in areas such as the Adriatic after a new base was established on the tiny island of Vis, allowing them easier access to the traffic present there, and causing considerable consternation.[70] Nevertheless, over the year they only managed to sink thirty-two vessels of generally very small types, totalling just 8,669 tons. By contrast, submarines had a much more successful year, although a lack of large targets hampered them somewhat. They sank 154 vessels, although these only totalled 75,500 tons as many were smaller types sunk in surface actions using the gun. When sinkings through minelaying are incorporated, the overall tally for 1944 comes to 422, totalling 421,285 tons. Ultimately, while the average size of vessels sunk was much smaller than previous years, the total number was actually greater than any year except 1943.[71] The effects on the crumbling Axis position in the Mediterranean were tangible.

The Final Collapse

While the Axis hoped to use the post-Tunisia lull in activity to supply their island outposts, they were met with the combined problem of steep demand and limited shipping. In May, the Italian Naval Ministry estimated the monthly cargo requirements of Sicily as 160,000 tons, along with 50,000 for Sardinia and 20,000 for Corsica.[72] In June, Kaufmann noted that supply of Sicily, Sardinia and Corsica was 'essential' and took stock of the remaining shipping still available for the task. There were still 350,000 tons of large Italian ships remaining, along with about 800 small vessels of 50–500 tons, plus a small remainder of the ex-French tonnage (around 27,500 tons) that was not going to be being sent to the Aegean (which would receive 69,000) or the Black Sea (22,964).[73]

Deeming this total inadequate, Kaufmann set out a schedule to supplement this with increased production of very small vessels; 85 ferry barges and 59 Siebel ferries were to be available in the Italian area by August. Yet this did not solve the immediate problem of supply and Kaufmann was also forced to acknowledge the need for greatly increased supply of both raw materials for construction and manpower to form the necessary crews, as current reserves in the theatre were exhausted. He appealed to the Fuehrer to have the Wehrmacht release necessary personnel to man the ships, with limited success.[74] By July, the proposed new construction had fallen well behind schedule, barely more than 50 per cent of the projected vessels having been delivered and the manpower shortage still unsolved. Thus, although Warlimont urged Kaufmann that the 'Transport situation in the Aegean and Black Sea requires the quickest possible reinforcement of shipping space in exploitation of all available resources', Kaufmann was forced to admit this was not possible with the ongoing difficulties and requirements in the central and western Mediterranean.[75]

The deficiency in shipping space frustrated the Axis hopes to exploit a period of relative calm and supply their island territories. In a conference of senior Italian military leaders on 5 July, Ambrosio announced that the supply situation for Sardinia was 'in crisis'. The quantity of supplies arriving was well below the capacity of the Sardinian ports, due to the lack of suitable vessels available. Thus, even though Allied sinkings were comparatively few on this route, they were having sufficient effect to degrade the island yet further. Despite efforts to alleviate it, the island was almost devoid of aviation fuel, having sufficient supplies for just two days of non-intensive operations. The following month supplies to the island by sea were ceased entirely in favour of supplying Corsica, whose much lower requirements proved far easier to fulfil.[76]

In the same meeting of 5 July, Ambrosio identified the primary difficulty in supplying Sicily as being the exact opposite of that in Sardinia: port capacity. The very short distances involved made the supply routes less vulnerable and the use of very small craft far more possible in comparison. Alternate ways of supplying the island and bolstering port capacity had been under examination since at least May, but several proposals proved difficult. Landing stores directly onto Sicilian beaches, for example, raised problems of their subsequent dispersal over underdeveloped road networks.[77] Thus reliance on the ports remained, and while traffic to places like Palermo could provide some of the total, the greatest burden fell on that coming across the straits of Messina. Allied bombing of ports on both sides of this narrow strip of water had certainly had some effect prior to 'Husky'. Damage to port facilities slowed their operation, while the ferries themselves were periodically damaged and put out of service, although never permanently.[78]

Allied disruption efforts spurred the Axis to prioritise military supplies for Sicily more ruthlessly over those for civil purposes as a countermeasure, and by the time of 'Husky' the supply situation on the island was rather mixed.[79] In May, the commander of Italian forces in Sicily, General Roatta, had delivered a scathing assessment of the forces under his command and the situation in Sicily. He noted the poor state of equipment and lack of munitions for his troops, the weakness of coastal and air defences and the lack of construction material to reinforce them or construct new ones. His feeling was that in the event of an Allied landing, 'we can only make an honourable resistance'. The provisions for both Italian units and coastal defences beyond the straits improved little up until the invasion.[80] Elsewhere, though, the situation was more positive. At the time of the collapse in Tunisia, there had been serious shortages in Sicily, and the scarcity of aviation fuel was considered bad enough that it was 'seriously imperilling' the use of fighter aircraft based on the island. Yet just before 'Husky', air forces in Sicily were conducting wide-ranging operations thanks to a sufficient fuel supply. One Italian Admiral reported that in the last ten days of June, the supplies shipped to Sicily averaged 1,737 tons a day.[81] When Operation 'Husky' was launched on 9 July, German forces were actually adequately provisioned. Italian forces were in a much less fortuitous position, as they relied increasingly on allocations of fuel and other materiel from the Germans, who were increasingly suspicious of the Italian will to fight.[82]

There is little evidence that anti-shipping operations had a significant effect on Axis fighting effectiveness during the Sicilian campaign, as it remained possible for the Axis to keep a steady flow of supplies moving across the straits of Messina. In fact, enough was transferred to cause congestion at Porto Molino on the Sicilian side.[83] Intercepted reports generally suggested that supplies of ammunition, fuel and rations were sufficient for the German forces on the island throughout the campaign. While there were occasions when certain types of ammunition ran low, these never reached the difficulties of the worst periods in North Africa, and could generally be quickly recognised by the transport authorities and acted against.[84]

Alongside this stream of supplies, it was also possible to send across reinforcements to the island, and much of the *Hermann Goering* division was transferred there successfully in the lead-up to and early stages of the campaign.[85] Additionally, the supply difficulties that were suffered were not necessarily the result of anti-shipping operations. Bombing raids and attacks on the straits were successful in causing heavy damage to the port facilities and berths at Villa San Giovanni and Reggio di Calabria, at one point reducing them to having only a single train ferry running. Yet the others were brought back into service, while the slack was picked up by the use of Siebel ferries and F-lighters. By contrast, the attacks on train stations and railway lines around Rome, Foggia, Salerno and Battipaglia hampered the Axis ability to send supplies south to Calabria, and so on to Sicily, which did cause a 'severe crisis' in supply for forces there late in the campaign.[86]

Anti-shipping operations also failed to prevent or seriously disrupt the evacuation of the island. The Italians successfully transferred 62,182 personnel, 41 guns, 227 vehicles and 41 mules to the mainland over twelve days using only two train ferries, four motorized rafts and two small steamers, for the loss of just one train ferry and a motor raft. The Germans managed 39,569 men, 9,605 vehicles, 47 tanks, 94 guns, 1,100 tons of ammo, 970 tons fuel and 15,700 tons of other supplies over just five days, for a handful of losses.[87] It is unlikely, however, that more intensive anti-shipping efforts could have achieved a vastly different result. The two well organised, and entirely separate evacuations over such short distances with such intensified defences presented an extremely difficult target. While more focused efforts started at an earlier date might have managed more sinkings, the ferry routes and terminals proved to be remarkably resilient, and supplementary efforts by additional small shipping were effective. The option of dual landings both on Sicily and the 'toe' of Calabria would have probably been the best option to prevent the escape, but it was discounted from an early stage by Allied planners. The dual reasons for this were the strength of enemy coastal defences and that it went beyond the parameters of the Mediterranean strategy agreed at Casablanca. It was a decision that drew disparaging post-war criticism from Axis commanders like Kesselring.[88]

Although anti-shipping operations had achieved minimal effect on the Sicilian campaign, the capture of the island added a new problem to German supply woes across the Mediterranean. It further restricted their ability to be flexible with their remaining shipping, by transferring it to where it was most needed. As their naval command in Italy lamented after the Italian armistice: 'With the loss of Sicily, the Mediterranean has been strategically cut into two parts which it will be impossible to link again. The bordering seas such as the Adriatic, Ionian, Aegean and the Black Sea cannot be separated from the eastern Mediterranean.'[89] This magnified the burden on existing shipping even further, and subsequently increased the impact of individual sinkings. Attrition to shipping had gone a long way towards neutering Axis air power on Sardinia since late 1942, and given the island's vulnerability, it had been earmarked for evacuation as part of Operation 'Achse'.

'Achse' had also included Corsica to act purely as a staging post for troops evacuated from Sardinia en route to Italy, but both OKW and the German naval command briefly held onto a hope that it could be retained.[90] Yet less than a week after the Italian armistice, it was definitively decided that remaining in Corsica was untenable. The Chief of the German Naval Staff's Operations Division was forced to admit that there was insufficient shipping in the Mediterranean to keep any garrison in Corsica supplied even in the short term. He also advised against the reinforcement of garrisons in Crete and the Dodecanese for the same reason. Around 80,000 tons of Italian shipping had been seized in Genoa, but it was in a poor state of repair and was expected to take a long time to be made ready for use. This was indicative of a wider picture; they had seized 575,000 tons of Italian shipping under 'Achse', but much of it was that which was no longer seaworthy, under repair or vessels that were completely unusable for current needs. In fact, the functional total was less than 230,000 tons.[91]

While attrition to shipping had neutered the threat from Sardinia and forced the abandonment of Corsica, the withdrawal from the islands was once again not prevented. The short jump from Sardinia to Corsica presented a difficult target over a brief timeframe during which the Allies were concentrated on cementing a vulnerable beachhead at Salerno. In that sense, it is perhaps unsurprising that the garrison of around 28,500 personnel was transferred to Corsica with little interference to the 'slight shipping resources' that were used. The only real resistance came from their former Italian allies and partisans on the ground.[92] The Corsica evacuation, however, presented a much clearer opportunity that was largely missed. The combined personnel from both islands had to be evacuated alongside as much equipment as possible, over a far greater distance between Bastia and Livorno, although the northerly position of the route favoured air defence and hampered attack.

The Germans had decided that due to a lack of escorts, and the need to evacuate Corsica quickly in the face of Allied advances, large convoys of minor vessels would be used to allow greater speed and safety in numbers. Initially, two steamers, two KT ships, ten naval landing craft and ten other small vessels were dedicated to the evacuation. These were later joined by another nine steamers of 10,000 tons plus a variety of small craft. Transport aircraft were also used to assist in the evacuation and constant fighter cover for both the sea and air transport was organised.[93] The Allies quickly became aware that the evacuation was underway and it was briefly discussed in the British War Cabinet, noting that some successes had been achieved against the shipping, yet they said nothing of a need to increase interdiction efforts. As Tomblin has noted, there were French destroyers available in the immediate region, as they had been involved in landing forces on Corsica, but they did not intervene.[94] Ultimately, the Germans successfully evacuated over 30,000 men, along with 3,026 vehicles, more than 100 tanks, 362 anti-aircraft guns and artillery pieces and over 6,000 tons of supplies. Hitler himself dubbed it 'an exceptional achievement; a complete success for which was scarcely to be hoped'. Roskill puts the combined total of shipping sunk during the evacuation of Sardinia and Corsica at only eighteen vessels of just 16,943 tons.[95]

While attrition to shipping and an altering strategic picture had led to Germany ceding its territories in the western basin, the British mounted their failed attempt to evict them from the Aegean by force. After successfully gaining a foothold with minimal forces against no opposition, attempts to safeguard these new possessions through anti-shipping operations floundered. Two submarines had been sent to intercept what turned out to be assault shipping to retake Kos, but failed to arrive in time. Destroyers that had been patrolling were already returning home to refuel, while air attacks were ineffective. Instead the landings by both sea and air proceeded without a hitch and the island fell within twenty-four hours.[96] The period between the loss of Kos and the German assault on Leros did see an increase in sinkings in the region, with some effect.

Scattered sinkings of merchantmen and landing craft hindered the German build-up of invasion forces and materiel, but the most damaging event was the destruction of the *Olympus* convoy. The sinking of eight of the nine vessels carrying equipment and men (400 of whom were killed) had several repercussions. First their Admiral in the Aegean immediately turned back other convoys at sea for fear of a similar ambush, which exacerbated the slowdown to the build-up caused by the loss of the convoy. Then, General Mueller, in charge of the German land component, argued that after the destruction of the convoy, Allied naval vessels continued to present a major danger operating in the area and then sheltering in Turkish waters. He warned that the operation to retake Leros would be 'condemned to failure from the outset' if it was attempted before the threat was dealt with. He ordered its postponement for 'a few days' until the Air Force was able to eliminate the destroyer presence or they otherwise left for good.[97] The British attempted to take advantage of this lull, which they learned of via intelligence, to use all methods of attack to increase sinking and prevent any German landings, but failed to achieve anything more than a postponement of around a month. After the landings were made, the Navy attempted to isolate the German force through interception at sea and bombardment of relevant harbours, but this all came to naught.[98]

After the termination of the disastrous Dodecanese campaign, Admiral Willis, Commander of the Royal Navy in the Levant, tried to salvage some positivity from the outcome. In conclusion he claimed that while the campaign had failed, the 'inroad made in the enemy shipping resources ... will prove a fatal handicap to him when the time comes for us to embark on an "all in" offensive in the Aegean, with adequate forces'.[99] This 'all in' offensive was destined to never appear, but Willis was partially correct: shipping losses were to prove a fatal flaw in the German Aegean position and contribute to their eventual withdrawal. Replacement of shipping was close to impossible, as they lacked any notable construction facilities there and had limited scope for the transferal of vessels from elsewhere. The Allied occupation of Sicily and then southern Italy severed first the western Mediterranean–Aegean route and then the Adriatic–Aegean route for in-theatre reinforcement. The Adriatic was in any case to see serious attrition to its stock of shipping over late 1943 into 1944, through increasingly effective Allied actions, led by coastal forces. At the end of March 1944, the German naval headquarters for the Adriatic was forced to admit that they had lost 50 per cent of all their small vessels that month.[100] Only a link to the Black Sea, which was itself resource starved, and to Germany via an increasingly dangerous Danube route, remained in any way viable to the Aegean.[101]

Given these difficulties, the supply situation across the Aegean Islands progressively worsened, as although total sinkings remained modest, they represented significant proportions of that available. The 10,000 tons lost in November was 23 per cent of the shipping space available in the Aegean at that point and an urgent request for another 15,000 was issued, but this was prevented by the increasingly isolated nature of the Aegean given Allied control of the broader Mediterranean. The islands frequently found themselves very short of food, fuel, munitions and other necessities. Such was the shortage in Crete in late November 1943 that authorities there warned that the sinking of a single cargo of food could cause an island-wide 'bread crisis', while some of the smaller islands were dangerously short of fresh water. The lack of food was the driving factor in the rise of a series of thriving black markets across the isolated territories.[102] The only brief improvement came in mid-1944 after the removal of some

Illustration 8.2 RAF Bristol Beaufighters of No. 201 (Naval Co-operation) Group attack a convoy in the Aegean Sea, which led to the sinking of the 5,300-ton cargo ship *Livenza* in February 1944. Through a combination of inter and intra-theatre learning and technical advances, the RAF and FAA significantly developed their anti-shipping procedures over the course of the war.
Source: www.gettyimages.co.uk/detail/news-photo/sinks-axis-supply-ship-in-the-aegean-news-photo/517362918?adppopup=true
Credit: Bettmann via Getty Images

troops to the mainland, thus reducing the requirement, but this was nothing more than a temporary palliative. Concerted efforts in 1944 to improve the shipping balance brought few dividends, as the tonnage available remained consistently below requirements.[103] After Hitler finally approved an evacuation of the Aegean, the dearth of shipping once more proved to be a great impediment. Hitler had urged 'that everything which can be got out of the Aegean islands should be withdrawn'. Of the 57,000 German troops and nearly 14,000 loyal Italian paramilitaries across the islands, 16,500 men had to be left on the fortified western end of Crete, and a further 16,700 across Rhodes, Kos and Leros. The majority of the withdrawal had to be conducted using transport aircraft due to both a lack of ships and fears of Allied naval superiority, meaning the bulk of the heavy equipment and weaponry also had to remain behind rather than be used in mainland Europe.[104]

By the end of 1944, anti-shipping operations had virtually ceased across the theatre. The Aegean had largely been evacuated, and both the quantity and utility of shipping in the Adriatic and off the Italian north-west coastline had drastically reduced. Over the course of the year, though, the attrition had contributed first to the German abandonment of the Aegean and then to their inability to successfully remove all troops and equipment. Elsewhere, the sinking of coastal shipping and Adriatic traffic continued in support of attempts to starve German troops in Italy and the Balkans of vital supplies, most notably during Operation 'Strangle'. These efforts demonstrated just how complete Allied dominion over the sea had become, as they were able to effectively shut down any Germans efforts to use coastal routes as a substitute for overland supply routes, reducing it to 'an unimportant minimum'.[105] The influence of this on the war in Italy was minimal, however, as the effects were inferior to the interdiction and disruption of overland communications, on which the Germans primarily relied.[106] Since the end in North Africa, the overall attrition to shipping had simply rendered any wider position across the Mediterranean impossible. Axis, and later solely German, mobility at sea had been denied, and Sardinia, Corsica and the Aegean all fell accordingly.

Conclusion

The surrender of the remaining German forces in Italy came into effect on 2 May 1945, five days before Jodl signed the unconditional surrender of all German armed forces. This concluded the Allies' war in the Mediterranean theatre, and post-war efforts transitioned to stabilisation, reconstruction and the construction of a bulwark against Soviet encroachment into the Balkans.[1] This was approached through a variety of political, military and economic means. A new alliance was soon forged in the form of the North Atlantic Treaty Organization, which saw the Mediterranean as its southern flank and a scene of increasing focus for the previously Mediterranean-sceptic Americans.

Money was also poured into the region for the dual purpose of both reconstruction and cementing political alignment against the Soviet Union. While Britain was the source of some of this financial input, it was limited by circumstance and the United States was by far the biggest contributor, operating under the newly enshrined 'Truman Doctrine' from 1947. Both countries would remain tied down with involvement in civil wars and against paramilitary violence in hotspots such as Greece for years to come, but the dynamics of power in the post-war Mediterranean bore little resemblance to those prior to or during the war.[2] The Italian empire had collapsed, British influence in the region had been considerably reduced while that of the United States grew rapidly, and the region's future became drawn into the broader picture of the emerging Cold War.

The road to this radically altered situation had been a long and destructive one, in which Axis efforts to dominate the Mediterranean came close to fruition. By the middle of 1941 they had conquered the Balkans, much of North Africa and held all the key contested islands across the theatre, bar Malta. They came close once more over the spring and summer of 1942, yet ultimately their grip on the theatre, held together across a network of maritime supply routes, collapsed. This was precipitated by a long but decisive anti-shipping campaign, which had simultaneously undermined the fighting efficiency of their forces in

North Africa and deprived them of the ability to sustain a theatre-wide position. Allied victory in the Mediterranean in turn had far wider ramifications, being a major contribution to final Allied victory in the war.

An Axis victory in the Mediterranean would have struck a powerful blow against the Allies, and a devastating one against Britain in particular, for which the area was vital and the scene of its greatest investment of men and materiel over 1940–43. Defeat there could have resulted in the loss of access to oil supplies that were significant yet replaceable for them, but whose capture would be a huge boon for the oil-starved Axis powers.[3] It would also have severed the British Empire into two halves, and even provided the European Axis powers the chance to co-ordinate more closely with Japan at the strategic and possibly operational levels. Finally, defeat in a theatre which Churchill had fashioned as the 'epicentre of Britain's resurrection' would have dealt serious damage to British national morale and willingness to continue the war.[4] As it was, success in the Mediterranean meant that oil supplies from the Middle East were secured, the Empire held together for the duration of the war, and the European and Asian Axis powers were kept separate. What is more, Allied victory in the theatre was an essential element of their overall victory in the European war. It was a key part of a strategy which was dependent on wearing down the Axis powers, sapping their long-term ability to wage war and shattering their alliance via the destruction of Fascist Italy.[5]

★★★

Defined in a broad sense, the Mediterranean theatre had been the scene of continuous fighting across a variety of heterogeneous settings since June 1940. Combat took place on, above and below the seas as well as in diverse environments on land. Campaigns were fought across the vast open spaces of the western desert, among the mountains and rivers of Italy and on the claustrophobic islands of Crete and the Dodecanese. For the vast majority of that time, it had been one of, if not the, most operationally 'joint' theatres of the war, rivalled perhaps only by the Pacific. In no other theatre had combat been so defined by interdependence on the roles of air, sea and land power. Time and again the successful application of any one of these instruments hinged on effective co-ordination with the other two. The impact of the war at sea on the land conflicts, which occurred around the periphery of the basin, is therefore essential when assessing the factors that determined the overall outcome of war in the theatre. It was undoubtedly true that the interdiction of Axis supplies at sea successfully degraded their combat efficiency at key junctures of the North African campaign, in a successful exploitation of their vulnerable supply lines. Yet it was also crucial because shipping was the key capability which allowed the Axis to sustain a theatre-wide presence across the Mediterranean as a whole. The attrition of this essential resource thus isolated the various Axis forces across the region, whether they were engaged in combat or not, and must be seen as the vital precursor to eventual Allied success in the theatre as a whole.

In order to fully appreciate why the Allies triumphed in this vital theatre of the war, it is essential to integrate these themes within the broader scope of total, industrialised warfare. All too often the war in the Mediterranean is treated as self-contained and distinct, and the role it played within the broader picture of total war has been under-appreciated. Some have examined Anglo-American tensions over the Mediterranean strategy and the changing dynamics of power between the Allies. Other avenues taken have included the place of the Mediterranean as a site of essential learning in the art of modern warfare for the western Allies. There are also numerous individual operational studies that assess the outcomes and importance of the war on land, at sea or in the air. Yet historians' tendency to assess these individual campaigns and environments has provided an incomplete picture of the theatre as a whole, whereas in reality it was connected by the lifeblood of seaborne supplies. Herein lies the first key element of the true significance of the anti-shipping campaign in the Mediterranean: the inability of the Axis to move troops and supplies across the region enabled the Allies to isolate and defeat key forces in detail in a series of campaigns, which culminated in their mass surrender in North Africa in 1943.

Depriving the Axis land and air forces of essential supplies such as fuel, weaponry, munitions, vehicles and spare parts denied them full use of their greatest advantage – manoeuvre warfare. When they did have an adequate supply base in place, their superior skill in this art frequently inflicted impressive and sometimes embarrassing defeats on their British and Commonwealth (and later Allied) opponents, who often had notable numerical and material superiority. The interdiction of supplies destined for them was of a sufficient priority and scale to deny them this advantage when it mattered most, however. It blunted their drive across Libya in mid-1941, and enabled the subsequent success of Operation 'Crusader' and the following (albeit temporary) expulsion of the Axis from Cyrenaica, by sinking up to 92 per cent of the fuel destined for them during key phases of the campaign. The Axis offensives in 1942 penetrated even more deeply, thrusting into Egypt and sparking panic and preparations for evacuation in Cairo, yet this offensive too was

Conclusion

first stopped and then forced into a withdrawal. While the improved leadership, doctrine, equipment and morale of the Eighth Army, along with their deeper integration with the RAF, were all-important to this pivotal triumph, its foundation was laid in the sinking of cargoes at sea. Crucial sinkings were achieved by air, surface and sub-surface arms that had integrated more effectively, and developed their procedures based on learning from experience in the theatre and elsewhere.[6]

During the Alamein period, the most important achievement was the prevention of significant use of the 'forward' ports and harbours that were much closer to the frontline, and thus to the forces that needed sustenance. Several historians have argued that the Axis supply woes were primarily the result of long overland routes and/or successful Allied interdiction of overland transport.[7] These issues were undoubtedly important, but stressing their significance ignores the key point that they were only made significant by the successful interdiction of Axis shipping across key trans-Mediterranean routes in the first place. The denial of forward ports, whose capacities were sufficient to have handled far larger quantities than they actually received, forced a greater reliance on those more remote from the frontline, thus stretching supply routes and hindering offensive action. This caused the domino effect of greater strain on a limited stock of motor transport (which was itself maintained through replacement vehicles and parts arriving by sea) that was forced to travel greater distances overland and spend a greater period of time exposed to attack.

After the Axis withdrawal to Tunisia, anti-shipping operations degraded the Axis supply base with much greater consistency than had been the case over 1940–42, thanks to easy access to vulnerable sea lanes with vastly superior air and naval forces. The quantity of shipping sunk ballooned in the December 1942–May 1943 period, totalling 477 vessels of 700,680 tons, nearly all of which were on the Tunisian routes. This resulted in the Tunisian ports receiving only a small fraction of the tonnages that they were capable of processing. The resulting supply shortages limited Axis ambitions and offensives as well as their ability to resist Allied attacks, which themselves grew in competence after a difficult start by unseasoned commanders and troops. The extent of the attrition to shipping also ensured that regardless of the result in Axis debates over whether Tunisia should be 'held to the last man', no major attempt at evacuation would ever be possible owing to the catastrophic shipping deficiencies. The potential of any portion of the 300,000 men contributing to the ongoing Axis war in the Mediterranean or elsewhere in Europe was thus removed, dealing a powerful blow to their ongoing war effort. Thanks to anti-shipping efforts, there would be no 'Dunkirk miracle' for the Axis forces in North Africa.

This leads to the second key element of the campaign's significance. Beyond a detrimental effect on Italo-German forces in North Africa, the attrition of shipping had a wider impact on the war in the Mediterranean. From June 1940 to May 1943, 1,033 vessels totalling 2,035,653 tons were sunk by Allied action, although these figures do not tell the full story. Alongside the total sunk by the Allies were those sabotaged, scuttled, captured and lost to friendly fire, accidents or unknown causes, which according to some sources might total as many as a further 317 vessels of 262,833 tons. Finally, patchy source material renders the number of vessels damaged and the proportion of them successfully repaired impossible to quantify fully, but damage certainly denied the use of a significant proportion of vessels for a time, while some were never repaired, a problem exacerbated by the lack of repair facilities available and their inefficiency.[8]

This rate of loss vastly outstripped the Axis ability to replace it by any means; after the internment of numerous vessels outside of the Mediterranean, they began the war with 548 ships totalling 1,749,441 tons in the theatre, plus a variety of smaller vessels fit for use as coastal traffic. From January 1940 through to the September 1943 armistice they managed to construct just 364,387 tons of new shipping in the theatre. Only the transferral of shipping constructed elsewhere and the seizure of tonnage from defeated enemies, primarily France, allowed them to retain any maritime transport capability at all, although these too fell far below initial expectations.[9] Transferrals from elsewhere never appeared in the numbers promised by officials like Kaufmann, while much of the vast French tonnage that was seized proved to be permanently or temporarily unseaworthy, or types that were completely unsuited to the tasks in hand.

The Allies therefore successfully outstripped the Axis's industrial capability to operate enough shipping in the theatre to maintain any presence overseas beyond the southern European mainland whatsoever. The irreplaceable cull of Axis shipping fundamentally undermined their ability to maintain a position across the theatre and precipitated a collapse. Beyond the operational shortage caused at key junctures in North Africa, the ability of the Axis to ship sufficient quantities of supplies, manpower, vehicles and munitions there over a sustained period of time was removed.

Even the shorter routes, which were more insulated from attack for reasons of geography and Allied priorities, thus became compromised. The use of Sardinia as an ideally positioned forward air base from which to menace Allied communications was nullified through the attrition of

Conclusion

shipping, leading to a lack of means to transport the necessary supplies to keep it operating. Any German hopes to retain a foothold in Corsica after the Italian armistice were dashed for the same reason. While British hopes to seize the Aegean islands with a 'shoestring' offensive around the same time proved to be abortive, the paucity of Axis shipping available there and continued attrition over 1944 contributed to a gradual degradation of the supply situation. Eventually this, combined with a changing strategic picture in eastern Europe, compelled the Germans to largely abandon the islands. Even then, they were forced to abandon some personnel and most of the heavy equipment to their fate for sheer lack of capability to remove them.

★★★

The compelling new thesis presented in this book is the result of the utilisation of a unique multinational, multilingual source basis and methodology. It demonstrates that the anti-shipping campaign was a key factor in the Axis defeat in the Mediterranean due to its combined impact in both the operational and industrial realms of the war. Overall, a combination of factors − increases in quality and quantity of forces available, operational learning, improved intelligence, attrition to Axis escorts and greater strategic and operational priority being accorded to anti-shipping operations − intertwined to deliver broadly increased efficiency and totals of sinking over 1940–43. This in turn enabled the creation of damaging operational shortages in supplies for the Axis in North Africa at those key junctures, but also bled the Axis supply network white by depriving it of the sole means of delivery.

The scale of attrition far outstripped the Axis's ability to replace their losses, whether from new construction or seizures from other nations. In this sense, events in the Mediterranean were influenced by similar factors to those Phillips O'Brien has argued decided the outcome in the Atlantic and Pacific, and rendered Germany and Japan incapable of prosecuting the wider war. The anti-shipping campaign placed 'unbearable pressure' on the Axis war fighting system in the Mediterranean, while air and sea power proved decisive by destroying Axis equipment long before it reached what would traditionally be described as 'the battlefield'.[10] Furthermore, the anti-shipping campaign was one of the key factors in placing 'unbearable pressure' on Italy in particular, ultimately contributing to its collapse and exit from the war.

Ultimately, the anti-shipping campaign was an essential ingredient in determining the outcome of the Mediterranean war by decisively influencing the fight in North Africa in the Allies' favour, and by fatally undermining the industrial capacity of the Axis to maintain a hold across the theatre. The British had been well aware that this was a weak link for the Axis prior to the war's beginning, yet the Axis powers were surprisingly slow to give its defence the priority it required. The reality dawned on the Axis military leadership only gradually, while for the political leadership the pace of realisation was glacial. When the recognition finally, truly hit home, it was sickening for them. As Mussolini put it in 1943: 'My illness has a name: convoys.'[11]

Notes

Note on Terminology

1 See Iain Johnston-White, *The British Commonwealth and Victory in the Second World War* (London: Palgrave Macmillan, 2017), pp. 228–9.
2 Richard Hammond, 'Fighting under a Different Flag: Multinational Naval Co-operation and Submarine Warfare in the Mediterranean, 1940–1944', *Journal of Military History*, 80, 2 (2016), p. 448.
3 Andrew Buchanan, 'A Friend Indeed? From Tobruk to El Alamein: The American Contribution to Victory in the Desert', *Diplomacy and Statecraft*, 15, 2 (2004), p. 287.

Introduction

1 MacGregor Knox, *Mussolini Unleashed, 1939–1941: Politics and Strategy in Fascist Italy's Last War* (New York: Cambridge University Press, 1982), pp. 124–5.
2 John Gooch, *Mussolini and His Generals: The Armed Forces and Fascist Foreign Policy, 1922–1940* (Cambridge: Cambridge University Press, 2007), pp. 218–19; Robert Mallett, *The Italian Navy and Fascist Expansionism, 1935–1940* (London: Frank Cass, 1998), pp. 1–2.
3 This is detailed further in the next chapter, but see MacGregor Knox, *Hitler's Italians Allies: Royal Armed Forces, Fascist Regime and the War of 1940–1943* (Cambridge: Cambridge University Press, 2003), p. 46; Georgina Elisabeth Angela Raspin, 'Some Aspects of Italian Economic Affairs 1940–43, with Particular Reference to Italian Relations with Germany' (PhD Thesis, London School of Economics, 1980), p. 66.
4 Generally, the term 'British' is used as shorthand throughout this book, but refers to all British, Commonwealth and imperial forces.
5 For an examination of the complexities in assessing the role of sea power during the First World War, see Paul Kennedy, 'The War at Sea' in Jay Winter (ed.), *The Cambridge History of the First World War, Vol. 1: Global War* (Cambridge: Cambridge University Press, 2014), pp. 321–48; David Morgan-Owen, 'War as It might Have Been: British Sea Power and the First World War', *Journal of Military History*, 83, 4 (2019), pp. 1095–131.

6 Richard Overy, *Why the Allies Won* (London: Norton, 1996), pp. 25–62; Phillips Payson O'Brien, *How the War Was Won: Air-Sea Power and Allied Victory in World War II* (Cambridge: Cambridge University Press, 2015), pp. 3, 184–5, 232.
7 See especially Craig L. Symonds, 'For Want of a Nail: The Impact of Shipping on Grand Strategy in World War II', *Journal of Military History*, 81, 3 (2017), 657–66 and also Symonds, *World War II at Sea: A Global History* (Oxford: Oxford University Press, 2018).
8 Douglas Porch, *The Path to Victory: The Mediterranean Theatre in World War II* (New York: Farrar, Straus and Giroux, 2004).
9 Simon Ball, *The Bitter Sea: The Brutal World War II Fight for the Mediterranean* (London: Harper Press, 2009) and for differing themes of conflict, see Ball, 'The Mediterranean and North Africa, 1940–1944' in John Ferris and Evan Mawdsley (eds.), *The Cambridge History of the Second World War*, Vol. 1 (Cambridge: Cambridge University Press, 2015), pp. 358–88.
10 Michael Howard, *The Mediterranean Strategy in the Second World War* (London: Weidenfeld and Nicolson, 1968); Matthew Jones, *Britain, the United States and the Mediterranean War, 1942–1944* (Basingstoke: Palgrave Macmillan, 1996); Andrew Buchanan, *American Grand Strategy in the Mediterranean during World War II* (New York: Cambridge University Press, 2014). A broader study of the wartime Anglo-American alliance that also covers the Mediterranean in depth is Niall Barr, *Yanks and Limeys: Alliance Warfare in the Second World War* (London: Jonathan Cape, 2015).
11 See particularly the emphasis placed on 'communications' in Julian Corbett, *Some Principles of Maritime Strategy* (London: Longmans, 1911).
12 Herbert Richmond, *Statesmen and Sea Power* (Oxford: Clarendon, 1946), p. ix. This author believes that this is a useful definition of sea power and its role during *wartime* (particularly during a total war) only.
13 The most recent, succinct discussion can be found in Symonds, 'For Want of a Nail'. For an earlier analysis, see the classic C. B. A. Behrens, *Merchant Shipping and the Demands of War* (London: HMSO, 1955).
14 See for instance Corelli Barnett, *Engage the Enemy More Closely: The Royal Navy in the Second World War* (New York: Norton, 1991).
15 Raymond De Belot, *The Struggle for the Mediterranean 1939–1945* (London: Oxford University Press, 1951); Donald MacIntyre, *The Battle for the Mediterranean* (London: Purnell Books Services, 1975); Bernard Ireland, *The War in the Mediterranean, 1940–1943* (London: Arms and Armour Press, 1993); Jack Greene and Alessandro Massignani, *The Naval War in the Mediterranean, 1940–1943* (London: Chatham, 1998); Joseph Attard, *The Struggle for the Mediterranean* (Valletta: Progress Press, 1999); Giorgio Giorgerini, *La guerra italiana sul mare: La marina tra vittoria e sconfitta, 1940–1943* (Milan: Mandadori, 2001); Naval Staff History (NSH), *The Royal Navy and the Mediterranean*, 2 Vols. (Abingdon: Routledge, 2002); Vincent P. O'Hara, *The Struggle for the Middle Sea: Great Navies at War in the Mediterranean* (London: Conway, 2009). See also James J. Sadkovich, *The Italian Navy in World War II* (Westport, CT: Greenwood, 1994).
16 Samuel Eliot Morison, *History of United States Naval Operations in World War II*, Vols. 2 and 9 (Boston: Little, Brown, 1947–54) contain some brief

details on anti-shipping operations; S. W. Roskill, *The War at Sea*, 3 Vols. (London: HMSO, 1954–61) is better but still has notable limitations. The quote is taken from Roskill, *War at Sea*, Vol. 2, p. 433.

17 Ufficio Storico della Marina Militare (USMM), *La marina italiana nella seconda guerra mondiale* (*LMI*), 19 Vols. (Rome: USMM, 1950–69). The relevant volumes are Vol. 1, *Dati Statistici* (1950); Vol. 6, *La difesa del traffico con l'Africa settentrionale dal 10 Giugno 1940 al 30 Settembre 1941* (1958); Vol. 7, *La difesa del traffico con l'Africa settentrionale dal 1 Ottobre 1941 al 30 Settembre 1942* (1962); Vol. 8, *La difesa del traffico con l'Africa settentrionale dal 1 Ottobre 1942 alla Caduta della Tunisia* (1964); Vol. 9, *La difesa del traffico con l'Albania, la Grecia e l'Egeo* (1965). For a more compact work on similar issues, see Giorgio Giorgerini, *La battaglia dei convogli in Mediterraneo* (Milan: Mursia, 1977).

18 See for instance the NSH, *The Royal Navy and the Mediterranean Convoys* (Oxford: Routledge, 2007); Douglas Austin, *Malta and British Strategic Policy, 1925–1943* (London: Taylor and Francis e-library, 2005); Richard Woodman, *Malta Convoys 1940–1943* (London: J. Murray, 2000); Paul Kemp, *Malta Convoys 1940–1943* (London: Arms and Armour Press, 1998); Joseph Attard, *The Battle for Malta: An Epic True Story of Suffering and Bravery* (Valetta: Progress Press, 1988) for specific studies, although these all receive a sizeable chunk of all histories of Malta and/or the Mediterranean War, most notably by Barnett and Roskill.

19 I. S. O. Playfair, G. M. S. Stitt, C. J. C. Molony, and S. E. Toomer, *The Mediterranean and the Middle East*, 6 Vols. (London: HMSO, 1954–88).

20 See Militärgeschichtliches Forschungsamt (MF), *Germany and the Second World War*, 9 Vols. (Oxford: Oxford University Press, 1990–2017), Vols. 3 and 6.

21 Some notable examples of these include Martin Kitchen, *Rommel's Desert War: Waging World War II in North Africa, 1941–1943* (Cambridge: Cambridge University Press, 2009); Niall Barr, *Pendulum of War: The Three Battles of El Alamein* (London: Penguin, 2004); Mario Montanari, *Le operazioni in Africa Settentrionale*, 4 Vols. (Rome: Ufficio Storico dello Stato Maggiore Esercito, 1984–93).

22 Martin van Creveld, *Supplying War: Logistics from Wallenstein to Patton* (Cambridge: Cambridge University Press, 2nd edition, 2004); Brad W. Gladman, 'Air Power and Intelligence in the Western Desert Campaign, 1940–43', *Intelligence and National Security*, 13, 4 (1998), pp. 144–62; Gladman, *Intelligence and Anglo-American Air Support in World War Two* (Basingstoke: Palgrave MacMillan, 2009); Alan Levine, *The War against Rommel's Supply Lines, 1942–1943* (Mechanicsburg, PA: Stackpole Books, 2008).

23 Austin, *Malta and British Strategic Policy*; Greg Kennedy, 'Sea Denial, Interdiction and Diplomacy: The Royal Navy and the Role of Malta, 1939–1943' in Ian Speller (ed.), *The Royal Navy and Maritime Power in the Twentieth Century* (Abingdon: Frank Cass, 2005); Tony Spooner, *Supreme Gallantry: Malta's Role in the Allied Victory, 1939–1945* (London: John Murray, 1996); Peter C. Smith and Edwin Walker, *The Battle of the Malta Striking Forces* (London: Littlehampton Book Services, 1974).

24 Giorgerini, *La Battaglia dei Convogli*, pp. 230–6, does include a 'chapter' on anti-shipping operations in the Adriatic and Aegean, but it is less than six pages long.

Chapter 1

1. For a broad guide to this history, see Peter Dietz, *The British in the Mediterranean* (London: Brasseys, 1994); and Robert Holland, *Blue Water Empire: The British in the Mediterranean since 1800* (London: Allen Lane, 2012).
2. Minutes of the meeting of 9 April 1940 in Ufficio Storico dello Stato Maggiore dell'Esercito (USSME), *Verbali delle riunioni tenute dal Capo di Stato Maggiore Generale*, Vol. 1 (Rome: USSME, 1982), p. 38.
3. Michael Simpson, 'Superhighway to the World Wide Web: The Mediterranean in British Imperial Strategy, 1900–45' in John B. Hattendorf (ed.), *Naval Strategy and Policy in the Mediterranean: Past, Present and Future* (Abingdon: Frank Cass, 2000), p. 51.
4. Dietz, *The British in the Mediterranean*, p. 87.
5. Lawrence Pratt, *East of Malta, West of Suez: Britain's Mediterranean Crisis, 1936–9* (Cambridge: Cambridge University Press, 1975), pp. 107, 172; Ball, *The Bitter Sea*, p. 32; Steven Morewood, *The British Defence of Egypt, 1935–1940: Conflict and Crisis in the Eastern Mediterranean* (London: Routledge, 2005), pp. 22–3.
6. Richard Hammond, 'An Enduring Influence on Imperial Defence and Grand Strategy: British Perceptions of the Italian Navy', *The International History Review*, 39, 5 (2017), pp. 810–11; John Darwin, 'Imperialism and the Victorians: The Dynamics of Territorial Expansion', *English Historical Review*, 112 (1997), p. 622; Simpson, 'Superhighway to the World Wide Web', pp. 51–77.
7. John Darwin, 'An Undeclared Empire: The British in the Middle East, 1918–1939', *Journal of Imperial and Commonwealth History*, 27, 2 (1999), pp. 160, 164, 166.
8. See for example the comments in The National Archives (TNA) CAB 23/76, 'Very Secret Addendum' to Cabinet Conclusions 45(33), 12 July 1933, p. 4, which details the desire to avoid League involvement in negotiations with Egypt at all costs.
9. Serious controls were introduced to the two services over the 1925–28 period. See John R. Ferris, 'Treasury Control, the Ten Year Rule and British Service Policies, 1919–1924', *Historical Journal*, 30, 4 (1987), pp. 864, 878–80.
10. On the crisis in general and Anglo-American talks see Christopher Thorne, *The Limits of Foreign Policy: The West, the League and the Far Eastern Crisis of 1931–1933* (London: Hamish Hamilton, 1972). On the COS and the 'defenceless' Far East, see TNA CAB 4/21, Committee for Imperial Defence memorandum, 'The Situation in the Far East', 22 February 1932.
11. N. H. Gibbs, *Grand Strategy, Vol. 1, Rearmament Policy* (London: HMSO, 1976), p. 188. On the naval risks see Arthur J. Marder, 'The Royal Navy and the Ethiopian Crisis of 1935–1936', *American Historical Review*, 75, 5 (1970), pp. 1327–56; and Hammond, 'Enduring Influence', pp. 813–17.
12. Culminating in some attacks on British warships. See Reynolds M. Salerno, *Vital Crossroads: Mediterranean Origins of the Second World War* (New York: Cornell University Press, 2002), pp. 24–9.
13. This is a strong theme across all the literature on British non-intervention in the Spanish Civil War, but for a succinct summary, see Alan Cassels, 'Britain,

Italy and the Axis: How to Make Friends with Mussolini and Influence Hitler' in Gaynor Johnson (ed.), *The International Context of the Spanish Civil War* (Newcastle: Cambridge Scholars, 2009), pp. 19–32.
14 Pratt, *East of Malta*, p. 79.
15 Zara Steiner, *The Triumph of the Dark: European International History, 1933–1939* (Oxford: Oxford University Press, 2011), pp. 157, 222, 316, 563, 685; W. C. Mills, 'Sir Joseph Ball, Adrian Dingli, and Neville Chamberlain's "Secret Channel" to Rome', *International History Review*, 24, 2 (2002), pp. 283–6, 305.
16 M. L. Roi, 'From Stresa Front to the Triple Entente: Sir Robert Vansittart, the Abyssinian Crisis and the Containment of Germany', *Diplomacy and Statecraft*, 6, 1 (1995), p. 65.
17 Earl of Perth to Viscount Halifax, 12 March 1938 in E. L. Woodward and Rohan Butler (eds.), *Documents on British Foreign Policy, 1919–1939*, 3, 1 (London: HMSO, 1949), pp. 37–8.
18 Gooch, *Mussolini and His Generals*, pp. 454–7.
19 Mussolini to Cavagnari, 27 May 1939 in Ufficio Storico della Marina Militare (USMM), *La Marina Italiana nella (LMI)*, Vol. 21, *L'organizzazione della Marina durante il Conflitto, Tomo I: Efficienza all'apertura delle ostilità* (Rome: USMM, 1972), p. 348; Knox, *Mussolini Unleashed*, pp. 39, 42.
20 Entries for 2 May, 21 and 26 August 1939 in Galeazzo Ciano, *Diario 1937–1943*, ed. Renzo de Felice (Milan: Rizzoli, 2010), pp. 292–3, 331–5; Salerno, *Vital Crossroads*, pp. 131–6; Knox, *Mussolini Unleashed*, pp. 30–43.
21 TNA GFM 36/10, Segretaria particolare del Duce (SPD), Verbali riunoni tenuta nella stanza del Duce a Palazzo Venezia, 29 May 1940, p. 1.
22 For a summary of British policy towards Italy during the period of non-belligerency, see Michael J. Budden, 'British Policy towards Fascist Italy in the Early Stages of the Second World War' (Unpublished PhD Thesis: University of London, 1999). On Italian deficiencies, see for example the pessimistic comments in TNA GFM 36/5, 'Verbali della seduta del 18 novembre 1939'.
23 TNA CAB 65/2/41, War Cabinet 107 (39), 7 December 1939, p. 342; for continued Italian opposition to war, see Gooch, *Mussolini and His Generals*, pp. 516–17.
24 For a summary of these opposing views and the reasoning behind them, see Christopher M. Bell, *The Royal Navy, Seapower and Strategy between the Wars* (Basingstoke: Palgrave Macmillan, 2000), pp. 117–25.
25 On this see in particular Steven Morewood, '"This Silly African Business": The Military Dimension of Britain's Response to the Abyssinian Crisis' in G. Bruce Strang (ed.), *Collision of Empires: Italy's Invasion of Ethiopia and Its International Impact* (Farnham: Ashgate, 2013), pp. 73–110; Marder, 'The Royal Navy'; Hammond, 'Enduring Influence', pp. 813–22.
26 TNA CAB 53/5, COS 149th meeting, 6 September 1935, pp. 3–5; Morewood, 'This Silly African Business', pp. 86–7.
27 Knox, *Hitler's Italians Allies*, p. 46; Raspin, 'Some Aspects of Italian Economic Affairs 1940–43', p. 66.
28 USMM, *LMI*, Vol. 6, *La difesa del traffico coll'Africa settentrionale, tomo I: dal 10 giugno 1940 al 30 settembre 1941*, pp. 4–5.

29 Archivio dell'Ufficio Storico della Marina Militare (AUSMM), Direttive generali operative (DG), Direttive Di. Na. no. 1 per le forze navali, 26 September 1938, pp. 9–10; Mallett, *The Italian Navy and Fascist Expansionism*, pp. 115–16.
30 'Di Na n. 0 (zero) Concetti generali di azione nel Mediterreaneo', 29 May 1940 in USMM, *LMI*, Vol. 21, *L'organizzazione, Tomo I*, pp. 354–5.
31 AUSMM, DG, 'Di. Na 0 – Concetti generali d'azione in Mediterraneo nell'attuale fase di conflitto', 14 July 1940, pp. 3–4.
32 Knox, *Hitler's Italian Allies*, p. 98; TNA HW 11/33, GC + CS Naval History, Vol. 20, p. 228.
33 USMM, *LMI*, Vol. 9, *La difesa del traffico con Albania, Grecia e l'Egeo* (Rome: USMM, 1964), pp. 17–19.
34 See for example the minutes of the meeting of 26 August 1940, in USSME, *Verbali delle riunioni tenute dal Capo di Stato Maggiore Generale*, Vol. 1, pp. 78–9.
35 TNA CAB 16/209, UK Delegation, Anglo-French Staff Conversations, 14 March 1939, p. 33. Blockade is not ignored as an option though, see ibid., p. 14.
36 TNA CAB 16/209, Strategic Appreciation Committee meeting, 6 April 1939, pp. 5–6; Pound to Cunningham, 24 July 1939 in Michael Simpson (ed.), *The Cunningham Papers*, Vol. 1 (Aldershot: Ashgate, 1999), p. 23.
37 TNA ADM 186/800, Naval Staff History (NSH), *Mediterranean*, Vol. 1, *September 1939–October 1940* (Historical Section, Admiralty, 1952), pp. 5, 8; see also the emphasis on anti-shipping operations in TNA ADM 1/9946, C-in-C Mediterranean to Admiralty, 13 May and 14 July 1939.
38 F. H. Hinsley et al., *British Intelligence in the Second World War*, Vol. 1 (London: HMSO, 1979), pp. 199, 206.
39 TNA CAB 16/209, UK Delegation, Anglo-French Staff Conversations, 14 March 1939, pp. 33–6; Playfair et al., *The Mediterranean and Middle East*, Vol. 1, pp. 27–9, 56.
40 TNA CAB 66/7, WP(40) 168, 'British Strategy in a Certain Eventuality', 27 May 1940, p. 2.
41 Austin, *Malta and British Strategic Policy*, p. 85.
42 TNA CAB 66/7, WP(40) 168, 'British Strategy in a Certain Eventuality', 27 May 1940, p. 3.
43 For details of these aspirational projects and their dismissal, see Mallett, *Italian Navy*, pp. 54–5; Brian R. Sullivan, 'Prisoner in the Mediterranean: The Evolution and Execution of Italian Naval Strategy, 1919–1942' in William B. Cogar (ed.), *Naval History: The Seventh Symposium of the US Naval Academy* (Wilmington, DE: Scholarly Resources Press, 1988), pp. 212–21; Gooch, *Mussolini and His Generals*, pp. 345–7.
44 Gooch, *Mussolini and His Generals*, pp. 232–3, 376–8, 482–3; Imperial War Museum (IWM), Italian Air Force Series (IAF), Box 24, 'Relazione statistica sull'attività operativa dell'Aeronautica dell'inizio delle ostilità al 30 settembre 1942', p. 3; Greene and Massignani, *Naval War in the Mediterranean*, p. 94.
45 Meetings of 5 and 26 June 1940, USSME, *Verbali delle riunioni tenute dal Capo di Stato Maggiore Generale*, Vol. 1, pp. 55, 66.

46 TNA GFM 36/7, Memorandum by Mussolini, 31 March 1940, pp. 9–10.
47 Mallett, *The Italian Navy and Fascist Expansionism*, pp. 150–1.
48 Roskill, *War at Sea*, Vol. 1, pp. 41–2, 271.
49 Howard, *Mediterranean Strategy*, p. 10.
50 Ibid., pp. 9, 16.
51 TNA CAB 66/11/42, WP(40) 362, 'Future Strategy', 4 September 1940, pp. 1–2, 10. On the Anglo-American dispute over the Mediterranean strategy, see Howard, *Mediterranean Strategy*; Jones, *Britain, the United States and the Mediterranean War*; Ball, *Bitter Sea*; Buchanan, *American Grand Strategy in the Mediterranean*.
52 Calculated from USMM, *LMI*, Vol. 1, *Dati Statistici*, p. 171. These figures are also used in Marc'Antonio Bragadin, *The Italian Navy in World War 2* (Annapolis: US Naval Institute Press, 1957), p. 355. Slightly different figures are given in Giorgerini, *La battaglia dei convogli*, p. 235, with a lower proportion to Libya and Tunisia. It seems likely that Giorgerini has included journeys to small harbours around the Libyan/Egyptian border alongside those to Albania, Greece and the Aegean. Given the Italian official history is used in this study for statistics on losses and deliveries of materiel, their figures on convoys have been as well.
53 These figures have been determined from TNA ADM 223/45, 'Special Intelligence Summaries: Analysis of Convoy Sailing from Italy to North Africa', September 1941–June 1943.
54 USMM, *LMI*, Vol. 6, *La Difesa*, p. 7.
55 Van Creveld, *Supplying War*, p. 184.
56 Austin, *Malta and British Strategic Policy*, pp. 125–6.
57 Brian R. Sullivan, 'The Italian Armed Forces, 1918–40' in Alan Millett and Williamson Murray (eds.), *Military Effectiveness*, Vol. 2, *The Interwar Years* (London: Unwin, 1988), p. 190.
58 Bragadin, *Italian Navy*, p. 7; USMM, *LMI*, Vol. 21, *L'organizzazione, Tomo I*, p. 253; Gooch, *Mussolini and His Generals*, pp. 446, 474–5.
59 Mallett, *The Italian Navy and Fascist Expansionism*, pp. 132–4; Brian R. Sullivan, 'A Fleet in Being: The Rise and Fall of Italian Sea Power, 1861–1943', *International History Review*, 10, 1 (1988), pp. 119–20; MacGregor Knox, 'The Italian Armed Forces, 1940–43' in Alan R. Millett and Williamson Murray (eds.), *Military Effectiveness*, Vol. 3, *The Second World War* (London: Unwin, 1988), p. 150.
60 TNA ADM 223/46, Special Intelligence Summary; Axis Merchant Shipping to Corsica and Sardinia, 11 April 1943, pp. 1–4.
61 Ibid., p. 3.
62 Charles W. Koburger, *Wine Dark, Blood Red Sea: Naval Warfare in the Aegean 1941–1946* (Westport, CT: Praeger, 1999), pp. 21–35.
63 TNA ADM 223/45, Special Intelligence Summary; Exchange of Shipping between the Aegean and the Black Sea, pp. 1–2.
64 Bragadin, *Italian Navy*, pp. 364–5; on pre-war warnings over shipping outside of the Mediterranean, see Gooch, *Mussolini and His Generals*, p. 446.
65 See Paul G. Halpern, *A Naval History of World War 1* (London: Routledge, 2003), pp. 335–45.

212   Notes to pages 28–32

66 See Duncan Redford, *The Submarine: A Cultural History from the Great War to Nuclear Combat* (London: Tauris Academic Studies, 2010), pp. 91–128.
67 Stephen Roskill, *Naval Policy between the Wars, Vol. 1, The Period of Anglo-American Antagonism 1919–1929* (London: Collins, 1968), pp. 81–2.
68 Ibid., pp. 327–8.
69 TNA CAB 24/202, WP 71(29), 'Maritime Belligerent Rights', 6 March 1929, pp. 18–19.
70 Stephen Roskill, *Naval Policy between the Wars, Vol. 2, The Period of Reluctant Rearmament 1930–1939* (London: Collins, 1976), p. 49.
71 TNA ADM 116/4155, Minute by DCNS, 11 October 1937.
72 See for example Williamson Murray, 'Strategic Bombing: The British, American and German Experiences' in Williamson Murray and Alan R. Millett (eds.), *Military Innovation in the Interwar Period* (Cambridge: Cambridge University Press, 1996), pp. 96–143; John Buckley, 'Contradictions in British Defence Policy, 1937–1939: The RAF and the Defence of Trade', *Twentieth Century British History*, 5, 1 (1994), pp. 100–13; Brian Bond, *British Military Policy between the Two World Wars* (Oxford: Oxford University Press, 1980), pp. 197–8, 283, 322–4.
73 TNA ADM 41/19, The RAF and Maritime War, Vol. 6, The Mediterranean and Red Sea, appendix B: Air Ministry Instructions on Air Action against Shipping at Sea, 14 February 1940.
74 Ibid.
75 Howard S. Levie, *Mine Warfare at Sea* (Dordrecht: Martinus Nijhoff, 1992), p. 78.
76 TNA ADM 234/380, NSH, *Submarines, Vol. 1, Operations in Home, Northern and Atlantic Waters*, 1954, p. 9.
77 Redford, *The Submarine*, pp. 147–8. A 'naval auxiliary' was defined as a vessel carrying troops or military stores.
78 TNA ADM 234/381, NSH, Submarines, Vol. 2, p. 3.
79 War Diary entry for 17 June 1940 in Simpson (ed.), *The Cunningham Papers*, Vol. 1, p. 78.
80 War Diary entries for 25 and 30 June and 14 July 1940 in ibid., pp. 80–1, 85, 112.
81 TNA CAB 66/9/37, WP(40) 257, 'Proposed Declaration of Dangerous Areas off the Coasts of Italy and Colonies', 10 July 1940. This came into being on 14 July.
82 TNA ADM 234/381, NSH, Submarines, Vol. 2, p. 4.
83 TNA CAB 66/9/42, WP(40) 262, Weekly Resume, 12 July 1940, p. 2.

Chapter 2

1 TNA ADM 187/8, Admiralty Pink List entry for 10 June 1940.
2 USMM, *LMI*, Vol. 1, *Dati Statistici*, p. 17.
3 RAFM, Longmore Papers, DC/74/102/14, 'Despatch on Middle East Air Operations', 1 February 1941, appendix B, 'Location of Units in Middle East Command as at 11 June 1940'.

4 RAFM, Longmore Papers, DC/74/102/14, 'Despatch on Middle East Air Operations', 1 February 1941, pp. 1, 9; Spooner, *Supreme Gallantry*, pp. 14–15.
5 TNA ADM 187/8, Admiralty Pink List entry for 10 June 1940.
6 TNA ADM 116/3900, 'The Strategical Aspect of the Situation in the Mediterranean on 1 October 1938', Part III, 14 November 1938.
7 TNA ADM 234/560, NSH, British Mining Operations, 1939–45, Vol. 1, pp. 559–60.
8 TNA ADM 234/560, NSH, British Mining Operations, Vol. 1, p. 559; TNA ADM 187/8, Admiralty Pink List entry for 10 June 1940.
9 ADM 116/3900, 'Situation in October–1st October 1938', Part III, Section II, 14 November 1938.
10 Cunningham to Pound, 7 June 1940, in Simpson (ed.), *The Cunningham Papers*, Vol. 1, p. 49.
11 RAFM, Longmore Papers, DC/74/102/14, 'Despatch on Middle East Air Operations', 1 February 1941, pp. 2–3.
12 Richard Hammond, 'British Policy on Total Maritime Warfare and the Anti-Shipping Campaign in the Mediterranean, 1940–1944', *Journal of Strategic Studies*, 36, 6 (2013), p. 796. In January 1941 it was discovered that this rule did not actually incorporate German shipping, and it was quickly rectified to do so.
13 For an appreciation of the potential role of Malta as a base to attack Italian shipping, see TNA ADM 1/9922, Pound to Secretary of the Admiralty, 19 January 1939, pp. 1–2; on the delay of building up Maltese defences immediately prior to the Italian declaration of war, see Michael J. Budden, 'Defending the Indefensible: The Air Defence of Malta, 1936–1940', *War in History*, 6, 4 (1999), pp. 461–3; on the primarily defensive fleet posture and focus on the eastern basin and Dodecanese, TNA CAB 80/12, COS(40), 421 JP, 'Policy in the Mediterranean', Annex I, C-in-C Mediterranean to Admiralty, 23 May 1940; Playfair et al., *The Mediterranean and Middle East*, Vol. 1, pp. 98–9.
14 RAFM, Longmore Papers, DC/74/102/14, 'Despatch on Middle East Air Operations', 1 February 1941, pp. 2, 11; appendix B, 'Location of Units in Middle East Command as at 11 June 1940'.
15 RAFM, Longmore Papers, DC/74/102/14, 'Despatch on Middle East Air Operations', appendix A, Air Council Instructions as to Responsibilities of Air Officer Commanding in Chief, Middle East, 11 June 1940, p. 2.
16 TNA AIR 41/19, Air Historical Branch Narrative (AHBN), The RAF and Maritime War, Vol. 6, p. 42.
17 Kenneth Poolman, *Night Strike from Malta: 830 Squadron RN and Rommel's Convoys* (London: Jane's Publishing, 1980), p. 22.
18 TNA CAB 80/12, COS(40), 421 JP, 'Policy in the Mediterranean', 30 May 1940, p. 3.
19 TNA AIR 2/7197, 'Notes on an Air Offensive against Italy', 3 May 1940, pp. 1–2 and 'Possible Bombing Operations against Italy', 29 May 1940, p. 1; Richard Overy, *The Bombing War: Europe 1939–1945* (London: Allen Lane, 2013), p. 511.

20 Raids listed in Marco Gioannini and Giulio Massobrio, *Bombardate l'Italia: Storia della guerra di distruzione aerea, 1940–45* (Milan: Rizzoli, 2007), website appendix. On the unprepared nature of Italian air defence see Stephen Harvey, 'The Italian War Effort and the Strategic Bombing of Italy', *History*, 70, 228 (1985), pp. 38–9; Achille Rastelli, 'I bombardamenti aerei nella seconda guerra mondiale: Milano e la provincia', *Italia Contemporania*, 195 (1995), pp. 309–42; Knox, *Hitler's Italian Allies*, pp. 67, 101; Overy, *The Bombing War*, pp. 513–16. For the unrest and anxiety caused, see Claudia Baldioli and Marco Finardi, 'Italian Society under Anglo-American Bombs: Propaganda, Experience and Legend, 1940–1945', *Historical Journal*, 52, 4 (2009), pp. 1019, 1026.
21 TNA CAB 80/16, COS(40) 629, Chiefs of Staff Committee, 14 August 1940.
22 TNA CAB 80/16, COS(40) 631, Chiefs of Staff Committee, 'Reinforcement of Garrisons Abroad', 24 August 1940, pp. 2–3.
23 TNA CAB 80/16, COS(40) 647, Chiefs of Staff Committee, 'Future Strategy' appreciation, 21 August 1940, p. 1, emphasis in original.
24 Ibid., p. 40.
25 TNA GFM 36/10, Mussolini to Graziani, 19 August 1940; Ball, *Bitter Sea*, p. 54.
26 Austin, *Malta and British Strategic Policy*, p. 89; War Diary entry for 25 September 1940, in Simpson (ed.), *The Cunningham Papers*, Vol. 1, p. 153.
27 TNA ADM 234/381, NSH, Submarines, Vol. 2, p. 14; TNA ADM 187/10, Admiralty Pink List entry for 30 December 1940.
28 War Diary entry for 25 October 1940, in Simpson (ed.), *The Cunningham Papers*, Vol. 1, p. 170.
29 On diminished threat of invasion, TNA CAB 69/11, Confidential Annex to DO(40) 39 War Cabinet Defence Committee (Operations) meeting 31 October 1940, p. 1; on Longmore–Portal correspondence, Christ Church Library, Oxford (CCO), Portal Papers, Folder 12, Longmore to Portal, 14 October 1940, p. 4; Longmore to Portal, 2 November 1940.
30 *I documenti diplomatici italiani* (DDI), Series 9, Vol. 5, Doc. 728, pp. 699–706; Playfair et al., *The Mediterranean and Middle East*, Vol. 1, p. 228; entry for 22 October 1940, Ciano, *Diario*, p. 472.
31 Martin van Creveld, 'Prelude to Disaster: The British Decision to Aid Greece, 1940–41', *Journal of Contemporary History*, 9, 3 (1974), pp. 66–7; TNA CAB 69/11, DO(40) 37, War Cabinet Defence Committee (Operations) meeting, 28 October 1940, p. 1; CCO, Portal Papers, Folder 1, COS Meeting Minutes, 1 November 1940; Folder 12, Portal to Longmore, 6 November 1940.
32 Drummond to D'Albiac, 5 November 1940, 'Directive to the Air Officer Commanding, British Air Forces in Greece', in Playfair et al., *The Mediterranean and Middle East*, Vol. 1, appendix 4, pp. 463–5.
33 TNA AIR 2/7397, Minute by DCAS, 5 November 1940; Air Ministry to HQ RAF Middle East, 11 November 1940.
34 Quoted in TNA AIR 2/7197, HQ Malta to Air Ministry, 18 November 1940.
35 War Diary entry for 3 November 1940, in Simpson (ed.), *The Cunningham Papers*, Vol. 1, pp. 173–4; TNA ADM 234/381, NSH, Submarines, Vol. 2, pp. 15–17.

36 USMM, *LMI*, Vol. 6, *La difesa del traffico*, pp. 21–2.
37 Jürgen Röhwer, *Allied Submarine Attacks of World War Two: European Theatre of Operations, 1939–1945*, (London: Greenhill, 1997), p. 126; TNA ADM 234/560, NSH, British Mining Operations, Vol. 1, pp. 560–3.
38 TNA ADM 199/1920, List of Patrols, June 1940; Hezlet, *British and Allied Submarine Operations*, p. 46.
39 Cunningham to Pound, 27 June 1940 in Simpson (ed.), *The Cunningham Papers*, Vol. 1, p. 83.
40 O'Hara, *Struggle for the Middle Sea*, p. 15; TNA ADM 234/323, 'Battle Summaries: No. 6, Bombardments of Bardia – Chapter I: 21 June 1940', p. 2.
41 Gioannini and Massobrio, *Bombardate l'Italia*, website appendix.
42 Royal Navy Submarine Museum (RNSM), Manuscript A1941/5, 'War Incidents December 1940, Enclosure A', p. 2.
43 Greene and Massignani, *Naval War in the Mediterranean*, pp. 63–5.
44 Playfair et al., *The Mediterranean and Middle East*, Vol. 1, p. 150; USMM, *LMI*, Vol. 3, *Navi Mercantili Perduti*, p. 22.
45 TNA ADM 234/323, 'Battle Summaries: No. 6, Bombardments of Bardia – Chapter II: 17 August 1940', pp. 6–7.
46 Hinsley et al., *British Intelligence*, Vol. 1, p. 210.
47 Attacks and results calculated from Röhwer, *Allied Submarine Attacks*, pp. 126–7.
48 TNA ADM 234/381, NSH, Submarines, Vol. 2, appendix 4, 'British and Allied Submarine losses in the Mediterranean', p. 276.
49 Cunningham to Pound, 3 August 1940, in Simpson (ed.), *The Cunningham Papers*, Vol. 1, pp. 123–4.
50 Hezlet, *British and Allied Submarine Operations*, p. 48.
51 TNA ADM 199/798, Report by CO 813 Squadron to CO HMS *Eagle*, 11 July 1940.
52 TNA ADM 199/798, C-in-C Mediterranean to Secretary of Admiralty, 13 September 1940; Report from CO HMS *Eagle* to C-in-C Mediterranean Station, 27 August 1940.
53 See Ben Jones, 'The Fleet Air Arm and the Struggle for the Mediterranean, 1940–1944' in Tim Benbow (ed.), *British Naval Aviation: The First 100 Years* (Farnham: Ashgate, 2011), pp. 79–85.
54 TNA ADM 207/13, 815 Squadron Diary, entry for 17 September 1940; TNA ADM 207/14, 819 Squadron Diary, January 1940–January 1941, p. 6; TNA ADM 199/798, Report from CO HMS *Illustrious* to Rear Admiral Aircraft Carriers, Mediterranean, 25 October 1940.
55 TNA AIR 27/614, No. 70 Squadron ORB, entries for 19 and 20 September 1940.
56 CCO, Portal Papers, Folder 12, Longmore to Portal, 14 October 1940, pp. 1, 4.
57 CCO, Portal Papers, Folder 12, Longmore to Portal, 2 November 1940, p. 2; David Gunby and Pelham Temple, *RAF Bomber Losses in the Mediterranean and Middle East*, Vol. 1, *1939–1942* (Hinckley: Midland Publishing, 2006), pp. 27–9.
58 Figure for raids against Valona in Denis Richards and Hilary Saunders, *The Royal Air Force at War, 1939–1945*, Vol. 1, *The Fight at Odds*

(London: HMSO, 1953), p. 258; losses calculated from Gunby and Temple, *RAF Bomber Losses in the Mediterranean and Middle East*, Vol. 1, pp. 29–49.

59 Report on Operation MB8, 6–14 November 1940, 3 March 1941 in Simpson (ed.), *The Cunningham Papers*, Vol. 1, p. 175; National Maritime Museum (NMM), Pridham-Wippell Papers, PWL/1, VALF to 7 CS, 13 November 1940, p. 1.

60 NMM, Pridham-Wippell Papers, PWL/1, VALF to C-in-C Mediterranean, 13 November 1940, 'Raid on Straits of Otranto, 11–12 November'; O'Hara, *Struggle for the Middle Sea*, p. 64.

61 Poolman, *Night Strike from Malta*, pp. 34–5.

62 CCO, Portal Papers, Folder 12, Longmore to Portal, 5 November 1940; TNA AIR 2/7937, Minute by DCAS, 5 November 1940, Air Ministry to HQ RAF Middle East, 11 November 1940; Gioannini and Massobrio, *Bombardate L'Italia*, website appendix; Spooner, *Supreme Gallantry*, p. 20.

63 TNA AIR 23/5697, 'Passage of Convoys to North Africa', 29 December 1940, pp. 1–2 for details of Naples build-ups and HUMINT; TNA AIR 27/1413, 228 Squadron ORB, Summary of Events, November–December 1940 for regular reconnaissance sorties. See entry for 6 November 1940 for Aegean flights.

64 TNA AIR 23/5697, 'Passage of Convoys to North Africa', 29 December 1940, p. 2.

65 TNA AIR 23/5697, Minute No. 3 by SASO, 12 December 1940; HQ RAF Mediterranean to 228 Squadron, 17 December 1940.

66 Figures calculated from Röhwer, *Allied Submarine Attacks*, pp. 16–17; sinking of the *Sardegna* and the actions and loss of *Proteus* in USMM, *LMI*, Vol. 9, *La difesa del traffico con l'Albania, la Grecia e l'Egeo*, pp. 50–5; losses from TNA ADM 234/381, NSH, Submarines, Vol. 2, appendix 4, 'British and Allied Submarine losses in the Mediterranean', pp. 276–7. The NSH actually gives three losses in September and places the loss of the *Narval* in early January. In fact, it was lost in late December.

67 Calculated from TNA AIR 20/9598, Table 3: 'Analysis of Enemy Merchant Shipping Sunk by all Causes, Scuttled, Captured or Surrendered in the Mediterranean'. Some revision of these figures has been undertaken using the data in Röhwer, *Allied Submarine Attacks*.

68 S. May, 'The British Submarine Campaign in the Mediterranean' (MPhil Thesis, University of Wales, Swansea, 2000), p. 40.

69 Figures from TNA ADM 189/159, Holerith Analysis, part one, pp. 1, 15–20.

70 See Ben Bryant, *One Man Band: The Memoirs of a Submarine CO* (London: William Kimber, 1958), pp. 57–61, 64–8.

71 John Campbell, *Naval Weapons of World War Two* (London: Conway Maritime Press, 2000), p. 80.

72 Ibid.

73 Simpson, *Periscope View*, pp. 101–2.

74 These arguments have been put forward extensively since the war. This list is by no means comprehensive, but see for instance Playfair et al., *The Mediterranean and Middle East*, Vol. 1, pp. 216–17; Roskill, *War at Sea*, Vol. 1,

pp. 305–6; Greene and Massignani, *Naval War in the Mediterranean*, p. 269; MacIntyre, *Battle for the Mediterranean*, p. 83; Simpson, *Periscope View*, p. 102; John Wingate, *The Fighting Tenth: The Tenth Submarine Flotilla and the Siege of Malta* (London: Periscope Publishing, 2003), p. 7; Spooner, *Supreme Gallantry*, p. 5; Andrew Browne Cunningham, *A Sailor's Odyssey: The Autobiography of Admiral of the Fleet Viscount Cunningham of Hyndhope* (London: Hutchinson, 1951), p. 269.
75 Cunningham to Pound, 3 August 1940 in Simpson (ed.), *The Cunningham Papers*, Vol. 1, pp. 123–4.
76 For full specifications, see Paul Akermann, *Encyclopedia of British Submarines 1901–1955* (Penzance: Periscope Publishing, 2002); D. K. Brown (ed.), *The Design and Construction of British Warships 1939–1945: The Official Record Vol. 2, Submarines, Escorts and Coastal Forces* (Annapolis: Naval Institute Press, 1996).
77 Wingate, *The Fighting Tenth*, p. 18.
78 Hezlet, *British and Allied Submarine Operations*, p. 417; D. K. Brown, *Nelson to Vanguard: Warship Development 1923–1945* (London: Chatham, 2006), p. 109.
79 RNSM, A1941/5, 'War Incidents December 1940', Enclosure A, p. 2.
80 Mallett, *The Italian Navy and Fascist Expansionism*, p. 172; Giorgerini, *La Battaglia dei Convogli*, pp. 42–4; Knox, *Hitler's Italian Allies*, p. 162; Greene and Massignani, *Naval War in the Mediterranean*, pp. 44–5, 257, 269; TNA ADM 199/311, Submarine intelligence summary No. 1, 10 October 1939, f. 236.
81 See Brown, *Nelson to Vanguard*, pp. 127–9, and Campbell, *Naval Weapons of World War 2*, pp. 88–93 for details of these weapons and their lethality.
82 TNA, ADM 219/583, 'Admiralty Wartime Research and Development 1939–1945: Submarines', 1950, p. 4; USMM, *LMI*, Vol. 4, *Le azioni navali dal 10 Giugno 1940 al 31 Marzo 1941* (Rome: USMM, 1959), p. 69.
83 USMM, *LMI*, Vol. 6, *La difesa del traffico*, p. 68.
84 Ibid., pp. 67–71; IWM IAF, Box 20, E. 2560, 'Attività bellica del 30 Stormo dall 11 giugno al 1 Agosto 1941', 7 August 1941.
85 Comment about poor suitability of SM 79 and lack of visual capability from IWM IAF, Box 20, E. 2560, '30 Stormo B.T: Relazione sull'attività del 1 anno di guerra', 7 August 1941, p. 19; Radios in Mallett, *The Italian Navy and Fascist Expansionism*, p. 173.
86 One example of such SIGINT giving a position and direction of a submarine just before the outbreak of war is in AUSMM, Fondo Supermarina, Intercettazioni Estere, No. 24, message 2143, 9 June 1940. However, direct evidence to link this knowledge to the sinking of one of the three submarines in June is lacking. For details of the 'avoidance' policy followed regarding SIGINT and convoys in 1942 see Vincent O'Hara and Enrico Cernucshi, 'The Other Ultra: Signal Intelligence and the Battle to Supply Rommel's Attack Towards Suez', *Naval War College Review*, 66, 3 (2013), pp. 117–38.
87 Figures on mines laid from TNA ADM 234/560, NSH, British Mining Operations, Vol. 1.

88 USMM, *LMI*, Vol. 19, *Il Draggagio*, p. 31.
89 See ibid., pp. 31–45.
90 TNA GFM 36/10, Mussolini to Graziani, 19 August 1940; Knox, *Mussolini Unleashed*, pp. 164–5, 190–1, 198, 208, 251–2.
91 Playfair et al., *Mediterranean and Middle East*, Vol. 1, p. 362.
92 Calculated from USMM, *LMI*, Vol. 1, *Dati Statistici*, Table LIV, p. 124.
93 Knox, *Hitler's Italian Allies*, pp. 57–8, 124; Brian R. Sullivan, 'The Italian Soldier in Combat, June 1940 to September 1943: Myths, Realities and Explanations' in Paul Addison and Angus Calder (eds.), *Time to Kill: The Soldiers' Experience of War in the West, 1939–1945* (London: Pimlico, 1997), pp. 178–8, 197.
94 On defensive frailties see the report by German observer Franz Reichart in TNA GFM 36/54, 'Relazione sulla mia permanenza presso l'Armata di Graziani dal 19 ottobre al 22 dicembre 1940', 26 December 1940; on warning signs, Knox, *Mussolini Unleashed*, p. 253.
95 Calculated from USMM, *LMI*, Vol. 1, *Dati Statistici*, Tables LXIII and LXV, pp. 147, 157.
96 MF, *Germany and the Second World War*, Vol. 3, pp. 420–2, 435, with further examples of logistical problems on pp. 439–40, 442, 444–5; for the Italian perspective on the war with Greece, see Mario Montanari, *L'Eserctio Italiano nella campagna di Grecia* (Rome: USSME, 3rd edition, 1999) and for the Greek see Alexandros Papagos, *The Battle of Greece, 1940–41* (Athens: J. M. Skazikis, 1949).
97 On this decision, see the minutes of meeting on 1 November 1940, USSME, *Verbali delle riunioni*, Vol. 2, pp. 107–12 and the entry for 1 November 1940 in Quirino Armellini, *Diario di guerra: nove mesi al Comando Supremo* (Milan: Garzanti, 1946), pp. 133–4.
98 USMM, *LMI*, Vol. 4, *Le Azioni Navali*, pp. 256–7; Vol. 9, *La difesa del traffico con Albania, Grecia e l'Egeo*, p. 18; AUSMM, Fondo Supermarina, Supermarina-Omologazioni danni nemico, b. 7, 'Economia bellica e linea di traffico', 11 December 1940, p. 2.
99 AUSMM, Fondo Supermarina, Supermarina-Omologazioni danni nemico, b. 7, 'Economia bellica e linea di traffico', 11 December 1940, pp. 1–2, 9, 11, 12.
100 See for example the Minutes of the Meeting of 14 October 1940 in USSME, *Verbali delle riunioni tenute dal Capo di Stato Maggiore Generale*, Vol. 1, pp. 87–96, especially 90–2.

Chapter 3

1 TNA CAB 80/56, COS(41), 2nd Meeting, 8 January 1941, Annexed minute on 'Future Strategy' by Churchill, pp. 1, 4–5.
2 Hinsley et al., *British Intelligence*, Vol. 1, pp. 259–61, 347–8; van Creveld, 'Prelude to Disaster', pp. 68–9, 90; Walter Ansel, *Hitler and the Middle Sea* (Durham, NC: Duke University Press, 1972), pp. 17–21, 191–203, 428; MF, *Germany and the Second World War*, Vol. 3, pp. 186–8, 197–246; Kitchen, *Rommel's Desert War*, p. 124.

3 TNA CAB 79/8, COS(41), 15th Meeting, 11 January 1941, annexed telegram from Churchill to Wavell and Longmore.
4 TNA CAB JP(41) 70, Joint Planning Staff Report, 28 January 1941, p. 4.
5 Playfair et al., *Mediterranean and Middle East*, Vol. 1, pp. 372, 377; TNA FO 371/24922, Memorandum by Sargent, 'Possibility of Greece making a separate peace', 12 December 1940 and minutes of 26, 28 and 30 December 1940.
6 J. R. M. Butler, *Grand Strategy*, Vol. 2, *September 1939–June 1941* (London: HMSO, 1957), pp. 384–5; Richards and Saunders, *The Royal Air Force at War*, Vol. 1, p. 284.
7 Klaus Schmider, 'The Mediterranean in 1940–41: Crossroads of Lost Opportunities?', *War and Society*, 15, 2 (1997), pp. 23–5.
8 An example of a positive response to calls for more aircraft in Greece is in CCO, Portal Papers, Folder 2, File 1, British Military Mission, Athens, to C-in-C ME, 12 Feb 1941; Beauforts in CAB 79/8, COS(41), 6th Meeting, 3 January 1941, pp. 1–2; Swordfish in 'Report from CO HMS *Ark Royal* to Flag Officer Commanding, Force H', 16 January 1941 in Ben Jones (ed.), *The Fleet Air Arm and the Second World War*, Vol. 1, *1939–1941: Norway, the Mediterranean and the* Bismarck (Farnham: Ashgate, 2012), pp. 320–2.
9 Based on the figures in TNA ADM 187/10, Admiralty Pink List entry for 30 December 1940 and TNA ADM 187/12, Admiralty Pink List entry for 31 March 1941. This does not mean no new submarines arrived at all; some replaced those that were transferred out of the theatre or lost.
10 Directive No. 22, 'German Support for the Battles in the Mediterranean Area', 11 January 1941 in Hugh Trevor-Roper (ed.), *Hitler's War Directives, 1939–1945* (London: Pan Books, 1966), pp. 98–100; Playfair et al., *The Mediterranean and Middle East*, Vol. 2, pp. 46–7; MF, *Germany and the Second World War*, Vol. 3, pp. 654, 670–3.
11 Hammond, 'British Policy on Total Maritime Warfare', p. 797.
12 TNA CAB 80/56, COS(41), 12th 'O' Meeting, 16 January 1941, annexed telegram from Longmore to Air Ministry, 15 January 1941.
13 CCO, Portal Papers, Folder 2, File 1, Portal to Churchill, 13 February and 16 March 1941.
14 Gioannini and Massobrio, *Bombardate l'Italia*, website appendix; ADM 207/13, 815 Squadron Diary, entries for 12 March–21 April 1941.
15 Basil Liddell-Hart (ed.), *The Rommel Papers* (London: Da Capo Press, 1950), p. 98.
16 Figures for evacuations from David Thomas, *Crete 1941: The Battle at Sea* (Athens: Efstathiadis, 1991), map 4.
17 See MF, *Germany and the Second World War*, Vol. 3, pp. 593–605, 611; Butler, *Grand Strategy*, Vol. 2, p. 519; Playfair et al., *Mediterranean and Middle East*, Vol. 2, pp. 177–205.
18 TNA CAB 79/55, COS(41), 10th 'O' Meeting, 4 April 1941, pp. 1, 3; TNA ADM 187/13, Admiralty Pink List Entry for 2 May 1941.
19 CCO, Portal Papers, Folder 2, File 1, Portal to Churchill, 24 April 1941; on inter-theatre learning see Richard Hammond, 'Inter and Intra-Theatre Learning and British Coastal Air Power in the Second World War', *War in History*, 26, 3 (2019), pp. 395–9.

20 Hammond, 'British Policy on Total Maritime Warfare', pp. 797–8 and figure 1 on p. 799.
21 Christina Goulter, *A Forgotten Offensive: Royal Air Force Coastal Command's Anti-shipping Campaign, 1940–45* (London: Frank Cass, 1995), p. 132, explains the detrimental effect of losing these aircraft to the Mediterranean on Coastal Command's own anti-shipping campaign.
22 TNA CAB 79/55, COS(41), 15th 'O' Meeting, 27 May 1941, Annex 2, 'Short Appreciation on the Situation in the Middle East As I See It' by J. G. Dill.
23 On the nature and achievements of aero-naval co-operation up to June 1941, see Richard Hammond, 'British Aero-Naval Co-operation in the Mediterranean, 1940–45, and the Creation of RAF No. 201 (Naval Co-operation) Group' in Michael LoCicero, Ross Mahoney and Stuart Mitchell (eds.), *A Military Transformed? Innovation and Adaptation in the British Military, 1792–1945* (Birmingham: Helion, 2014), pp. 232–4.
24 Austin, *Malta and British Strategic Policy*, p. 121.
25 Quoted in Michael Simpson, 'Wings over the Sea: The Interaction of Air and Sea Power in the Mediterranean, 1940–1942', in N. A. M. Rodger (ed.), *Naval Power in the Twentieth Century* (Basingstoke: Macmillan, 1996), p. 144.
26 CCO, Portal Papers, Folder 2, File 1, Portal to Churchill, 24 April 1941.
27 Cunningham to Pound, 10 April 1941; Pound to Cunningham, 11 April 1941 in Simpson (ed.), *The Cunningham Papers*, Vol. 1, pp. 337–9.
28 Both quotes in Austin, *Malta and British Strategic Policy*, p. 106.
29 Chiefs of Staff to C-in-C Middle East, 16 April 1941, in Simpson (ed.), *The Cunningham Papers*, Vol. 1, pp. 351–2.
30 Barnett, *Engage the Enemy More Closely*, pp. 365–6.
31 NMM, Dick Papers, DCK/20/13, Bombardment of Tripoli, 21 April 1941, p. 1.
32 Pound to Cunningham, 23 April 1941; Cunningham to the Admiralty, 25 April 1941 in Simpson (ed.), *The Cunningham Papers*, Vol. 1, pp. 354–6; it is important to note that despite the successes at Taranto and Cape Matapan, the potential threat of the Italian Navy was not considered to have been eliminated, see Hammond, 'Enduring Influence', pp. 824–8.
33 Cunningham to Pound, 22 April 1941 in Simpson (ed.), *The Cunningham Papers*, Vol. 1, pp. 353–4; CCO, Portal Papers, Folder 2, File 1, Portal to Churchill, 24 April 1941.
34 Churchill to Cunningham, 26 April 1941 in Simpson (ed.), *The Cunningham Papers*, pp. 357–8.
35 TNA AIR 22/398, RAF Middle East fortnightly operational summary No. 13, 21 April–4 May 1941, pp. 6–7.
36 Calculated from Thomas, *Crete 1941*, appendix 1.
37 TNA AIR 8/961, C-in-C Mediterranean to Admiralty, 3 June 1941.
38 Joint Services Command and Staff College (JSCSC), AHB Translations, Vol. 5, Translation VII/41, 'Appreciation of the Air Situation in the Mediterranean Theatre during the period 11/7–31/8 1941', report by German liaison officer to Italian Air Force, p. 1; Vol. 7, Translation No. VII/63, 'Reports on Axis Problems of Supply and on German–Italian co-operation, May–August 1941', pp. 1–2; Hinsley et al., *British Intelligence*, Vol. 2, p. 282.

39 Hugh Lloyd, *Briefed to Attack: Malta's Part in Allied Victory* (London: Hodder and Stoughton, 1949), pp. 13, 27–8, 62–9. Lloyd's predecessor, Maynard, had wanted, and often attempted, expansion and improvement of facilities, but was frequently thwarted first by a lack of personnel, and later by the aerial siege.
40 TNA CAB 79/12, COS(41), 212th COS Committee Meeting, 14 June 1941, annexed telegram from COS to C-in-C Mediterranean.
41 TNA AIR 8/961, Air Ministry to HQ RAF ME, 5 June 1941; increase in bombing based on statistics in TNA AIR 22/398, RAF Middle East fortnightly operational summary Nos. 16–17, 2–29 June 1941.
42 TNA AIR 22/398, RAF Middle East fortnightly operational summary No. 17, 16–29 June 1941, p. 4.
43 TNA CAB 79/12, COS(41), 220th COS Committee Meeting, 21 June 1941, pp. 2–3.
44 Middle East Commanders in Chief Committee, 4 and June 18 1941 in Simpson (ed.), *The Cunningham Papers*, Vol. 1, pp. 476–7, 481.
45 TNA CAB 79/55, COS(41), 22nd 'O' Meeting, 27 July 1941, p. 2.
46 Poolman, *Night Strike*, pp. 74–5.
47 Alberto Santoni and Francesco Mattesini, *La partecipazione tedesca alla guerra aeronavale nel Mediterraneo, 1940–1945* (Rome: Edizione dell'Ateneo & Bizzarri, 1980), p. 98.
48 Portal had wanted major attacks on Naples with subsequent high publicity, in revenge for Axis air attacks on Alexandria. He felt this would have an important effect on Egyptian morale and that this would justify diversion from attacks on Tripoli. The rest of the Cabinet disagreed and Naples only received a few small raids at this stage. TNA CAB 79/12, COS(41), 233th COS Committee Meeting, 3 July 1941, p. 7; Gioannini and Massobrio, *Bombardate l'Italia*, website appendix.
49 TNA AIR 23/5697, 'Minutes of Conference held at HQ, RAF Mediterranean, on 1st January 1941, on the Subject of Interception and Attack of Enemy Convoys', p. 1.
50 Ibid., pp. 1–2.
51 Ibid.; Cunningham to Pound, 5 January 1941 in Simpson (ed.), *The Cunningham Papers*, Vol. 1. p. 227; Roy Conyers Nesbit, *The Armed Rovers: Beauforts and Beaufighters over the Mediterranean* (Shrewsbury: Airlife, 1995), pp. 18–19.
52 TNA AIR 23/5697, Air Operation Instructions, 10 January 1941; RAFM, Longmore Papers, DC/74/102/14, 'Despatch on Middle East Air Operations', 1 February 1941, p. 10.
53 Playfair et al., *The Mediterranean and Middle East*, Vol. 1, p. 316.
54 TNA ADM 199/108, 'Attack on Italian Convoy by 830 Squadron on 27/1/41', 24 June 1941; Poolman, *Night Strike*, pp. 40–4.
55 Calculated from TNA ADM 199/108.
56 TNA ADM 234/381, NSH, Submarines, Vol. 2, p. 21; TNA ADM 234/560, NSH, British Mining Operations, Vol. 1, pp. 569–70; sinkings calculated from Röhwer, *Allied Submarine Attacks*, p. 130.
57 TNA ADM 234/323, Battle Summaries: No. 7, Bombardment of Genoa, p. 22.

58 Playfair et al., *The Mediterranean and Middle East*, Vol. 1, pp. 330–1; O'Hara, *Struggle for the Middle Sea*, p. 81.
59 Playfair et al., *The Mediterranean and Middle East*, Vol. 2, p. 75; Richards and Saunders, *The Royal Air Force*, Vol. 1, p. 286.
60 TNA AIR 22/398, Summary of Bombing Operations in Support of Greece, 18 March–6 April 1941.
61 ADM 207/13, 815 Squadron Diary, entries for 12 March–21 April 1941; vessels sunk from TNA AIR 20/9598.
62 Calculated from TNA AIR 22/398, 'Summary of Bombing Operations, Part II – in Egypt and Libya', 18 March–6 April 1941.
63 TNA AIR 8/961, Governor and C-in-C Gibraltar to War Office, copy of signal from Secretary of State for Foreign Affairs to Prime Minister, 9 April 1941.
64 Calculated from TNA AIR 22/398, Fortnightly Operational Summaries Nos. 11–15, 18 March–1 June 1941.
65 For a good example, see the results of a raid on 1 May as reported in the war diary of the Benghazi Sea Transport Hub, National Archives and Records Administration (NARA) T-1022, Roll 2525, PG 45221, Kriegstagebuch der Seetransporthauptstelle Bengasi, entries for 1–2 May 1941.
66 TNA DEFE 3/686, Enigma Signal OL 26, 2 April 1941; USMM, *LMI*, Vol. 6, *La difesa*, pp. 99–100.
67 USMM, *LMI*, Vol. 6, *La difesa*, p. 105; Greene and Massignani, *Naval War in the Mediterranean*, pp. 161–4.
68 'Operations MD2 and MD3: The Bombardment of Tripoli, 21 April 1941' in Simpson (ed.), *The Cunningham Papers*, Vol. 1, pp. 363–4.
69 TNA ADM 207/23, 826 Squadron Diary, entry for 7 May 1941.
70 TNA ADM 234/560, NSH, British Mining Operations, Vol. 1, pp. 572–3.
71 Claim of 4,000 killed in 'Cunningham's Report on the Battle of Crete', 4 August 1941 in Simpson (ed.), *The Cunningham Papers*, Vol. 1, p. 429; figures of 3–400 dead from Thomas, *Crete 1941*, p. 144; accounts of Italian escorts in Bragadin, *Italian Navy*, pp. 108–9.
72 Lloyd, *Briefed to Attack*, p. 45.
73 Austin, *Malta and British Strategic Policy*, p. 120.
74 O'Hara, *Struggle for the Middle Sea*, pp. 137–8. Details of some of the information on convoy sailings provided by this intelligence are located in TNA ADM 223/31, 'Italian Convoy Reports, October 1941–May 1943' and TNA ADM 223/45, 'Analysis of Convoy Sailings from Italy to North Africa, September 1941–June 1943'.
75 Ralph Bennett, *Ultra and Mediterranean Strategy, 1941–1945* (London: Hamish Hamilton, 1989), p. 24; Hinsley et al., *British Intelligence*, Vol. 2, p. 283.
76 Austin, *Malta and British Strategic Policy*, p. 127.
77 Most notably, Sadkovich has overstated the effect of the breaking of C38m, including an incorrect claim that the cypher was broken in autumn 1940 and contributing to sinkings from that point onward. See Sadkovich, *Italian Navy*, pp. 126–7.
78 Calculated from Röhwer, *Allied Submarine Attacks*, pp. 134–41.

79 Calculated from ibid., pp. 130–41.
80 Mediterranean War Diary, 'General Appreciation' for February 1941, in Simpson (ed.), *The Cunningham Papers*, Vol. 1, p. 293; Simpson, *Periscope View*, p. 126.
81 May, 'British Submarine Campaign in the Mediterranean', p. 43.
82 TNA ADM 199/1888, Captain (S), First Submarine Flotilla to C-in-C China Station, 8 March 1941.
83 TNA ADM 189/159, 'British Submarine Wartime Patrols: Holerith Analysis. Part 1', p. 2; TNA ADM 189/166, Holerith Analysis Part 8, pp. 10–11.
84 TNA ADM 234/381, NSH, Submarines, Vol. 2, p. 32.
85 Mediterranean War Diary, April 1941, Summary and Appreciation of Events in Simpson (ed.), *The Cunningham Papers*, Vol. 1, p. 368.
86 Hinsley, *British Intelligence*, Vol. 2, p. 281; a good example of the sometimes overly slow nature of determining the running of the shipping routes can be found in Enrico Cernuschi, *'Ultra' la fine di un mito: La guerra dei codici tra gli inglesi e le Marine italiane, 1934–1945* (Milan: Mursia, 2014), p. 216.
87 Cunningham to Pound, 11 June 1941, in Simpson (ed.), *The Cunningham Papers*, Vol. 1, p. 478.
88 As they did not take place during anti-shipping operations, losses during the evacuation have not been included here.
89 MF, *Germany and the Second World War*, Vol. 3, pp. 659, 686–8.
90 USMM, *LMI*, Vol. 6, *La difesa*, pp. 70–1.
91 IWM, IAF, Box 20, 'Relazione sull'impiego del 30 Stormo nel primo anno di Guerra', 7 August 1941, pp. 16–20; 'Attività bellica del 30 Stormo dal Giugno 1941 al 1 Agosto 1941'.
92 IMW, IAF, Box 20, Foglio 21572/9, Memorandum by Generale Biffi, 6 October 1941.
93 Knox, *Hitler's Italian Allies*, pp. 113–14, 164.
94 IWM, IAF, Box 25, E.2530, 'Relazione Statistica sull'attività operativa dell'Aeronautica nel trimestre Aprile–Giugno, 1941'; Austin, *Malta and British Strategic Policy*, pp. 113, 117.
95 Playfair et al., *The Mediterranean and Middle East*, Vol. 2, p. 299.
96 Knox, *Mussolini Unleashed*, pp. 258–60; MF, *Germany and the Second World War*, Vol. 3, pp. 446–8.
97 MF, *Germany and the Second World War*, Vol. 3, pp. 500–16; Christopher Buckley, *Greece and Crete 1941* (Athens: Efstathidis Group, 1993), pp. 47–154.
98 On the course of the battle for Crete, see MF, *Germany and the Second World War*, Vol. 3, pp. 543–55; Buckley, *Greece and Crete*, pp. 161–317; Tony Simpson, *Operation Mercury: The Battle for Crete, 1941* (London: Hodder and Stoughton, 1981), pp. 152–274.
99 Riccardi to Ministero delle Comunicazioni, 16 June 1941 in USMM, *LMI*, Vol. 9, pp. 99–100.
100 USMM, *LMI*, Vol. 9, p. 103; TNA HW 11/33, GC + CS Naval History, Vol. 20, pp. 60–1.
101 JSCSC, AHB Translations, Vol. 7, Translation No. VII/63, 'Conference with the Italian General Staff', 2 June 1941, pp. 5–6.

102 The difficulties of establishing the latter figures (beyond the DAK) are well discussed in Austin, *Malta*, p. 132.
103 Kitchen, *Rommel's Desert War*, pp. 56–8.
104 TNA DEFE 3/686, Signals OL 235, 259 338 and 448, 6, 9, 16 and 28 May 1941.
105 Meeting of 17 April 1941 in USSME, *Verbali*, Vol. 2, pp. 40–2.
106 Kitchen, *Rommel's Desert War*, pp. 71, 75–6.
107 TNA CAB 146/19, Enemy Documents Section (EDS) Appreciation 11, 'The Axis Supply Situation in North Africa, February 1941–December 1942', pp. 12, 19.
108 Wolf Heckmann, *Rommel's War in Africa* (New York: Doubleday, 1981), p. 232.
109 TNA DEFE 3/686, Signals OL 69 and OL 103, 8 and 16 April 1941.
110 TNA HW 13/1, 'Transport in the Libya Campaign', 15 June 1941, pp. 1–3.
111 Calls for greater use of Benghazi had been coming from the moment of its capture. See TNA DEFE 3/686, Signals OL 83 and OL 84, 11 April 1941.
112 TNA DEFE 3/686, Signals OL 177, 184, 197 and 212, 27, 28 and 30 April and 4 May 1941; NARA T-1022, Roll 2525, PG 45221, Kriegstagebuch der Seetransporthauptstelle Bengasi, entries for 1–2 May 1941.
113 *The Rommel Papers*, pp. 114, 134–8; TNA HW 11/33, GC + CS Naval History, Vol. 20, pp. 116–17.
114 TNA DEFE 3/686, Signals OL 269 and OL 280, 11 and 12 May 1941; TNA HW 13/1, 'Transport in the Libya Campaign', 19 May 1941, pp. 2, 7.
115 Conference of 25 July 1941, in *Fuehrer Conferences on Naval Affairs, 1939–1945* (London: Greenhill, 1990), p. 224; TNA CAB 146/19, Enemy Documents Section (EDS) Appreciation 11, 'The Axis Supply Situation in North Africa, February 1941–December 1942', pp. 12, 19.
116 TNA CAB 146/19, Enemy Documents Section (EDS) Appreciation 11, 'The Axis Supply Situation in North Africa, February 1941–December 1942', p. 50.
117 TNA HW 11/33, GC + CS Naval History, Vol. 20, p. 117.
118 JSCSC, AHB Translations, Vol. 7, Translation No. VII/63, Cavallero to Keitel, 12 June 1941, pp. 7–8.
119 See Rintelen's minute to JSCSC, AHB Translations, Vol. 7, Translation No. VII/63, Cavallero to Keitel, 12 June 1941, pp. 7–8.
120 Van Creveld, *Supplying War*, p. 187.
121 Kitchen, *Rommel's Desert War*, p. 130; for the sinkings of very small vessels, see the listings held in TNA AIR 20/9598.
122 JSCSC, AHB Translations, Vol. 9, Translation No. VII/81, Keitel to C-in-C Army, 20 May 1941.
123 JSCSC, AHB Translations, Vol. 7, Translation No. VII/63, 'Conference held in the Presence of the Duce between Chef OKW and General Cavallero', 29 August 1941, appendix 2: 'The Shipping Space Situation in the Mediterranean', p. 20.
124 Cristiano Andrea Ristuccia, 'The Italian Economy under Fascism: The Rearmament Paradox' (DPhil thesis, University of Oxford, 1998), pp. 226, 233–5, 238–9.

125 Calculated from AUSMM, Maristat-Statistiche Generali, pacco no. 3, Situazione naviglio mercantile, 'Situazione al 1° Ottobre 1941 naviglio *Italiano* affondato o danneggiato per fatti di guerra', undated.
126 Ristuccia, 'Italian Economy under Fascism', p. 237; TNA HW11/33, GC+CS Naval History, Vol. 20, The Mediterranean, 1940–1943, p. 109; for an example of the long delay in repair and inadequate repair capacities, see F. W. Deakin, *The Brutal Friendship: Mussolini, Hitler and the Fall of Fascism* (London: Weidenfield and Nicolson, 1962), p. 81.
127 JSCSC, AHB Translations, Vol. 9, Translation No. VII/81, Keitel to C-in-C Army, 20 May 1941.
128 TNA CAB 79/55, COS(41), 24th 'O' Meeting, 30 July 1941, p. 3.

Chapter 4

1 MF, *Germany and the Second World War*, Vol. 3, pp. 706–7, 725.
2 TNA CAB 69/2, D.O.(41), 51st Meeting, 17 July 1941, p. 1.
3 TNA CAB 69/2, D.O.(41), 53rd Meeting, 1 August 1941, pp. 3–4.
4 TNA CAB 79/55, COS(41), 27th 'O' Meeting, 25 August 1941, p. 2.
5 TNA AIR 23/1376, Cunningham to Tedder, Letter on 'Air Co-operation', 14 August 1941.
6 TNA AIR 23/1376, Tedder to Cunningham, 18 September 1941.
7 See Hammond, 'British Aero-Naval Co-operation in the Mediterranean', pp. 234–7.
8 TNA AIR 8/961, Churchill to Pound, 22 August 1941.
9 TNA AIR 8/961, Cunningham to Pound, 24 August 1941.
10 TNA CAB 79/55, COS(41) 27th 'O' Meeting, 25 August 1941, p. 3.
11 Ibid., p. 4.
12 Pound to Cunningham, 31 August 1941 in Simpson (ed.), *The Cunningham Papers*, Vol. 1, p. 506; TNA AIR 8/961, C-in-C Mediterranean to Admiralty, 19 September 1941.
13 TNA AIR 8/961, DoP to CAS, 20 September 1941; Gioannini and Massobrio, *Bombardate l'Italia*, online appendix.
14 CCO Portal Papers, Folder 12, Tedder to Portal, 5 September 1941; Hinsley et al., *British Intelligence*, Vol. 2, p. 285.
15 TNA AIR 8/961, Air Ministry to HQ RAF ME, 30 September 1941; HQ RAF ME to Air Ministry, 1 October 1941; CCO Portal Papers, Folder 12, Portal to Tedder, 4 October 1941.
16 Playfair et al., *Mediterranean and Middle East*, Vol. 2, appendix 7, p. 361; TNA ADM 187/16, Admiralty Pink List Entry for 3 November 1941; on Allied submarines see Richard Hammond, 'Fighting under a Different Flag: Multinational Naval Co-operation and Submarine Warfare in the Mediterranean, 1940–1944', *Journal of Military History*, 80, 2 (2016), pp. 447–76. At this stage there were Greek, Dutch and Polish vessels, along with one non-operational Yugoslav boat. French and Italian vessels were later added.
17 Spooner, *Supreme Gallantry*, p. 71; Poolman, *Night Strike*, p. 128.

18 This brief account is built from the following sources: Playfair et al., *Mediterranean and Middle East*, Vol. 3, pp. 1–102; MF, *Germany and the Second World War*, Vol. 3, pp. 725–54; Kitchen, *Rommel's Desert War*, pp. 141–80; Jack Greene and Alessandro Massignani, *Rommel's North Africa Campaign: September 1940–November 1942* (Conshohocken, PA: Combined Books, 1994), pp. 91–134, 249–53.
19 Kitchen, *Rommel's Desert War*, p. 161.
20 For a breakdown of respective losses in men and armour, see Playfair et al., *Mediterranean and Middle East*, Vol. 3, p. 97.
21 'Report of Proceedings, 5–14 August 1941' in Simpson (ed.), *The Somerville Papers*, pp. 299–300.
22 TNA ADM 234/560, NSH, Minelaying, Vol. 1, p. 576.
23 TNA ADM 223/553, VA Malta to C-in-C Mediterranean, 11 May 1942.
24 TNA AIR 8/961, C-in-C Mediterranean to Admiralty, 2 September 1941.
25 Calculated from CCO, Portal Papers, Folder 12, Lloyd to Portal, 13 October 1941.
26 Calculated from TNA AIR 22/398, HQ RAF ME Fortnightly Summaries Nos. 20–24, 28 July–5 October 1941.
27 TNA AIR 20/5306, Operational Research Section (Middle East), Report No. 4; 'An Account of Anti-Shipping Operations Carried out by Aircraft Operating from Malta between Oct. 1 and Dec. 12 1941', p. 1.
28 TNA ADM 199/108, 'Night Operations of Swordfish Aircraft of No. 830 Squadron Fleet Air Arm Based on Malta against Convoys in the Central Mediterranean', 22 November 1941. These techniques appear to have been used from September onwards, prior to being formalised.
29 Calculated from TNA AIR 22/398, HQ RAF ME Fortnightly Summaries Nos. 20–24, 28 July–5 October 1941.
30 Calculated from ibid.
31 TNA ADM 234/381, NSH, Submarines, Vol. 2, pp. 47, 51.
32 Simpson, *Periscope View*, pp. 150–3; Röhwer, *Allied Submarine Attacks*, p. 143; Giogerini, *La Battaglia dei Convogli*, p. 146.
33 TNA DEFE 3/690, Signals OL 1847–50, 8–9 November 1941. For an account of the role of both SIGINT and aerial reconnaissance in notifying the British of the departure of the convoy and assisting in its destruction, see Alberto Santoni, *Il vero traditore: Il ruolo documentato di ULTRA nella Guerra del mediterraneo* (Milan: Mursia, 1981), pp. 116–20.
34 TNA ADM 199/677, HMS *Aurora* Senior Officer Report of Proceedings, No. BS/10, 11 November 1941 and attached minute by Director of Training and Staff Duties Division, 25 January 1942; Greene and Massignani, *The Naval War in the Mediterranean*, pp. 193–5; Roskill, *War at Sea*, Vol. I, pp. 532–3; MF, *Germany and the Second World War*, Vol. 3, pp. 718–19.
35 TNA DEFE 3/745, Signals MK 67, 168, 22–24 November 1941.
36 TNA ADM 199/677, Letter of Proceedings for period 23–25 November, No. BS/14, 3 December 1941; on the comprehensive tracking data provided from SIGINT, see Santoni, *Il vero traditore*, pp. 121–6.
37 Entry for 2 December 1941, Ciano, *Diario*, pp. 562–3. For *Procida* and *Maritza*, TNA DEFE 3/745, Signal MK 168, 24 November 1941.

38 TNA ADM 199/677, 'Interception of Enemy Convoys for Benghazi. Letter of Proceedings, 30 Nov to 1 Dec', 13 December 1941, p. 3.
39 MF, *Germany and the Second World War*, Vol. 3, p. 720.
40 Greene and Massignani, *The Naval War in the Mediterranean*, pp. 196, 198–200; Roskill, *War at Sea*, Vol. I, p. 534; Spooner, *Supreme Gallantry*, pp. 97–101; details of cargoes carried and casualties taken from DEFE 3/745 Signal MK 485, 5 December 1941, and O'Hara, *Struggle for the Middle Sea*, p. 153.
41 Report of the C-in-C Navy to the Fuehrer at Wolfsschanze, 13 November 1941 in *Fuehrer Conferences*, p. 240.
42 Minutes of meeting of 4 December 1941, USSME, *Verbali delle riunioni*, Vol. 2, p. 119.
43 Greene and Massignani, *The Naval War in the Mediterranean*, pp. 159–60. For an in-depth account of the role of SIGINT in enabling anti-shipping operations, see Santoni, *Il vero traditore*, passim.
44 Giorgerini, *La Battaglia dei Convogli*, pp. 164–7; Playfair et al., *Mediterranean and Middle East*, Vol. 3, pp. 110–14. On sackings and court-martials in the Italian Navy, see Greene and Massignani, *The Naval War in the Mediterranean*, p. 196.
45 TNA ADM 199/897, Report of Proceedings for the Period 18/19th December 1941, including the Loss of HM Ships 'Neptune' and 'Kandahar'; Roskill, *War at Sea*, Vol. 2, p. 535.
46 Fuehrer Directive No. 38, 2 December 1941 in Trevor-Roper (ed.), *Hitler's War Directives*, pp. 163–5.
47 MF, *Germany and the Second World War*, Vol. 6, p. 655.
48 The number of damaged vessels is calculated from AUSMM, Maristat-Statistiche Generali, pacco no. 3, Situazione naviglio mercantile, 'Naviglio Danneggiato', undated, pp. 2–3. There are figures for tonnages of damaged vessels in AUSMM, Maristat-Statistiche Generali, pacco no. 3, Situazione naviglio mercantile, 'Situazione al 1° Ottobre 1941 naviglio Italiano affondato o danneggiato per fatti di guerra', undated, but this only covers August and September. It also gives a higher number of ships damaged in those two months than the first source but these have not been incorporated. The figure of forty-five ships for August–December is therefore likely a conservative one, and the reality probably higher.
49 May, 'British Submarine Campaign in the Mediterranean', p. 37.
50 Ibid., p. 40; Röhwer, *Allied Submarine Attacks*, p. 147. Although this did not translate into an immediate attack, the *Proteus* did manage to sink a merchant ship the following morning.
51 War Diary entry for 21 December 1941 in Simpson (ed.), *The Cunningham Papers*, Vol. 1, p. 553.
52 TNA ADM 189/161, Holerith Analysis, Part 3, pp. 12–15.
53 Calculated from Röhwer, *Allied Submarine Attacks*, pp. 141–50.
54 TNA ADM 234/381, NSH, Submarines, Vol. 2, p. 47.
55 Report of the C-in-C Navy to the Fuehrer at Wolfsschanze, 13 November 1941 in *Fuehrer Conferences*, p. 241.
56 TNA AIR 20/1057, Operational Research Section (Middle East) Report No. 4, 'An account of anti-shipping operations carried out by aircraft

operating from Malta between Oct 1 and Dec 12, 1941', p. 4. On the parallel introduction of a formalised approach to learning alongside the ongoing ad hoc work, see Hammond, 'Inter and Intra-Theatre Learning', pp. 12–16.

57 TNA AIR 8/961, C-in-C Mediterranean to Admiralty, 18 September 1941.
58 TNA AIR 23/1376, Cunningham to Tedder, Letter on 'Air Co-operation', 14 August 1941, p. 2.
59 Hammond, 'British Aero-Naval Co-operation', p. 238.
60 For a dedicated analysis of the role of air power in the campaign, see Richard Hammond, 'Air Power and the British Anti-Shipping Campaign in the Mediterranean, 1940–44', *Air Power Review*, 16, 1 (2013), pp. 50–69.
61 TNA ADM 234/381, NSH, *Submarines*, Vol. 2, p. 262.
62 On mine detector units, see May, 'British Submarine Campaign in the Mediterranean', p. 110; for quality of Italian mines, see USMM, *LMI*, Vol. 18, *La Guerra di Mine*.
63 There are certainly fewer decrypts in AUSMM, Fondo Supermarina, regarding Royal Navy submarine movements from mid-1941 onwards than exist for 1940 and early 1941, but this is not necessarily an accurate reflection of intelligence capability due to the large quantity of material that was destroyed around the time of the September 1943 armistice.
64 Calculated from TNA AIR 22/398, HQ RAF ME Fortnightly Summaries Nos. 20–25, 28 July–14 October 1941; TNA AIR 22/165, AMWR Weekly Statistical Analysis, Nos. 1–11, 12 October 1941–4 January 1942.
65 CCO, Portal Papers, File 12, Lloyd to Tedder, 18 August 1941.
66 CCO, Portal Papers, File 12, Lloyd to Portal, 13 October 1941; MF, *Germany and the Second World War*, Vol. 3, pp. 659, 686–8.
67 Some examples of such accidents are highlighted in CCO, Portal Papers, File 12, Lloyd to Portal, 13 October 1941.
68 IWM, IAF, Box 20, Marzucco to subordinate units, 22 August 1941.
69 Santoni and Mattesini, *La partecipazione*, pp. 145–6, 147–55.
70 TNA AIR 20/5306, Operational Research Section (Middle East), Report No. 4, pp. 4, 7.
71 JSCSC, AHB Translations, Vol. 7, Translation No. VII/63, 'Conference held in the Presence of the Duce between Chef OKW and General Cavallero', 29 August 1941, appendix 2: 'The Shipping Space Situation in the Mediterranean', pp. 20–1.
72 Gabriella Gribaudi, 'The True Causes of "Moral Collapse": People, Fascists and Authorities under the Bombs. Naples and the Countryside, 1940–1944' in Claudia Baldoli, Andrew Knapp and Richard Overy (eds.), *Bombing, States and Peoples in Western Europe, 1940–1945* (London: Continuum, 2011), p. 229.
73 See for example TNA GFM 36/8, Hitler to Mussolini, 21 June 1941, pp. 6–7; JSCSC, AHB Translations, Vol. 7, Translation No. VII/63, 'Conference with the Italian General Staff', 2 June 1941, p. 5; JSCSC, AHB Translations, Vol. 7, Translation No. VII/63, 'Supplies for Fliegerfuhrer Afrika and the German Afrika Korps', 12 August 1941, p. 13.
74 TNA HW 13/4, NI/MSS/16, 9 January 1942, p. 3.
75 JSCSC AHB Translations, Vol. 7, Translation No. VII/63, 'Supplies for Fliegerführer Afrika and the German Afrika Korps', 12 August 1941, p. 13;

Translation No. VII/65, 'Review of the Situation in the Central and South-Eastern Mediterranean for the period July 11–August 31 1941', 9 September, 1941, pp. 8–9.
76 TNA HW 13/4, 'Libyan Transport', 21 September 1941, p. 8; TNA HW 13/4, 'Libyan Transport', 12 October 1941, p. 8.
77 Kitchen, *Rommel's Desert War*, p. 134.
78 Ibid., p. 148.
79 TNA DEFE 3/690, Signals OL 1635, 21 October 1941 and OL 1769, 2 November 1941; TNA DEFE 3/745, Signal MK 481, 5 December 1941; TNA CAB 146/19, EDS Appreciation 11, 'The Axis Supply Situation in North Africa, February 1941–December 1942', pp. 20, 23.
80 Kitchen, *Rommel's Desert War*, pp. 148, 151.
81 'Probabilità di offensive nemico contro la Libia', 27 October 1941 in USSME, *Seconda offensiva Britannica in Africa settentrionale e ripiegamento italo-tedesco nella Sirtica orientale (18 novembre1941–17 gennaio 1942)* (Rome: USSME, 1949), pp. 191–6; Kitchen, *Rommel's Desert War*, pp. 141–3, 149.
82 'Probabilità di offensive nemico contro la Libia', 27 October 1941 in USSME, *Seconda offensiva Britannica*, p. 196.
83 TNA CAB 146/19, EDS Appreciation 11, 'The Axis Supply Situation in North Africa, February 1941–December 1942', pp. 48, 54, 60.
84 'Azione offensive per la presa di Tobruch', 11 November 1941 in USSME, *Seconda offensiva Britannica*, p. 198.
85 TNA HW 13/4, NI/MSS/16, 9 January 1942, p. 3.
86 Santoni, *Il vero traditore*, pp. 109–10.
87 TNA CAB 146/19, EDS Appreciation 11, 'The Axis Supply Situation in North Africa, February 1941–December 1942', p. 50.
88 TNA DEFE 3/833, Signal ZTPI 1785, 7 November 1941; TNA CAB 146/19, EDS Appreciation 11, 'The Axis Supply Situation in North Africa, February 1941–December 1942', pp. 52, 55.
89 MF, *Germany and the Second World War*, Vol. 3, p. 719. This did not apply to warships/submarines carrying cargo.
90 TNA DEFE 3/745, Signal MK 98, 23 November 1941; Kitchen, *Rommel's Desert War*, p. 166.
91 NARA, T-821, Roll 211, Frame 737, Comando Supremo Ufficio Servizi to Superesercito, 20 December 1941; Frame 738, Comando Supremo to Supermarina, 19 December 1941; TNA CAB 146/19, EDS Appreciation 11, 'The Axis Supply Situation in North Africa, February 1941–December 1942', p. 56.
92 'Verbale del colloquio avvenuto il giorno 8 Dicembre', 8 December 1941 and 'Verbale della riunione avvenuta a Berta il 14 Dicembre', 14 December 1941 in USSME, *Seconda offensiva Britannica*, pp. 214–18, 229–33; Greene and Massignani, *Rommel's North Africa Campaign*, pp. 125–6.
93 TNA DEFE 3/690, Signals OL 1613 and OL 1670, 20–23 October 1941; TNA DEFE 3/745, Signals MK 93, MK 98 and MK 191, 23–25 November 1941; TNA DEFE 3/746, Signals MK 591, MK 669 and MK 991, 8–18 December 1941.

94 TNA DEFE 3/690, Signal OL 1670, 23 October 1941; TNA DEFE 3/745, Signal MK 93, 23 November 1941; TNA DEFE 3/746, Signals MK 669, 703, 10–11 December 1941.
95 TNA HW 13/4, 'Libyan Transport', 5 November 1941, p. 3.
96 NARA, T-1022, Roll 2525, PG 45557, Kriegstagebuch der Seetransporthauptstelle Tripolis, entry for 7 February 1942.
97 Van Creveld, *Supplying War*, p. 190; TNA DEFE 3/745, MK 191, 23 November 1941.
98 Van Creveld, *Supplying War*, p. 190.
99 Santoni, *Il vero traditore*, pp. 140–1.
100 See Playfair et al., *Mediterranean and Middle East*, Vol. 3, pp. 100–2; David French, *Raising Churchill's Army: The British Army and the War against Germany, 1919–1945* (Oxford: Oxford University Press, 2000), pp. 216–39.
101 'War Diary for December 1941: Summary of Events for December' in Simpson (ed.), *The Cunningham Papers*, Vol. 1, p. 554.
102 Playfair et al., *Mediterranean and Middle East*, Vol. 3, p. 118.

Chapter 5

1 TNA CAB 79/56, COS (42) 2nd 'O' Meeting, 9 January 1942.
2 Admiralty to Cunningham, 24 December 1941 in Simpson (ed.), *The Cunningham Papers*, Vol. 1, p. 556; TNA AIR 2/7654, VCAS to Tedder, 25 December 1941.
3 Playfair et al., *Mediterranean and Middle East*, Vol. 3, pp. 135–7; MF, *Germany and the Second World War*, Vol. 6, pp. 635–8.
4 Hinsley et al., *British Intelligence*, Vol. 2, pp. 331–2; Kitchen, *Rommel's Desert War*, pp. 183, 187.
5 Kitchen, *Rommel's Desert War*, pp. 201–2.
6 Playfair et al., *Mediterranean and Middle East*, Vol. 3, p. 150.
7 TNA CAB 69/4, DO(42) 7th Meeting, 2 March 1942, p. 1; TNA CAB 79/20, JP(42) 348, 'Relation of Strategy in Middle East and India', 3 April 1942, p. 2.
8 Austin, *Malta and British Strategic Policy*, pp. 137–40.
9 TNA CAB 79/56, COS(42) 39th 'O' Meeting, 10 May 1942, p. 2.
10 TNA CAB 79/56, COS(42) 44th 'O' Meeting, 21 May 1942, p. 1.
11 TNA CAB 69/4, DO(42) 9th Meeting, 26 March 1942, p. 3.
12 TNA CAB 69/4, DO(42) 31st Memorandum, Annexed telegram from Cripps to Churchill, 20 March 1942.
13 TNA CAB 79/56, COS(42) 14th 'O' Meeting, 27 March 1942, p. 2.
14 TNA CAB 79/56, COS(42) 16th 'O' Meeting, 30 March 1942, p. 2
15 CCO, Portal Papers, Folder 3, File 1, Portal to Churchill, 29 March 1942, p. 1.
16 See Overy, *The Bombing War*, p. 496, for 'the most bombed place on earth'; for Simpson's decision to withdraw S10, see his report in Simpson, *Periscope View*, appendix 3: Captain S10 to Captain S1, 10 May 1942, pp. 294–300.
17 TNA CAB 79/20, COS(42), 121st Meeting, 16 April 1942, p. 1; COS(42), 133rd Meeting, 28 April 1942, p. 1.

18 TNA FO 837/1329, Minutes of the fourth meeting held between MEW and the Naval Staff, 9 April 1942, p. 3.
19 Austin, *Malta and British Strategic Policy*, pp. 137–42. The best dedicated study of the tortured Axis planning to invade Malta remains Mariano Gabriele, *Operazione C3: Malta* (Rome: USMM, 1965).
20 TNA CAB 79/56, COS(42) 42nd 'O' Meeting, 13 May 1942, p. 4; CCO Portal Papers, Folder 3, File 2, Portal to Churchill, 18 May 1942.
21 TNA AIR 23/1376, Tedder to Harwood, 8 June 1942; for the continued threat of the Italian Navy and the subsequent tying down of British resources, see Hammond, 'An Enduring Influence', pp. 826–7.
22 Playfair et al., *Mediterranean and Middle East*, Vol. 3, p. 220; Hinsley et al., *British Intelligence*, Vol. 2, p. 365; MF, *Germany and the Second World War*, Vol. 6, pp. 666–7.
23 For a full account of the Battles of the Gazala line and the fall of Tobruk, see Playfair et al., *Mediterranean and Middle East*, Vol. 3, pp. 223–73; MF, *Germany and the Second World War*, Vol. 6, pp. 661–98; Kitchen, *Rommel's Desert War*, pp. 216–55. On morale, see Jonathan Fennell, *Combat and Morale in the North African Campaign: The Path to El Alamein* (Cambridge: Cambridge University Press, 2011). On Fellers, see Barr, *Pendulum of War*, pp. 19–21.
24 Barr, *Yanks and Limeys*, p. 179.
25 Entry for 12 June 1942 in Charles Burdick and Hans-Adolf Jacobsen (eds.), *The Halder War Diary, 1939–1942* (Novato, CA: Presidio Press, 1988), p. 623.
26 Kitchen, *Rommel's Desert War*, p. 247; JSCSC, AHB Translations, Vol. 8, Translation No. VII/80, Rommel to OKW Operations Staff, 23 June.
27 TNA GFM 36/8, Mussolini to Hitler, 21 June 1942; Entries for 20, 22, 23 and 25 June in Ciano, *Diario*, pp. 631–3. For an expanded discussion of the debate over taking Malta, see Gabriele, *Operazione C3*.
28 Cavallero to Mussolini, 23 June 1942 in USSME, *Diario Storico del Comando Supremo (DSCS)*, Vol. 7, Tomo 2, (Rome: USSME, 1997), pp. 201–2; Albert Kesselring, *The Memoirs of Field Marshal Albert Kesselring* (London: William Kimber, 1954), pp. 122–9.
29 Ball, *Bitter Sea*, pp. 145–6; Roskill, *War at Sea*, Vol. 2, pp. 73–4.
30 Barr, *Pendulum of War*, pp. 23–5; Barr, *Yanks and Limeys*, pp. 180–1.
31 For an excellent account of 1st Alamein see Barr, *Pendulum of War*, pp. 69–184.
32 CCO Portal Papers, Folder 3, File 3, Smuts to Churchill, 30 June 1942.
33 CCO Portal Papers, Folder 3, File 3, 'Suggested draft telegram from Prime Minister to General Smuts, 4 July 1942'.
34 CCO, Portal Papers, Folder 3, File 3, PM Minute, 11 July 1942.
35 On American assistance around the time of El Alamein, see Buchanan, 'A Friend Indeed?'.
36 Austin, *Malta and British Strategic Policy*, p. 151; Barnett, *Engage the Enemy More Closely*, p. 517; Greene and Massignani, *Naval War in the Mediterranean*, pp. 243–4; Playfair et al., *Mediterranean and Middle East*, Vol. 3, p. 314.
37 Austin, *Malta and British Strategic Policy*, p. 152.
38 Mediterranean War Diary, entry for 23 January 1942 in Simpson (ed.), *The Cunningham Papers*, Vol. 1, p. 566.

39 MF, *Germany and the Second World War*, Vol. 6, pp. 655–6; Austin, *Malta and British Strategic Policy*, p. 146.
40 Roskill, *War at Sea*, Vol. 2, p. 58.
41 See Playfair et al., *Mediterranean and Middle East*, Vol. 3, pp. 155–75.
42 Austin, *Malta and British Strategic Policy*, p. 145.
43 War Diary entry for 15 March 1942 in Simpson (ed.), *The Cunningham Papers*, Vol. 1, p. 582; TNA PREM 3/274/2, Alexander to Churchill, 21 July 1942; USMM, *LMI*, Vol. 3, *Navi Mercantili Perdute*, p. 52.
44 'Summary and Appreciation of Events for January 1942' in Simpson (ed.), *The Cunningham Papers*, Vol. 1, p. 568.
45 For details of storing runs, see TNA ADM 199/1926, 'Admiral Submarines: Statistics, 1939–1945', f. 305; for the *Clyde* see Simpson, *Periscope View*, p. 174.
46 TNA ADM 187/16–19, Admiralty pink list entries from December 1941–June 1942; TNA ADM 199/1916, First Submarine Flotilla monthly letter for September 1942, f. 9.
47 TNA AIR 20/1057, Middle East ORS Report R.20; 'An account of anti-submarine and anti-shipping operations in the Middle East during May 1942', 14 July 1942, pp. 4–5.
48 The greatly increased number of attacks in August compared to the preceding months in 1942 is evidenced in Röhwer, *Allied Submarine Successes*, pp. 150–62. For the return of S10, see Roskill, *War at Sea*, Vol. 2, p. 75.
49 Playfair et al., *Mediterranean and Middle East*, Vol. 3, p. 326; Röhwer, *Allied Submarine Successes*, pp. 159–62.
50 TNA ADM 199/108, Report of Proceedings of 830 Squadron during January 1942, 11 February 1942; USMM, *LMI*, Vol. 3, *Navi Mercantili Perdute*, p. 48.
51 Lloyd, *Briefed to Attack*, p. 149.
52 Austin, *Malta and British Strategic Policy*, p. 145.
53 Sorties calculated from TNA ADM 199/108–9; serviceability in Playfair et al., *Mediterranean*, Vol. 3, p. 185.
54 'Telegram from Rome to the Army High Command at the Fuehrer Headquarters, Wolfsschanze', 12 April 1942 in *Fuehrer Conferences*, p. 278.
55 TNA AIR 20/1057, Middle East ORS Report R.11; 'An account of anti-submarine and anti-shipping operations in the Eastern Mediterranean during March 1942', 14 April 1942, pp. 1, 4.
56 TNA AIR 20/1057, Middle East ORS Report R.14; 'An account of anti-shipping operations in the Central and Eastern Mediterranean during April 1942', 14 June 1942, p. 1; Middle East ORS Report R.20; 'An account of anti-submarine and anti-shipping operations in the Middle East during May 1942', 14 July 1942, p. 4.
57 See Hammond, 'Inter and Intra-Theatre Learning', pp. 14–15.
58 Damage figures calculated from AUSMM, Maristat-Statistiche Generali, pacco n. 3, Situazione naviglio mercantile, 'Diagramma del naviglio da trasporto italiano e tedesco danneggiato nel mediterraneo dal 1 gennaio al 30 agosto 1942'. For the 'Annus Horribilis' claim, see van Creveld, *Supplying War*, pp. 192, 196, 198–200 and similar comments in Barnett, *Engage the Enemy More Closely*, pp. 491–526, who focuses entirely on Malta, and discounts attacks from elsewhere.

59 Three submarines (HMS *P. 36*, *P. 39* and *Pandora*) were sunk in March and April in the harbour at Malta. As they were not at sea, they have not been included as losses from the anti-shipping campaign.
60 Sortie numbers calculated from TNA AIR 22/165, Air Ministry War Room Weekly Statistics entries for 28 June–30 August 1942; on the wider efforts by air power at this time see Ehlers, *Mediterranean Air War*, pp. 213–22.
61 Kitchen, *Rommel's Desert War*, p. 202.
62 Meeting of 24 January 1942 in USSME, *Verbali delle riunioni*, Vol. 3, p. 82.
63 JSCSC, AHB Translations, Vol. 8, Translation No. VII/80, GHQ *Panzerarmee* to Army General Staff, Operations Division, 5 April 1942; German General at Comando Supremo to Army General Staff, Operations Division, 5 April 1942. An explanation of CUs can be found in TNA CAB 146/19, EDS Appreciation, 'The Axis Supply Situation in North Africa', February 1941–December 1942, p. 4.
64 JSCSC, AHB Translations, Vol. 8, Translation No. VII/80, GHQ *Panzerarmee* to Army General Staff, Operations Division, 5 April 1942.
65 TNA CAB 106/753, CC(42) 41, Commanders-in-Chief Committee, 'Enemy Maintenance Cyrenaica: Note by DMI', 19 April 1942.
66 TNA CAB 106/753, CC(42) 41, Commanders-in-Chief Committee, 'Enemy Maintenance Cyrenaica: Note by DMI', 19 April 1942.
67 'Riunione tenutasi preso il Comando Supremo sotto la Presidenza dell'Ecc Riccardi', 4 May 1942 in USSME, *DSCS*, Vol. 7, Tomo 2, pp. 3–4; TNA HW 13/4, 'Libyan Coastal Traffic', 4 April 1942; JSCSC, AHB Translations, Vol. 8, Translation No. VII/80, German General at Comando Supremo to Army General Staff, Operations Division, 7 May 1942.
68 NARA Microfilm T-821, Roll 211, Frame 783, Ufficio Servizi to Superesercito, 9 January 1942; JSCSC, AHB Translations, Vol. 8, Translation No. VII/80, German General at Comando Supremo to Army General Staff, Operations Division, 7 May 1942.
69 'Verbali delle riunioni tenutasi presso il Comando Supremo sotto la presidenza del generale Cavallero', 11 May 1942 in USSME, *DSCS*, Vol. 7, Tomo 2, pp. 35–7; *The Rommel Papers*, p. 192; MF, *Germany and the Second World War*, Vol. 6, p. 668; Playfair et al., *Meidterranean and Middle East*, Vol. 3, pp. 216–21.
70 See for instance the entries for 5, 8 and 24 June in JSCSC, AHB Translations, Vol. 9, Translation No. VII/88, 'War Diary of the German Africa Corps, June 1942', pp. 10, 18, 40; TNA AIR 40/2345, Y Daily Reports Middle East for 20 May 1942.
71 On supply captures, see MF, *Germany and the Second World War*, Vol. 6, pp. 681, 692; on the failure to integrate different arms into combined operations and problems with Ritchie's leadership, see French, *Raising Churchill's Army*, pp. 219–23, 225, 229–30, 231–2. A partial exception to this poor performance was an improvement in air–land integration.
72 Playfair et al., *Mediterranean and Middle East*, Vol. 3, p. 274; JSCSC, AHB Translations, Vol. 8, Translation No. VII/80, Rommel to OKW Operations Staff, 23 June 1942. Barr, *Pendulum of War*, p. 38 gives statistics of the huge amount of ammunition lost by the Eighth Army, but it is unknown exactly how much of this was captured versus that lost/destroyed.

234   Notes to pages 123–128

73 On aerial interdiction of Axis land supply routes, see Gladman, 'Air Power and Intelligence', pp. 144–62.
74 TNA HW 13/221, Mediterranean Daily Report, 8 June 1942, p. 2; JSCSC, AHB Translations, Vol. 8, Translation No. VII/80, Rintelen to Army General Staff, Operations Division, 24 June 1942.
75 Cavallero to Comando Superiore Forze Armate Africa Settentrionale, 26 June 1942 in USSME, *DSCS*, Vol. 7, Tomo 2, pp. 280–1.
76 See Cavallero to Keitel, undated June 1942 in USSME, *DSCS*, Vol. 7, Tomo 2, pp. 141–2.
77 JSCSC, AHB Translations, Vol. 8, Translation No. VII/80, Rommel to OKW Operations Staff, 21 July 1942, pp. 17–18.
78 TNA HW 13/221, Mediterranean Daily Report, 1 July 1942, p. 7; TNA HW 13/221, Mediterranean Daily Report, 5 July 1942, p. 5.
79 See JSCSC, AHB Translations, Vol. 8, Translation No. VII/80, Rommel to OKW Operations Staff, 21 July 1942, pp. 15–19.
80 Report on a Conference between the C-in-C Navy and the Fuehrer at the Berghof, 15 June 1942 in *Fuehrer Conferences*, p. 285.
81 See for instance JSCSC, AHB Translations, Vol. 8, Translation No. VII/80, Rintelen to Army General Staff, Operations Division, 4 July 1942; the entries for 1, 3, 4, 5 and 18 July in JSCSC, AHB Translations, Vol. 9, Translation No. VII/87, 'War Diary of the German Africa Corps, July 1942', pp. 2, 4–5, 7–8, 29.
82 Santoni, *Il vero traditore*, pp. 162–9; TNA HW 13/221, Mediterranean Daily Report, 27 July 1942, pp. 3–4; TNA HW, Mediterranean Daily Report, 28–9 August 1942, p. 2. The *Pozarica* was critically damaged and forced to beach at Corfu.
83 TNA HW 13/221, Mediterranean Daily Report, 30–31 July 1942, p. 5; TNA HW 13/221, Mediterranean Daily Report, 9 August 1942, p. 9; TNA HW 13/221, Mediterranean Daily Report, 28–9 August 1942, p. 5.
84 TNA HW 13/221, Mediterranean Daily Report, 28–9 August 1942, pp. 6–7.
85 Kitchen, *Rommel's Desert War*, pp. 290–3; JSCSC, AHB Translations, Vol. 8, Translation No. VII/80, Rommel to OKW operations staff, 15 August 1942, p. 20.
86 Kitchen, *Rommel's Desert War*, pp. 294–300.

Chapter 6

1 Ehlers, *Mediterranean Air War*, p. 215.
2 TNA HW 13/221, Mediterranean Daily Report, 2 July 1942, p. 1.
3 Kitchen, *Rommel's Desert War*, pp. 288–9; Barr, *Pendulum of War*, pp. 185–217. Montgomery replaced Auchinleck as head of Eighth Army, Harold Alexander took over as C-in-C Middle East.
4 TNA AIR 23/1376, Mideast to Air Ministry, 30 July 1942.
5 Submarine numbers calculated from TNA ADM 187/21, Admiralty Pink List entry for 4 September 1942, on their eastern concentration see Roskill, *War at Sea*, Vol. 2, p. 311. On air reinforcements, see Ehlers, *Mediterranean Air War*, pp. 224–7.
6 TNA CAB 79/23, COS(42) 273rd Meeting, 28 September 1942, p. 3.

7 Playfair et al., *Mediterranean and Middle East*, Vol. 3, p. 371; MF, *Germany and the Second World War*, Vol. 6, pp. 762–3; on morale see Fennell, *Combat and Morale*.
8 Kitchen, *Rommel's Desert War*, p. 299; MF, *Germany and the Second World War*, Vol. 6, pp. 756–7.
9 Kitchen, *Rommel's Desert War*, pp. 313, 315. On his repeated accusation towards the authorities in Rome (especially the Italians), see *The Rommel Papers*, pp. 265–70, 359.
10 On the American contribution, see Buchanan, 'A Friend Indeed'.
11 Kitchen, *Rommel's Desert War*, pp. 325–6; Playfair et al., *Mediterranean and Middle East*, Vol. 4, pp. 1–2.
12 CCO, Portal Papers, Folder 12, Portal to Tedder, 24 September 1942.
13 CCO, Portal Papers, Folder 3, File 3, PM Minute, 28 September 1942.
14 Austin, *Malta and British Strategic Policy*, pp. 152–3.
15 Playfair et al., *Mediterranean and Middle East*, Vol. 4, pp. 1–7; MF, *Germany and the Second World War*, Vol. 6, pp. 774–5; Barr, *Pendulum of War*, pp. 255–61, 271–3, 274–81.
16 Playfair et al., *Mediterranean and Middle East*, Vol. 4, p. 36.
17 See Barr, *Pendulum of War*, pp. 306–82.
18 TNA CAB 79/24, COS(42) 303rd Meeting, 29 October 1942, pp. 3–4; TNA ADM 187/22, Admiralty Pink List entry for 2 November 1942.
19 Barr, *Pendulum of War*, pp. 342, 371–2, 383–405.
20 Hitler to Rommel, 3 November 1943, in *The Rommel Papers*, p. 321.
21 Barr, *Pendulum of War*, pp. 400–4.
22 Ibid., p. 404.
23 For an example of this pressure, see TNA GFM 36/8, Mussolini to Hitler, undated November 1942.
24 Kitchen, *Rommel's Desert War*, pp. 391–3, 396–400.
25 'Sintesi del colloquio delle ore 12 con il Führer, partecipano', 18 December 1942 in USSME, *DSCS*, Vol. 8, Tomo 2, (Rome: USSME, 1999), p. 113.
26 TNA CAB 79/24, COS(42) 318th Meeting, 17 November 1942, p. 3.
27 TNA CAB 79/24, COS(42) 322nd Meeting, 20 November 1942, p. 3.
28 Playfair et al., *Mediterranean and Middle East*, Vol. 3, p. 379.
29 Calculated from TNA AIR 22/165, AMWR weekly statistical analysis, 30 August–8 November 1942.
30 These ratios have been calculated from the figures given in TNA AIR 20/1057, Map of 'Anti-Shipping Efforts and Results, October 1942' and Map of 'Anti-Shipping Efforts and Results, November 1942'.
31 For an example of ongoing learning and refinement within 201 Group at this time, see Bodleian Library Special Collections (BLSC), Kendrew Papers, NCUACS 11.4.89, B. 34, 'Minutes of a meeting held at Advanced Headquarters, No. 201 Group', 15 August 1942. On the process of learning in general, see Hammond, 'Inter and Intra Theatre Learning'.
32 TNA AIR 20/1057, ORS Report No. R.33: An account of anti-shipping operations in the Eastern Mediterranean, p. 2.
33 TNA AIR 20/1057, ORS Report No. R.33: An account of anti-shipping operations in the Eastern Mediterranean, p. 7.

34 BLSC, Kendrew Papers, NCUACS 11.4.89, B.60, 'The Air–Sea War in the Mediterranean, Jan 1942–May 1943', undated, p. 17; TNA AIR 20/1057, ORS Report No. R.33: An account of anti-shipping operations in the Eastern Mediterranean, p. 7.
35 TNA AIR 23/1282, 'Air Tactics and Operational Notes on 201 Group HQ RAFME', undated, likely June 1943, p. 3.
36 Austin, *Malta and British Strategic Policy*, pp. 152–3; TNA CAB 79/24, COS (42) 318th Meeting, 17 November 1942, p. 3.
37 TNA ADM 199/109, 'Naval Air Squadrons, Malta: Reports of Proceedings, September 1942', 7 October 1942; 'Naval Air Squadrons, Malta: Reports of Proceedings, October 1942', 1 November 1942.
38 TNA AIR 20/5306, 'Anti-Shipping operations in the Eastern Mediterranean, October–December 1942', p. 1.
39 Hezlet, *British and Allied Submarine Operations*, pp. 165–8.
40 Playfair et al., *Mediterranean and Middle East*, Vol. 4, p. 201.
41 TNA AIR 23/1282, 'Air Tactics and Operational Notes on 201 Group HQ RAFME', undated, likely June 1943, p. 3.
42 Playfair et al., *Mediterranean and Middle East*, Vol. 4, p. 203; Austin, *Malta and British Strategic Policy*, p. 164; Röhwer, *Allied Submarine Attacks*, pp. 167–70.
43 TNA ADM 234/560, NSH, Minelaying, Vol. 1, pp. 587–8, 592–3.
44 'Costituzione presso Supermarina di un Comitato misto navale ed aeronautico, italiano e germanico, per l'organizzazione e la protezione dei trasporti per l'Africa', 15 September 1942 in USSME, *DSCS*, Vol. 8, Tomo 2, pp. 20–1.
45 Archivio dell'Ufficio Storico dello Stato Maggiore Esercito (AUSSME), Repertorio I-4, Busta 42, Cartella 14, Studio sulle cause delle perdute di naviglio, 8 September 1942, pp. 1–3; 'Verbale sintetico del colloquio Mussolini-Kesselring a rocca delle caminate il 13 settembre 1942' in USSME, *La terza offensiva in Africa Settentrionale, tomo I: 6 September 1942–4 February 1943* (Rome: USSME, 1961), pp. 387–9.
46 Greene and Massignani, *Naval War in the Mediterranean*, p. 278; Nesbit, *The Armed Rovers*, p. 61.
47 BLSC, Kendrew Papers, NCUACS 11.4.89, B.60, 'The Air–Sea War in the Mediterranean, Jan 1942–May 1943', undated, p. 21 and appendix 'B', 'Attack on F-Boats', p. 1.
48 TNA HW 11/33, Government Code and Cypher School Naval History (GC +CS NH), Vol. 20, 'The Mediterranean, 1940–1943', p. 224. On Italian armaments see John Campbell, *Naval Weapons of World War Two* (London: Conway Maritime Press, 2000), pp. 319, 338–47.
49 BLSC, Kendrew Papers, NCUACS 11.4.89, B.60, 'The Air-Sea War in the Mediterranean, Jan 1942-May 1943', undated, p. 27.
50 Calculated from TNA AIR 22/165, AMWR weekly statistics for 30 August–29 November 1942.
51 BLSC, Kendrew Papers, NCUACS 11.4.89, B.60, 'The Air–Sea War in the Mediterranean, Jan 1942–May 1943', undated, p. 26.
52 TNA ADM 234/381 NSH, Submarines, Vol. 2, p. 276.
53 See O'Hara and Cernuschi, 'The Other Ultra'.

54 NARA, T-821, Roll 211, Frames 878–9, Ufficio Servizi to Delease, 31 August 1942; *The Rommel Papers*, pp. 274–5; Albert Kesselring, *The Memoirs of Field Marshal Kesselring* (London: Greenhill, 1988), p. 131.
55 TNA GFM 36/6, 'Dispozione date ecc. Cavallero circa l'intensificazione delle scorte aeree ai convogli per l'A.S.I.', 7 September 1942, pp. 6–7; the intended destination of the *Pozarica* is given in TNA HW 13/221, Mediterranean Daily Report, 19 August 1942 and the *Sanandrea* in Playfair et al., *Mediterranean and Middle East*, Vol. 3, p. 382.
56 TNA GFM, 36/6, 'Potenziamento delle Forze Armate', 1 October 1942, p. 5.
57 Barr, *Pendulum of War*, p. 237; TNA CAB 146/20, EDS Appreciation 11, 'The Axis Supply Situation in North Africa, February 1941–December 1942. Part II: March–August 1942', pp. 212, 215.
58 JSCSC, AHB Translations, Vol. 8, Translation No. VII/80, GHQ *Panzerarmee Afrika* to von Rintelen, 3 September 1942; on bomb damage to Tobruk, see TNA DEFE 3/773, Signal QT 551, 1 September 1942; for the permanent defensive shift, TNA DEFE 3/773, Signal QT 844, 6 September 1942. Losses on 4–5 September from USMM, *LMI*, Vol. 3, *Navi mercantili perduti*, p. 54.
59 JSCSC, AHB Translations, Vol. 8, Translation No. VII/80, GHQ *Panzerarmee Afrika* to von Rintelen, 3 September 1942.
60 Barr, *Pendulum of War*, p. 225.
61 For some examples of these criticisms, see Kitchen, *Rommel's Desert War*, pp. 297–9; MF, *Germany and the Second World War*, Vol. 6, pp. 749–50.
62 JSCSC, AHB Translations, Vol. 8, Translation No. VII/80, Deputy Chief of German Naval Command in Italy to Chief of Naval Staff, Operations Division, 7 September 1942; Rommel to OKW operations staff, 11 September 1942.
63 JSCSC, AHB Translations, Vol. 8, Translation No. VII/80, Warlimont to Chief of OKW Operations Staff, 14 September 1942. Criticisms of the anti-shipping operations are in van Creveld, *Supplying War*, pp. 192–8; Barnett, *Engage the Enemy*, pp. 525–6; Gladman, 'Air Power and Intelligence', p. 158. Losses of MT at sea are calculated from USMM, *LMI*, Vol. 1, *Dati Statistici*, Table LIV, p. 126.
64 JSCSC, AHB Translations, Vol. 8, Translation No. VII/80, Warlimont to Chief of OKW Operations Staff, 14 September 1942.
65 Stumme to Cavallero, 3 October 1942 in USSME, *La terza offensiva*, pp. 387–9.
66 IWM FD 4195/45, Kaufmann to Borman, 1 October 1942.
67 Kitchen, *Rommel's Desert War*, pp. 329, 333–4.
68 'Comunicazione dell'Armata corazzata Africa', 6 October 1942 in USSME, *DSCS*, Vol. 8, Tomo 2, pp. 36–7.
69 'Comando Supremo, IV Reparto, 'Promemoria della riunione operativa del 7 ottobre 1942' in USSME, *DSCS*, Vol. 8, Tomo 2, p. 53.
70 Minutes of meetings on 11, 12 and 15 October 1942 in USSME, *Verbali delle riunioni*, Vol. 3, pp. 851–5.
71 Minutes of meetings on 15, 16, 21 and 22 October 1942 in USSME, *Verbali delle riunioni*, Vol. 3, pp. 854–64.

72 The attacks are described in Nesbit, *Armed Rovers*, pp. 90–101.
73 'Verbale delle riunione a Taormina presso la sede dell'OBS', 22 October 1942 in USSME, *La terza offensiva*, p. 69.
74 TNA DEFE 3/780, Signal QT 4120, 23 October 1942.
75 Quoted in Barr, *Pendulum of War*, p. 333.
76 JSCSC, AHB Translations, Vol. 7, Translation No. VII/66, 'Air Operations of the 5th Squadra Aerea between October 20 1942 and January 31 1943', pp. 2, 8; *The Rommel Papers*, p. 313.
77 TNA HW 13/221, Mediterranean Daily Report, 28–29 August 1942, p. 5; van Creveld, *Supplying War*, p. 197 places the monthly capacity of Tobruk below 20,000 tons, which does not tally with the potential to unload 1,800 in a single day.
78 MF, *Germany and the Second World War*, Vol. 3, p. 768; TNA DEFE 3/780, Signals QT 4077, 4251, 4383, 4474, 22–27 October 1942; Kitchen, *Rommel's Desert War*, pp. 333, 351.
79 MF, *Germany and the Second World War*, Vol. 3, p. 807.
80 'Comunicazione Armata Corazzata Africa', 8 November 1942 in USSME, *La terza offensiva*, pp. 222–4. One issue was the equivalent of 250 small-calibre rounds, 150 medium-calibre and 100 large-calibre.
81 Kitchen, *Rommel's Desert War*, pp. 386, 388; 'Comunicazione del Fieldmaresciallo Rommel', 17 November 1942 in USSME, *La terza offensiva*, p. 256.
82 JSCSC, AHB Translations, Vol. 5, Translation No. VII/44, 'Extracts from Reports of Fuhrer Conferences', entry for 12 December 1942, p. 1. For a short summary on the issue of pursuit, including both criticisms and mitigating factors, see Porch, *Path to Victory*, pp. 322–5.
83 JSCSC, AHB Translations, Vol. 3, Translation No. VII/25, 'The Battle for Tunis, November 1942–May 1943', German Air Historical Branch appreciation, 17 July 1944, pp. 8–9.
84 'Comando Supremo, I Reparto – Ufficio Operazioni – Apprezzamento della situazione', 30 December 1942 in USSME, DSCS, Vol. 8, Tomo. 2, p. 145; entry for 31 December 1942 in Ciano, *Diario*, p. 682.

Chapter 7

1 On the troubled genesis of 'Torch', see Jones, *Britain, the United States and the Mediterranean War*, pp. 25–40; Buchanan, *American Grand Strategy*, pp. 33–52; Howard, *Mediterranean Strategy*, pp. 19–35.
2 MF, *Germany and the Second World War*, Vol. 6, pp. 792–3, 822–7; Entries for 8–12 November 1942 in Ciano, *Diario*, pp. 664–7.
3 Deakin, *The Brutal Friendship*, pp. 78–9; MF, *Germany and the Second World War*, Vol. 6, p. 794; Bruce Allen Watson, *Exit Rommel: The Tunisian Campaign, 1942–1943* (Westport, CT: Praeger, 1999), 63–4.
4 Kitchen, *Rommel's Desert War*, pp. 377–9.
5 TNA CAB 79/24, COS(42) 322nd Meeting, 20 November 1942, p. 1.
6 TNA AIR 8/719, Air Ministry to Commanders-in-Chief, Middle East, 22 November 1942; Mideast to Air Ministry, 22 November 1942.

7 CCO, Portal Papers, Folder 3, File 4, Portal to Churchill, 24 November 1942; Pound to Churchill, 26 November 1942.
8 Cunningham to Pound, 20 November 1942 in *Cunningham Papers*, Vol. 2, pp. 56–7.
9 TNA AIR 8/721, Extract from COS(42) 339th Meeting, 8 December 1942; Admiralty to C-in-C Mediterranean, 24 November 1942; Minute by CAS, 24 November 1942.
10 TNA CAB 69/4, DO(42) 17th Meeting, 16 November 1942, p. 4, and attached annex on 'Extension of Mediterranean Sink at Sight Zone to Franco-Spanish Border'.
11 Austin, *Malta and British Strategic Policy*, p. 165; TNA 69/4, DO(42) 18th Meeting, 23 November 1942, p. 1.
12 TNA CAB 79/24, JIC(42) 463, 'Enemy Reinforcements to Tunisia', 27 November 1942.
13 TNA CAB 79/24, JIC(42) 465, 'Axis Supply and Reinforcement Plans in the Central Mediterranean', 30 November 1942; TNA CAB 79/24, COS (42) 336th Meeting, 5 December 1942, pp. 1–2; TNA CAB 79/24, COS(42) 339th Meeting, 8 December 1942, pp. 1–2.
14 Kitchen, *Rommel's Desert War*, p. 409.
15 Watson, *Exit Rommel*, pp. 101–3.
16 For a narrative of this stage, see George F. Howe, *Northwest Africa: Seizing the Initiative in the West* (Washington, DC: OCMH 1957), pp. 283–344.
17 Kitchen, *Rommel's Desert War*, pp. 440–3.
18 TNA GFM 36/8, Hitler to Mussolini, 14 March 1943, pp. 3–5; Letter from Mussolini to Hitler, 25 March 1943, pp. 4–5.
19 Jones, *Mediterranean War*, pp. 40–5.
20 TNA CAB 79/59, JP(43) 85, Operation 'Husky', Report by Joint Planning Staff, annexed telegram from Eisenhower, 17 February 1943.
21 TNA CAB 79/59, COS(43) 51st Meeting, 26 February 1943, p. 5.
22 TNA AIR 8/721, Eisenhower to Chiefs of Staff, 6 January 1943.
23 TNA AIR 8/721, Chiefs of Staff to Eisenhower, 8 January 1943; Admiralty to NCXF, 19 January 1943.
24 Ehlers, *Mediterranean Air War*, p. 269.
25 TNA AIR 20/5323, ACAS (Operations) to C-in-C Bomber Command, 20 February 1943; BLSC, Kendrew Papers, NCUACS 11.4.89, B.60, 'The Air-Sea War in the Mediterranean, Jan 1942–May 1943', undated, p. 17.
26 Howe, *Northwest Africa*, pp. 501–9; Kenneth Macksey, *Crucible of Power: The Fight for Tunisia, 1942–1943* (London: Hutchinson, 1969), pp. 179–86; Playfair et al., *Mediterranean and Middle East*, Vol. 4, pp. 322–31; Kitchen, *Rommel's Desert War*, pp. 439–40.
27 Playfair et al., *Mediterranean and Middle East*, Vol. 4, pp. 329–31.
28 Ibid., pp. 334–56, 362.
29 Gibbs et al., *Grand Strategy*, Vol. 4, by Michael Howard, pp. 351–2; Playfair et al., *Mediterranean and Middle East*, Vol. 4, pp. 383–4.
30 TNA AIR 8/719, C-in-C Mediterranean to Admiralty, 24 April 1943, p. 1.
31 Greene and Massignani, *Naval War in the Mediterranean*, p. 282.

32 See for instance Playfair et al., *Mediterranean and Middle East*, Vol. 4, p. 460; MF, *Germany and the Second World War*, Vol. 8, p. 1109.
33 TNA ADM 1/14262, 'Force Q: Action on night of 1–2 December 1942', 21 January 1943; Santoni, *Il vero traditore*, pp. 192–4.
34 Playfair et al., *Mediterranean and Middle East*, Vol. 4, pp. 205–6.
35 TNA ADM 223/578, Message 1737A from VA Malta, 7 December 1942; Message 1500A from VA Malta, 20 December 1942; Message 1630A from VA Malta, 15 January 1943; Message 0937A from VA Malta, 19 January 1943.
36 TNA ADM 223/578, Message 0755A from NO i/c Malta, 20 January 1943.
37 Playfair et al., *Mediterranean and Middle East*, Vol. 4, p. 203; Austin, *Malta and British Strategic Policy*, p. 164.
38 Calculated from TNA AIR 22/165, AMWR weekly statistical analysis, 29 November–6 December 1942.
39 Calculated from TNA AIR 22/342, AMWR Monthly Summaries, January and February 1943.
40 TNA AIR 20/1057, ORS Report No. R.33: An account of anti-shipping operations in the Eastern Mediterranean, p. 7; Levine, *War against Rommel's Supply Lines*, p. 98; TNA AIR 8/721, NCXF to Admiralty, 16 January 1943.
41 TNA AIR 8/721, Tedder to Portal, 8 January 1943; CCO, Portal Papers, Folder 4, File 1, Portal to Churchill, 26 February 1943.
42 BLSC, Kendrew Papers, NCUACS 11.4.89, B.60, 'The Air–Sea War in the Mediterranean, Jan 1942–May 1943', undated, pp. 24–5.
43 'Costituzione presso Supermarina di un Comitato misto navale ed aeronautico, italiano e germanico, per l'organizzazione e la protezione dei trasporti per l'Africa', 15 September 1942 in USSME, *DSCS*, Vol. 8, Tomo 2, pp. 20–1.
44 IWM FD 4195/45, 'Third Report by the Reichskommissar for Shipping on Further Development in the Mediterranean', 3 February 1943, p. 18; Minutes taken at Conference of the C-in-C Navy, 14 March 1943 in *Fuehrer Conferences*, p. 314; TNA HW 11/33, GC+CS Naval History, Vol. 20, 'The Mediterranean, 1940–43', p. 224.
45 TNA AIR 23/926, 'An Account of Anti-shipping Operations in the Eastern Mediterranean, January–February 1943', p. 1.
46 Ehlers, *Mediterranean Air War*, pp. 259–60.
47 TNA AIR 8/719, Mediterranean Air Command to Air Ministry, 15 March 1943.
48 Ehlers, *Mediterranean Air War*, pp. 263–4, 278–9; TNA GFM 36/6, 'Verbali delle riunione a Palazzo Venezia presso il Duce sul'argomento "Potenziamento dell forze armate"', 29 January 1943, pp. 11–12.
49 TNA AIR 8/719, C-in-C Mediterranean to Admiralty, 24 April 1943, p. 1.
50 TNA AIR 20/1057, ORS Report No. R.45: Operations against enemy shipping in the Mediterranean, March–May 1943, 20 July 1943, p. 8; on the diversionary operations, see Roskill, *War at Sea*, p. 438.
51 TNA GFM 36/6, 'Verbali delle riunione a Palazzo Venezia presso il Duce sul'argomento "Potenziamento dell forze armate"', 29 January 1943, p. 17; IWM FD 4195/45, 'Third Report by the Reichskommissar for Shipping on

Further Development in the Mediterranean', 3 February 1943, p. 18; NARA, T-821, Roll 211, Frames 720-1, 'Prospetti Operativi Navali', 24 February 1943, p. 2.
52 TNA ADM 234/381, NSH, Submarines, Vol. 2, p. 277.
53 TNA HW 11/33, GC+CS Naval History, Vol. XX, 'The Mediterranean, 1940–43', p. 225.
54 Santoni, *Il vero traditore*, p. 217.
55 JSCSC, AHB Translations, Vol. 3, Translation No. VII/25, 'The Battle for Tunis', p. 9; Kitchen, *Rommel's Desert War*, p. 415.
56 *The Rommel Papers*, p. 417; Minutes of meeting on 29 January 1943, USSME, *Verbali delle riunioni*, Vol. 4, p. 29.
57 Minutes of meetings on 6 and 12 February 1943, USSME, *Verbali delle riunioni*, Vol. 4, pp. 37, 50.
58 JSCSC, AHB Translations, Vol. 3, Translation No. VII/25, 'The Battle for Tunis', p. 9.
59 Kaufmann had initially been extremely positive about 'solving' the shipping crisis through these seizures, but quickly became disillusioned: IWM FD 4195/45, Kaufmann to Hitler, 16 December 1942; 'Report by the Reichskommissar for Shipping on the further Development in the Mediterranean', 23 December 1942; 'Third Report by the Reichskommissar for Shipping on the further Development in the Mediterranean', 3 February 1943, p. 18.
60 Levine, *War against Rommel's Supply Lines*, p. 79.
61 The 225,000 is based on a thirty-day month, calculated from the daily figure of 7,500 tons given in Ehlers, *Mediterranean Air War*, p. 259. On port capacity claims and the dismissal of attrition as a factor, see USMM, *LMI*, Vol. 6, *La difesa del traffico*, pp. 11–12; van Creveld, *Supplying War*, p. 198.
62 Barr, *Yanks and Limeys*, pp. 203, 207, 208–13, 226–7, 231; French, *Raising Churchill's Army*, pp. 265, 269–71; Macksey, *Crucible of Power*, pp. 108–11.
63 Macksey, *Crucible of Power*, pp. 136–9.
64 Playfair et al., *Mediterranean and Middle East*, Vol. 4, pp. 278–85, 287–303; Macksey, *Crucible of Power*, pp. 140–62.
65 Playfair et al., *Mediterranean and Middle East*, Vol. 4, pp. 274–5; Howe, *Northwest Africa*, p. 370; Watson, *Exit Rommel*, p. 78; Levine, *War against Rommel's Supply Lines*, p. 81; Porch, *Path to Victory*, p. 407.
66 Walter Warlimont, *Inside Hitler's Headquarters, 1939–45* (London: Weidenfeld and Nicolson, 1964), pp. 309–11.
67 Levine, *War against Rommel's Supply Lines*, p. 81.
68 TNA DEFE 3/807, Signals VM 7588, 7647, 26–27 March 1943.
69 TNA DEFE 3/807, Signals VM 7634, 7647, 27 March 1943.
70 TNA DEFE 3/807, Signals VM 7770, 7810, 7835, 28–29 March 1943.
71 Kitchen, *Rommel's Desert War*, p. 450.
72 TNA DEFE 3/808, Signals VM 8070, 8128, 31 March–1 April 1943.
73 TNA DEFE 3/808, Signal VM 8158, 1 April 1943.
74 TNA DEFE 3/808, Signals VM 8269, 8276, 2 April 1943.
75 TNA CAB 146/27, EDS Appreciation 12: 'The Axis in Tunisia: The End in Africa, April–May 1943', p. 112; TNA HW 1/1633, Signal ML 241, AOC-in-C

South to C-in-C South East, 21 April 1943; TNA DEFE 3/809, Signals VM 8902, 8984, 9–10 April 1943. TNA DEFE 3/809, Signal VM 8152, 5 April 1943 gives the complex and resource-intensive methods planned in order to ensure the arrival of the *Regina*.
76 TNA DEFE 3/814, Signals ML 1129, 1141, 1329, 5–7 May 1943; Playfair et al., *The Mediterranean and Middle East*, Vol. 4, p. 455.
77 Playfair et al., *Mediterranean and Middle East*, Vol. 4, pp. 357–405, 429–62.
78 *The Rommel Papers*, pp. 419, 421; Playfair et al., *The Mediterranean and Middle East*, Vol. 4, p. 431; TNA CAB 146/27, EDS Appreciation 12: 'The Axis in Tunisia: The End in Africa, April–May 1943', p. 27.
79 Minutes of meeting on 22 April 1943, USSME, *Verbali delle riunioni*, Vol. 4, pp. 86–7.
80 Playfair et al., *The Mediterranean and Middle East*, Vol. 4, p. 431.
81 NARA T-821, Roll 211, Frame 596, Ufficio Traffico, 'Appunto per il Capo Stato Maggiore Generale', 3 May 1943; Frame 577, 'Notizie ore 16000805', 8 May 1943; JSCSC, AHB Translations, Vol. 3, Translation No. VII/25, 'The Battle for Tunis', p. 23.
82 Barbara Tomblin, *With Utmost Spirit: Allied Naval Operations in the Mediterranean, 1942–1945* (Lexington: University of Kentucky Press, 2004), pp. 119–21; Roskill, *War at Sea*, Vol. 2, pp. 441–2; Hinsley et al., *British Intelligence*, Vol. 2, p. 614; Playfair et al., *The Mediterranean and Middle East*, Vol. 4, pp. 423–4; Ehlers, *Mediterranean Air War*, p. 283.
83 The figures for new-build tonnage are calculated from Ristuccia, 'The Italian Economy under Fascism', p. 226. The combined total for Italian and German construction, seized vessels, purchases, those transferred to the theatre and those returned to service after repair up to 31 December 1942 in USMM, *LMI*, Vol. 1, *Dati Statistici*, pp. 30–2 totals 773,586 tons. It should be noted that figure includes the first tranche of seizures from France in late 1942.
84 AUSSME, Repertorio I-4, Busta 42, Cartella 15, Marina Mercantile, Programma costruzione in corso e programma 1943, 9 September 1942, pp. 1–3.
85 AUSSME, Repertorio I-4, Busta 42, Cartella 15, Programma Regia Marina, 1943, 9 September 1942, pp. 3–5, 7.
86 TNA GFM 36/6, 'Potenziamento delle Forze Armate', 1 October 1942, pp. 10–11.
87 TNA GFM 36/6, 'Potenziamento delle Forze Armate', 1 October 1942, pp. 18–19, 24.
88 IWM FD 4195/45, Kaufmann to Borman, 1 October 1942; Kaufmann to Borman, 9 November 1942; JSCSC, AHB Translations, Vol. 2, Translation No. VII/13, 'Minutes of a Conference held in Goering's Special Train in Rome', 30 November 1942, p. 1.
89 IWM FD 4195/45, Kaufmann to Hitler, 16 December 1942; 'Report by the Reichskommissar for Shipping on the further Development in the Mediterranean', 23 December 1942; TNA GFM 36/6, 'Verbali delle riunione a Palazzo Venezia presso il Duce sul'argomento "Potenziamento dell forze armate"', 29 January 1943, p. 38.

90 IWM FD 4195/45, 'Third Report by the Reichskommissar for Shipping on the further Development in the Mediterranean', 3 February 1943, pp. 17–18; JSCSC, AHB Translations, Vol. 5, Translation No. VII/44, 'Extracts from Reports of Fuhrer Conferences', entry for 4 March 1943, p. 1.
91 The quote is from JSCSC, AHB Translations, Vol. 5, Translation No. VII/44, 'Extracts from Reports of Fuhrer Conferences', entry for 12 December 1942, p. 3. For other examples of suggestions to increase available shipping, see TNA GFM 36/6, 'Verbali delle riunione a Palazzo Venezia presso il Duce sul'argomento "Potenziamento dell forze armate"', 29 January 1943, p. 42; IWM FD 4195/45, 'Fourth Report by the Reichskommissar for Shipping on the Situation in Holland/Belgium/France and further Developments in the Mediterranean', 6 March 1943, pp. 1–2, 5, 6; IWM FD 4195/45, Kaufmann to Kesselring, 12 March 1943.
92 IWM FD 4195/45, 'Fifth Report by the Reichskommissar for Shipping on the further Development in the Mediterranean and on the Position in Dutch Shipyards', 27 April 1943, p. 2.
93 TNA CAB 146/21, EDS Appreciation 11, 'The Axis Supply Situation in North Africa, February 1941–December 1942. Part III: September–December 1942', pp. 265, 271.
94 TNA DEFE 3/897, Signal QT 6942, 25 November 1942.
95 TNA DEFE 3/807, Signal VM 7710, 28 March 1943.
96 TNA AIR 20/5399, Sardinian Aeronautical Command to Minister for Air, 3 March 1943, p. 1; TNA AIR 20/5397, Italian report on air raid on Cagliari, 13 May 1943, pp. 6–9.
97 TNA DEFE 3/809, Signals VM 8869, 8870, 8 April 1943. Serviceability rates for the accompanying Italian aircraft are unknown.
98 TNA DEFE 3/814, Signal ML 1345, 7 May 1943.
99 Roskill, *War at Sea*, Vol. 2, appendix O, Table 2, p. 486; Playfair et al., *The Mediterranean and Middle East*, Vol. 4, pp. 252–4; Hinsley et al., *British Intelligence*, Vol. 2, pp. 605–6; TNA AIR 20/5399, Sardinian Aeronautical Command to Minister for Air, 3 March 1943, p. 1; TNA AIR 41/54, AHBN, The RAF and Maritime War, Vol. 7, appendix 30: 'British, Allied and Neutral Merchant Shipping Losses in the Mediterranean and Indian Ocean due to Enemy Action'.
100 Playfair et al., *The Mediterranean and Middle East*, Vol. 4, pp. 116, 124–5, 387.
101 Tomblin, *With Utmost Spirit*, p. 109.
102 TNA CAB 146/28, EDS Appreciation 14: 'Axis Plans and Policies in the Mediterranean, May–September 1943', p. 41.
103 TNA DEFE 3/769, Signal MKA 1544, 11 August 1942; TNA DEFE 3/776, Signal QT 2071, 24 September 1942.
104 TNA DEFE 3/780, Signal QT 4052, 22 October 1942; TNA DEFE 3/897, Signal PK 78, 8 November 1942.
105 TNA DEFE 3/780, Signal QT 4419, 26 October 1942.
106 TNA DEFE 3/807, Signal VM 7918, 30 March 1943; TNA DEFE 3/809, Signal VM 8792, 7 April 1943; TNA DEFE 3/884, Signal JP 6576, 8 October 1943.

Chapter 8

1. See for instance TNA CAB 79/57, COS(42) 279th Meeting, 5 October 1942, p. 4; TNA AIR 23/1333, JPS M.E. Paper No. 110: 'Capture of Crete and the Dodecanese', 4 October 1942. On Churchill's ambitions over Turkey, see Nicholas Tamkin, *Britain, Turkey and the Soviet Union, 1940–45* (Basingstoke: Palgrave Macmillan, 2009).
2. Howard, *Grand Strategy*, Vol. 4, pp. 409–34.
3. Quoted in ibid., p. 422.
4. Maurice Matloff, *Strategic Planning for Coalition Warfare 1943–1944* (Washington, DC: Centre of Military History, United States Army, 1994), pp. 120–35. Although there remain questions over Roosevelt's opinion of a Mediterranean strategy, he broadly backed the JCOS and planners at the Trident conference.
5. TNA WO 201/2070, CC(43) 9th Meeting of the Commanders-in-Chief Committee, 28 March 1943, pp. 3–5.
6. TNA AIR 41/54, AHBN, The RAF and Maritime War, Vol. 7, appendix 30: 'British, Allied and Neutral Merchant Shipping Losses in the Mediterranean and Indian Ocean due to Enemy Action'.
7. TNA CAB 79/59, JP(43) 1035 (Final), Operation 'Brimstone' report by the Joint Planning Staff, 10 January 1943, p. 11; TNA AIR 8/719, C-in-C Mediterranean to Admiralty, 24 April 1943; TNA ADM 234/381, NSH, *Submarines*, Vol. 2, pp. 144–52.
8. JSCSC, AHB Translations, Vol. 10, Translation No. VII/93, 'The Invasion of Sicily, 1943', p. 3; 'Conference with Field Marshal Kesselring', 13 May 1942 in *Fuerer Conferences*, pp. 322, 326; IWM FD 4195/45, 'Sixth Report by the Reichskommissar for Shipping on the Position in the Norwegian Area and of the making available of small tonnage for the Western Mediterranean and Norway', 6 June 1943, p. 41.
9. Michael Howard, *Strategic Deception in the Second World War* (London: Pimlico, 1990), pp. 73, 85–93 (Vol. 5 of Hinsley et al., *British Intelligence*), offers an engaging narrative of these events and where they achieved some success; Klaus-Jürgen Müller, 'A German Perspective on Allied Deception Operations in the Second World War' in Michael Handel (ed.), *Strategic and Operational Deception in the Second World War* (London: Frank Cass, 1987), pp. 303–16 offers a persuasive warning against overstating the effects of these deception operations, as the early historiography has. On anti-shipping operations, see Roskill, *War at Sea*, Vol. 2, p. 438.
10. On the defences and state of Italian coastal units, see the comments by Mario Roatta that 'we can only make an honourable resistance' in the minutes of the meetings of 2 May 1943, USSME, *Verbali delle riunioni*, Vol. 4, pp. 103–24. See also Alberto Santoni, *Le operazioni in Sicilia e in Calabria, luglio–settembre 1943* (Rome: Stilografica, 1983), pp. 481–7. Kesselring commented three days after the landings that most Italian troops had 'fallen by the way side', see MF, *Germany and the Second World War*, Vol. 8, p. 113.
11. TNA GFM 36/8, Comando Supremo, Il Duce, 'Situazione', 14 July 1943.
12. Roskill, *War at Sea*, Vol. 3, Part 1, p. 114.

13 Ehlers, *Mediterranean Air War*, p. 295.
14 Roskill, *War at Sea*, Vol. 3, Part 1, p. 109.
15 Hammond, 'An Enduring Influence', p. 828; TNA ADM 234/381, NSH, *Submarines*, Vol. 2, pp. 161–72.
16 TNA ADM 234/356, Battle Summary No. 35, 'The Invasion of Sicily: Operation Husky', pp. 90–1.
17 Samuel W. Mitcham and Friedrich von Stauffenberg, *The Battle of Sicily: How the Allies Lost Their Chance for Total Victory* (Mechanicsburg, PA: Stackpole, 2007), pp. 285–93.
18 Hinsley et al., *British Intelligence*, Vol. 3, Part 1, p. 96.
19 'Report on Operation "Husky"', 1 January 1944 in Simpson (ed.), *The Cunningham Papers*, Vol. 2, p. 114; Eduard Mark, *Aerial Interdiction: Air Power and the Land Battle in Three American Wars* (Washington, DC: Centre for Air Force History, 1994), pp. 67–8; TNA AIR 41/54, AHBN, The RAF and Maritime War, Vol. 7, p. 128.
20 Ehlers, *Mediterranean Air War*, p. 305 gives figures of 287 aircraft used in raids on Rome and southern France, while Overy, *The Bombing War*, p. 591 states that 175 were used in the August attack on Ploesti.
21 See for example 'Discussion with Sonderfuhrer von Neurath concerning Italy on 20 May 1943' and 'Briefing Conference, 25 July 1943' in Warlimont, *Inside Hitler's Headquarters*, pp. 319–31, 344–53.
22 MF, *Germany and the Second World War*, Vol. 8, pp. 1118–22; US Naval War College (USNWC), Record Group (RG) 8, War Diary, German Naval Staff, Operations Division, Vol. 49, Part A, 8 September 1943, p. 118 and 12 September 1943, pp. 168–9.
23 USNWC, RG 8, War Diary, German Naval Staff, Operations Division, Vol. 48, Part A, 1 August 1943, p. 2.
24 For an in-depth account of the armistice period, see Elena Agarossi, *A Nation Collapses: The Italian Surrender of September 1943* (Cambridge: Cambridge University Press, 2000), pp. 91–124.
25 Warlimont, *Inside Hitler's Headquarters*, pp. 383–8.
26 Peter Smith and Edwin Walker, *War in the Aegean: The Campaign for the Eastern Mediterranean in World War II* (London: William Kimber, 1974), p. 35.
27 The hope of Italian collaboration had existed before the fall of Mussolini. See for example TNA WO 201/2070, CC(43) 17th Meeting of the Commanders-in-Chief Committee, 16 July 1943, p. 5.
28 Ian Gooderson, 'Shoestring Strategy: The British Campaign in the Aegean, 1943', *Journal of Strategic Studies*, 25, 3 (2002), pp. 6–8.
29 'Conference minutes of the C-in-C Navy, at the Fuehrer's Headquarters', 24 September 1943 in *Fuehrer Conferences*, pp. 368–9.
30 Churchill College Archives Centre (CCAC) Algernon Willis Papers (WLLS) 6/2, 'General Report on Aegean Operations', 27 December 1943, p. 2 and attached report by Captain(S) First Submarine Flotilla.
31 TNA WO 201/2070, CC(43) 32nd Meeting of the Commanders-in-Chief Committee, 7 October 1943, p. 2; CC(43) 34th Meeting of the Commanders-in-Chief Committee, 10 October 1943, pp. 1–2.

32 TNA WO 201/2070, CC(43) 46th Meeting of the Commanders-in-Chief Committee, 7 December 1943, p. 2.
33 TNA AIR 23/6257, Memorandum by AOC-in-C Middle East, 'Operations in the Aegean', 2 December 1943, p. 1.
34 See F. M. Sallagar, *Operation "Strangle" (Italy, Spring 1944): A Case Study of Tactical Air Interdiction* (Santa Monica, CA: RAND, 1972), p. 18.
35 Warlimont, *Inside Hitler's Headquarters*, p. 471; MF, *Germany and the Second World War*, Vol. 8, pp. 1091–2.
36 TNA AIR 20/5397, Italian Report on Enemy Air Raids from 28 January to 10 February 1943, pp. 3, 6; TNA AIR 23/7085, Middle East Interpretation Unit: Messina Train Ferry Service, 10 July 1943, pp. 5–9; TNA CAB 79/59, JP(43) 7 (Final), Operation 'Husky' report by the Joint Planning Staff, 10 January 1943, Annex 1, p. 5.
37 Calculated from TNA AIR 22/342, AMWR Monthly Summaries for May–July 1943, and TNA AIR 20/1174, Summary of shipping attacks, 1–22 August 1943.
38 Calculated from TNA AIR 22/342, AMWR Monthly Summaries for May–July 1943, and TNA AIR 20/1174, Summary of shipping attacks, 1–22 August 1943.
39 Ehlers, *Mediterranean Air War*, p. 304.
40 TNA CAB 79/59, JP(43) 7 (Final), Operation 'Husky' report by the Joint Planning Staff, 10 January 1943, Annex 1, p. 1.
41 TNA DEFE 3/873, Signals JP 1257 and 1274, 17 August 1943.
42 Dudley Pope, *Flag 4: The Battle of Coastal Forces in the Mediterranean, 1939–1945* (London: Chatham, 2006), pp. 121–2.
43 TNA AIR 41/54, AHBN, The RAF and Maritime War, Vol. 7, p. 128.
44 TNA ADM 234/381, NSH, *Submarines*, Vol. 2, pp. 162–72 and Plan (map) 13; sinkings calculated from Röhwer, *Allied Submarine Attacks*, pp. 188–96.
45 Röhwer, *Allied Submarine Attacks*, pp. 188–96.
46 NARA, T-821, Roll 211, Comando Supremo, Ufficio Traffico, 'Appunto per il Sotto Capo di Stato Maggiore Generale', 9 May 1943; NARA, T-821, Roll 211, Comando Militare in Sicilia to Comando Supremo, 25 July 1943.
47 TNA DEFE 3/873, Signal JP 1257, 17 August 1943.
48 TNA AIR 23/7085, Middle East Interpretation Unit: Messina Train Ferry Service, 10 July 1943, pp. 5, 9.
49 Mark, *Aerial Interdiction*, p. 66; Barnett, *Engage the Enemy More Closely*, p. 649; Mitcham and Stauffenberg, *The Battle for Sicily*, pp. 286–7.
50 Calculated from TNA AIR 22/342, AMWR Monthly Summaries for June–July 1943, and TNA AIR 20/1174, Summary of shipping attacks, 1–22 August 1943.
51 TNA ADM 234/381, NSH, *Submarines*, Vol. 2, p. 277.
52 See for instance the mission reports held in TNA AIR 23/5748.
53 TNA AIR 20/5396, 'Report of the Result of the Enemy Air Raid on 18 June 1943'; TNA AIR 20/5397, 'Damage to Ships under Construction at Leghorn', 4 July 1943, pp. 1–5; TNA AIR 20/1174, Summary of shipping attacks, 29 August–3 October 1943.

54 Röhwer, *Allied Submarine Attacks*, pp. 197–203; USNWC, RG 8, War Diary, German Naval Staff, Operations Division, Vol. 49, Part A, 26 September 1943, p. 378.
55 Tomblin, *With Utmost Spirit*, p. 301.
56 On the numbers of fighters, see Hinsley et al., *British Intelligence*, Vol. 3, p. 122; on the distance of airfields, see Gooderson, 'Shoestring Strategy', p. 8.
57 TNA WO 201/2070, CC(43) 29th Meeting of the Commanders-in-Chief Committee, 2 October 1943, p. 2.
58 CCAC WLLS 6/2, Middle East Interpretation Unit: Report on Enemy Preparations for the Attack on Leros – A Summary of the Information derived from Air Reconnaissance, 18 December 1943, pp. 3–4; Hinsley et al., *British Intelligence*, Vol. 3, pp. 123–4, 126–7, 132–3.
59 Calculated from TNA AIR 20/1174, Summary of shipping attacks, 5 September–21 November 1943.
60 CCAC WLLS 6/2, 'General Report on Aegean Operations', 27 December 1943, p. 2 and attached report by Captain(S) First Submarine Flotilla.
61 TNA ADM 234/381, NSH, *Submarines*, Vol. 2, pp. 208–14; Röhwer, *Allied Submarine Attacks*, pp. 198–204.
62 Gooderson, 'Shoestring Strategy', pp. 19–20; CCAC WLLS 6/2, 'General Report on Aegean Operations', 27 December 1943, p. 3.
63 CCAC WLLS 6/2, 'General Report on Aegean Operations', 27 December 1943, pp. 5–7; Roskill, *War at Sea*, Vol. 3, Part 1, pp. 199–202. German-laid mines also accounted for two destroyers running supplies to Leros and caused serious damage to a third, but as these were not engaged in anti-shipping operations, they are not included in the losses listed in this chapter.
64 CCAC WLLS 6/2, 'Naval Operations in the Aegean: 7 September–28 November 1943', 27 December 1943, appendix 1.
65 TNA ADM 234/381, NSH, *Submarines*, Vol. 2, pp. 217–18; C. J. C. Molony et al., *The Campaign in Sicily, 1943 and the Campaign in Italy, 3rd September 1943 to 31st March 1944* (London: HMSO, 1973), pp. 563–5 (Vol. 5 of I. S. O. Playfair et al., *Mediterranean and Middle East*).
66 Figures taken from TNA AIR 20/2034, 'Mediterranean Allied Air Force: miscellaneous statistics'.
67 Hammond, 'Air Power and the British Anti-Shipping Campaign', p. 63; Hammond, 'Inter and Intra-Theatre Learning', p. 15.
68 Nesbit, *The Armed Rovers*, pp. 207–8.
69 Calculated from TNA AIR 20/9598, Table 3: 'Analysis of Enemy Merchant Shipping Sunk by All Causes, Scuttled, Captured or Surrendered in the Mediterranean'.
70 'Minutes of the conference of the C-in-C Navy and the Fuehrer at the Headquarters, Berghof, 12–13 April 1944 in *Fuehrer Conferences*, pp. 389–90.
71 Calculated from TNA AIR 20/9598, Table 3: 'Analysis of Enemy Merchant Shipping Sunk by All Causes, Scuttled, Captured or Surrendered in the Mediterranean'. Some revisions to the statistics regarding sinkings by submarine have been made using Röhwer, *Allied Submarine Attacks*.
72 TNA AIR 41/54, AHBN, The RAF and Maritime War, Vol. 7, p. 70.

248   Notes to pages 190–192

73 IWM FD 4195/45, 'Sixth Report by the Reichskommissar for Shipping on the Position in the Norwegian Area and of the making available of small tonnage for the Western Mediterranean and Norway', 6 June 1943, pp. 41–3.
74 IWM FD 4195/45, 'Sixth Report by the Reichskommissar for Shipping on the Position in the Norwegian Area and of the making available of small tonnage for the Western Mediterranean and Norway', 6 June 1943, pp. 41–3.
75 USNWC, RG 8, War Diary, German Naval Staff, Operations Division, Vol. 48, Part A, 3 August 1943, p. 47; IWM FD 4195/45, Warliamont to Kaufmann, 7 July 1943; 'Seventh report by the Reichskommissar for shipping on the situation in the Mediterranean, in the Aegean in the Black Sea and in the North Sea and Baltic Area', undated, likely July 1943, p. 47.
76 TNA DEFE 3/824, Signal ML 6106, 4 July 1943; Minutes of meeting on 5 July, 1943, USSME, *Verbali delle riunioni*, Vol. 4, p. 179. There was a slight increase in quantities landed at Sardinia at the time of 'Husky', before quantities receded once again. On the cessation of supplies to Sardinia and satisfactory supply in Corsica, see TNA DEFE 3/826, Signal ML 7127, 12 July 1943; TNA DEFE 3/873, Signals JP 1327 and JP 1373, 18 August 1943.
77 Minutes of meeting on 2 July 1943, USSME, *Verbali delle riunioni*, Vol. 4, p. 179; NARA T-821, Roll 211, letter to Adriacono (Undersecretary for Merchant Marine) from undisclosed, 3 May 1943.
78 NARA T-821, Roll 211, Comando Supremo, Ufficio Traffico, 'Appunto per il Sotto Capo di Stato Maggiore Generale', 9 May 1943; TNA AIR 23/7085, Middle East Interpretation Unit: Messina Train Ferry Service, 10 July 1943, pp. 4, 7.
79 NARA T-821, Roll 211, Ministero della Guerra, Gabinetto, 'Concorso militare in occassione di incursion aeree', 16 June 1943; Il Ministro delle Comunicazioni, Promemoria per il Comando Supremo, 14 July 1943.
80 See Minutes of the meetings of 2 May 1943, USSME, *Verbali delle riunioni*, Vol. 4, pp. 103–24. See also the reproduced report on the state of the Italian forces and defences in Italy in Santoni, *Le operazioni in Sicilia e in Calabria*, pp. 481–7.
81 TNA DEFE 3/814, Signal ML 1391, 7 May 1943; TNA DEFE 3/825, Signals ML 6777, 6860, 6919, 6993, 9–10 July 1943; TNA DEFE 3/826, Signal ML 7187, 12 July 1943; Minutes of the meeting of 5 July, 1943, USSME, *Verbali delle riunioni*, Vol. 4, p. 183.
82 TNA DEFE 3/825, Signal ML 6557, 8 July 1943; Minutes of the meeting of 5 July, 1943, USSME, *Verbali delle riunioni*, Vol. 4, pp. 181–4; Hinsley et al., *British Intelligence*, Vol. 3, Part I, pp. 75–7. The reproduced Italian report in Santoni, *Le operazioni in Sicilia e in Calabria*, pp. 481–7, is damning towards the state of the Italian forces and defences in Italy.
83 As evidenced by decrypted intelligence reports: TNA DEFE 3/826, Signals ML 7026, 7125, 7221, 7247, 7422, 11–14 July 1943.
84 TNA DEFE 3/826, Signal ML 7431, 7440, 7461, 14–15 July 1943; TNA DEFE 3/873, Signal JP 1018, 15 August 1943.
85 TNA DEFE 3/826, Signal ML 7342, 7424, 7490 14–15 July 1943.

86 NARA T-821, Roll 211, Supertrasporti to Comando Supremo Ufficio Traffico, 23 July 1943; Comando Militare in Sicilia to Comando Supremo, 25 July 1943; Supertrasporti to Comando Supremo Ufficio Traffico, 7 August 1943.
87 Tomblin, *With Utmost Spirit*, pp. 227, 230.
88 Carlo D'Este, *Bitter Victory: The Battle for Sicily 1943* (London: Collins, 1988), pp. 76, 524–7.
89 USNWC, RG 8, War Diary, German Naval Staff, Operations Division, Vol. 49, Part A, 20 September 1943, p. 285.
90 MF, *Germany and the Second World War*, Vol. 8, p. 1120, 1133–4; USNWC, RG 8, War Diary, German Naval Staff, Operations Division, Vol. 49, Part A, 8 September 1943, p. 118.
91 USNWC, RG 8, War Diary, German Naval Staff, Operations Division, Vol. 49, Part A, 12–13 September 1943, pp. 168–9, 183–4, 192–3; MF, *Germany and the Second World War*, Vol. 8, pp. 1133–4; IWM FD 4195/45, 'Eighth Report by the Reichskommissar for Shipping covering the Period August–November 1943 inclusive', 13 December 1943, pp. 60–1.
92 TNA DEFE 3/880, JP 4589, 16 September 1943; Tomblin, *With Utmost Spirit*, p. 300; Agarossi, *A Nation Collapses*, pp. 110–11.
93 USNWC, RG 8, War Diary, German Naval Staff, Operations Division, Vol. 49, Part A, 19 September 1943, p. 273; TNA DEFE 3/880, Signals JP 4667, 4863, 17–19 September 1943; TNA DEFE 3/883, Signal JP 6109, 2 October 1943.
94 TNA DEFE 3/883, Signal JP 6026, 2 October 1943; TNA CAB 66/35/42, War Cabinet Conclusions, 28 September 1943, p. 55; Tomblin, *With Utmost Spirit*, p. 301.
95 The figures for the evacuation come from MF, *Germany and the Second World War*, Vol. 8, pp. 1133–4. Slightly different figures for this, including a claim of over 40,000 men are to be found in Tomblin, *With Utmost Spirit*, pp. 301–2 and also TNA DEFE 3/883, Signal JP 6411, 6 October 1943. For the Hitler quote and sinking figures, see TNA DEFE 3/884, Signal JP 6531, 7 October 1943; Roskill, *War at Sea*, Vol. 3, Part I, p. 187.
96 Roskill, *War at Sea*, Vol. 3, Part 1, pp. 194–5; Jeffrey Holland, *The Aegean Mission: Allied Operations in the Dodecanese, 1943* (Westport, CT: Greenwood, 1988), pp. 121–2.
97 TNA DEFE 3/884, Signals JP 6574, 6603, 6637, 6713, 6745, 6824, 6896, 6971, 8–12 October 1943.
98 Hinsley et al., *British Intelligence*, Vol. 3, pp. 126–7; CCAC WLLS 6/2, 'General Report on Aegean Operations', 27 December 1943, pp. 5–8.
99 CCAC WLLS 6/2, 'Naval Operations in the Aegean: 7 September–28 November 1943', 27 December 1943, p. 20.
100 Molony et al., *Mediterranean and Middle East*, Vol. 5, p. 825.
101 USNWC, RG 8, War Diary, German Naval Staff, Operations Division, Vol. 48, Part A, 5 and 10 August 1943, pp. 68, 127; Vol. 49, Part A, 20 September 1943, p. 284; TNA HW 11/33, GC + CS Naval History, Vol. 20, pp. 246–7.

102 TNA HW 13/11, CX/MSS/EC.21, 27 November 1943, CX/MSS/EC.24, 16 and 25 November 1943, 2 December 1943; IWM FD 4195/45, 'Eighth report by the Reichskommissar for Shipping covering the Period August–November 1943 inclusive', 13 December 1943, pp. 60–1; TNA GFM 36/36, Rennato Burrini to Ministro degli Esteri, 17 April 1944.

103 IWM FD 4195/45, 'Report by the Representative for Greece for the Reichskommissar for Shipping concerning sea transport and the supply position in the Aegean', 17 December 1943, p. 64; 'Tenth report by the Reichskommissar for Shipping on the Position of Shipping on 31 May 1944', 12 June 1944, pp. 69–70; TNA HW 1/3194, CX/MSS/T291/126, 29 August 1944.

104 Warlimont, *Inside Hitler's Headquarters*, p. 471; MF, *Germany and the Second World War*, Vol. 8, pp. 1090–2.

105 Quoted in Sallagar, *Operation 'Strangle'*, p. 39.

106 Although notable quantities of shipping were sunk, the coastal routes were only supplying around 15 per cent of the total traffic, with the rest coming by road and rail, where disruption was more effective. See Ehlers, *Mediterranean Air War*, pp. 332–3, although Sallagar, *Operation "Strangle"*, passim, disputes the overall effectiveness in causing supply shortages. For an example of interdiction of shipping in the Adriatic regarding the Balkans, see JSCSC, AHB Translations, Vol. 10, Translation No. VII/96, War Appreciation No. 16, 10 November 1944, p. 4.

Conclusion

1 For details on Anglo-American stabilisation and reconstruction efforts in Italy in the period immediately after the surrender, as well as their concerns over communism in the north of the country, see David Ellwood, *Italy, 1943–1945* (Leicester: Leicester University Press, 1985), pp. 184–235.

2 On the establishment of NATO's southern flank, see Dionysius Chourchoulis, *The Southern Flank of NATO, 1951–1959: Military Strategy or Political Stabilisation* (Lanham, MD: Lexington Books, 2015), which also includes a summary of events in 1945–50 on pp. xxiii–xxx. For a summary of British and American involvement in Greece, see Amikam Nachmani, 'Civil War and Foreign Intervention in Greece: 1946–49', *Journal of Contemporary History*, 25, 4 (1990), pp. 489–522. On American financial aid to the region, particularly in Greece and Turkey, see Stephen E. Ambrose, *Rise to Globalism: American Foreign Policy since 1938* (London: Allen Lane, 1971), pp. 142, 147–52.

3 On the gaping disparity between the Allied wartime control of oil resources and the Axis lack thereof, and failed Axis attempts to compensate, see Overy, *Why the Allies Won*, pp. 228–34.

4 On the potential repercussions of defeat, see Porch, *Path to Victory*, pp. 6–7, 26–7; Gerhard Weinberg, *A World at Arms: A Global History of World War II* (Cambridge: Cambridge University Press, 1994), pp. 171–2, 213, 350–1.

5 Porch, *Path to Victory*, p. 662.

6 Hammond, 'Inter and Intra-Theatre Learning', pp. 10–16.

7 Most notably in van Creveld, *Supplying War*, and Gladman, 'Air Power and Intelligence'.
8 Figures for sinkings, losses to sabotage, scuttling, capture, friendly fire, accident and unknown causes are calculated from TNA AIR 20/9598, Table 3: 'Analysis of Enemy Merchant Shipping Sunk by all Causes, Scuttled, Captured or Surrendered in the Mediterranean', with some revisions to the statistics regarding sinkings using Röhwer, *Allied Submarine Attacks*. On the poor quality and capability of Italian repair facilities, see Ristuccia, 'The Italian Economy under Fascism', p. 237; Deakin, *Brutal Friendship*, pp. 81, 212.
9 Bragadin, *Italian Navy*, pp. 364–5. The figures for new-build tonnage are calculated from Ristuccia, 'The Italian Economy under Fascism', p. 226.
10 O'Brien, *How the War Was Won*, pp. 4–5.
11 Deakin, *Brutal Friendship*, p. 275.

Bibliography

Unpublished Primary Sources

Italy

Archivio dell'Ufficio Storico dello Stato Maggiore dell'Esercito, Rome (AUSMME)
　1 Repertorio I-4
Archivio dell'Ufficio Storico della Marina Militare, Rome (AUSMM)
　1 Direttive Generali
　2 Fondo Supermarina
　3 Intercettazioni

United Kingdom

The National Archives, Kew, London (TNA)
　1 Admiralty (ADM)
　2 Air Ministry (AIR)
　3 Cabinet (CAB)
　4 Ministry of Defence (DEFE)
　5 Copies of Captured Records of German, Italian and Japanese Governments (GFM)
　6 Government Communications Headquarters (HW)
　7 War Office (WO)
Imperial War Museum, London (IWM)
　1 Italian Air Force series (IAF)
　2 Foreign Documents section (FD)
Bodleian Library Special Collections, Oxford (BLSC)
　1 John Cowdrey Kendrew Papers
Churchill College Archives, Cambridge (CCAC)
　1 Algernon Willis Papers (WLLS)
Joint Services Command and Staff College Archive, Shrivenham (JSCSC)
　1 Air Historical Branch Translations
National Maritime Museum, Greenwich, London (NMM)
　1 Roger Dick Papers
　2 Henry Pridham-Wippell Papers
Royal Air Force Museum, Hendon, London (RAFM)
　1 Arthur Longmore Papers

Royal Navy Submarine Museum, Gosport (RNSM)
United Kingdom Hydrographic Office, Taunton
1 Admiralty Distance Tables

United States of America

National Archives and Records Administration, College Park, Maryland (NARA)
1 T-821
2 T-1022
United States Naval War College Archive (USNWC)
1 Record Group 8: Intelligence and Technical Archives (RG 8).

Published Primary Sources

Armellini, Quirino, *Diario di guerra: nove mesi al Comando Supremo, 1940–1941* (Milan: Garzanti, 1946).
Ciano, Galeazzo, *Diario 1937–1943*, ed. Renzo de Felice (Milan: Rizzoli, 2010).
The Cunningham Papers, ed. Michael Simpson, 2 Volumes (Aldershot: Ashgate, 1999–2006).
Diario Storico del Comando Supremo (DSCS), ed. Ufficio Storico dello Stato Maggiore dell'Esercito (USSME), 9 Volumes (Rome: USSME, 1986–2000).
Documents on British Foreign Policy, 1919–1939, ed. Woorward, E. L. and Rohan Butler, Series 1, Volume 3 (London: HMSO, 1949).
Fuehrer Conferences on Naval Affairs, 1939–1945 (London: Greenhill, 1990).
The Halder War Diary, 1939–1942, ed. Charles Burdick and Hans-Adolf Jacobsen (Novato, CA: Presidio Press, 1988).
Hitler's War Directives, 1939–1945, ed. Hugh Trevor-Roper (London: Pan Books, 1966).
I documenti diplomatici italiani, Series 9, Volume 5 (Rome: Istituto Poligrafico dello Stato, 1965).
The Rommel Papers, ed. Basil Liddell-Hart (London: Da Capo Press, 1950).
Verbali delle riunioni tenute dal Capo di Stato Maggiore Generale, ed. Ufficio Storico dello Stato Maggiore dell'Esercito (USSME), 4 Volumes (Rome: USSME, 1983–85).

Newspapers

The Hull Daily Mail
The Times

Secondary Sources: Official Histories

Gibbs, N. H., J. R. M. Butler, J. M. A. Gwyer, Michael Howard, and John Ehrman, *Grand Strategy*, 6 Volumes (London: HMSO, 1957–76).
Volume 1 *Rearmament Policy* (1976).
Volume 2 *September 1939–June 1941* (1957).
Volume 4 *August 1942–September 1943* (1972).

Hinsley, F. H., E. E. Thomas, G. F. G. Ransom, R. C. Knight, Michael Howard, *British Intelligence in the Second World War*, 5 Volumes (London: HMSO, 1979–90).
  Volume 1 *Its Influence on Strategy and Operations* (1979).
  Volume 5 *Strategic Deception* (1990).
Howe, George F., *Northwest Africa: Seizing the Initiative in the West* (Washington, DC: Office of the Chief Military Historian, 1957).
Jones, Ben (ed.), *The Fleet Air Arm and the Second World War, Vol. 1, 1939–1941: Norway, the Mediterranean and the Bismarck* (Farnham: Ashgate, 2012).
Matloff, Maurice, *Strategic Planning for Coalition Warfare, 1943–1944* (Washington, DC: Centre of Military History, United States Army, 1994).
Militärgeschichtliches Forschungsamt (MF), *Germany and the Second World War*, 9 Volumes (Oxford: Oxford University Press, 1990–2017).
  Volume 3 *The Mediterranean, South-East Europe and North Africa, 1939–1941* (1995).
  Volume 6 *The Global War* (2001).
  Volume 8 *The Eastern Front 1943–1944; The War in the East and on the Neighbouring Fronts* (2017).
Morison, Samuel Eliot, *History of United States Naval Operations in World War II*, 15 Volumes (Boston: Little, Brown, 1947–62).
  Volume 2 *Operations in North African Waters, October 1942–June 1943* (1947).
  Volume 9 *Sicily – Salerno – Anzio, January 1943–June 1944* (1954).
Naval Staff History (NSH), *Mediterranean, Vol. I, September 1939–October 1940* (Historical Section, Admiralty, 1952).
  The Royal Navy and the Mediterranean, 2 Volumes (Abingdon: Routledge, 2002).
  The Royal Navy and the Mediterranean Convoys (Oxford: Routledge, 2007).
Playfair, I. S. O., G. M. S. Stitt, C. J. C. Molony, S. E. Toomer, *The Mediterranean and the Middle East*, 6 Volumes (London: HMSO, 1954–88).
  Volume 1 *The Early Successes against Italy* (1954).
  Volume 2 *The Germans Come to the Help of Their Ally* (1956).
  Volume 3 *British Fortunes Reach Their Lowest Ebb* (1960).
  Volume 4 *The Destruction of the Axis Forces in Africa* (1966).
  Volume 5 *The Campaign in Sicily, 1943 and the Campaign in Italy, 3rd September 1943 to 31st March 1944* (1973).
Richards, Denis and Hilary Saunders, *The Royal Air Force at War, 1939–1945*, 3 Volumes (London: HMSO 1953–54).
  Volume 1 *The Fight at Odds* (1953).
Roskill, Stephen, *War at Sea*, 3 Volumes (London: HMSO, 1954–61).
  Volume 1 *The Defensive* (1954).
  Volume 2 *The Period of Balance* (1956).
  Volume 3, Parts 1 and 2 *The Offensive* (1960–61).
Ufficio Storico della Marina Militare (USMM), *La Marina Italiana nella seconda guerra modiale* (*LMI*), 21 Volumes (Rome: USMM, 1950–78).
  Volume 1 *Dati statistici* (1950).
  Volume 3 *Navi mercantili perduti* (1952).
  Volume 4 *Le azioni navali dal 10 Giugno 1940 al 31 Marzo 1941* (1959).

Volume 5 *Le azioni navali dal 1 Aprile 1941 al 8 Settembre 1943* (1960).
Volume 6 *La difesa del traffico con l'Africa settentrionale, tomo I: dal 10 Giugno 1940 al 30 settembre 1941* (1958).
Volume 7 *La difesa del traffico con l'Africa settentrionale, tomo II* (1958).
Volume 8 *La difesa del traffico con l'Africa settentrionale dal 1 Ottobre 1942 alla Caduta della Tunisia* (1964).
Volume 9 *La difesa del traffico con Albania, Grecia e l'Egeo* (1964).
Volume 19 *Il Dragaggio* (1969).
Volume 21 *L'organizzazione della Marina durante il conflitto, tomo I: Efficienza all'apertura delle ostilità* (1972).
Ufficio Storico dello Stato Maggiore dell'Esercito (USSME), *Seconda offensiva Britannica in Africa settentrionale e ripiegamento italo-tedesco nella Sirtica orientale (18 novembre 1941–17 gennaio 1942)* (Rome: USSME, 1949).
La terza offensive in Africa settentrionale, tomo I: 6 September 1942–4 February 1943 (Rome: USSME, 1961).
Verbali delle riunioni tenute dal Capo di Stato Maggiore Generale, Volume 1 (Rome: USSME, 1982).

Secondary Sources: Articles and Chapters

Baldioli, Claudia and Marco Finardi, 'Italian Society under Anglo-American Bombs: Propaganda, Experience and Legend, 1940–1945', *Historical Journal*, 52, 4 (2009), pp. 1017–1038.
Ball, Simon, 'The Mediterranean and North Africa, 1940–1944' in John Ferris and Evan Mawdsley (eds.), *The Cambridge History of the Second World War*, Volume 1 (Cambridge: Cambridge University Press, 2015), pp. 358–388.
Buchanan, Andrew, 'A Friend Indeed? From Tobruk to El Alamein: The American Contribution to Victory in the Desert', *Diplomacy and Statecraft*, 15, 2 (2004), pp. 279–301.
Buckley, John, 'Contradictions in British Defence Policy, 1937–1939: The RAF and the Defence of Trade', *Twentieth Century British History*, 5, 1 (1994), pp. 100–113.
Budden, Michael J., 'Defending the Indefensible: The Air Defence of Malta, 1936–1940', *War in History*, 6, 4 (1999), pp. 447–467.
Cassels, Alan, 'Britain, Italy and the Axis: How to Make Friends with Mussolini and Influence Hitler' in Gaynor Johnson (ed.), *The International Context of the Spanish Civil War* (Newcastle: Cambridge Scholars, 2009), pp. 19–32.
Darwin, John, 'Imperialism and the Victorians: The Dynamics of Territorial Expansion', *English Historical Review*, 112, 447 (1997), pp. 614–642.
'An Undeclared Empire: The British in the Middle East, 1918–1939', *Journal of Imperial and Commonwealth History*, 27, 2 (1999), pp. 159–176.
Ferris, John, 'Treasury Control, the Ten Year Rule and British Service Policies, 1919–1924', *Historical Journal*, 30, 4 (1987), pp. 859–883.
Gladman, Brad, 'Air Power and Intelligence in the Western Desert Campaign, 1940–43', *Intelligence and National Security*, 13, 4 (1998), pp. 144–162.

Gooderson, Ian, 'Shoestring Strategy: The British Campaign in the Aegean, 1943', *Journal of Strategic Studies*, 25, 3 (2002), pp. 1–36.

Goulter, Christina, 'The Politicization of Intelligence: The British Experience in Greece, 1941–1944' in Martin S. Alexander (ed.), *Knowing your Friends: Intelligence inside Alliances from 1914 to the Cold War* (London: Frank Cass, 1998), pp. 165–194.

Gribaudi, Gabriella, 'The True Causes of "Moral Collapse": People, Fascists and Authorities under the Bombs. Naples and the Countryside, 1940–1944' in Claudia Baldoli, Andrew Knapp and Richard Overy (eds.), *Bombing, States and Peoples in Western Europe, 1940–1945* (London: Continuum, 2011), pp. 219–238.

Hammond, Richard, 'Air Power and the British Anti-Shipping Campaign in the Mediterranean during the Second World War', *Air Power Review*, 16, 1 (2013), pp. 50–69.

'British Policy on Total Maritime Warfare and the Anti-Shipping Campaign in the Mediterranean, 1940–1944', *Journal of Strategic Studies*, 36, 6 (2013), pp. 789–814.

'British Aero-Naval Co-operation in the Mediterranean, 1940–45, and the Creation of RAF No. 201 (Naval Co-operation) Group', in Michael LoCicero, Ross Mahoney and Stuart Mitchell (eds.), *A Military Transformed? Innovation and Adaptation in the British Military, 1792–1945* (Birmingham: Helion, 2014), pp. 229–245.

'Fighting under a Different Flag: Multinational Naval Co-operation and Submarine Warfare in the Mediterranean, 1940–1944', *Journal of Military History*, 80, 2 (2016), pp. 447–476.

'An Enduring Influence on Imperial Defence and Grand Strategy: British Perceptions of the Italian Navy', *The International History Review*, 39, 5 (2017), pp. 810–835.

'Inter and Intra-theatre Learning and British Coastal Air Power in the Second World War', *War in History*, 26, 3 (2019), pp. 384–405.

Harvey, Stephen, 'The Italian War Effort and the Strategic Bombing of Italy', *History*, 70, 228 (1985), pp. 32–45.

Jones, Ben, 'The Fleet Air Arm and the Struggle for the Mediterranean, 1940–1944' in Tim Benbow (ed.), *British Naval Aviation: The First 100 Years* (Farnham: Ashgate, 2011), pp. 79–98.

Kennedy, Greg, 'Sea Denial, Interdiction and Diplomacy: The Royal Navy and the Role of Malta, 1939–1943' in Ian Speller (ed.), *The Royal Navy and Maritime Power in the Twentieth Century* (Abingdon: Frank Cass, 2005), pp. 50–66.

Kennedy, Paul, 'The War at Sea' in Jay Winter (ed.), *The Cambridge History of the First World War, Vol. 1: Global War* (Cambridge: Cambridge University Press, 2014), pp. 321–348.

Knox, MacGregor, 'The Italian Armed Forces, 1940–43' in Alan R. Millett and Williamson Murray (eds.), *Military Effectiveness*, Volume 3, *The Second World War* (London: Unwin, 1988), pp. 136–179.

Marder, Arthur J., 'The Royal Navy and the Ethiopian Crisis of 1935–1936', *American Historical Review*, 75, 5 (1970), pp. 1327–1356.

Mills, W. C., 'Sir Joseph Ball, Adrian Dingli, and Neville Chamberlain's "Secret Channel" to Rome', *International History Review*, 24, 2 (2002), pp. 278–317.

Morewood, Steven, '"This Silly African Business": The Military Dimension of Britain's Response to the Abyssinian Crisis' in G. Bruce Strang (ed.), *Collision of Empires: Italy's Invasion of Ethiopia and Its International Impact* (Farnham: Ashgate, 2013), pp. 73–110.

Morgan-Owen, David, 'War as It Might Have Been: British Sea Power and the First World War', *Journal of Military History*, 83, 4 (2019), pp. 1095–1131.

Müller, Klaus-Jürgen, 'A German Perspective on Allied Deception Operations in the Second World War' in Michael Handel (ed.), *Strategic and Operational Deception in the Second World War* (London: Frank Cass, 1987), pp. 301–326.

Murray, Williamson, 'Strategic Bombing: The British, American and German Experiences' in Williamson Murray and Alan R. Millett (eds.), *Military Innovation in the Interwar Period* (Cambridge: Cambridge University Press, 1996), pp. 96–143.

Nachmani, Amikam, 'Civil War and Foreign Intervention in Greece: 1946–49', *Journal of Contemporary History*, 25, 4 (1990), pp. 489–522.

O'Hara, Vincent and Enrico Cernuschi, 'The Other Ultra: Signal Intelligence and the Battle to Supply Rommel's Attack towards Suez', *Naval War College Review*, 66, 3 (2013), pp. 117–138.

Rastelli, Achille, 'I bombardamenti aerei nella seconda guerra mondiale: Milano e la provincia', *Italia Contemporania*, 195 (1995), pp. 309–342.

Roi, M. L., 'From Stresa Front to the Triple Entente: Sir Robert Vansittart, the Abyssinian Crisis and the Containment of Germany', *Diplomacy and Statecraft*, 6, 1 (1995), pp. 61–90.

Schmider, Klaus, 'The Mediterranean in 1940–41: Crossroads of Lost Opportunities?', *War and Society*, 15, 2 (1997), pp. 19–41.

Simpson, Michael, 'Wings over the Sea: The Interaction of Air and Sea Power in the Mediterranean, 1940–1942' in N. A. M Rodger (ed.), *Naval Power in the Twentieth Century* (Basingstoke: Macmillan, 1996), pp. 134–150.

'Superhighway to the World Wide Web: The Mediterranean in British Imperial Strategy, 1900–45' in John B. Hattendorf (ed.), *Naval Strategy and Policy in the Mediterranean: Past, Present and Future* (Abingdon: Frank Cass, 2000), pp. 51–77.

Sullivan, Brian R., 'A Fleet in Being: The Rise and Fall of Italian Sea Power, 1861–1943', *International History Review*, 10, 1 (1988), pp. 106–124.

'The Italian Armed Forces, 1918–40' in Alan Millett and Williamson Murray (eds.), *Military Effectiveness*, Volume 2, *The Interwar Years* (London: Unwin, 1988), pp. 169–217.

'Prisoner in the Mediterranean: The Evolution and Execution of Italian Naval Strategy, 1919–1942' in William B. Cogar (ed.), *Naval History. The Seventh Symposium of the US Naval Academy* (Wilmington, DE: Scholarly Resources Press, 1988), pp. 212–221.

'The Italian Soldier in Combat, June 1940 to September 1943: Myths, Realities and Explanations' in Paul Addison and Angus Calder (eds.), *Time to Kill: The Soldiers' Experience of War in the West, 1939–1945* (London: Pimlico, 1997), pp. 177–205.

Symonds, Craig L., 'For Want of a Nail: The Impact of Shipping on Grand Strategy in World War II', *Journal of Military History*, 81, 3 (2017), 657–666.
Van Creveld, Martin, 'Prelude to Disaster: The British Decision to Aid Greece, 1940–41', *Journal of Contemporary History*, 9, 3 (1974), pp. 65–92.

Secondary Sources: Books

Agarossi, Elena, *A Nation Collapses: The Italian Surrender of September 1943* (Cambridge: Cambridge University Press, 2000).
Akermann, Paul, *Encyclopedia of British Submarines 1901–1955* (Penzance: Periscope Publishing, 2002).
Ambrose, Stephen E., *Rise to Globalism: American Foreign Policy since 1938* (London: Allen Lane, 1971).
Ansel, Walter, *Hitler and the Middle Sea* (Durham, NC: Duke University Press, 1972).
Attard, Joseph, *The Battle for Malta: An Epic True Story of Suffering and Bravery* (Valetta: Progress Press, 1988).
The Struggle for the Mediterranean (Valletta: Progress Press, 1999).
Austin, Douglas, *Malta and British Strategic Policy, 1925–1943* (London: Taylor and Francis e-library, 2005).
Ball, Simon, *The Bitter Sea: The Brutal World War II Fight for the Mediterranean* (London: Harper Press, 2009).
Barnett, Corelli, *Engage the Enemy More Closely: The Royal Navy in the Second World War* (New York: Norton, 1991).
Barr, Niall, *Pendulum of War: The Three Battles of El Alamein* (London: Penguin, 2004).
Yanks and Limeys: Alliance Warfare in the Second World War (London: Jonathan Cape, 2015).
Barros, James, *The Corfu Incident of 1923: Mussolini and the League of Nations* (Princeton, NJ: Princeton University Press, 1965).
Behrens, C. B. A., *Merchant Shipping and the Demands of War* (London: HMSO, 1955).
Bell, Christopher M., *The Royal Navy, Seapower and Strategy between the Wars* (Basingstoke: Palgrave Macmillan, 2000).
Bennett, Ralph, *Ultra and Mediterranean Strategy, 1941–1945* (London: Hamish Hamilton, 1989).
Bond, Brian, *British Military Policy between the Two World Wars* (Oxford: Oxford University Press, 1980).
Bragadin, Marc'Antonio, *The Italian Navy in World War 2* (Annapolis, MD: US Naval Institute Press, 1957).
Brown, D. K. (ed.), *The Design and Construction of British Warships 1939–1945, the Official Record*, Volume 2, *Submarines, Escorts and Coastal Forces* (Annapolis, MD: Naval Institute Press, 1996).
Brown, D. K., *Nelson to Vanguard: Warship Development 1923–1945* (London: Chatham, 2006).
Bryant, Ben, *One Man Band: Memoirs of a Submarine C.O.* (London: William Kimber, 1958).

Bibliography

Buchanan, Andrew, *American Grand Strategy in the Mediterranean during World War II* (New York: Cambridge University Press, 2014).
Buckley, Christopher, *Greece and Crete 1941* (Athens: Efstathidis Group, 1993).
Campbell, John, *Naval Weapons of World War Two* (London: Conway Maritime Press, 2nd edition 2002).
Cernuschi, Enrico, *'Ultra' la fine di un mito: La guerra dei codici tra gli inglesi e le Marine italiane, 1934–1945* (Milan: Mursia, 2014).
Chourchoulis, Dionysius, *The Southern Flank of NATO, 1951–1959: Military Strategy or Political Stabilisation* (Lanham, MD: Lexington Books, 2015).
Corbett, Julian, *Some Principles of Maritime Strategy* (London: Longmans, 1911).
Cunningham, Andrew Browne, *A Sailor's Odyssey: The Autobiography of Admiral of the Fleet Viscount Cunningham of Hyndhope* (London: Hutchinson, 1951).
Darwin, John, *The Empire Project: The Rise and Fall of the British World System, 1830–1970* (Cambridge: Cambridge University Press, 2009).
De Belot, Raymond, *The Struggle for the Mediterranean 1939–1945* (London: Oxford University Press, 1951).
Deakin, F. W., *The Brutal Friendship: Mussolini, Hitler and the Fall of Fascism* (London: Weidenfeld and Nicolson, 1962).
Dietz, Peter, *The British in the Mediterranean* (London: Brasseys, 1994).
Ehlers Jr., Robert S., *The Mediterranean Air War: Airpower and Allied Victory in World War II* (Lawrence: University Press of Kansas, 2015).
Ellwood, David, *Italy, 1943–1945* (Leicester: Leicester University Press, 1985).
Fennell, Jonathan, *Combat and Morale in the North African Campaign: The Path to El Alamein* (Cambridge: Cambridge University Press, 2011)
French, David, *Raising Churchill's Army: The British Army and the War against Germany, 1919–1945* (Oxford: Oxford University Press, 2000).
Gabriele, Mariano, *Operazione C3: Malta* (Rome: USMM, 1965).
Gioannini, Marco and Giulio Massobrio, *Bombardate L'Italia: Storia della Guerra di distruzione aerea, 1940–45* (Milan: Rizzoli, 2007).
Giorgerini, Giorgio, *La battaglia dei convogli in mediterraneo* (Milan: Mursia, 1977).
La guerra italiana sul mare: La marina tra vittoria e sconflitta, 1940–1943 (Milan: Mandadori, 2001).
Gladman, Brad W., *Intelligence and Anglo-American Air Support in World War Two* (Basingstoke: Palgrave MacMillan, 2009).
Gooch, John, *Mussolini and His Generals: The Armed Forces and Fascist Foreign Policy* (Cambridge: Cambridge University Press, 2007).
Goulter, Christina, *A Forgotten Offensive: Royal Air Force Coastal Command's Antishipping Campaign, 1940–45* (London: Frank Cass, 1995).
Greene, Jack and Alessandro Massignani, *Rommel's North Africa Campaign: September 1940–November 1942* (Conshohocken, PA: Combined Books, 1994).
The Naval War in the Mediterranean 1940–1943 (London: Chatham Publishing, 1998).
Gunby, David and Pelham Temple, *RAF Bomber Losses in the Mediterranean and Middle East, Volume 1, 1939–1942* (Hinckley: Midland Publishing, 2006).
Halpern, Paul G., *A Naval History of World War 1* (London: Routledge, 2003).
Heckmann, Wolf, *Rommel's War in Africa* (New York: Doubleday, 1981).

Bibliography

Hezlet, Arthur, *British and Allied Submarine Operations in World War II* (Gosport: Royal Naval Submarine Museum, 2002).
Holland, Jeffrey, *The Aegean Mission: Allied Operations in the Dodecanese, 1943* (Westport, CT: Greenwood, 1988).
Holland, Robert, *Blue Water Empire: The British in the Mediterranean since 1800* (London: Allen Lane, 2012).
Howard, Michael, *The Mediterranean Strategy in the Second World War* (London: Weidenfeld and Nicolson, 1968).
Ireland, Bernard, *The War in the Mediterranean, 1940–1943* (London: Arms and Armour Press, 1993).
Johnstone-White, Iain, *The British Commonwealth and Victory in the Second World War* (London: Palgrave Macmillan, 2017).
Jones, Matthew, *Britain, the United States and the Mediterranean War, 1942–1944* (Basingstoke: Palgrave Macmillan, 1996).
Kemp, Paul, *Malta Convoys 1940–1943* (London: Arms and Armour Press, 1998).
Kesselring, Albert, *The Memoirs of Field Marshal Albert Kesselring* (London: William Kimber, 1954).
Kitchen, Martin, *Rommel's Desert War: Waging World War II in North Africa, 1941–1943* (Cambridge: Cambridge University Press, 2009).
Knox, MacGregor, *Mussolini Unleashed: 1939–1941: Politics and Strategy in Fascist Italy's Last War* (New York: Cambridge University Press, 1982).
  Hitler's Italian Allies: Royal Armed Forces, Fascist Regime, and the War of 1940–1943 (Cambridge: Cambridge University Press, 2000).
Koburger, Charles W., *Wine-Dark, Blood Red Sea: Naval Warfare in the Aegean 1941–1946* (Westport, CT: Praeger, 1999).
Levie, Howard S., *Mine Warfare at Sea* (Dordrecht: Martinus Nijhoff, 1992).
Levine, Alan, *The War against Rommel's Supply Lines, 1942–1943* (Mechanicsburg, PA: Stackpole Books, 2008).
Lloyd, Hugh, *Briefed to Attack: Malta's Part in Allied Victory* (London: Hodder and Stoughton, 1949).
MacIntyre, Donald, *The Battle for the Mediterranean* (London: Purnell Books Services, 1975).
Macksey, Kenneth, *Crucible of Power: The Fight for Tunisia, 1942–1943* (London: Hutchinson, 1969).
Mallett, Robert, *The Italian Navy and Fascist Expansionism, 1935–40* (London: Frank Cass, 1998).
Mark, Eduard, *Aerial Interdiction: Air Power and the Land Battle in Three American Wars* (Washington, DC: Centre for Air Force History, 1994).
Mitcham, Samuel W. and Friedrich von Stauffenberg, *The Battle of Sicily: How the Allies Lost Their Chance for Total Victory* (Mechanicsburg, PA: Stackpole, 2007).
Montanari, Mario, *Le operazioni in Africa settentrionale*, 4 Volumes (Rome: Ufficio Storico dello Stato Maggiore Esercito, 1984–93).
  L'Eserctio Italiano nella campagna di Grecia (Rome: USSME, 3rd edition 1999).
Morewood, Steven, *The British Defence of Egypt, 1935–1940: Conflict and Crisis in the Eastern Mediterranean* (London: Routledge, 2005).

Nesbit, Roy Conyers, *The Armed Rovers: Beauforts and Beaufighters over the Mediterranean* (Shrewsbury: Airlife, 1995).
O'Brien, Phillips Payson, *How the War Was Won: Air–Sea Power and Allied Victory in World War II* (Cambridge: Cambridge University Press, 2015).
O'Hara, Vincent P., *Struggle for the Middle Sea: The Great Navies at War in the Mediterranean Theatre, 1940–1945* (Annapolis: Naval Institute Press, 2009).
Overy, Richard, *Why the Allies Won* (London: Norton, 1995).
The Bombing War: Europe, 1939–1945 (London: Allen Lane, 2013).
Papagos, Alexandros, *The Battle of Greece, 1940–41* (Athens: J. M. Skazikis, 1949).
Poolman, Kenneth, *Night Strike from Malta: 830 Squadron RN and Rommel's Convoys* (London: Jane's Publishing, 1980).
Pope, Dudley, *Flag 4: The Battle of Coastal Forces in the Mediterranean 1939–1945* (London: Chatham Publishing, 2nd edition, 2006).
Porch, Douglas, *The Path to Victory: The Mediterranean Theatre in World War II* (New York: Farrar, Straus and Giroux, 2004).
Pratt, Lawrence R., *East of Malta, West of Suez: Britain's Mediterranean Crisis, 1936–1939* (Cambridge: Cambridge University Press, 1975).
Redford, Duncan, *The Submarine: A Cultural History from the Great War to Nuclear Combat* (London: Tauris Academic Studies, 2010).
Richmond, Herbert, *Statesmen and Sea Power* (Oxford: Clarendon, 1946).
Röhwer, Jürgen, *Allied Submarine Attacks of World War Two: European Theatre of Operations, 1939–1945* (London: Greenhill, 1997).
Roskill, Stephen, *Naval Policy between the Wars*, 2 Volumes (London: Collins, 1968–76).
Sadkovich, James J., *The Italian Navy in World War II* (Westport, CT: Greenwood Press, 1994).
Salerno, Reynolds M., *Vital Crossroads: Mediterranean Origins of the Second World War* (Ithaca, NY: Cornell University Press, 2002).
Sallagar, F. M., *Operation "Strangle" (Italy, Spring 1944): A Case Study of Tactical Air Interdiction* (Santa Monica, CA: RAND, 1972).
Santoni, Alberto, *Le operazioni in Sicilia e in Calabria, luglio–settembre 1943* (Rome: Stilografica, 1983).
Il vero traditore: Il ruolo documentato di ULTRA nella guerra del mediterraneo (Milan: Mursia, 1981).
Santoni, Alberto and Francesco Mattesini, *La partecipazione tedesca alla guerra aeronavale nel mediterraneo, 1940–1945* (Rome: Edizioni dell'Ateneo & Bizzarri, 1980).
Simpson, G. W. G., *Periscope View: A Professional Autobiography* (London: Macmillan, 1972).
Simpson, Tony, *Operation Mercury: The Battle for Crete, 1941* (London: Hodder and Stoughton, 1981).
Smith, Peter and Edwin Walker, *The Battle of the Malta Striking Forces* (London: Littlehampton Book Services, 1974).
War in the Aegean: The Campaign for the Eastern Mediterranean in World War II (London: William Kimber, 1974).
Spooner, Tony, *Supreme Gallantry: Malta's Role in the Allied Victory, 1939–1945* (London: John Murray, 1996).

Steiner, Zara, *The Triumph of the Dark: European International History, 1933–1939* (Oxford: Oxford University Press, 2011).
Symonds, Craig L., *World War II at Sea: A Global History* (Oxford: Oxford University Press, 2018).
Tamkin, Nicholas, *Britain, Turkey and the Soviet Union, 1940–45* (Basingstoke: Palgrave Macmillan, 2009).
Thomas, David, *Crete 1941: The Battle at Sea* (Athens: Efstathiadis, 1991).
Thorne, Christopher, *The Limits of Foreign Policy: The West, the League and the Far Eastern Crisis of 1931–1933* (London: Hamish Hamilton, 1972).
Tomblin, Barbara, *With Utmost Spirit: Allied Naval Operations in the Mediterranean, 1942–1945* (Lexington: University of Kentucky Press, 2004).
Van Creveld, Martin, *Supplying War: Logistics from Wallenstein to Patton* (Cambridge: Cambridge University Press, 2nd edition, 2004).
Warlimont, Walter, *Inside Hitler's Headquarters, 1939–45* (London: Weidenfeld and Nicolson, 1964).
Watson, Bruce Allen, *Exit Rommel: The Tunisian Campaign, 1942–1943* (Westport, CT: Praeger, 1999).
Weinberg, Gerhard, *A World at Arms: A Global History of World War II* (Cambridge: Cambridge University Press, 1994).
Wingate, John, *The Fighting Tenth: The Tenth Submarine Flotilla and the Siege of Malta* (London: Periscope Publishing, 2003).
Woodman, Richard, *Malta Convoys 1940–1943* (London: J. Murray, 2000).

Secondary Sources: Unpublished Theses

May, S. 'The British Submarine Campaign in the Mediterranean' (MPhil Thesis, University of Wales, Swansea, 2000).
Raspin, Georgina Elisabeth Angela, 'Some Aspects of Italian Economic Affairs 1940–43, with Particular Reference to Italian Relations with Germany' (PhD Thesis, London School of Economics, 1980).
Ristuccia, Cristiano Andrea, 'The Italian Economy under Fascism: The Rearmament Paradox' (DPhil thesis, University of Oxford, 1998).

Index

Abyssinian crisis (1935–36), 13, 15, 19
Accolade, Operation (1943), 179–80
Achse, Operation (1943), 178, 193
Admiralty, the, 88, 94, 107
  First Lord of, 109
  veiws on attacking merchant ships and, 28–30
  war planning and, 19
Adriatic Sea, the, 5, 12, 193
  anti-shipping operations in, 7, 42, 44–5, 53–5, 63–4, 76, 89, 117, 175, 180, 186, 188–9
  Axis uses of for supply, 19, 24, 27, 37–8, 50, 75–6, 79, 162, 169, 185, 195, 197
Aegean Sea, the, 5, 10, 12, 27, 43, 97, 193
  Allied strategy and, 24, 36, 42, 53, 173, 175, 179–81, 195, 203
  anti-shipping operations in, 56, 65, 72, 89, 95, 117, 133, 144, 159, 171, 175, 180–1, 184, 186–8
  Axis uses of for supply, 2, 19, 24, 27, 79, 85, 99, 110, 162, 169, 171, 178, 190, 194–7
  German withdrawal from, 10, 179–81, 195, 197
Agedabia, 108, 132
Air Ministry, the
  control of air assets and, 43, 83
  strategy and, 34–5
  views on attacking merchant ships and, 29
  war planning and, 20
Air-Surface Vessel Radar (ASV), 62–3, 65, 85, 89–90, 95, 109, 116–18, 134–5, 138, 158
Albania *See also* Adriatic Sea, the; Durazzo; Valona
  Axis shipping to, 18–19, 27, 37, 42, 49–50, 54–5, 64–5, 167
  Axis withdrawal from, 181
  Greek campaign and, 36, 50, 75–6
Alexander, Field Marshal Harold, 128–9

Alexandria, 20–1, 35, 90, 92, 106, 109, 127
  anti-shipping operations from, 44, 64, 69, 89, 115–16, 136, 187
  Royal Navy withdrawal from, 112
Algeria, 148, 150, 153, 169–70
Algiers, 148, 157
Allied Army formations
  Eighth Army (UK), 86–7, 105, 108, 111–13, 124–33, 143, 145–7, 149, 151–5, 163, 175, 201
  First Army (UK/US), 151–2, 154–5, 163, 170
  Seventh Army (US), 175
  Western Desert Force (UK), 53
Ambrosio, General Vittorio, 160, 190
Anderson, General Kenneth, 151, 154–5
Anton, Operation (1943), 148
Arnim, General Hans-Jürgen von, 149, 152, 154, 160, 163–6
Athens, 25, 43, 55, 218–19, 223
Auchinleck, Field Marshal Claude, 81–2, 87, 108, 112, 127
Axis Army formations
  Army Group Africa (Ger/It), 151, 153, 155, 165
  Deutsches Afrikakorps (Ger/It), 55, 77, 79–80, 87, 103
  Divisions
    10th Panzer Division (Ger), 164–5
    15th Panzer Division (Ger), 66, 77, 87, 103, 131, 145, 151, 165
    164th Division (Ger), 126
    21st Panzer Division (Ger), 77, 87, 131, 145, 165
    Ariete Division (It), 86, 131
    Folgore Division (It), 126
    Hermann Goering Division (Ger), 192
    Littorio Division (It), 131
    Trieste Division (It), 50, 131
  Fifth Panzer Army (Ger/It), 147, 149, 152, 161, 163, 165

263

Axis Army formations (cont.)
  First Italian Army (Ger/It), 151, 164
  Panzerarmee Afrika (Ger/It), 82, 101, 108, 119–21, 125–6, 128, 131–3, 140–6, 149, 151–2
  Tenth Army (It), 41, 46, 49–50

Badoglio, Marshal Pietro, 176, 178
Bardia, 49, 87
  Allied attacks on, 39–40, 89
  Axis use of as supply port, 26, 78, 100, 123
Bari, 25
  Allied attacks on, 37, 43
Bastia, 25, 185, 193
Bastico, General Ettore, 102, 123
Battleaxe, Operation (1941), 60–2, 69, 79
Beirut
  Allied attacks on, 61, 69
  Royal Navy units withdrawn to, 110, 112, 116
Benghazi, 49, 52, 87, 104, 108, 131
  Allied attacks on, 32, 35–6, 41–2, 58, 60–1, 66–7, 69, 75, 85, 89, 91, 97–8, 104, 109, 113–14, 118–19, 123, 133, 140, 144, 146
  Axis use of as supply port, 2, 25–6, 60, 77–80, 85, 88, 91–2, 100–4, 119, 121–4, 127, 130, 132, 144–6
Bir Hakeim, 111
Bizerte, 21, 154–5
  Allied attacks on, 149, 157
  Axis use of as supply port, 25, 150, 157
Black Sea, the
  Axis sea communications with, 19, 27, 99, 169, 178, 190, 193, 195, 211, 248
Bône *See also* Algeria
  anti-shipping operations from, 150, 155, 158
Brindisi
  Allied attacks on, 37–8, 43, 65
  Axis use of as supply port, 25, 42, 54, 77–8
British Army *See* Allied Army formations
  pre-war spending cuts to, 13

Cagliari
  Allied attacks on, 38–9, 170
  Axis use of as supply port, 25
Capri, Operation (1943), 154, 164
Casablanca conference (1943), 153, 173–4, 192
Cavagnari, Admiral Domenico, 11, 22, 76, 209

Cavallero, General Ugo
  Axis shipping/supply shortages and, 99–100, 139, 142, 144
  Axis strategy and, 111–12, 123, 132
Chamberlain, Neville, 14
Chiefs of Staff (British)
  Allied strategy and, 173
  anti-shipping operations and, 52, 54–5, 61, 81, 82–4, 114, 128, 130, 132, 134, 149, 153
  pre-war imperial defence and, 13
  pre-war relations with Italy and, 15
  views of attacking merchant shipping and, 9
  war in North Africa and, 108
  war planning and, 16, 34–5
China, 46
Churchill, Winston
  Allied strategy and, 23, 52–3, 82, 86, 107–8, 129–30, 153, 173, 179, 199
  anti-shipping operations and, 54–5, 57–9, 66, 83–5, 109, 113–14, 132, 149–50, 158
  control of air assets and, 56–7
  sacking of Auchinleck and, 127
  sacking of Longmore and, 62
  vote of no confidence in, 112
Ciano, Count Galeazzo, 15, 36, 91
Comando Supremo (Italian Armed Forces High Command), 139, 143, 154
Comitato per la organizzazione e la protezione dei trasporti per l'Africa, 136–7, 158
Compass, Operation (1940), 49, 52–3
Corsica *See also* Bastia
  Allied attacks on, 184–5
  Allied strategy and, 173
  Axis seizure of, 148
  Axis supplies to, 24, 27, 150, 169, 170–2, 175, 184, 189–90
  German withdrawal from, 2, 10, 178–9, 188, 193–4, 197, 203
  Italian war planning and, 21
Crete, 54, 179, 199
  Allied deception operations and, 175
  Axis aircraft based in, 74, 85–6, 174, 185
  Axis shipping to North Africa via, 88, 134
  Axis supplies to, 27
  Axis supply shortages in, 171, 193, 195
  Battle of (1941), 55, 67–8, 73, 76
  British aim to secure, 36–7, 53
  British evacuation of, 56, 59–60, 68
  German withdrawal from, 196
Cripps, Stafford, 109

Index

Crotone, 43
Crusader, Operation (1941-42), 8–9, 82–3, 85–7, 99, 102–5, 107, 119, 200
Crüwell, General Ludwig, 86–7
Cunningham, Admiral of the Fleet Andrew
 anti-shipping operations and, 33, 36, 38–41, 45–7, 55, 57–61, 63, 67, 71–2, 84, 88, 94, 96, 98, 107, 116, 149
 control of air assets and, 56–7, 62, 83
 evacuation of Crete and, 59
 loss of battleships to Italian special forces and, 106
 Operation Retribution (1943) and, 155
 policy on attacking merchant shipping and, 30
 relationship with Tedder and, 62
Cyprus, 20, 56, 69, 185
Cyrenaica, 49, 52, 55–6, 66, 81–2, 86–7, 93, 96, 103, 107, 109, 111, 132, 149
 airfields in, 66, 108, 114
 Axis supply shortages in, 8, 78–9, 91, 100–2, 104, 120–1, 123, 125–6, 133, 135, 200
 ports in *See* Bardia; Benghazi; Derna; Tobruk

Derna, 49, 78
 Allied attacks on, 34, 89, 140
 Axis use of as supply port, 2, 78, 100, 121, 123
Dill, Field Marshal John, 56, 60
Dodecanese campaign (1943), 179–80, 185–8, 194–5, *See also* Accolade, Operation (1943); Aegean Sea, the
Dodecanese islands, 27, 33–4, 36, 41, 54, 60, 193, 199, *See also* Aegean Sea, the
Dönitz, Admiral Karl, 152, 158, 171
Durazzo
 Allied attacks on, 42, 54, 65
 Axis use of as supply port, 50

Eisenhower, General Dwight, 151
 Allied strategy and, 153, 179–80
 anti-shipping operations and, 9, 176
El Agheila
 Axis defensive positions at, 49, 53, 87, 105, 107, 119, 132, 146, 150

Fellers, Colonel Bonner, 112–13, 231
Flax, Operation (1943), 166
Fleet Air Arm, 32
 aircraft
  Fairey Albacore, 85, 88–9, 117, 127–8, 135, 153, 158

Fairey Swordfish, 32, 34, 39–41, 43, 49, 54–5, 62–7, 69, 88–9, 98, 117, 135, 158
 Air-Surface Vessel Radar and, 96
 anti-shipping operations and, 34, 38, 41, 43–5, 48–9, 51, 54–5, 60–1, 63–4, 65–6, 67, 69, 73, 85, 88–9, 117, 129, 153, 175
 control of air assets and, 83
 Squadrons
  813 Squadron, 39, 41
  815 Squadron, 41, 54, 65
  819 Squadron, 41
  830 Squadron, 43–4, 96
France
 Allied invasion of southern (1944), 24
 anti-shipping operations by prior to armistice, 39, 48
 Axis forces in south of, 173, 177
 Axis shipping and south of, 150, 169
 Axis war planning and, 22, 26
 Battle of (1940), 15, 20–1, 31, 34
 fall of (1940), 1, 11, 26, 31, 34, 38–9
 Italian expectations of war with, 26
 ports in south of, xiv, 24, 27, 148, 178, 188
 war planning and, 14, 16–17, 19–21
Free/Fighting France, 39, 45, 111, 163, 185, 194
Freeman, Air Chief Marshal Wilfrid, 61
French Air Force, 34
French Navy, 22, 26, 148, *See also* Vichy France; Free/Fighting France, *See also* France:anti-shipping operations prior to armistice
 Battleships
  Lorraine, 39
 scuttling of, 148
 Submarines
  La Turquoise, 38
  Le Nautilus, 38
  Narval, 39, 45, 47
  Saphir, 38

Gazala
 Axis defensive positions at, 87, 103
 Battle of (1942), 111–12, 119, 122, 125, 128
 Eighth Army defensive positions at, 108
Genoa
 Allied air attacks on, 84
 Allied naval bombardments of, 39, 65
 Axis shipping at, 193
 as Italian economic hub, 34

266 Index

German Air Force, 57, 74
  attacks on Royal Navy and, 73, 187
  bombing of Malta and, 84
  Formations
    Fliegerführer Afrika, 120
    Fliegerkorps Afrika, 104
    Fliegerkorps II, 93, 98, 105
    Fliegerkorps VIII, 75
    Fliegerkorps X, 54, 60, 104, 111
    Luftflotte II, 93
  supply shortages and, 78, 104, 139–40, 171
German Army *See* Axis Army formations
German Navy, 79, 152
  F-lighter, 134, 137, 158, 192
  Siebel Ferry, 134, 137, 158, 184, 190, 192
  U-boats, 28–9, 87, 93, 115–16, 173
Gibraltar, 7, 11, 16, 20–2, 32, 157
  anti-shipping operations from, 36–7, 44, 65, 89, 116, 135
Greece *See also* Adriatic Sea, the: Axis uses of for supply purposes; Adriatic Sea, the: anti-shipping operations in
  Allied deception operations and, 159, 175
  anti-shipping operations from, 42, 44, 65
  Axis aircraft based in, 54, 60, 85, 185
  Axis shipping to North Africa via, 88, 96, 101
  Axis supplies to, 38, 53, 167, 184–5, 188
  British decision to aid, 7, 37, 52
  British withdrawal from, 56, 59
  campaign in (1940–41), 19, 50, 53, 55, 66, 75–6
  German withdrawal from, 181
  Italian ultimatum to, 36
  post-war paramilitary violence in, 198
Greek Army, 55, 65, 75–6
Greek Navy, 37, 42, 44, 64
  Submarines
    Proteus, 44–5

Haifa, 32
  Royal Navy units withdrawn to, 110, 112, 116
Harwood, Admiral Henry, 111
Hitler, Adolf
  Axis strategy and, 102, 112, 117, 131–2, 148–9, 152, 166, 177–9, 181, 188, 194, 196
  relationship with Mussolini, 14
  shipping losses and, 92, 95, 100, 158
  shipping shortages and, 169, 196
  supply shortages and, 160

Host-Venturi, Giovanni, 168
Hube, General Hans-Valentin, 177, 182
Husky, Operation (1943), 175, *See also* Sicily
  Allied strategy after, 174
  Axis supply situation during, 191
  planning of, 153, 175–6, 181–3

India, 12, 109, 131, 230
Iraq, campaign in (1941), 55, 82
Italian Air Force
  aircraft
    Cant Z.501, 21
    Savoia-Marchetti 79, 48
  bombing of Malta and, 60
  convoy escort and, 47, 73–4, 140
  relationship with Italian Navy and, 19, 74
  supply shortages and, 139
  war planning and, 21
Italian Army *See* Axis Army formations
  collapse of after armistice, 178
  war planning and, 21, 26
Italian Navy, 31, 60, 84, 111
  Allied war planning and, 16
  anti-submarine warfare and, 47
  convoy escort and, 50, 76, 80, 91, 137, 152
  cruisers
    Da Barbiano, 91–2
    Di Giussano, 91–2
    Scipione Africano, 183
  destroyers
    Espero, 44
    Luca Tarigo, 67
    Zeffiro, 39
  relationship with Italian Air Force and, 74
  signals intelligence and, 20
  Torpedo Boats
    Lupo, 67
  war planning and, 17–19, 21

Japan
  as Axis power, 107, 199, 203
  entry to the war (1941), 8, 98, 107
  expansionism in 1930s, 13
  possible alliance with Germany and/or Italy, 13, 16
Jodl, General Alfred, 149, 198
Joint Chiefs of Staff (American), 148, 153, 170, 174, 244
Joint Planning Staff, 35, 108, 174

Index

Kasserine Pass, Battle of (1943), 152, 163–4
Kaufmann, Karl
  Axis shipping losses and, 158
  Axis shipping shortages and, 142, 161, 168–9, 175, 189–90, 202
  defence of Axis shipping and, 159
Keitel, Field Marshal Wilhelm
  Axis shipping shortages and, 80, 99–100
  Axis strategy and, 123, 152
  Axis supply shortages in North Africa and, 77, 80, 101
Kesselring, Field Marshal Albert
  Axis shipping shortages and, 168–9, 175
  Axis strategy and, 112, 131–2, 149, 152, 163, 175
  Axis supply shortages and, 139, 144, 160–1
  end of Tunisian campaign and, 165–6
  post-war views and, 192
  use of Axis air power and, 93, 117, 170
Kos *See* Accolade, Operation (1943); Dodecanese campaign (1943); Dodecanese islands

La Spezia, 65, 153
Leros *See* Accolade, Operation (1943); Dodecanese campaign (1943); Dodecanese islands
Lightfoot, Operation (1942), xiii, 129–30, 133, 145
Livorno
  Allied attacks on, 65, 88, 185
  Axis use of as supply port, 25, 185, 193
Lloyd, Air Chief Marshal Hugh
  anti-shipping operations and, 55, 60, 68, 84, 97–8, 111, 117
  requests for additional aircraft at Malta and, 60, 96
Longmore, Air Chief Marshal Arthur
  anti-shipping operations and, 33–4, 36–7, 41–2, 44, 53–4
  control of air assets and, 43, 64
  relationship with Cunningham, 56
  sacking of, 62

Malta, 178, 198
  anti-shipping operations from, 5–6, 37–8, 42–6, 54, 58–9, 61, 64–6, 68–73, 88–91, 97, 100, 113, 115, 117, 130, 132–5, 156, 185, 187
  as a base for mining operations, 32
  Axis war planning and, 22–3
  defences of, 32–3
  forces based on, 34–7, 39, 43, 54–6, 60–3, 84–5, 88, 94, 96, 116, 149–50

  possible Axis invasion of, 112
  siege of, 5, 8, 54, 60, 74, 93, 98, 108–11, 114–15, 117, 119, 137
  supply of, 53, 88, 92, 108–9, 111, 114, 128, 149, 169
  war planning and, 15, 20–1
Mareth Line
  Axis attacks from, 152, 154
  Axis defensive positions at, 151, 153–4
  Battle of (1943), 164
Maynard, Air Vice Marshal Foster
  anti-shipping operations and, 37, 43
  control of air assets and, 43
  replacement at Malta, 55
Mediterranean Air Command, 153, 186
Mediterranean Allied Air Forces, 188
Mersa Matruh, 112, 122
  Allied attacks on, 113, 116, 118–19, 134
  Axis use of as supply port, 123, 143
Messe, General Giovanni, 151–2, 154, 166
Messina
  Allied attacks on, 64, 176, 181, 183–4
  Axis use of as supply port, 25, 191
Messina, straits of, 20
  Allied attacks on, 159, 176
  Axis defence of, 183–4
  Axis transport across, 191
Metaxas, General Ioannis, 36, 53
Mincemeat, Operation (1942), 175
Montgomery, Field Marshal Bernard
  Allied strategy and, 127
  Battles of El Alamein and, 129–30
  methodical nature and, 132, 146, 151, 163
  Tunisian campaign and, 151, 163
Mueller, General Friedrich-Wilhelm, 194
Mussolini, Benito
  Alliance with Germany and, 14–15
  Axis strategy and, 35–6, 49, 112, 132, 149, 152, 166
  Axis supply shortages and, 129
  declaration of war and, 1, 20, 27, 168
  deposal of, 176–8
  shipping losses and, 77, 100, 140, 159, 204
  shipping shortages and, 99, 167
  Sicilian campaign and, 176
  war planning and, 15–16

Naples
  Allied attacks on, 37, 43, 62, 64, 135, 157
  Axis use of as supply port, 25, 73, 77–8, 100
Nehring, General Walter, 149, 151, 163
North Atlantic Treaty Organization, 198
Northwest African Air Forces, 153, 155, 177

Oberkommando der Wehrmacht (OKW)
  Axis strategy and, 102, 123, 129, 149, 178, 181, 193
  Axis supply shortages and, 77, 124, 142, 164, 168
Oberkommando des Heeres (OKH)
  Axis strategy and, 82, 108, 112, 129
  Axis supply shortages and, 101
  siege of Malta and, 117
Ochsenkopf, Operation (1943), 154
Olbia, 170, 185

Palermo
  Allied attacks on, 64, 89, 157, 181
  Axis use of as supply port, 25, 191
Pedestal, Operation (1942), 114
Phillips, Admiral Tom, 61
Poland, 14–15
Portal, Marshal of the Royal Air Force Charles
  aircraft allocation and, 36–7, 54, 57, 109, 113, 128, 131
  anti-shipping operations and, 42–3, 54–5, 59, 61, 84–5, 98, 129, 133, 149, 158
  control of air assets and, 43, 56–7, 62
  strategic bombing and, 37
Pound, Admiral of the Fleet Dudley
  aircraft allocation and, 57, 62, 128, 149
  anti-shipping operations and, 38, 55, 58–9, 63, 72, 84–5
  control of air assets and, 56
  war planning and, 19, 32–3
Pricolo, General Francesco, 73
Pridham-Wippell, Vice Admiral Henry, 40, 42, 252
Pugilist, Operation (1943), 154

Raeder, Admiral Erich, 79, 92, 95
Retribution, Operation (1943), 155, 166
Rhodes *See* Accolade, Operation (1943); Dodecanese campaign (1943); Dodecanese islands
Riccardi, Admiral Arturo, 76, 92, 160
Rintelen, General Enno von, 79, 111, 144
Ritchie, General Neil, 87, 112
Roatta, General Mario, 191
Romania, 52–3, 173, 178
Rooster (location technology), 85, 89, 91, 99, 116, 135
Royal Air Force, 32, 128
  aircraft
    Bristol Beaufighter, 61, 89, 107, 131, 134, 150, 159, 186
    Bristol Beaufort, 54, 56, 85, 88, 107, 111, 134–5, 150

    Bristol Blenheim, 34, 42, 53, 55–6, 61, 65, 68–9, 73–4, 84, 88–9, 97–8, 117
    Consolidated B-24 Liberator, 108–9, 111, 133
    Gloster Gladiator, 34
    Martin Baltimore, 159, 186
    Martin Maryland, 35, 43, 61, 63–4, 67, 68–9, 90, 96
    Short Sunderland, 35, 39, 43, 54, 63–4
    Vickers Wellington, 37, 41–4, 54, 59, 61–6, 69, 85, 89–91, 109, 111, 117–18, 134–5, 150, 158–9, 182, 185
  aircraft allocation and, 127
  aircraft losses and, 73, 75
  air–land integration and, 201
  anti-shipping operations and, 39, 41, 44–5, 49, 57, 60–2, 65, 69, 96, 116, 129, 135–6
  campaign in Greece and, 37, 50, 53
  Commands
    Coastal Command, 107, 109, 118, 188
    Middle East Command, 20, 32–4, 36, 43, 109, 114, 153, 186
  control of air assets and, 62
  convoy escort and, 111
  Groups
    No. 2 Group, 60
    No. 201 (Naval Co-operation) Group, 83, 91, 96, 117, 133, 136, 144, 159, 171
  Operation Lightfoot and, 130–1
  pre-war spending cuts to, 13
  signals intelligence and, 48
  Squadrons
    148 Squadron, 37
    228 Squadron, 32, 35, 39, 43
  strategic bombing and, 34, 84, 113
  tactical development and, 63–4
  war planning and, 16, 33
Royal Navy
  aircraft carriers
    Argus, 32
    Ark Royal, 54, 65, 93, 105
    Eagle, 32, 41
    Formidable, 67, 107
    Illustrious, 107
    Indomitable, 107
  Allied strategy and, 34
  anti-shipping operations and, 38, 44, 48, 58, 68, 88, 110, 187, 195
  battleships
    Barham, 93, 105
    Centurion, 58
    Queen Elizabeth, 106
    Valiant, 106

Index

cruisers
  Aurora, 85, 91, 93, 98
  Carlisle, 187
  Galatea, 93, 105
  Naiad, 115
  Neptune, 93, 98
  Penelope, 85, 115
destroyers
  Dulverton, 187
  Javelin, 157
  Kandahar, 93, 98
  Kelvin, 157
  Lance, 85
  Lively, 85
  Mohawk, 67, 73, 91
  Panther, 187
  Quentin, 156
  Rockwood, 187
evacuation of Crete and, 55, 60, 73
evacuation of Dodecanese islands and, 187–8
Force H, 65, 88, 92
Force K, 85, 90–1, 93, 98, 103–5, 114–16, 150, 156
Force Q, 150, 155–6, 177, 183
Force X, 42, 50
minelayers
  Abdiel, 67
  Manxman, 88, 136
  Welshman, 88
policy on attacking merchant ships and, 28, 30
pre-war spending cuts to, 13
strength of Mediterranean Fleet and, 31, 106, 114
submarines
  10th Flotilla, 69, 94, 109, 114, 116–17, 135, 138, 186
  1st Flotilla, 34, 64, 69, 109–10, 116–17, 135–6, 138, 171, 179, 186
  8th Flotilla, 89, 135, 157, 175, 186
  Clyde, 116
  Grampus, 32, 38, 48
  Medway (depot ship), 116
  Odin, 38
  Orpheus, 38
  Osiris, 47
  Oswald, 41
  P33, 68
  Parthian, 38, 71
  Pheonix, 40
  Proteus, 38, 94
  Rorqual, 32, 38, 40, 64
  Sokol (Polish), 186, 188
  Unique, 90
  Upholder, 90

  Uproar, 188
war planning and, 19–20

Samos *See* Accolade, Operation (1943); Dodecanese campaign (1943); Dodecanese islands
Sardinia *See also* Cagliari; Olbia
  Allied attacks on, 88, 135, 159, 170, 175, 183–5
  Allied deception operations and, 175
  Allied strategy and, 173–4
  Axis aircraft based in, 174, 202
  Axis supplies to, 2, 27, 155, 167, 175, 189–90
  Axis supply shortages in, 171–2, 189–90, 193
  German withdrawal from, 2, 10, 178–9, 194, 197
  Italian war planning and, 17
Sfax, 157, 164
Sicily
  Allied deception operations and, 159, 175
  Allied invasion of *See* Husky, Operation (1943)
  Allied strategy and, 173
  Axis aircraft based in, 47, 54, 60, 66, 73, 84, 93, 98, 137, 139, 174
  Axis defence of, 17, 40, 175, 191
  Axis seaborne supply problems after loss of, 192, 195
  Axis supplies to, 10, 24–5, 155, 167, 169–71, 181–5, 189–92
  Axis supplies to North Africa and, 66–7
  Axis withdrawal from, 2, 10, 177–8
  campaign in, 10, 24
Sidi Rezegh, 86–7
Smuts, Field Marshal Jan, 113
Sollum, 26, 86–7
Somerville, Admiral of the Fleet James, 88
Sousse, 157, 164
Soviet Union
  Allied assistance to, 179
  Axis war with, 52, 60, 82, 181
  post-war Allied relationship with, 198
Spain
  Axis shipping and, 99, 144, 150
  neutrality of, 21, 23, 150
Spanish Civil War, 13
Stoneage, Operation (1942), 149
Strangle, Operation (1944), 181, 185, 197
Stumme, General Georg, 142
Suez Canal
  Axis attacks on, 52–3, 112, 128
  defence of, 20–1, 34

Suez Canal (cont.)
  importance of to British Empire, 6, 13, 23
  importance of to Italy, 16, 21–2
Suez, port of, 11
Supercharge II, Operation (1943), 154
Supercharge, Operation (1942), 131
Supermarina (Italian Navy High Command), 48, 68, 78
Syria
  Allied attacks on shipping to, 56, 60–1, 63
  campaign in (1941), 55, 82

Taranto
  Allied attacks on, 42–3, 76, 135
Tedder, Marshal of the Royal Air Force Arthur
  anti-shipping operations and, 61, 62, 85, 97–8, 109, 111, 114, 129, 133, 149, 153, 158–9
  control of air assets and, 62, 83
  strategic bombing and, 177
Tobruk, 49, 52, 131
  Allied attacks on, 34, 39–42, 89, 113–14, 118–19, 124, 133–4, 140–1, 143–4
  Axis use of as supply port, 25, 122–7, 130, 132, 143–5
  siege of, 55, 60, 77–9, 82, 86–7, 93, 99–104, 111–12
Torch, Operation (1942), 148, 151, 157, 163, 173
Tripoli, 53, 107
  Allied attacks on, 38, 43–4, 57–9, 61, 63–7, 70, 79, 84, 90–1, 97–8, 104–5, 108–9, 135, 144
  Axis use of as supply port, 2, 25–6, 42, 61, 73, 77–8, 84, 88, 92–3, 100–3, 119–24, 127, 129, 132–3, 145, 150–1

Tripolitania, 55, 104, 142, 149, 151, 156
Tunis, 148, 151, 154–5, 163
  Allied attacks on, 149
  Axis use of as supply port, 25, 150, 157, 169
Turkey
  neutrality of, 23, 33, 53, 173, 178–80

United States Army *See* Allied Army formations
United States Army Air Force (USAAF)
  aircraft
    Consolidated B-24 Liberator, 134
    Lockheed P-38 Lightning, 186
  anti-shipping operations and, 134–5, 157–8
  loan of long-range fighter aircraft to Britain and, 180, 186
  strategic bombing and, 177

Valona, 52
  Allied attacks on, 42, 54, 65
  Axis use of as supply port, 25, 42, 50
Vichy France, 23, 55, 88, *See also* Anton, Operation (1943)
  Axis acquisition of shipping from, 10, 80, 99, 143, 160–1, 166, 168–9, 189, 202
  British hostility with, 40, 55, 63, 69
Vulcan, Operation (1943), 155

Warlimont, General Walter
  Axis shipping shortages and, 190
  Axis supply shortages and, 142, 160–1, 163–4
Washington Conference (1943), 173–4
Weichold, Admiral Eberhard, 77, 171
Willis, Admiral Algernon, 195

Yugoslavia, 27, 55, 75, 188